Dr Romain Pizzi BVSc MSc Phd DZooMed DipECZM MACVS(Surg) FRES FRGS FRSB FRCVS, is a Royal College of Veterinary Surgeons Recognised Specialist in Zoo & Wildlife Medicine, and the world's leading expert in wildlife surgery. He has travelled the globe pioneering many world-first operations in endangered wild animals. Pizzi was born and grew up in South Africa, where he qualified as a veterinary surgeon. He was an honorary professor at the University of Nottingham in zoo and wildlife medicine, and has taught and mentored wildlife veterinarians from around the globe. He has worked with conservation charities, wildlife rescue and rehabilitation centres, and zoos across the world. His work has featured on numerous TV documentaries on the BBC, Animal Planet, National Geographic, CNN and other international media. He lives in Scotland, 10 minutes walk from the ruins of Rosslyn castle, with his vet cardiologist wife and their two young children.

Praise for Romain Pizzi

'Romain Pizzi, who pioneered keyhole surgery for animals, is arguably the most versatile and inventive vet in the world.'
Guardian

'A highly entertaining and thought-provoking tour de force. Thoroughly recommended.' *Veterinary Record*

'We have other vets who are incredibly talented, but Romain is one of a kind.' Matt Hunt, CEO of Free the Bears

'One of the most innovative wildlife surgeons in Europe and perhaps the world ... he has operated on giraffes and tarantulas, penguins and baboons, giant tortoises and at least one shark, and m   cases others won't. If   nes, or a suspiciou   magazine

Exotic Vetting

Extraordinary Stories
of Treating Amazing Animals

Romain Pizzi

BVSc MSc PhD DZooMed
DipECZM MANZCVS(Surg)
FRES FRGS FRSB FRCVS

Royal College of Veterinary Surgeons
Recognised Specialist in Zoo & Wildlife Medicine

WILLIAM
COLLINS

William Collins
An imprint of HarperCollins*Publishers*
1 London Bridge Street
London SE1 9GF

WilliamCollinsBooks.com

HarperCollins*Publishers*
Macken House
39/40 Mayor Street Upper
Dublin 1
D01 C9W8
Ireland

First published in Great Britain in 2022 by William Collins

This William Collins paperback edition published in 2023

1

A catalogue record for this book is available from the British Library

ISBN 978-0-00-835678-1

Typeset in Palatino by Palimpsest Book Production Ltd, Falkirk, Stirlingshire
Printed and Bound in the UK using 100% Renewable Electricity at CPI Group (UK) Ltd

To all my animal patients

Contents

Introduction

How to operate on a mammoth

The technicalities of operating on a mammoth are not something many veterinarians spend any time thinking about. Very few vets ever need to treat an elephant, and even fewer of us have ever operated on one. Surprisingly, there were still mammoths alive three and a half thousand years ago on Wrangel Island in the East Siberian Sea. Until human hunters arrived. By the time of their man-made extinction the Great Pyramids of Giza were already a thousand years old. But there is a possibility we could see mammoths resurrected in our lifetime, thanks to clever geneticists. If so, they will invariably need veterinarians at some stage. So how would I go about operating to fix a broken leg, for example? It would, pardon the pun, be a mammoth undertaking.

Yet we have already addressed more demanding problems in treating the enormous diversity of wildlife patients that myself and other wildlife vets see in the course of our work. We anaesthetise fish for hours for complex surgery, despite them breathing underwater. We can get blood from a hippo despite veins that are invisible deep under the skin, X-ray a penguin, or ultrasound scan a manta ray's heart. We can even perform surgery on a scorpion. They can all be a challenge, and we treat them very differently to people, pet dogs or farm cows.

1

I could never have imagined any of this as a child growing up in South Africa. Neither surrounded by elephants nor the son of a game warden, I had a more mundane upbringing in a small town. One of my first experiences with animals came when I hand-reared an injured fledgling Cape turtle dove, hiding it among the socks in my cupboard, after it was caught by the African wildcat my parents had rescued when its mother was shot. Other injured and orphaned birds soon followed, with my only guide a dog-eared copy of *Stroud's Digest on the Diseases of Birds*, written by the 'Birdman of Alcatraz' in 1943. I could never have envisaged myself one day treating Komodo dragons, giant pandas or wild orangutans.

This book is a brief glance at how we anaesthetise, diagnose, operate on, medicate, and finally return to the wild a great variety of creatures on the planet. How do you catch a kangaroo or anaesthetise a shark? Why do deer have bizarre red blood cells, and how can you see inside a Galapagos giant tortoise to diagnose a problem? Why is orthopaedic surgery on a tarantula bizarre, and how do you treat a walrus with toothache? Lastly, having prodded, poked, fixed and fed your armadillo, how do you return him to his life in the wild?

Come with me on a journey around the world's wild places and sanctuaries, as I and other wildlife veterinarians – using a mix of science and sometimes just guesswork – treat some of the strangest creatures on the planet. And you may end up pondering how to treat a de-extinct mammoth too.

Walruses are awkward patients. Out of water, they seem to collapse under their own weight. Their tendency to hold their breath under anaesthesia, as if they were under-water, makes keeping them alive challenging. In care, they have a tendency to damage their tusks' enamel, with bacteria invading the pores in the dentine to cause painful pulp infections. To prevent this, we may need to place titanium tusk caps.

1

The problem with a suicidal walrus

The walrus tries its best to commit suicide under anaesthesia by holding its breath. It has a dive reflex, allowing it to breath-hold for more than half an hour underwater. To save oxygen underwater, the heart slows down and blood vessels supplying the brain, heart and kidneys widen, to maximise blood and oxygen supply to these important organs. In other places vessels constrict, shifting blood flow away from less critical sites such as the skin, blubber and intestines. Unfortunately, when anaesthetised, all a walrus's natural mechanisms are confused and don't work normally. While the brain is away, not even dreaming of clams, the body thinks it is underwater. The walrus holds its breath, its heart slows, and the longer the anaesthesia the higher the risk of disaster unfolding.

Anaesthesia is controlled death. It is easy to forget this when disguised by the veneer of respectability in a modern human hospital. Despite over 150 years of anaesthesia, with millions of people anaesthetised yearly for everything from ingrown toenails to brain surgery, and wildlife vets like me anaesthetising everything from seahorses to elephants, we still don't actually understand the precise physiological mechanisms that make anaesthetic drugs work. Why, when we give some compounds, does the brain lose consciousness, and patients don't feel pain? It isn't at all like sleep. Give too much and the patient dies. Anaesthetic drugs are after all toxic chemicals: poisons given in just the precise amount to keep the patient oblivious, in the narrow corridor between life and death.

Anaesthesia in the walrus is complicated by its massive weight and blubber. The thick blubber layer makes it difficult to inject into muscle. Drugs in the blubber are absorbed unreliably, and it can take ages for the walrus to become anaesthetised, making everything even more unpredictable. Its hind limbs are tiny with small muscles, so we inject drugs in the back muscles instead. The blubber makes it almost impossible to get a catheter in a vein to give injectable drugs in an emergency. A large bull can weigh one and a half tonnes. In water this is not a problem, as the weight is evenly supported by external pressure. On land, however, it is a different story. All the pressure is exerted in one direction by gravity. It's like trying to breathe with a small car parked on your chest. Under anaesthesia, this is hardly helpful to a walrus's wellbeing. Even with a ventilator to breathe for the unconscious animal, and using drugs to encourage a less sluggish heartbeat, walrus anaesthesia is usually nerve-racking and occasionally fatal.

Thankfully, walrus anaesthesia is not needed that often. Still, having anaesthetised over 300 wild seals, I am all too familiar with them trying to suffocate themselves under anaesthesia by holding their breath. But there are other alarming anaesthesia patients besides walruses and seals.

Anaesthesia is hours of boredom, interspersed with moments of sheer terror. My patients, if they happen to wake up inadvertently, can quickly kill me. Having an endangered Asiatic lion blink and lick her lips while I had her anaesthetised, makes one think rather quickly. She won't be writing a letter of complaint to hospital management if she wakes up unexpectedly.

Anaesthetising the same wild animal can be completely different in disparate scenarios. Despite an intimidating appearance, white rhinos are often absurdly easy to anaesthetise in a zoo. The simplest thing is to give them a half bucket of fresh vegetables, and when they stick their head in to guzzle, to put a thin needle in one of the fine veins on the outer edge of their ear. They flick the ear once or twice as if a fly were biting them, then seem not to notice. I used to apply a local anaesthetic cream with gloves and wait 15 minutes for it to take effect, until I realised that most of them simply don't care. I attach a long thin drip-line, so the needle isn't pulled out, and then I will slowly inject, until, with a few big sighs, their legs crumple beneath them, and they are off to the land of oblivion. Feeding an animal while I anaesthetise it is not seen as best-practice among many anaesthetists – choking or breathing in regurgitated food are their biggest fears, and much of the human anaesthetic process is to limit the risk of this as much as possible. But a small bucket of fruit for a 3 tonne animal is like me eating half a chocolate bar. Still this horrifies some, until I explain the alternative. Would they rather have an hysterical patient running around in Accident and Emergency while you try to inject drugs into their butt-cheek? Stress hormones have a detrimental effect on the heart under anaesthesia, so this can quickly turn into an even worse scenario.

While anaesthesia for zoo rhinos is often simple and stress-free initially, this is only the getting them to sleep phase, or induction. Keeping rhinos safely asleep under anaesthesia, or maintenance, is a whole different matter. They don't breathe well under anaesthesia, but for different reasons to walruses. Broad, flat ribs are great protection for your vital organs from another rhino charging you, but make your chest rigid. Rhinos breathe mainly with their diaphragm, and so need to move their abdomen to breathe. Lying on your belly when anaesthetised doesn't make this easy. As anaesthesia slows down the gut's involuntary wave-like constriction and relaxation (peristalsis), gas accumulates in puffed-up intestines, further putting pressure on the diaphragm. Again, keeping anaesthesia as short as possible is the secret to success.

Capturing wild white rhinos in South Africa, where I qualified as a vet, requires slightly more effort. Much of the time they behave like a large grey cow, only with very poor

7

eyesight and a single horn on their nose. Rhinos don't enjoy being darted, and can be difficult to get close to, so they are often darted from a small helicopter. As helicopter fuel is horrendously expensive, helicopters like the Robinson R22 are so lightweight they almost appear made of paper, with no doors, and an engine hardly bigger than a garden lawn-mower's. Swooping down at speed to dart a rhino from as close a distance as possible means that when things go wrong, it is the equivalent of dropping out of the sky on a moped.

Things are considerably worse outside Africa, where other rhino species are far more endangered and rare, and dense forest makes finding them very difficult. I was once asked to come up with a way to safely anaesthetise rhinos for a project that had found a tiny number of a critically endangered rhino species in a geographic region where none were supposed to exist. But they were in dense jungle, in a low-grade war zone, where the only access was via freedom fighters, or terrorists, whichever perspective you prefer. Wandering around as a foreigner in camouflage on foot with a dartgun slung over your shoulder in a rebel-held war zone for months was never going to be an easy sell to my wife.

Wildlife vets refer to a bewildering array of different things as anaesthesia. Anaesthesia is usually defined as a controlled, temporary loss of sensation or awareness induced for medical purposes, with general anaesthesia being unconsciousness and a total lack of sensation. We rarely use local anaesthesia on its own in wildlife. A dentist attempting local anaesthesia on its own in a lion would be a one-patient wonder. In many cases we simply want to be able to handle, take a blood sample, or even just put an animal in a transport crate, and don't need the same depth of anaesthesia to block pain as for an operation. This is immobilisation, rather than anaesthesia, although the terms are often interchanged. Usually, when moving animals such as rhinos, we actually want them to be standing, so a lightly sedated rhino can be walked, although stumbling, with guiding ropes into a truck without the risks that come with full anaesthesia. This also has the benefit of the rhino doing the hard work for us, rather than needing a crane to lift it.

Standing sedation is the secret to safe capture of one of the least favourite anaesthetic patients of any wildlife vet: giraffes. Although their necks can be more than 2 metres long, they still only have seven neck bones, the same as most mammals. They also have a surprisingly thin skull. An anaesthetised giraffe keeling over and hitting the ground risks fatally breaking its neck. Better if we can dart the giraffe, then rush over before it falls down, and partly reverse the anaesthetic drugs. With some leg ropes and a blindfold the giraffe is dozy, but can be safely walked into a transport truck.

The dartgun

In July 1850, the *Times* newspaper reported the first successful anaesthesia in a wild animal. A cheetah at London Zoo had managed to break its leg. A sponge of chloroform on a long stick was held to its face until it become unconscious, and a successful amputation of its mangled leg was carried out under chloroform anaesthesia. But a chloroform-soaked sponge, even on a stick, is useless for lions or elephants running around the African savanna or orangutans swinging through the Bornean rainforest.

Enter the dartgun. While its invention may seem obvious, it wasn't so at the time. There were several insurmountable problems. Syringes, even after World War II, were made of glass, so hardly suitable for being shot out of a gun. Early human anaesthetic drugs needed injection via a vein, which was impossible with a dart, and most needed large volumes to be given.

First attempts at remote anaesthesia differed little from how South African bushmen and South Americans hunted wildlife with poison-coated arrows. Animals were shot with arrows coated with drugs such as curare and strychnine that their muscles had to dissolve and absorb slowly. One early attempt was actually a metal drill bit, the grooves filled with gallamine and glucose, shot into white-tailed deer with a carbon dioxide gun. Curare was used by native South Americans in blowpipe darts to kill animals for thousands of years. Gallamine was similar to curare, and both were terrible for anaesthesia. They paralysed muscles, so an animal couldn't move but was totally awake and could still feel pain normally. A tiny bit too much and it also paralysed the breathing muscles, with the patient suffocating. Another early design, powered by thick elastic bands, was lovingly named the bazooka, which perhaps wasn't the greatest endorsement.

Veterinarians have always proved to be extremely inventive. We have vet John Dunlop to thank for the pneumatic tyres we take for granted on our cars and bicycles. New Zealand vet Colin Murdoch was even more creative. Aged only 10 years, he made his own gunpowder, and a few years later his own homemade gun. Working after World War II, his most remarkable invention was the disposable plastic hypodermic syringe. He knew that despite boiling for sterilisation, glass syringes frequently spread infections between patients. The New Zealand Department of Health wasn't convinced of the merits of the plastic syringe and so he couldn't progress its development for several years, but it paved the way for another of his 46 other patented inventions.

Faced with the difficulties of catching Himalayan tahr, a large hairy wild goat introduced to New Zealand 50 years earlier for sport hunting, Murdoch invented the first dartgun. This would completely revolutionise wildlife veterinary work, particularly in Africa, with its many large dangerous wildlife species. However, there were still few suitable drugs. Murdoch started testing his dartgun using curare, which unfortunately killed many of the animals. Over the next two decades, a host of different companies came up with their own systems. Some used blank firearm cartridges, and without care the metal syringes could fatally shoot straight through smaller animals. Others used carbon dioxide, or a foot pump. Dart syringes also had different designs and mechanisms for injecting the drugs. Some were powered by butane or compressed air, while others used springs or bicarbonate-driven reactions caused by a tumbling eccentric weight.

In the late 1950s, the first successful dartgun captures of African game animals were carried out, on the kob, a beautiful orange-brown antelope with spiral horns, using a muscle paralysing drug similar to curare called succinylcholine. While this worked, better more potent drugs were clearly needed. The man who made these first captures and almost single-handedly started modern African game capture was Antonie 'Toni' Harthoorn. A tall and lanky Sandhurst-trained officer and commando during World War II, he graduated from the Royal Veterinary College in London, before ending up in East Africa. He started trialling strong opioids, drugs derived from morphine or other opium poppy compounds, in as many wildlife species as he could. He had plenty of opportunity, when rescuing wildlife stranded by the new Kariba Dam on the Zambezi river. In the early 1960s, he invented a breakthrough drug combination called M99. It contained etorphine, an opioid that was a thousand times as potent as morphine. Two to three millilitres was enough to anaesthetise an adult bull elephant. Etorphine is still one of the mainstays of anaesthesia in African wildlife today. It was originally discovered by Edinburgh researchers studying new anti-inflammatory medicines, when someone stirred the cups of tea with a glass lab rod that, unbeknown to them, had tiny traces of etorphine on it. Their shoddy hygiene almost killed them, but helped discover the drug for anaesthetising elephants in Africa. Etorphine was even investigated by British American Tobacco, who hoped it might create an additional addictive craving for cigarettes.

The benefit of such a concentrated drug was dramatic. When Harthoorn needed to move 100 white rhinos from the Hluhluwe-Imfolozi game park in South Africa, he had started first with morphine combinations for anaesthesia. The volumes were huge, requiring big 20-millilitre darts with considerable impact force. Ian Player, the park warden, describes wounds so large that he was forced to insert almost his whole arm into the depths of the animals to clean them out. Morphine was quickly abandoned for the slightly more potent opioid diethylthiambutene, but the huge volumes and wounds remained a problem until etorphine arrived.

Harthoorn went on to run a wildlife orphanage, and with his vet wife Sue Hart treated George Adamson's lions, made famous by the film *Born Free*. He inspired the TV show *Daktari* and the film *Clarence the Cross-Eyed Lion*, although he shunned the limelight himself. Abruptly losing his job at Nairobi University following Kenyan independence in 1963, he moved to South Africa where he continued pioneering wildlife capture, anaesthesia and medicine, some of which has still hardly changed. He wrote scientific papers and a 416-page book on the chemical capture of wildlife, which I still treasure on my bookshelf. Then, in a bizarre twist after retiring, he became a homeopath. The scientific pioneer of wildlife veterinary anaesthesia changed career to a human alternative medicine with no scientific basis at all. And he was still happily practising while I was studying at veterinary school.

Etorphine worked wonderfully in large herbivores, but not for carnivores. In South Africa we used phencyclidine, a human anaesthetic with the street drug name of 'Angel dust', to anaesthetise lions. For a while some North American wildlife vets used this on mountain lions as well. A long-retired colleague described how, in desperation, he once smuggled Angel dust in an aftershave bottle across Europe to anaesthetise his safari park lions. It can't have been pleasant. It took ages to work, lions were very twitchy, vomited and sometimes had seizures. It was thankfully replaced by the new human anaesthetic drug ketamine during the Vietnam War, when the American army also switched away from phencyclidine. Ketamine remains one of our main wildlife anaesthetic drugs today.

It seems logical that most cat species would metabolise drugs similarly; however, that isn't the case. Bizarrely, tigers don't tolerate the same anaesthetic drug dosages that lions do, despite being a similar size and are more prone to seizures under anaesthesia. Another group that reacts to anaesthetics very differently is bears. The first time I anaesthetised rescued sun bears in Cambodia a decade ago to transport them, I used drugs that work well in brown bears, and even moon bears, which live in the same region. But the sun bears' bodies drank the drugs up, and I had to use huge doses to get them asleep. They stayed anaesthetised for hours, and I had to stop the trucks every 15 minutes to wet the bears down so that they didn't overheat. Thankfully they were fine, but I never used that combination again. Even giant pandas react to medications very differently, particularly opioid drugs. Tramadol is a common painkiller for people and animals. At worst, side effects in humans are nausea and feeling slightly groggy. But in large animals, the consequences can be more far-reaching. A colleague once gave an arthritic giant panda a single low dose of tramadol, and was horrified to find she slept non-stop for almost four days without eating or drinking.

Concentrated drugs via the flying syringe, as dartguns were originally called, still have limitations. Darting a black wildebeest bull should be easy. Males are territorial during breeding season, unlike their crazy blue cousins. In good bushveld, you can see a male every few hundred metres just standing in his little area, keeping an eye out for passing females, or a neighbouring male drifting into his area to be chased off. You can drive to within 50 metres of a bull, if you approach slowly and obliquely. Approaching head-on is a guaranteed way to scare off any animal. You can get a long but reasonable shot with a well-maintained dartgun, but not if there are plains zebra around. These wandering pyjama-donkeys are far more suspicious, and before you can ever get close enough to be within dartgun range, with a loud bark from the stallion they all stampede off, triggering the wildebeest bull to do the same. You can waste a whole day staring at the jumble of bouncing striped bums running away, never able to take even a single shot at your wildebeest bull. Yet a zebra's flight zone, the distance it lets you approach before galloping off, is modest compared to some animals. Gemsbok are possibly the most beautiful of all antelope. But living in the Namib desert they can spot you kilometres away. Sometimes the only sight you can glimpse of a small herd is a tiny puff of dust on the horizon, making them impossible to reach with a dartgun from your Land Rover.

While it's easier to use a dartgun in a zoo, there is still a risk of injury, and at the least it is unpleasant and painful for the patient. It is often not much fun for the vet, either. I remember early in my career having to dart a gorilla. She knew what was going to happen and quivered in the corner, trying to hide herself in straw and crying. It was nerve-racking trying to dart her, but also distressing. Over the years I have seen all sorts of mishaps, from a pregnant antelope being darted directly into the brain, to broken bones and unfortunate deaths from unlucky shots.

Zoos now design enclosures with squeeze cages for us to safely inject patients by hand, or even better, train animals for hand injection. An adult tiger trained to calmly accept an anaesthetic injection is better for both patient and vet. Without surging adrenaline, anaesthetic onset is rapid, and much safer. This is now common for everything from chimpanzees to giant pandas.

There are other ways to make anaesthesia less stressful for our patients. We can sometimes anaesthetise animals like bears by putting drugs in their food. Carfentanil is an opioid that is ten thousand times the potency of morphine, even more potent than etorphine. Mixing it with a tablespoon of honey means bears will happily anaesthetise themselves. Even better, they seem happy to take it again in future, making repeated anaesthetics easy, rather than getting the animal stressed and wary. It even works in the most suspicious of zoo anaesthesia patients: chimpanzees.

Potent opioids would appear useless outside elephant anaesthesia, as even a tiny dose could be fatal to humans. In October 2002, when Chechen terrorists occupied a theatre in Moscow and took 900 people hostage, the Russian author-ities pumped a chemical agent into the ventilation system to incapacitate the terrorists. Sadly, more than a hundred hostages also died. While the Russian government never divulged what it used, later analysis of clothing at the Porton Down military research centre demonstrated that the chemical cocktail contained carfentanil.

Carfentanil was also used to cut heroin, with the predictable result of accidental deaths due to drugs being more potent than addicts had expected. These problems have led to opioids such as etorphine and carfentanil, which we so heavily rely on in wildlife anaesthesia, becoming very restricted. It is now impossible to import them for genuine wildlife work in much of the world. In some cases, we now have to use less safe and effective drug combinations than we were using half a century ago. I recently had my first giraffe anaesthesia death in two decades, because I couldn't get etorphine imported into the country I was working in, which was very sad and extremely frustrating.

Oral anaesthetics have also been used in wild birds. Sandhill cranes have been caught by mixing alpha-chloralose, a barbiturate, with corn and then catching them by hand when heavily sedated and unable to fly. It takes cranes 24 hours to recover, during which they have difficulty regulating their body temperature. It is essential to prevent them from overheating or becoming cold, both of which would be fatal. Alpha-chloralose is actually mainly marketed as an avicide – a poison to kill birds eating farm crops – highlighting the fine line anaesthesia treads between life and death.

There is the real danger that birds will gobble the anaesthetic corn and fly away before the half an hour it takes to have effect, so it is best offered late afternoon. Then if the cranes do fly away, they will likely roost nearby. Many birds have a crop, a dilation of the oesophagus that temporarily stores food. This is a clever evolutionary adaptation that allows them to quickly guzzle more than their stomach can hold before they fly away, so it's useful for avoiding predators. But the crop can delay alpha-chloralose taking effect after ingestion. If a crane flies far away before falling into an anaesthetised state, it is at real risk of being caught and eaten by predators, which may then also be affected.

Darting won't work well on a great hammerhead shark. Sharks have amazingly tough skin, covered with denticles. These are microscopic overlapping teeth made of dentine and containing a pulp cavity with nerves and blood vessels, just like those in your mouth. Sadly, this wonder has simply led to their skin being used as cheap sandpaper. Humans have little appreciation for the wonders of evolution. To anaesthetise a shark or other fish we can dissolve drugs in the water. One of the most effective and least toxic is eugenol, the main component of clove oil, but also found in nutmeg, cinnamon and basil. Eugenol also has local anaesthetic effects, and is used in dentistry to pack small wounds. A clownfish can be anaesthetised in a container of the diluted solution, gradually slowing down before floating to the surface. For a quick examination, you can remove the fish and place it on a wet incontinence pad, with its nice non-abrasive surface. To reverse anaesthesia we simply place Nemo in seawater again. Containers with different concentrations let us change anaesthesia depth like the dial on a gas anaesthetic machine for mammals and birds. For long procedures, such as surgery in a conger eel, a water pump anaesthetic machine is useful. This consists of a small pump pushing water through the fish's mouth and out through its gills, so it gets oxygen. Water has 25 times less oxygen available than air, so gills have evolved with lamella and fine filaments to have a very large surface area. Anaesthetic depth is altered by placing the pump's intake tube into the different concentrations of eugenol.

For an ultrasound examination, we can get away without any anaesthesia in a 3 metre long sand tiger shark, despite its formidable appearance, by using tonic immobility. Manipulating the shark in a stretcher onto its back, it freezes, giving us 10 minutes for our ultrasound exam. A golden pheasant can also be hypnotised by gently placing it on its back, as has been done with chickens by everyone from Friedrich Nietzsche to Ernest Hemingway. We can even mesmerise black iguanas. If we press gently down on their closed eyelids with our fingertips for a minute, the iguana's heartbeat slows and it will stay still for a few minutes, enough to take some X-rays without needing anaesthesia. In sharks, tonic immobility is unfortunately stressful, as can be shown by measuring stress hormones. It is probably a fright response similar to when attacked by an orca. Virginia opossums and hognose snakes also play dead to avoid being eaten. It is common advice to pretend to be dead if attacked by a bear, which is far easier said than done. Yet in iguanas it doesn't appear to be stressful, as the mechanism is different. Many people also gently press their closed eyelids during a stressful day to slow their heart rate and relieve their anxiety, using the same oculocardiac reflex.

For me to pass a long endoscope into a sand tiger shark's stomach, tonic immobility is insufficient, unless I want it to chew up the endoscope to join whatever it is I am trying to retrieve from the shark's stomach in the first place. But on its back, it is perfectly positioned to inject the same anaesthetic drugs we use in other animals. We need a long needle to reach the vein deep in the underside of the tail, just below the tail vertebrae and completely invisible. This is actually the same way I can anaesthetise an emerald tree boa, rhinoceros iguana, or even an alligator snapping turtle, with intravenous drugs, safely away from a biting mouth.

I can't use gaseous anaesthesia induction for a rhinoceros iguana, even if it has come some way from the days of ether and chloroform. Modern inhalation anaesthetics like isoflurane and sevoflurane are extremely safe, even in critically ill patients, and make it possible to fully anaesthetise a trumpeter hornbill in just two minutes with a face mask. Gas anaesthesia revolutionised bird anaesthesia, once halothane became available in the 1960s. Before this time, it was easy to kill birds with the available injectable drugs. It's remarkable that the respiratory systems of birds are extremely sensitive to inhaled substances. Coal miners used canaries as sentinels to detect any dangerous explosive gases, and just overheating a non-stick frying pan is enough to kill a pet scarlet macaw from the fluorocarbons given off by the polytetrafluoroethylene coating.

Ingeniously, evolution gave birds a breathing system only half the size and weight of mammals, keeping them light for flight, but twenty times as efficient for oxygen exchange, with their sets of air sacs acting as billows, and fine sponge lungs without any alveoli or diaphragm. Air flows in a circle, and birds absorb oxygen as air moves from air sacs at the rear of their body through the lungs to air sacs in the front. But this means birds must move their chest, like the bellows of an old church organ, to keep air moving around the system. Gases don't simply diffuse from the internal airways, as they do in mammals. Simply holding a bird tightly will cause it to suffocate. Under anaesthesia, chest movement is reduced. Inadvertently leaning our fingers on a tiny Scottish crossbill's body while operating, or taping the wings and legs out to take symmetrical X-rays of a racket-tailed roller bird, doesn't help matters. If anaesthesia is very brief, the patient is usually fine. But if it drags on, carbon dioxide builds up and fatally poisons our sleeping patient.

To help prevent this, we insert an endotracheal tube down into the windpipe. This allows us to move air through the system with a mechanical ventilator, or more simply by periodically squeezing a balloon-like bag with our hand. This keeps the oxygen and carbon dioxide exchange going even if the bird doesn't move its chest. We can now safely keep delicate patients asleep for hours for even the most complex surgery. Sometimes, we just make tubes ourselves from an intravenous catheter for tiny patients like an Egyptian tortoise.

Airway tubes were reported over five thousand years ago in Egyptian tablets, but had to be placed after cutting open the neck and windpipe – a tracheotomy. Thankfully, it's not something we need to perform for every anaesthesia. Alexander the Great is even purported to have performed a tracheotomy on an injured soldier on the battlefield, cutting the windpipe open with the tip of his sword. Nonsense or not, even in ancient times the importance of an open airway to breathing was well understood. Two centuries ago, metal coils covered in leather were inserted to resuscitate new-born babies, inflating their lungs like a party balloon. The tubes saved lives but risked severe injury from being rammed blindly down the invisible windpipe. The delicate vocal cords also lie at the entrance to the windpipe, and are easily damaged. These were replaced by metal, and eventually plastic ones. About a hundred years ago laryngoscopes, basically a metal tongue depressor with a light on the end, finally allowed one to see the windpipe opening to insert the tube, without needing to slash anything or brutalise the vocal cords.

Tubes inserted in the windpipe were also used to help revive drowning victims, and thanks to Arthur Guedel – known as the 'motorcycle anaesthetist' during World War I because he would rush between different field hospitals – and his success in preventing a dog from drowning, we have the modern tubes we use today. Guedel developed soft plastic tubes surrounded by a small inflatable balloon; essential in keeping a gorilla alive using a ventilator when I am doing open chest surgery, otherwise the lungs would fatally collapse; or to prevent regurgitated fluid from the large rumen stomach of a sable antelope going down the windpipe during anaesthesia and causing a catastrophic aspiration pneumonia. Back in the day, Guedel decided the best way of testing his contraption was to sedate the family dog, insert his tube and keep the animal submerged in the bath for an hour. It worked, but who knows what his family thought of him when they found out?

We employ endotracheal tubes in everything from spectacled bears to leaf-tailed geckos, to maintain them on gas anaesthesia. Some animals are difficult to entubate. Giant anteaters, with their long, thin mouth that hardly opens, are a challenge. Their windpipe entrance actually sits in their chest, so a special half-metre-long tube inserted with a thin flexible endoscope is needed. There are other hurdles too. King penguins have a dividing strut for most of their windpipe, preventing it from buckling or getting crushed when diving deep. Cocoi herons have a funnel-shaped windpipe that narrows, with a little ridge at the entrance, which helps prevent small fish going down their windpipe, but also makes inserting a tube more tricky. The windpipe of a bird is made up of overlapping cartilage rings, unlike the c-shaped rings in mammals. Inflating the balloon cuff on a tube needs care if you are not to catastrophically burst this delicate windpipe. Reptiles also pose challenges. A green anaconda's windpipe can be a metre long, but narrow, while a Burmese star tortoise's windpipe separates just behind its mouth into two separate tubes, to allow it to pull its head back quickly into its shell if a predatory golden jackal appears.

Gas anaesthesia works well in reptiles, so why can't we use a mask, just as we would in their avian relatives for induction? Anaesthetic gases like isoflurane have an irritant smell, and reptilian breath-holding ability is prodigious. Loggerhead turtles hold their breath while swimming for an hour or two, and breath holding of up to ten hours has been recorded. This is far from exceptional. It is not that rare for a pet Greek tortoise that has fallen into a garden pond to be found and safely retrieved by the traumatised owner several hours later, apparently no worse for the ordeal. Being able to hold your breath for hours and sometimes only eat a few times a year, as some crocodiles can, makes the old taxonomists' descriptions of reptiles as primitive or lower animals farcical. Our big human brains are not much good in those situations, whereas reptiles are clearly superbly adapted for their lives in the wild.

Yet there are big-brained mammals that need to hold their breath for long periods, and they too pose significant anaesthetic challenges. Bottlenose dolphins may live in water, but they breathe air. Researchers have always wanted to study dolphins' brains, as they are intelligent social animals, with a brain 10 per cent larger than ours. But anaesthesia has been a hurdle. The first primitive attempts to use ether in a cone facemask on stranded dolphins in the 1920s simply killed the animals. Different attempts after that fared little better for half a century. Eventually, it was the huge resources of the military during the Cold War that heralded progress. The Naval Undersea Warfare Centre looked into dolphin anaesthesia to treat the wild-caught dolphins they kept and trained at huge expense. Watching an old, declassified film from Naval Missile Centre at Point Mugu, California, when researching how I would perform needle-prick-sized keyhole surgery in bottlenose dolphins, was fascinating. It is common knowledge that dolphins can sleep with one half of their brain at a time so they don't drown. It is far less well known that dolphins can also sleep with both sides of their brain, just as we do.

A neurosurgeon friend describes being awake as a state of continuous low-grade brain damage. Sleep is vital to survival, despite the risks of a dolphin drowning, or a lion sneaking up on a sleeping giraffe. In calm seas, dolphins sleep with both sides of their brain, by floating in an upright position with just their blowhole emerging. Similar to walruses and seals, they normally take short fast breaths, with long periods of holding their breath. Ingeniously, when fully asleep they have a reflex to beat their tail just before they breathe, ensuring their blowhole is above the surface. When inducing anaesthesia in a dolphin, this tail flick is a unique reflex we can use to help us monitor our anaesthetic depth. Dolphin anaesthesia is full of challenges. Their unique breathing makes normal ventilators harmful, so special ventilators that mimic their normal breath-holding pattern are needed. Placing a breathing tube is challenging thanks to their breath-holding, strong gag reflex, and the unique anatomy between their blowhole and windpipe. Evolved to be surrounded by the even pressure of water, rather than squashed by gravity on land, dolphins also do better if anaesthetised in a water bath, making life difficult for everything else we need to do as vets.

Even if risky, at least we can anaesthetise dolphins. The animals no one has yet cracked for anaesthetic purposes are whales. We haven't even managed to effectively sedate them yet, although a few brave pioneers have tried various drug combinations, delivered by dartgun from a boat when the

21

whale surfaces. Why on earth would anyone need to try to sedate a wild whale, you might ask? The sad answer is: humans. With careless consumerism, the oceans are brimming with plastic, abandoned fishing gear and other rubbish. Whales are commonly entangled, but removing twisted and embedded netting and lines is extremely difficult. Your patient can suddenly plunge to two kilometres depth, stay underwater for an hour or two, before surfacing a kilometre away. A slap from a tail weighing several tonnes is also no small risk. One dedicated whale rescuer was sadly killed in this way a few years ago. A few wildlife vets are persevering to find a way to at least sedate whales to try and make the whole process safer and less stressful. But we are not there yet.

Despite all our scientific progress, anaesthesia of wildlife is still difficult. But to try and 'calm the wild beast', sometimes we face an even greater challenge just trying to catch it in the first place.

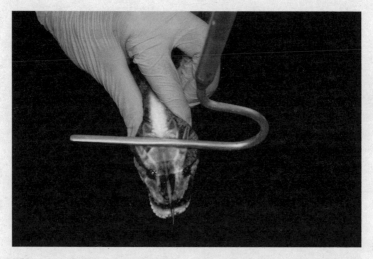

When using a hook to pin a snake, we press down on the head, squashing the flexible
jaw bones out of the way, as the brain is well protected. It is essential to avoid the
neck, as there is only a single weak joint at the back of the skull.

2

Catching crocodiles with shoelaces

Of all the things my wife made me give up when we got married, I miss catching venomous snakes on police drug raids the most. The early morning police station briefing, surrounded by muscular officers wearing bullet-proof vests; watching them take down the steel reinforced door with the small battering ram they called 'the enforcer'; the characters hurriedly bundled out the door in various stages of restraint, and occasional undress. Then I would be given a brief nod, and clutching my snake hooks and some empty pillowcases, I would step inside, never sure exactly what I would find.

Darting a roaring lion, operating on a giant panda, running away from a grumpy buffalo, or performing an ultrasound scan on a fully conscious crocodile can all give my adrenal glands a healthy massage. But nothing beats the sheer mental clarity and focus from the blast of adrenaline I get when catching a venomous snake.

It appears strange to write about capturing my patients. It's hardly medical. My human physician colleagues don't usually have to run around the Accident and Emergency ward trying to grab their patients; except on the psychiatric ward, perhaps. Like a paediatrician, I can't explain to my patient that I am trying to help, or what I am planning to do. The difference is, small children can't maul you like a leopard, or gore you like an angry gaur.

But why catch anything, I hear you ask? You can simply dart them. Unlike a James Bond movie where someone falls instantly asleep after being darted in the neck with something the size of a fruit fly, the reality is disappointingly different. Anaesthesia darting is far from instantaneous. I have watched in despair as a collared peccary still galloped around madly half an hour after being darted. Stress often makes an adrenaline-infused body oblivious to the fact it is so full of drugs that it should, at least according to the scientific papers, be unconscious by now. Stress is also not helped by darting. You are, after all, shooting an animal. Some dartguns are powered by blank gun cartridges and shot from a modified gun. Old cruder models not infrequently killed wild patients by blasting the dart straight through them. The metal darts were the same diameter as an elephant gun bullet, and on a bad day had the same effect.

The dart (syringe) is lightweight plastic, but the needle is still a metal needle. I even saw an adult cheetah's back leg bone break just with a blowpipe. Darting is often not our first option for capturing wild animals for treatment. Who wants to risk breaking an antelope's leg when you only need to remove a stone stuck between its toes?

My wildlife patients occasionally capture themselves, such as a hedgehog caught in a discarded ice-cream tub, or an angry ratel that's fallen into a septic tank. However, on most occasions a little more effort is needed. Over the years I have caught snakes with clothes hangers, a tiger's vaginal speculum, pillowcases, a variety of sticks, and old yoga mats. On drug raids, when I was tasked with catching snakes for the police (which I did to earn extra money while studying to become a specialist), despite informers swearing to numerous king cobras roaming loose, on most occasions there were only a couple of small non-venomous rat snakes, or a tiny ball python in a little glass fish tank. These would never be able to kill you, even if someone tried to strangle you with one. Most of the time the dealers only told people the snakes were lethal, but just occasionally someone really would be crazy enough to have a room full of diamond-back rattlesnakes.

Snake hooks, improvised coat-hangers, sticks or brooms all lift a snake and keep the head well away from any part of you it can bite. You can then chaperone it into a bag or container. Bags, like pillowcases closed with cable ties, are simple and safe, as you can see exactly where the snake is inside. Opening a wooden box lid blindly risks a snake exploding out in your face. Naturally, the best way of handling venomous snakes is to avoid actually using your hands. Dangling snakes by their tail, yo-yo style, despite its popularity by Australian TV presenters, is bad news. Heavy snakes like a puff adder will damage their spine, while intelligent snakes like the black mamba may realise they can still bite you by striking sideways. To handle them for veterinary procedures such as taking a blood sample from their tail, we encourage them into a tight-fitting clear tube, in which they can't turn. On one occasion, the only thing to hand was a Perspex tube used as a tiger vaginal speculum, which I put to good use restraining the front end of an injured coral snake to clean a lacerated wound on its side, when it tried to squeeze through a drain. It is reassuring to observe an Eastern coral snake's bright stripes through the transparent tube while you recite to yourself 'Red on black, venom lack; red on yellow, kill a fellow' to differentiate these from similar-looking but harmless king snakes. The rule is sadly useless outside North America, as several venomous Asian coral snakes have red on black stripes.

Occasionally, I do have to handle venomous snakes by hand. A firm, slightly springy surface, like a rubber mat, works best for this. Snake hooks are often just made by chopping the head off a golf club, and replacing this with a slender flat-sided hook, but in an emergency even a wire coat-hanger can be quickly fashioned into a suitable hook. Snakes can be lifted using the hook into a bag without using your hands, but you can also pin a snake's head down securely, so you can grasp it safely just behind the head without being bitten. Pinning a lizard would crush its skull, but snake anatomy helps us out. Aside from the small but strong cranium bones protecting its brain, other skull and jaw bones are only loosely connected by ligaments. This allows a snake to swallow animals much wider than its head – such as an African rock python slowly walking its individual upper and lower jaw bones, with backward-pointing teeth, over the springbok it has just suffocated by constriction. The joints don't dislocate, they are just very flexible. They also act as a shock-absorber when pinning the visibly squashed head for treatment, while the brain is safely protected in its tiny, thick cranium.

Snakes only have a single joint or condyle attaching their head to their neck. Humans and most mammals have two, and this is a weak point in snake design. Carelessly pinning a snake down behind its head can dislocate the spine and sever the spinal cord. Despite offering superb protection of their brain, the rest of a snake's body is surprisingly fragile. The entire body length consists of hundreds of slender ribs, easily broken if grasped too firmly by a fearful human.

Snakes are deserving of our respect. Black mambas are a venomous species that can slither almost as fast as a man can run, chasing anyone getting too close to their precious eggs. Even after pinning them, you treat them with the utmost care and precision. Gaboon vipers have long front-hinged fangs, which can still pierce you even though their mouth is supposedly held securely. They have even bitten handlers by piercing their fang through the skin of their own lower jaw. Boomslangs have short back fangs but can catch you by wriggling their jaws up and down while being held. Their tiny bites and lack of any apparent symptoms for the first few hours can lull you into a false sense of a lucky escape, until their anticoagulant venom kicks in fatally. Snakes are also deceptively strong. Seeing a cottonmouth suddenly jerking free from a handler to fly through the air and land at your feet is not reassuring. And we never stand directly in front of a snake, as some, like the Mozambique spitting cobra, can eject venom forcefully from their fangs into your eyes, even if they can't bite you. One reason I am grateful to wear glasses.

Capture equipment is sometimes more bizarre and ad hoc, such as using a shoelace to catch a crocodile. A large Nile crocodile may appear more fearsome than a snake, but it is often easier to catch. Approaching from the rear, and with others distracting it, once you're on the crocodile's back their jaws can usually be held closed with your hands until tied shut. A trouser belt, duct tape, or even shoelaces are all sufficiently strong to hold these fearsome beasts' mouths safely closed. While they can snap a half-tonne plains zebra's leg bone in half, all their muscle power is for clamping those ferocious jaws closed. They only have weak muscles to open their mouths. We always try to catch crocodiles on land, so they are unable to attempt their aquatic death-roll. They are also best caught early in the morning, before they warm up. Being cold-blooded, or poikilothermic, all their metabolic processes are regulated by their environmental temperatures. A colder crocodile is more lethargic, and less likely to grab your arm and rip it off.

A broom is one of the most useful pieces of capture equipment. Whether approaching an anaesthetised zoo leopard that may still wake up, or encouraging a grumpy cape porcupine into a crate, a broom gives just enough safe distance from being bitten or impaled, and is unlikely to hurt your patient. A golden jackal can be pinned in a trap just long enough for an injection, without the risk to both parties from actually trying to grab it. An old, discarded cupboard door with its handle also makes an excellent aide to moving unruly collared peccaries without being bitten, although professionally made pig boards, resembling riot shields, can also be bought.

Cling film, pencils, and artist paintbrushes are all excellent for wrangling small but tetchy patients. As children in South Africa, we dared each other to catch scorpions by hand. Not a particularly sensible pastime. Even as kids we knew not to catch scorpions with small pincers and muscular tails. These are usually highly venomous and kill their prey by their venom. Instead we caught larger, more fearsome-looking scorpions with scary pincers but thinner tails. Their sting, should they catch you, wasn't so severe. Scorpions can only sting directly in front of their mouth, and they have to position their whole body to face their prey. They can't move their tail to the side to sting. This makes them easy to catch. Approaching from behind, then gripping the tail from either side with thumb and forefinger as high up the raised tail and as close to the scary stinger as possible, is the ideal way. They can more professionally be caught with a long pair of padded forceps, instead of your fingers, to be safely ushered into a suitable receptacle.

Catching tarantulas is more interesting. Cambodian children search out zebra leg tarantula burrows and simply stick their hands in lightning fast and pull them out. The secret must be their fearless manner, as these spiders have a reputation for being grumpy and quick to bite. The alternative is to carefully dig out the burrow until one reaches the spider, then lift it into a bucket with a spade. In Cambodia, spiders are sold to be cooked, or exported to food markets in Thailand. Many tourists try fried tarantula for the novelty, but sadly are unaware that a large tarantula may be over 30 years old. Capturing tarantulas for food is totally unsustainable; they have now disappeared from many areas, and this allows a proliferation of insects and mice to damage rice and other crops.

Catching a captive Brazilian salmon-pink, bird-eating tarantula is quite easy. Despite being one of the largest spiders in the world, with a leg span the size of a dinner plate, they are less prone to bite than Asian tarantulas such as the zebra leg, or aggressive African baboon spiders. The main defence for many South American tarantulas is not to bite, but instead to kick irritating hairs off their body into a predator's face. This is actually far worse than a bite. With barbs on either end, the hairs cause itching in the skin or nose, and even bronchospasm, as if you were asthmatic. But the eyes are the real target. Incredibly painful, these hairs render any foe blind. Their tiny size and barbed nature make them impossible to remove, and can cause long-term problems. Even when just cleaning a tarantula container, we are paranoid never to touch our eyes.

You can safely pin a Mexican red knee tarantula down with a piece of stretched cling film to examine it. I still prefer catching tarantulas by hand to hold them for an examination. I use a small artist's watercolour brush and a pencil with a small eraser on the back. With the paintbrush, I will gently stroke what appear to be the smaller first pair of legs. These are actually the pedipalps or false legs. They contain more nerves and receptors than the actual legs, and allow tarantulas to taste and sense their environment. A tarantula's eight tiny eyes are pretty useless for any detailed sight. Ground-dwelling tarantulas detect and catch prey by sensing air movements via the hairs on their pedipalps, legs and body. Each hair has a nerve at its base. Stroking pedipalps is like the nerve stim-ulation of whispering in a tiger's ear – it lets me know what mood the spider is in. An irritable spider will immediately rear up, baring its fangs, and may strike at the brush, whereas a more amenable bird-eater will stay still. Although I will have to catch both, I now have a better idea of what to expect. Using the back of the pencil, we quickly pin the tarantula down gently but firmly. The eraser provides friction so the pencil doesn't slide off and the tarantula flip over and bite me as I reach to pick it up. Replacing the pencil with my index finger to pin the spider down, I place my thumb and middle finger on either side between the legs, and lift the spider up. It really is that easy. I can now flush the mouth to sample a discharge, or treat an injured leg. But you have to avoid the waving legs. Each foot has two barely visible small hooks. If they attach, the spider will flip around, sinking its fangs into the palm of my hand.

Each animal species has its own quirks to being safely caught and handled. If you catch and handle lemur frogs with dry hands, you damage their invisible layer of protective mucus, and some will be dead within the week from skin infections. Using wet rubber gloves helps prevent this. Gloves also help prevent the spread of diseases such as chytridiomycosis, currently implicated in amphibians declining worldwide. However, if you handle tadpoles with latex gloves for a conservation project, most will be dead within a day. You instead need to use vinyl gloves if handling can't be avoided. Amphibian skin is very thin, in many places only a few cells thick. Many substances innocuous to us can cross this barrier and prove toxic. Even holding them in some plastic containers can be fatal, as bioactive chemicals can leach into the water in tiny quantities. The mucus layer is vital protection, as most deadly infections in amphibians, like aquatic tuberculosis, will enter through the skin. So a wet incontinence pad is an ideal non-abrasive surface upon which to handle frogs and newts.

When grabbing an African crowned eagle, gloves are not particularly useful. Their large hooked beak, more obvious than the crown of feathers that sits flat most of the time, is not the end to be cautious of. It's the eagle's feet you have to be careful with. While not the biggest African eagle, these impressive birds easily take small antelope and monkeys as meals. When removing an eagle from a trap, a leather falconry glove, unless covered in chain mail, is pretty useless protection from a bird of prey that is capable of penetrating your skull with its long talons and strong feet.

Wild eagles and falcons are caught using numerous small fishing-line snares set over a cage containing food. Many a long boring hour is spent watching traps with binoculars from a distance. Catching nestling eagles is considerably faster, but even with tree-climbing rope skills you risk losing your footing when dive-bombed by angry parents, and end up inadvertently bungee-jumping through branches halfway down a towering tree. After you have spent hours watching a trap, when an eagle finally swoops down to try and grasp its meal through the cage, it finds its feet tangled in the numerous looped snares covering the cage surface. The long wait over, you sprint over, and the part of extricating the bird without either party getting injured begins. While teaching young vets for decades on the perils of injury and to focus on a bird of prey's feet rather than its beak, I myself have a small facial scar, where a white-tailed eagle once ripped a small chunk out of my cheek when I grabbed it.

Leather welding gloves, a cheap version of traditional falconry gauntlets, are often touted as the best animal handling accessory for everything from iguanas and macaws to small carnivores and primates. They are the perfect combination of being thin, unwieldy, poor fitting, and insensitive to what your hands are doing. Lulling you into a false sense of protection, they are well suited to allow a scarlet macaw to lacerate your hand through the glove, or a Hamlyn's monkey to mutilate your fingers by chewing through the thin leather. I have been unfortunate enough to have an eagle owl skewer its talons through my wrist when the handler was using leather gloves, and the foot slipped from their grasp.

The best handling equipment for eagles, owls and most birds of prey is the humble bath towel. Throwing this over the bird's head allows you to grab the legs without being mangled by the talons. The towel also stops birds flailing their wings around and injuring themselves. Hessian rice sacks, a jacket, sleeping bag or almost anything similar can be used as effectively. Modestly sized birds, from a saker falcon to a cockatoo, can then simply be wrapped completely in the towel, while just leaving a wing, head, or other part to be examined or treated, protruding in what I refer to as the burrito technique.

Swan bags work similarly. These were invented by a wildlife rescuer friend, Colin Seddon, who first bundled a fractious mute swan into a cloth tool bag to restrain it while removing a fishing hook from its beak. Nowadays circular bags of waterproof canvas with Velcro straps and handles are used everywhere by those handling and moving swans, geese, cranes and pelicans. Easy to clean and store, they keep birds calm while restrained, and have the benefit of keeping any poop produced inside the bag, rather than splattered everywhere inside your car.

Some birds have dangerous beaks. Hyacinth macaws have a natural nutcracker attached to their face, although garden secateurs, able to prune a finger off, is perhaps a more accurate description. Towels are again our handling equipment of choice, so the parrot can't see where your fingers are beneath the cloth. Parrots use their beak like a third leg to climb with. That gives you a split second to grab a bird safely while the beak is otherwise occupied with climbing.

The risk from other beaks can be underestimated. As I tried rescuing a heron tangled in fish line, the stressed bird desperately tried its only defence – stabbing lightning fast at my eyes with its stiletto beak, like a snake striking. My spectacles saved me, the blow glancing off to nick my brow. All feathers and chopstick legs, the main handling risk with herons is the ease with which their long fragile legs are injured. Northern gannets will similarly strike at the eyes in self-defence. My spectacles probably wouldn't be able to protect me from this largest of gannet species. Living just half an hour away from the world's largest breeding colony, I am always careful when handling these striking and delicate creatures.

Many birds use their beaks as their only form of defence, even if they are pretty useless at inflicting any injury. Treating flamingos, I find it's not even worth the effort avoiding them biting you, as the pinches they furiously administer with the tips of their angled beaks are little more than amusing pin pricks. Flamingos have little defence except fleeing, hence why they live in large colonies and breed in inhospitable caustic lakes. Yet they are one of the longest-living birds. A greater flamingo reached 83 years of age at Adelaide Zoo, not so bad for a defenceless bird.

There is, however, one bird whose beak I am particularly cautious of. One of the most intelligent and by far the most difficult birds I have ever had to trap in the wild, it took us four months to catch just two vultures. Unlike other birds of prey, they have stubby unimpressive talons on their feet but ferociously strong beaks. The first to arrive at the scene of dead animals, they use their beaks to hurriedly rip open the thick hide to get to the meat and organs before other animals arrive and chase them away.

Catching crocodiles with shoelaces

I was a young vet working in a team in India investigating the collapse of the Indian vulture population, which had gone from one of the most common birds to almost extinct in a decade. It was an ecological tragedy. Feral dog populations exploded, and so did human rabies deaths, as a result. The Parsi community had a particular problem, having for centuries relied on vultures to dispose of their dead in the towers of silence as part of their Zoroastrian faith.

We needed to catch some birds for a breeding programme, as insurance against extinction. Previous attempts had been spectacularly unsuccessful. Even visiting specialists, who had caught the last remaining Californian condors, failed to catch a single Indian vulture. In despair, the project turned to traditional bird-trappers.

Vultures have a sense of safety in large groups. They are extremely cautious about descending to a carcass when no other animals are around. This had become more pronounced with their low numbers. Circling out of sight kilometres high, crossing between India and Pakistan and back, they could see us setting traps below in the Thar desert. So we would be up at four in the morning in the dark, tiptoeing, with just a small torchlight, through a stinking carcass dump in the desert, trying to avoid the baying feral dogs, some of which clearly had rabies. All sorts of hidden spring traps failed to work. There would invariably be feral dogs standing on the edges of the traps and preventing them snapping closed when triggered. And once triggered, vultures would avoid that area for weeks.

Our local bird-trapper, Ali Hussain, used a traditional trapper's method that was unique. He would build a small hide out of a mound of sticks and grass and sit hunched inside this, a few metres from the carcass. He would then wait, spending up to ten hours curled up in a tiny taut ball without moving, waiting for a vulture to come down. By the early afternoon, if no vultures had appeared, the thin grey-haired 60-something-year-old would abandon his post and emerge from the sweltering oven of a hide sweating and encrusted with grass and twigs.

If vultures did land, Ali would need to hold his nerve and wait until a small group had arrived and were engrossed in feeding and squabbling. Ever so slowly over 10 minutes, he would advance a thin bamboo pole. Carefully he would extend this with a series of carefully trimmed bamboo poles, fitting each one into the next, to be able to reach the target vulture. The tip was a thin fork, resembling a snake's tongue, which he had smeared with a thick glue of boiled fig-tree sap, a recipe passed down in his family for generations, and jealously guarded. Finally, Ali would jab the stick at the vulture. The vulture would immediately try to take off, but impeded by the attached stick would be slowed down for a few seconds, just enough for Ali to explode out of the hide, sprint towards the vulture and jump on top of it. Sometimes he won, but often the precious vulture still got away. When the capture was successful, Ali and his son always ended up with gashes from the vulture's hooked beak, as evident from their heavily scarred hands and arms. A vulture beak is strong enough to sever a finger, but despite this Ali and his son didn't seem to mind. I suspect they preferred the injuries to going back into the hot sweaty hide for days.

Some animals are almost impossible to catch alive. My friend Kirsty Officer spent months in Vietnam trying to catch a splinter group of Cat Ba langurs with no success. With only 65 individuals left on their mountainous island, the hope was to catch and relocate a handful of isolated females stranded on another island. But catching the previously hunted primates on sheer limestone cliffs proved impossible. In more than a decade's efforts, only two females were ever successfully caught and translocated to the main group.

Sometimes intelligence makes animals easier to catch. The method for catching chacma baboons remains unchanged for hundreds of years in South Africa. Nuts are placed inside a dried calabash shell with a hole in it, and the shell is secured to a post. The baboon figures out there is food inside the calabash shell, inserts his hand and grabs the food but then is unable to pull his closed hand out of the small hole. The baboon refuses to let go of his precious find, and sits at the trap until the hunter comes along to dispatch him, or during the 1980s bundle him into a cage for sale as a laboratory animal overseas. We can still use this method today to catch baboons in order to fit radio-collars.

Talk about wildlife capture, and most will immediately think of large African animals. While the 1950s and 60s was a heyday for catching large wild animals from Africa for zoos, chasing them down with vehicles and ropes, the most extensive African wildlife capture period was actually under ancient Rome. Humans had already been catching wild animals for thousands of years. There are hieroglyph panels of Egyptians parading antelopes, cheetahs and even giraffes on leads, although there are no known records of how they managed to catch them. The Romans possibly made an entire North African elephant species extinct, and decimated many wild animal populations in the Mediterranean and North Africa. During Augustus's reign alone, over 3,500 elephants were killed in games.

The stress of capture

The first vets in zoos were constantly presented with new species of patients and all manner of unknown ailments. The results of these early zoo veterinarians were pretty rubbish. With blood-letting, blistering, administering mercury, arsenic, and other toxic drenches, and a lack of any anaesthesia or aseptic surgery, it is little surprise that vets probably did most patients more harm than good. The only vaguely scientific aspect to the whole endeavour was the post-mortem understanding of anatomy. As a cantankerous old zoo vet said, when questioned about what appeared to be a pointless treatment, 'One needs to be seen to do something.' Yet it wasn't just vets' limited abilities or knowledge that was to blame. The stress and trauma animals went through before arriving at a zoo often sealed their fate. Some elephants living in zoos and sanctuaries today still clearly have the mental trauma from their capture and breaking-in from distant lands decades ago. We still deal with these problems in other animals arriving at rescue sanctuaries across the world. Confiscated from smugglers, the majority of pangolins will still die, despite our modern knowledge and drugs. Stress hormones like cortisol dampen down the activity of white blood cells and suppress the immune system, leading to all manner of infections.

Without due care, today's wildlife researchers can cause harm to their subjects during capture, mesmerised by a belief in the scientific value of the data they will get. There can be disappointingly little thought about the impact on wild subjects' remaining lives, once precious research samples have been harvested. Wildlife veterinarians, as custodians of animal welfare and health, sometimes have to disagree with colleagues, striving to bring balance to research projects.

A snare is one of the most horrible ways of catching a wild animal. The fear and distress of an animal caught in these primitive traps is difficult to imagine. Stuck in the open and vulnerable to attack by predators, as the wire bites deep into their flesh, some animals will gnaw their own leg off in desperation. Exhausted, thirsty and in pain, if lucky they are only trapped a day or so, before the hunter arrives to kill them. Millions of animals are killed or maimed by snares every year worldwide. Snares are indiscriminate, killing not just their intended targets. From chimpanzees that have lost their fingers, to sun bears with missing legs, strangled otters, and the dead mother babirusa with her confused hungry piglets keeping vigil by her side, I hate snares with all my being, having witnessed the damage they cause through treating victims of all shapes and sizes in the countries I've worked in. I live for the day when they are illegal worldwide, recognised for the barbaric and inhumane devices they are.

Despite this, occasionally wildlife vets have still needed to use these horrid devices to catch a patient when there were no other options. Unlike Bengal tigers in the Sundarbans mangrove swamps that can still be captured by darting, Siberian tigers roaming the expanse of far eastern Russia are much more sparsely distributed. Freezing temperatures will jam all sorts of trap mechanisms. As a last resort, vets may turn to snares. These are not ordinary snares but have thick plastic-padded wires with loud clanging bells attached. Now replaced by mobile phone alarms, wildlife vets waiting remotely at camp immediately know if they are triggered. Vets then rapidly dart the trapped tiger they would never otherwise even glimpse. This is sometimes the only way to catch a handful of animals over many months of patient waiting. Even with skilled snare placement for the desired animal's natural behaviour, occasionally one arrives to find a furious black bear in the trap, which still needs to be anaesthetised, just to free it. A wildlife veteran of Russian winters told me how different the behaviour of various animals caught in these snares was. A snared tiger could be heard furiously roaring and thrashing around over a kilometre away. Yet its cortisol stress levels were not as high as the tiger's noisy demeanour made you expect. Catching a rare Amur leopard in the snare, one of the most critically endangered cats on the planet with fewer than a hundred left in the wild, you would be forgiven for thinking it's a false alarm, until arriving, where you would see her silently crouching. Yet her cortisol stress hormone levels measured in a blood sample would be sky high. She had clearly realised she was an easy snack for any passing tiger or bear.

I avoid snares unless absolutely nothing else is possible. But place a thick plastic-coated wire loop, in essence a snare, on a long pole, and you have a useful grabbing device. The catch-pole is used by wardens catching rabid dogs; rangers retrieving a raccoon stuck down a drain or getting a coyote trapped in a basement; for handling a harbour seal entangled in a fishing net; catching a Tasmanian devil with a facial tumour; or snaring a stump-tailed macaque causing a riot in a fruit market.

Traps can be less traumatic than graspers. The best traps are those built into wildlife sanctuary and zoo enclosures. We can then use the animals' own behaviour to catch them safely and with minimal stress. Animals moved daily between outside and indoor enclosures, for cleaning and feeding, become accustomed to the routine. Including cage tunnels with sliding doors allows easy separation of a yellow-breasted capuchin when it needs to be caught. If the tunnel is removable we can transport the capuchin to a hospital. Including an internal sliding wall and handles makes this a squeeze-cage. Squashing him immobile to the side for a few seconds, we can then safely inject him. This is far less stressful than trying to catch an adrenaline-infused capuchin with nets on poles while it bounces off enclosure walls; or trying to dart your delicate patient as it jumps and swings between ropes to avoid you.

In the wild, trapping becomes more difficult. We can usually use contraptions less risky than snares. Most simply have a pressure plate that, when a wolverine steps on it once inside, closes the door. Some instead have a mechanism to which food is attached. When a bobcat tugs on it, this releases the door. Spring clips hold doors locked once closed, to prevent clever animals like raccoons from figuring out a way to open the trap. There are all manner of cage traps, some even remote-controlled, to safely catch alive most mammals you can think of.

Traps can take ages to work, as I learned over a decade catching and testing European beavers for their reintroductions to England and Scotland. We needed to check they were not carrying infections, and especially a nasty zoonotic tapeworm called *Echinococcus multilocularis*. This marked the first return of a wild mammal to the United Kingdom; unfortunately the wheels of bureaucracy had turned too slowly for some enthusiastic beaver fans and a considerable number of beavers had supposedly escaped, and were happily breeding and spreading along the River Tay. We were given eight months to catch and health screen as many as possible, which seemed like loads of time. We had an expert beaver biologist, and suitable spring-operated cage traps loaded with beaver favourites like turnip, apple and aspen. The traps were left unlocked and open for a week beforehand to get beavers used to taking food from them, and they were widely spread and remote from roads. We caught three beavers in the first week, and felt confident. But the beavers naturally had other plans, and it took a further two months before we caught another one.

On another project in England, we resorted to expert trappers from Scandinavia for the single-week period we had. They spent nights hiding in trees and jumped down on the beavers when they emerged, like something out of a *Rambo* movie. We caught 18 beavers with no injuries. Once caught, the easiest way to handle this largest of European rodents is to bundle them into a large hessian potato sack. The beavers stay calm inside. A hole in one corner lets you squeeze the beaver like a tube of toothpaste, until its nose emerges, for gas anaesthesia with a mask, or the tail can be careful extended from the sack opening so a blood sample can be taken.

Attracting animals to traps is a challenge, especially if your patient is intelligent and can eat almost anything in an environment where there is plenty of food. For a beaver, an apple may prove tempting enough to enter the unfamiliar trap. For a leopard, this won't work. These clever animals are very adaptable, often living invisibly inside cities, and can eat anything from termites to antelopes. They have one dietary weak-spot. This can't be used to trap them, but it may alert people to their presence, and be the reason they need to be moved somewhere safer. Leopards seem to have a bizarre taste for dogs.

In India this is seen as a benefit, with massive numbers of feral dogs, and the highest numbers of human rabies cases in the world. One study found leopards living in Mumbai eat 1,500 feral dogs a year. It is estimated they prevent over a thousand human dog bites annually and a hundred fatal human rabies cases a year. Dogs appear to make up half the entire diet of these leopards. In Africa, leopards may live on a farm for many years, never tempted to eat the livestock. No one ever realises they are there, until one eats a dog. Once this happens, they may return to eat more dogs, even entering houses via windows or dog flaps to hunt pet dogs once the taste has been acquired. Strange and risky behaviour from an adaptable animal that is otherwise the ultimate survivor. Leopards normally avoid human contact, and can live just on termites and small rodents if they need to.

While dogs are there to protect livestock, the loss of a dog is normally more upsetting to the farmer, who then wants rid of the leopard. But how to trap them? There is plenty of other food available safely outside the trap, and you clearly can't use a dog as bait. Instead, we can turn to high fashion.

Calvin Klein's fragrance, Obsession For Men, was marketed as having 'notes of bergamot, mandarin and vanilla, with a heart of sandalwood and oakmoss'. Less charitably, the scent is simply musky. But it seems alluring to leopards, who seem unable to resist the smell. It is perfect to bait a trap to catch one. It has also been used to try to catch man-eating tigers in India, and perfumed camera traps are more likely to be visited by jaguars in the South American jungle, making studying their numbers easier. Perhaps the house of Calvin Klein didn't appreciate its scent's growing reputation in the animal world, as they discontinued it a few years ago. But popular for decades, there is still plenty of stock, and none of us have run out yet.

We can also use a scent favoured by past frontier fur-trappers. Castoreum, a pungent secretion from beavers' glands used to mark their territory, is preferred by bears and wolves. Once used in perfumes by Chanel, Lancôme and Givenchy to suggest notes of leather, I still wouldn't recommend it on a date night. Other animal baiting scents we use include drop-pings from rock hyrax and smeared secretions from badgers' subcaudal glands.

Traps can be the last resort to prevent extinction. The black-footed ferret is a specialist prairie dog predator that declined even faster than prairie dogs, as its habitat was converted to farmlands. The species was affected by the same bubonic plague bacteria that killed the prairie dogs, after it arrived in North America. Believed extinct in 1979, a tiny group was found two years later, after a dog brought a dead ferret back. The last 18 black-footed ferrets were caught in 1987 for captive breeding to save the species. The traps could not have been more simple: just wire mesh tubes, with a basic mousetrap closing door. But they worked. Today, more than a thousand ferrets survive in the wild, with hundreds more in captive breeding programmes still being released back into the wild.

One obvious aspect of trapping can still be missed. The species you are trying to catch needs to actually be living where you are trapping. One of the largest gardening store chains in Northern Ireland ran promotions for mole traps and repellents for months, until it was pointed out that there are no moles at all on the island of Ireland. Sea levels rose too quickly at the end of the last ice age to allow them to cross from England. Other mammals found on the mainland also didn't make it. For example, Ireland also has no weasels.

Traps are not suitable for everything. Watching the film *Hatari* gives an idea of how large African wild animal capture was carried out during much of the twentieth century. Animals were simply chased and then roped with nooses on long poles, or nets, and moved into large crates. Originally this was done on horseback, then the motorcar made it possible to chase down animals that could run much faster than a horse, or were simply too dangerous to chase. It also kept Hollywood stars safe from a cantankerous black rhino, while still being able to chase the animals for the film.

The film promoters for *Hatari* were eager to publicise that John Wayne and the actors did their own stunts and caught the animals themselves, in a display of ultimate manliness. There is one scene in which a now endangered beisa antelope stands absolutely exhausted after a long chase, in the hot sun, visibly panting with its mouth open. Beisa, and their close relatives the gemsbok, are possibly the most heat-resistant antelopes in sub-Saharan Africa. They have a unique circulation system in their head, able to cool blood flowing to their brain using the capillaries in their nose as they breathe. It's the zoological equivalent of a car radiator. They can tolerate raised body temperatures which would cause fatal brain damage in other animals, and conserve water otherwise needed for sweat, another useful trick for an arid-region antelope. They are supreme athletes and long-distance runners. Seeing it chased to exhaustion, I am certain this particular beisa died after filming from capture myopathy.

Capture myopathy

Capture myopathy disastrously occurs after excessive muscle exertion. A beisa running full-out for ages is unable to get sufficient blood and oxygen to its active muscles. Anaerobic metabolism inside muscle fibres is a useful survival mechanism for ultra-short bursts of speed; enough for a beisa to run away from a lion, or a human sprinter to win the 100 metres gold. But this produces lactic acid in the muscles, and the runner, human or animal, needs a decent recovery period for the blood to remove this. This is why marathon runners have a slower pace than sprinters. They rely on not exceeding muscle metabolism that can be supported by the blood flow and oxygen.

With over-exertion, there is a production of large quantities of lactic acid and heat. Acid in muscles does what acid does to most things – it starts destroying them. The excess heat makes things worse, cooking the muscle. Sometimes, having pumped so vigorously, the heart muscle itself is fatally damaged, and an animal drops dead shortly after capture. More commonly, an antelope is simply stiff the next day, then dies a few days later. The muscle destruction releases large amounts of myoglobin, the oxygen-storing protein in muscle. Myoglobin is a massive molecule, and difficult for the kidney to filter. Large quantities simply block the kidney tubules, causing kidney failure and death. The same myoglobin-induced kidney failure also often kills deer and moose that initially survive being hit by a car, only to die a few days later.

Showing clips from *Hatari* to students to explain capture myopathy, I get tearful seeing a now critically endangered black rhino being chased, goaded, bashed and caught simply for the film: as disposable as an old vehicle in a movie car crash scene. From what it endured on film, I am doubtful that rhino survived.

Capture myopathy doesn't just affect mammals. Ostriches, with their massive muscular legs, are also vulnerable. Trapped since ancient Rome for use in the arena, ostriches are difficult to catch simply by chasing, as they weave to and fro, and are far more manoeuvrable than any off-road vehicle at speed. Classic capture myopathy is thankfully rare in ostriches.

I learned to handle ostriches in South Africa while at vet school there. Most of the world's ostrich farming still takes place in a small region of South Africa around Oudtshoorn, where it started 150 years ago to supply hat feathers for wealthy Europeans. Besides riding an ostrich, tourists can eat ostrich omelettes and steaks, buy carved eggs and ostrich leather shoes, or even purchase an ostrich foot ashtray, although who would want one is a mystery.

I was hugely disappointed to learn how silly ostriches are when I started working with them. It's all on account of their eyes. Ostriches have the largest eyes of all birds, and indeed of all land animals. More than five times the volume of our own eyes, they are just slightly smaller than a billiard ball. Humongous eyes give them excellent night vision to avoid nocturnal predators, and good sight when running at speed, although their resolution is not nearly as good as an eagle's. But massive eyes come at a cost – there is little space left in the skull for their brain. The ostrich brain is actually a quarter the size of just one of its eyes.

My favourite way to catch an ostrich is to use an old sock. Standing at the side of the fence, sock rolled up on my wrist, fingers and thumb where the toes should go, I simply offer some quartz pebbles, and perhaps a silver coin, in my outstretched hand. Unquenchably inquisitive, the ostrich can't help but come over, even if I have caught it the same way just a few days earlier. Ostriches are attracted to almost anything shiny they can swallow; not just stones, but coins, sweet wrappers, nuts and bolts, and watches. Like all birds, ostriches have no teeth, an evolutionary adaptation for balance in flight. Nature then decided to evolve ostriches into large flightless cows, living on grass and shrubs. But without teeth they must constantly swallow stones to grind their food in their large muscular stomach.

Attracted by the handful of shiny stones, the ostrich happily pecks away. Suddenly, I close my thumb and forefinger, gripping the upper and lower beak together. With my other hand I quickly slip the sock over its head and neck, covering the eyes, and let go of the beak. Eyes covered, the world gone dark, the ostrich stands still, evidently confused about what is going on. I can now safely march it off somewhere to take a blood sample, or treat an injury.

Sadly, this method doesn't work with similar birds. If hooded, an emu's response is to blindly dash around, jumping and kicking madly, until it dislodges the hood, is totally exhausted, or knocks itself out against an obstacle. While all the large flightless birds are called ratites, none of them are actually related. They have all evolved from separate ancestors, explaining their different behaviours despite their similar appearance.

Another way of handling an ostrich is to use an ostrich crook. Similar to the usual shepherd's crook, but longer and with an S-shaped end, it can fend off a charging male. Its main purpose, however, is to catch an ostrich's neck. Hooked gently behind the neck, the head is then brought down towards the ground. This prevents the ostrich being able to kick you.

My grandmother always warned me how an ostrich could disembowel a man with just a single kick. While numerous people are injured or killed by ostriches every year, I cannot find a single scientific report of anyone being disembowelled. The nail on the foot could cause lacerations, but a powerful kick to the abdomen is sufficient to fatally rupture your liver and other internal organs. Their other martial art is simply to knock you over and then trample and jump on you. Weighing up to 90 kilograms, this is pretty effective at fatally mashing your innards.

Catching smaller ratites such as Darwin's rhea is much less fraught, even if we can't use a hood. We can use pig-handling boards, riot shields or old cupboard doors to move them around without being kicked. If we need to grab one, it can usually be bundled into a fence corner with an old duvet and grabbed. Duvets are always in plentiful supply in zoos. Local hospitals and hotels are constantly replacing those stained by incontinent or over-amorous guests. A duvet, however, is not much use for catching an injured wild emu running around in Northern Queensland. For that you will likely need a net.

Nets are versatile. A sock net on a pole can catch most medium-sized animals in a rescue centre or zoo, from a flying fox to a siamang gibbon. They are perfect for catching a red-necked wallaby bounding past. Wild walla-bies can be caught by pop-up net traps, like in pirate movies, or chased into a net slung between trees. There is even an ingenious net tunnel for wild wallabies and kangaroos, placed between fences, with drawstrings at either end. This allows you to catch a wallaby bounding through, give it an injection, then release it, all within a few minutes. Wallabies, despite being far smaller than kangaroos, can still give you a thumping kick or painful bite. Caught in a net, the best place to grab and hold a wallaby is at the base of their thick muscular tail. Grabbing the tail conveniently prevents them kicking you in the face. Watching males fighting, boxing each other with their feet, kangaroos are as accurate as any prize kickboxer, but only to the front.

For most animals, grabbing tails is a complete no-no. Birds' long feathers will simply come out, leaving a bald stump and a bird unable to manoeuvre while flying. Monkeys will whip around to grab and bite you to bits if you grasp their tail. Most patients with long slender tails, you risk injuring by dislocating the tail bones. Degus have the horrible tendency for their entire tail skin to come off in your hand, if you make the mistake of grabbing one. There is then nothing that can be done for the now bleeding exposed tail bones but to amputate the injured tail. Green iguanas go further. Don't make the mistake of trying to pull one from its branch by its dangling tail. Snap. With a powerful shake, off the whole thing comes, and you are left with the writhing tail, while the offended iguana runs off among the branches with only a stump. This isn't as disastrous as it sounds. Many lizards have evolved this ability, called autotomy, to survive a predator grabbing their tail. Sawtail lizards have a bright blue tail to aid the distraction. Speckled stone geckos have large tails that act as a fat store. They shed their fat tails easily, bribing any predator grabbing them. Many geckos will grow a new tail, although never as pretty as the original. As vets we can use the technique to remove an injured tail rather than amputating, as this way they will grow a new one. But try autotomising a savanna monitor tail and you will end up with a bloody mangled mess. Not all lizard species can do this trick. Eyelash geckos, for example, can drop their tails, but they don't regrow them. You need to know your species.

Nets are excellent for catching everything from fish to small birds, and we can use mist nets hung between poles for disease-screening projects. Even bighorn rams can be caught, with nets dropped out of low swooping helicopters. Sometimes, a trapper even jumps out with the net. Helicopters are perhaps an extreme way to launch nets. Netguns are more practical. They can be used from a helicopter, but also to catch a rogue rhesus macaque, snapping TV aerials off as it jumps between Mumbai rooftops, just as India goes in to bat in the Cricket World Cup. Netguns, useful as they are, carry risks. Shot nets have weights around the perimeter, and hitting a baby macaque directly can fracture its arm, or even kill it.

Impala can be caught by chasing them into nets hidden among trees and suspended on wooden sticks. These drop nets are knocked down when animals run into them. They can catch several animals at once, but netted antelope can get horribly tangled, breaking their legs. Mothers may even strangle themselves trying to get to calves bleating in distress. It can be difficult to get to all individuals in a large group before some injure themselves. Members of the capture team also risk injury in the rush to free individuals.

Catching a herd of nervous, easily spooked greater kudu is tricky. They are difficult to dart and behave unpredictably with some drugs. Caught in nets, they panic, injuring themselves, and males are dangerous with their long spiral horns. The best thing is to catch them as a group in dry season, using their normal behaviour, and without having to handle them at all. An ingenious system does just this, using only plastic, but it needs planning and a skilled team to pull it off.

It was the brainchild of a game ranger in 1968, watching the carnage during efforts to catch surplus antelope on horseback with nooses and nets in the Imfolozi and Hluhluwe nature reserves. Jan Oelofse realised that antelope may not know how strong a barrier was but would avoid running into it as long as they could see it. Building a massive funnel of opaque plastic sheeting, hidden among trees, meant that animals such as antelope could be chased into this, leading into an enclosure. It's not that different to the role of a sheepdog, only performed by people on horseback or in vehicles. The chasing is not vigorous, and is more herding, using their normal behaviour to move away from disturbance. Keeping antelope in their natural herds also reduces stress, helping prevent capture myopathy. It is safest when performed in winter, when coolest, and as early in the day as possible, and for staff this means rising at 4 a.m.

The funnel can be built with sections that close with curtains, to catch separate groups, or can simply lead to an enclosure, called a boma. The funnel can even lead directly to transport containers on trucks. The truck-loading area is dug down into the ground, so the ground the antelope run on is the same height as the truck bed. There are only two disadvantages. It is expensive, needing a lot of time for planning and preparation. It also only really works in the southern African bushveld, where plastic sheeting walls can be hidden from approaching animals by vegetation. Animals can simply avoid the funnel in open East African grassland. With sparser trees, more work and preparation are needed. Plastic walls hidden in trenches have to be made pop-up, or constructed like curtains hanging from steel cables, pulled closed once animals are in position. Some species like springbok can't be caught with this system, but many antelope, buffalo, giraffe and even African hunting dogs can.

Mass capture bomas are not glamorous. Documentary makers prefer filming a single rhino being darted from a helicopter. However, they have been revolutionary, reducing animal stress and injuries. They have also enabled large-scale wildlife capture and movement all over southern Africa. This has allowed more land to be used for wildlife ranching than ever before. In South Africa alone, over a third of a million large wild animals are moved every year. With an estimated 10,000 private game farms in South Africa, covering 15 million hectares, and separate to national parks and regional nature reserves, almost 20 per cent of the total private land in South Africa is managed as game ranches. So perhaps southern Africa wildlife capture now does rival the wildlife caught during Roman times, even if mainly antelope, which the Romans had little interest in. This capture technique would have been possible in Roman times using cloth and poles, so perhaps we can be grateful they didn't think of it first. The results of our game capture two millennia later are vastly different. Healthy, well-fed animals, caught with little stress, always do far better.

So we have finally caught our patient. And with the furious tiger in a trap, wallaby gripped firmly by the tail, or the buffalo in the boma, we have also carried out the correct anaesthetic procedure to enable us to tackle the problem in a safe environment. Yet, we still have to figure out what that problem is . . .

South American kissing bugs, hungry and ready to be deployed as living syringes, can collect blood samples from uncooperative wildlife patients without the need for anaesthesia.

3

When a bird in the hand is not better

Swifts are astounding. They spend almost their entire life in the air. They catch and eat insects, drink, mate, sleep in the air while flying, and may not land for almost a year. They can fly almost as fast as I can legally drive, and can cover 200,000 kilometres in a year. Weighing less than a Mars bar, with legs a quarter of a matchstick's length, their leg blood vessels are the thickness of a cotton thread. Even catching a swift risks breaking their tiny bones, and it is near impossible to draw blood from their leg veins on a cold day. Far better if we can safely get our blood sample without ever having to touch one.

Vampire or Mexican kissing bugs are the bedbugs from hell. In their native South America, these large insects live in armadillo burrows and animal nests, sucking blood when their victim is asleep with long piercing mouthparts. No animal would stay asleep while being stabbed, so they have evolved an anaesthetic in their saliva which is injected into their victim.

We can breed bugs in a sterile lab, ensuring they are free of any disease. We put a large ravenous bug in an artificial egg with small holes, just large enough to stick its head out, but not escape, and our living syringe is ready. After we have placed this in a nest, the swift doesn't even realise it has had a blood sample taken. Retrieving the dummy egg and balloon-like bug a few hours later, we now have our sample. A kissing bug frequently manages to get a larger sample than I would get even under anaesthesia. The only loser is the bug, which is executed and robbed of its meal. Biting bugs have also been used on various zoo animals, getting up to 1 millilitre of blood from hippos, rhinos and giraffes, which would otherwise not co-operate with blood sampling while awake.

Wildlife veterinarians have become masters of maximising the health information we can get from animals without actually catching them. The most disgusting samples are frequently the most revealing. All excrement is a bonanza, helping us to assess the health of wild populations without disturbing them. A coughed-up bit of sputum on a leaf from a gorilla's nest can be tested for respiratory disease viruses transmitted from visiting foreign tourists. A piece of washed-up sperm-whale afterbirth can tell us if the animal is infected with the monstrous 8 metre long parasitic worm *Placentonema gigantissima*. Drops of urine from a golden takin splashed on a Himalayan rock can tell us if a female is pregnant. A tuft of hair from a Barbary sheep, tangled on a thorn bush in the Atlas mountains, lets us measure stress hormone levels and judge how they are coping with climate change. And a smear of grey seal dung on the beach can highlight antibiotic-resistant bacteria, thanks to human sewage contaminating what appears to be a pristine bay.

While getting samples without catching animals is better for them, it poses challenges. Marine biology sounds glamorous with images of diving with whale sharks springing to mind. The reality can be less exciting. Those studying skin bacteria of humpback whales spend months at sea following a whale pod, trying to collect a few fragments of shed skin. Tiny particles of sloughed skin come loose when whales breach, and collectors race around trying to be close enough to scoop them up with fine nets on long poles before they sink. More high-tech sampling uses a small drone to fly over whales with a petri dish to try and catch samples of respiratory vapour or 'whale blow', to analyse bacteria and fungi, and to assess an individual's health. The samples can also be tested for DNA to look at the population's genetic health. This sounds simpler than the reality of trying to guess where whales will surface, keeping up in boats, and trying to steer the drone via video link while buffeted by waves. All while trying not to crash the drone into the whale or the sea.

Why sample wild animals?

There are many reasons to sample truly wild animals, and not just because an individual appears ill or injured when viewed through binoculars. In our increasingly disturbed planet, it is important to discover what toxins are building up in the environment. We can also better understand why some species are declining, and act to try and change this.

Thanks to documentaries, the world has been alerted to the risks posed by plastics. Shearwaters on the remotest islands have plastic fragments in their stomachs. Green sea turtles choke on plastic straws. A rockhopper penguin half-strangled by a six-pack plastic ring even features as an animated character in children's movies. I have spent hours retrieving plastic from a harbour seal's stomach with an endoscope, or removing nylon line embedded in the legs of a razorbill. The world's wildlife seems to be drowning in a sea of plastic. Yet it is easier to appreciate and act on things we can see. Far more deadly pollution is invisible, and so more difficult to mobilise the public against.

We have invented chemical compounds for every need. It is only after decades of use that we sometimes discover they cause a problem. Dioxins form as by-products during industrial processes such as bleaching paper, manufacturing pesticides and making PVC plastic. They have been linked to cancers, liver damage, immunity suppression, growth abnormalities, and the disruption of hormones in many wild animals. But they are only one of the more well-known environmental toxins out there. There are thousands, from formaldehyde used in carpet glue, to propylene glycol in cosmetics; from triclosan used in disinfectant soaps and mattresses, to diethanolamine in shampoo, and benzene from rubber and lubricants. More recent compounds may have effects that are not yet clear, unless they are monitored. Heavy metals like lead, cadmium, arsenic and mercury are still abundant in the Arctic region half a century after manufacturing processes stopped using them.

The twentieth century was the pinnacle of industrial chemistry. Scientists and researchers gave us remarkable, almost magical, products. Polytetrafluoroethylene made non-stick cookware and GoreTex waterproof outdoor clothing. It is also used in aerospace computer wiring and musicians' trumpet valve oil, and it lines hospital intravenous catheters so bacteria can't stick to their surface. There are hundreds of useful applications. But this miraculous substance's manufacture needs nastier compounds such as perfluorooctanoic acid, which causes serious health harms to humans and animals, and is linked with multiple types of tumour. Almost all humans worldwide now have detectable levels in their blood, as do animals, from fish and seals to eagles and polar bears.

It is obvious that a dead shearwater with its stomach filled with plastic has died from pollution, and it makes for a powerful photograph. A slow decline in beluga whales over decades due to accumulated effects from numerous different toxins is much more difficult to pin down. There is also nothing photographic to engage public concern. Belugas and polar bears are apex predators and accumulate toxins found in all the animals below them in the food chain. Because of the complexity of the problem, samples are needed over prolonged time periods, monitoring toxin levels and correlating them with how a population is doing. Samples from dead animals help, but may not tell the whole story. Repeated darting of polar bears from helicopters every year for decades to take blood samples is expensive, time consuming, and not great for the polar bears involved either.

Handling or anaesthetising animals always carries risks. How much better if we can get health information without ever having to catch them. We can measure pesticides in discarded peregrine falcon eggshells. Thanks to conservationist Rachel

Carson's book *Silent Spring*, first published in 1962, a whole generation learned that the organochloride pesticide dichloro-diphenyl-trichloroethane (DDT) caused thin, easily broken eggshells. Plummeting falcon populations eventually helped get DDT banned in many countries. Wood treated with the preservative chromated copper arsenate (CCA) gives timber a slightly green appearance. Unfortunately, arsenic leaches out into the soil over time. Arsenic levels can even be detected in crocodile eggs, letting us know how contaminated an area is. Various toxins, from organochlorine pesticides and polychlorinated biphenyls (PCBs) to flame retardants, can be detected in eggs ranging from northern gannets to common snapping turtles, depending on which environment you want to assess.

While eiderdown feathers may stuff expensive duvets, we can also measure toxins like heavy metals in the discarded feathers that sea ducks use to insulate eggs in their nest. Mercury levels in moulted feathers from sooty albatrosses tell us how much contamination is reaching their isolated nesting islands. Feathers are an ideal test sample. They grow rapidly, sometimes in just a few weeks. Their amazing structure emerges wrapped in a waxy sheath, looking like an obese hair, before the bird preens the sheath away and the feather emerges. They are moulted every year, often during a specific season, as birds renew their insulation, waterproofing, and flight abilities. This allows us to be very accurate in determining when exactly a toxin was in the body and laid down in the feather. It isn't just useful in large seabirds. Cadmium can be accurately monitored in the great tit's feathers. While environmental contamination with cadmium comes from metal mining and battery recycling, it also comes from cigarette smoke. With 1–2 milligrams per cigarette, and 18 billion cigarettes sold worldwide every day, cadmium quickly adds up in some urban areas. Heavy metals like cadmium even cause personality changes in great tits. They show less exploratory behaviour, and so may be less able to find food and survive in cities and parks, the very places they need their skills the most.

Monitoring feathers also highlights risks to human health. Kentish plovers in Venice have such high mercury levels that it affects their ability to breed. Mercury contamination can naturally occur with volcanic eruptions, but this clearly isn't the cause in Venice. Power stations and incinerators are the likely sources. Mercury bioaccumulates in the tiny invertebrates the plovers eat, but also in the local seafood tourists pay a premium to eat. And just as medical incinerators can be a source of mercury for birds, barium used in human hospital X-ray studies is found in feathers from ill sparrows. In our quest for better individual health treatment, we need to be careful we don't inadvertently poison each other too.

Something similar can happen with food. Hunters shoot ducks and geese. Or at least they try to. The frequent misses cause problems. Lead shot sinks to the bottom of lakes and streams. In dry years, ducks take up lead particles with the small stones and sand from the riverbed, to grind food in their stomach. Lead shot is also slowly ground down by the river's motion, contaminating the water and everything in it. Severe lead toxicity is obvious, with mute swans staggering around with bizarre nervous signs and diarrhoea. But low levels of accumulated lead are not obvious and simply result in weaker birds, which, ironically, are more likely to be shot, and slowly poison the hunter and his family. Lead particularly affects children and young animals. Even small amounts cause lifelong intellectual stunting and learning disabilities. So hunters from families with long shooting traditions may quite literally be intellectually impaired, as claimed by opponents.

Hair sampling

Carnivorous birds are the most affected by heavy metals, accumulating it from the birds they eat, just as we do. White-bellied sea eagles in the Derwent estuary in Tasmania have more than 200 times as much mercury in their feathers as the geese they feed on, and mercury levels are particularly high in Bonelli's eagles catching birds in the vicinity of power stations in Portugal. Shed feathers again help us monitor the environment between different years, without a single bird ever needing to be caught.

Feathers grow rapidly and then are inert and non-growing for most of the year. Hair grows slowly but continually. Between different species, hair may grow less than a millimetre to more than 2 centimetres a month. Reindeer and Arctic foxes moult their coats seasonally to cope with temperature changes, but a maned sloth will have continuously growing hairs for up to a decade. The same toxins that we detect in feathers can be found in hair, but the information it gives us is different. Rather than a snapshot of what happened in a few weeks, a clump of hair tangled on a thorn bush can tell us what an animal was exposed to over several years. Hair can be analysed to give us the total amount of toxin taken in over the period it was growing. But if you know when a hair was plucked out, and how fast it grows in that species, its length gives you a calendar of when the animal was exposed to different compounds. Mercury, copper and zinc in grizzly bear hairs correlate with the brief periods they guzzle spawning salmon in Canadian rivers. Hair samples don't have to be big. A single hair from a wood mouse is enough to analyse lead levels.

Hair can tell us about more than just toxins. As children we were told that predators like wolves only pick off the old and weak animals, doing the herds a service. Thanks to hair, we can test this. Hair from Saskatchewan bison killed by wolves has much higher levels of the stress hormone cortisol than bison shot by hunters. These stressed bison also have much less fat stored in their bone marrow, confirming they are thin and struggling to survive. So wolves do indeed pick off the weak, poorly nourished and stressed members of a herd, helping to keep groups fit and healthy. Conversely, trophy hunters take pride in shooting the best animals, depriving populations of the strongest genes.

In some animals, from coyotes to chimpanzees, hair cortisol levels are the same no matter which part of the body the hair comes from. But in species like the Canadian lynx, hair cortisol levels vary, even from different places on the same leg. Hair cortisol gives us a timeline for stressful events in animals' lives. We can glean information we would never learn in any other way, no matter how long we observed the species. Some findings are puzzling at first. Male black bears have higher hair cortisol than females, but in grizzly bears it is the females with higher cortisol. Grizzly bears eating the least salmon have the highest stress levels, while black bears in areas with few fish have the highest stress, no matter how much the individual bear ate. We think grizzly bears are more stressed by not getting enough food for hibernation, while black bears appear more stressed by other bears, and by the fights and social competition when food is scarce, rather than being stressed by food scarcity itself.

Brown bears in Scandinavia are stressed when living near humans. Even trapping bears raises hair cortisol; an unexpected finding when you consider that trapping only lasts a few hours, while hair can grow for over a year. Cortisol levels are highest with culvert traps, a large metal pipe with a trap door used to catch bears in North America. Surprisingly, these cause higher cortisol than even bears chased and darted by helicopter.

While wind farms are useful in reducing carbon emissions, they have been criticised for their impact on birds. The effect of wind farms on mammals is less obvious. European badgers don't obviously show stressed behaviour, so hair cortisol is a useful aid. The hair of badgers living within a kilometre of one wind farm had over 250 per cent higher cortisol levels than badgers 10 kilometres away. Hair cortisol didn't decrease over subsequent years, meaning badgers could not adapt and continued to be extremely stressed by the noise.

In contrast, I was surprised to find that reindeer with intestinal parasites don't have higher hair cortisol than reindeer treated with medication. Reindeers and their normal gut parasites have probably co-evolved for thousands of years.

In our distant primate relatives, Madagascan grey mouse lemurs, higher hair cortisol is linked to lower survival. Chronic stress kills. In other primates, we would imagine stresses to be similar to those we experience, but this is not always so. Male vervet monkeys living close to humans have higher hair cortisol, as expected, but levels of cortisol in hair from wild chimpanzee nests in Uganda don't increase in areas with high ecotourism or even illegal logging. With their intelligence, perhaps chimpanzees rapidly adapt and normalise change, much as humans do. Move chimpanzees between different zoos, however, and it will be over a year before hair cortisol levels return to normal. Like humans, chimpanzees find social disruption extremely stressful. It is also no surprise that bullied individuals have the highest hair cortisol levels. Hair cortisol from ring-tailed lemurs also helps us understand what climate events they find stressful. All ages find drought stressful, but young lemurs also find cyclones stressful, just as human children fear violent storms.

It isn't just in captive primates that social stress can be measured from hair. In zoos, Dorcas gazelles' hair cortisol levels can help assess social stress, and the effects of captive animal husbandry. This information can be used to improve an individual animal's welfare by altering its care. Animal sanctuaries can also use hair cortisol to show that newly built rescue animal enclosures, whether for gibbons or moon bears, result in lower stress, justifying their expense.

In zoo bonobos, our closest relatives, hair plucking correlates with high stress levels, but ironically needs to be demonstrated by checking urine cortisol levels, due to the hair damage. Oxytocin can also be measured in urine. This happy hormone is responsible for bonding, and surges in a mother's body after giving birth. It helps us judge if a bonobo will look after her new baby or reject it. It also tells us if chimpanzees are strongly bonded socially, or if a group may descend into violent fighting.

Urine sampling

We can test urine for a variety of hormones and substances excreted via the kidneys. A zoo bonobo's urine can be syringed up from a concrete floor for a cheap supermarket pregnancy test, but urine from a wild bonobo disappears into the soil.

Urine is still a great non-invasive diagnostic sample in animals in sanctuaries and those being rehabilitated for return to the wild. Cheap urine test strips give a host of information from just a drop of urine. Urine glucose may hint that a cotton-top tamarin has diabetes. There shouldn't be glucose entering the urine, unless blood levels rise very high. The more likely cause, however, is stress. This may be due to a tamarin feeling bullied. The tamarin doesn't need insulin therapy, just a change from its companions.

Whether acidic or alkaline, urine also gives us valuable health information. Carnivorous mammals and many primates normally produce acidic urine. Alkaline urine hints at problems ranging from kidney disease in an elderly clouded leopard or cystitis in a Barbary macaque, to more unusual causes like vomiting in a maned wolf, or a crab-eating monkey swallowing a rag blocking its stomach.

More often than not, alkaline urine has just been on the ground for some time, during which bacteria have enjoyed their free meal while altering the urine's pH. It's essential to remember this before rushing to treat a non-existent disease.

Unlike carnivores, most herbivores normally have alkaline urine. If acidic, this can indicate problems ranging from a fallow deer gorging on wheat, to a pregnant Patagonian mara that is anorexic. Small changes in urine pH can hint that a problem is developing. Sanctuary visitors may be slipping food over the fence to a group of southern serows, unbalancing their diet. We can detect this in decreasing urine pH before they develop painful laminitis (inflammation) of their hooves.

In wildlife rescue centres in developing countries with limited funds, we can make our urine pH test strips simply by boiling red cabbage and adding a little alcohol to the liquid after it cools, then drying dipped paper strips in the sun for later use. These are just as useful as expensive medical versions, with the benefit that the animals and staff can eat the cabbage too.

Infectious diseases and toxins can also be detected in the urine. Bacteria such as Leptospira can be detected in the urine of patients from camels to prairie dogs. Antibodies to simian T-lymphotropic virus can be detected in chimpanzee urine, and antibodies to the microscopic tear-drop shaped Babesia parasites that live inside red blood cells can be detected in urine from wapiti. Even worm eggs from bizarre Schistosoma parasites that spend their lives swimming through the blood vessels of common hippopotamuses can be found in a hippo's urine. The problem is actually getting a urine sample to test. Even in a zoo or sanctuary this can be difficult.

Urine screening in zoos has an important role. Feeding zoo carnivores like lions and tigers with a variety of afford-able meat for their health is challenging, and zoos often resort to meat from fallen stock. Cows, sheep, pigs and deer that have been found dead are deemed unfit for human consump-tion, and are collected by the knackerman. Instead of being rendered into glue and soap, some are fed to zoo animals. Occasionally, a farm animal euthanised with drugs will mistakenly, or dishonestly, be collected by the knackerman, and inadvertently poison a zoo carnivore. I have seen stag-gering, disorientated lions, collapsed tigers and unconscious wolves. Urine can be screened for drugs by the local human hospital, so the correct treatment can be started.

Bird and reptile urine is very different. Laying eggs that can form less than 30 hours after fertilisation, there is no pregnancy to test. Urine and faeces are voided through a single opening, the cloaca, which also passes eggs. Birds have three obvious parts to their droppings. One is faeces, one is liquid urine, and the third is the white urates unique to birds and reptiles. Mainly insoluble uric acid, which causes painful gout in people's joints after over-indulgence, the chalky white sediment is the normal waste produced from proteins eaten by birds. Annoying motorists by soiling their cars, it is a handy visual signpost when collecting faeces for testing. Changes in urate colour can alert us to problems. Green urates often indicate a liver problem, such as a psittacosis infection, a zoonotic disease that can pass to humans.

Pregnancy testing

Human pregnancy tests don't work for many mammals, with different types of gestation and placentas, and varying changes in hormones. Six-banded armadillos can even delay implantation of their fertilised embryo. This is called embryonic diapause, and the fertilised armadillo embryo floats unattached in the uterus for months. There are minimal hormone changes, so pregnancy testing is difficult until implantation occurs. Ethiopian wolves can have false pregnancies. A *corpus luteum* forms on the ovary after ovulation, giving off hormones like progesterone that help maintain pregnancy. If the ovum is not fertilised no pregnancy occurs, but the ovary still develops a *corpus luteum*, producing normal pregnancy hormones. Wolves behave as if pregnant, build dens, and even develop enlarged mammary glands that produce milk. The body believes it is pregnant. Except, of course, it isn't.

Possibly no animal's pregnancy diagnosis is as frustrating as that of the giant panda. Pandas undergo both embryonic diapause and false pregnancy to complicate hormone analysis. Only recently down-classified from endangered, every zoo birth is important, although perhaps more for the financial implications of increased visitor numbers than actual conservation impact. As I have seen for myself, specialist panda breeding centres in China have no difficulty making panda babies. Breeding naturally, pairing compatible personalities, recognising the 36-hour fertile period that only occurs once a year, and detecting from subtle behavioural cues which females are likely pregnant – all appears within a day's work. Experience with large numbers of giant pandas and their subtle differences in behaviour is key.

With only one female in a Western zoo, you can't compare subtle behaviours between different pandas. With intense pressure on vets from the zoo and media, a number of tests have been trialled and published. A test may correlate wonderfully to a pregnancy, but when used in another zoo the following year it may demonstrate the same results when the panda isn't pregnant at all. Urinary oestrogens, progestogens, pregnanediol, prostaglandin F2α, relaxin, acute phase proteins such as ceruloplasmin, and other compounds have been measured daily for months on complex graphs, with judgements on various spikes, drops, ratios, and cross-overs relative to other hormones. After a decade of examining months of panda graphs and seeing results prove a lottery, I must admit to being no wiser than when I started. I was happy to leave the intense discussions over their meanings to leading reproduction scientists, while limiting my involvement to simply sucking up urine from the ground with a syringe for testing.

Leaving the convoluted technological testing of pandas, we can use cheap simple pregnancy tests that the ancient Egyptians used 3,000 years ago. The Egyptians diagnosed pregnancy by getting women to urinate on barley or wheat seeds. Urine during pregnancy causes the seeds to sprout faster. The test is about 70 per cent accurate compared to modern techniques like ultrasound. It also works in monkeys such as hamadryas baboons. Herbivores are different. The Punyakoti test, named after a sacred cow in Sanskrit, can be used in ruminants from blackbuck to banteng, using mung beans. Urine from pregnant animals prevents seeds sprouting for five days, and stunts their growth. High concentrations of the plant hormone abscisic acid is found in the urine of pregnant herbivores, which maintains seeds' dormancy. Yak urine is like a sleeping pill if you are a mung bean.

Faeces sampling

One collection trick we have learnt from kestrels. Field voles mark their paths with urine. This is an olfactory signpost, just as in many other animals. But voles can see into the near ultraviolet spectrum, which we can't. Their urine is brightly visible under this spectrum of sunlight, although invisible to us, acting as a visual warning to other voles to respect their territory. Kestrels can also see in this ultraviolet spectrum. They patiently hover, watching freshly marked vole paths. At the slightest sign of movement they swoop down on the vole, making it a meal. We can search for rodent samples at dusk using a strong blacklight torch, which emits ultraviolet light that shows up normally invisible objects with a faint fluorescence. Stomping around at night with an ultraviolet torch looking for Namibian ground squirrel urine will highlight scorpions that also glow under UV light. While we avoid those, the glowing urine can lead us to what we are really after, the droppings, which also glow faintly. The fresher the droppings, the brighter they glow, helping us to select the freshest samples, for testing for gut infections such as cryptosporidium. Cryptosporidium can afflict humans, and droppings can indicate if perhaps chipmunks are to blame for a human outbreak, or conversely if poor human sanitation is to blame for infecting the chipmunks.

Of all hands-off samples we can collect, poo is really the gift that keeps giving. Human doctors and domestic animal vets typically only use faecal samples for testing a small number of things, such as gut parasites and intestinal bacterial infections. After all, why take a smelly unpleasant sample, when you can simply ask the patient questions, or perform an ultrasound examination? It is also more socially acceptable to take a blood sample than ask a human patient to shove some of their noxious stool into a plastic pot. In contrast, with wild animals we have to work with what we can get.

But poo can look the same, whether hours or days old.

For some tests, the freshest possible sample is critical. It is confusing to zookeepers seeing the veterinarian ignoring an ill giant panda, watching them instead peer at the different piles of poo with a thermal camera to tell which is warmest, and hence freshest. The bacteria species causing the gut problem can quickly be overgrown by other invading bacteria at this microbial all-you-can-eat buffet. If this happens, then the laboratory won't give you the correct diagnosis. High-tech poo-spotting is also useful when collecting elephant dung early in the morning. With piles everywhere near congregated Sri Lankan elephants in a national park, quickly finding the warmest pile to sample keeps you from overly annoying the pachyderms.

While good for solitary animals like giant pandas, in a big troop of capuchin monkeys how do we tell which poo belongs to a specific individual? For this we need a bit of glamour. Mixing different colours of make-up glitter into foods such as jam or peanut butter, and watching which individual eats which colour through binoculars, means we can tell whose poo belongs to whom. More boring natural alternatives are corn or lentils.

So you have fresh faeces and you know which animal it is from. What can you test it for? Well, almost anything. You can analyse diets; identify nutrition and vitamin status and how well digestion is working; analyse the DNA from shed intestinal cells; look for parasites; check for infectious diseases of all sorts; and judge stress hormones. You can even diag-nose pregnancy. Using faeces rather than urine to diagnose pregnancy is more difficult, and needs more specialist labo-ratory equipment. However, cheetahs are one species where faeces can be reliable for pregnancy testing. This is really useful, as male fertility is often so poor that simply observing cheetahs mating predicts nothing.

Even diseases in distant organs can be detected. European badgers with cattle tuberculosis in their lungs may be detected just from droppings. It isn't the best TB test for badgers, but it's still impressive that tiny numbers of bacteria, coughed up and swallowed, digested and mixed with a host of other bacteria in the stool, can still be detected.

We can learn valuable information when no infections are present. Magellanic penguin populations have been declining, the cause blamed on everything from overfishing to climate change. Knowing what penguins eat is critical to understanding the problem, but not easy in birds spending most of their lives at sea. When I first saw Magellanic penguins in Ushuaia, Argentina, decades ago, our knowledge was based on a rather unpleasant test. Ambushing parent penguins returning to feed their chicks, we filled their stomachs with water via a tube, until the poor bird vomited up all the food it had collected to feed its chick. The stomach contents were then analysed to see what birds were catching. Now we study penguin diets in a friendlier manner, with no water torture needed. By collecting poo we can simply analyse this for the DNA of different fish. The results have been surprising. We now know that several penguin species regularly catch jellyfish. These break down as soon as they are swallowed, but we never realised this from our old stomach-pumping exploits. Jellyfish numbers appear to be increasing due to warming oceans, so are penguins eating them to cope with overfishing and climate change, or do they just like them? We still don't know.

At the other end of the digestion process, saliva can also be a useful test sample. As young vets, we could test anaesthetised African buffalo for foot and mouth disease by shoving a long metal wire with a small cup on the end, called a probang, down its throat to collect saliva and mucus. With newer tests, we now get away with far less saliva. To test wild boar in a Bulgarian forest, we can use corn cobs strung on a rope, with a few kernels replaced with cotton bud tips, to soak up saliva for later testing. Without corn cobs to test African forest hogs, we can use thick, soft cotton rope tied to a tree, rubbed with tasty-smelling fruit for them to chew on, while their saliva soaks in. Saliva from chimpanzees can be used for disease testing too, but is also useful to detect stress. Unlike hair, which gives a picture over many months, saliva cortisol changes in less than an hour. In sanctuaries and zoos, it can help us to investigate whether noisy school groups, or barbecue smells from a nearby restaurant, are stressful for the chimpanzees.

Parasites are one of the easiest things to test for in poo. Dissolving faeces and as much table salt in water as possible, worm eggs will float to the top, to be collected and examined under the microscope. This is simple, cheap, and works in everything from mountain gorillas to golden mantella frogs. If we find eggs, we know that our Sudanese sulcata tortoise has intestinal worms. Domestic animal vets spend much professional time treating worms, fleas and ticks in domestic dogs, cats, cattle, sheep and horses. But wild animals have evolved alongside their parasites for millions of years. Treating a tortoise for worms can actually be detrimental. Some drugs that kill worms can paralyse or kill tortoises. We also believe some wild tortoises actually rely on worms to gently churn the food as it slowly moves down the intestines, helping expose more of the food to the intestinal surface where nutrients can be absorbed. Useful if your diet consists of grasses low in nutritional value.

Faeces is sometimes the only sample possible, for animals practically impossible to catch. A few dried faecal pellets from reintroduced scimitar-horned oryx can tell us if they are getting enough nutrition from sparse desert vegetation, what plants they are eating, or if they are afflicted by parasites. One can only see these oryx with the aid of binoculars before they disappear in a puff of dust galloping over the horizon. That is, if you can even find them. Aristotle claimed one of these almost extinct antelopes, seen from a distance with a broken horn, was the source of unicorn mythology. Extinct in the wild until 2016, in Chad twenty-five oryx were reintroduced into a desert nature reserve the size of Scotland. Finding small, dry faecal pellets in a desert reserve is difficult. But so too is finding tiger droppings in dense mountainous jungle. Tracker dogs trained with zoo tiger droppings are one of the most effective ways of finding wild tiger droppings.

But dogs are no good for animals living in the forest tree canopy.

We can enlist insect helpers to assist us in dense vegetation where finding fresh poo is impossible. In the Ivory Coast, some species of fly are especially attracted to sooty mangabeys and follow the small groups of smoky-coloured monkeys through the dense rainforest. Different fly species are attracted to the monkeys' smelly droppings, while others prefer hanging around the sweaty mangabeys themselves. Testing the different flies can tell us if anthrax infection is causing skin sores, or if anthrax is actually in the intestinal tract and likely to kill more of the mangabeys. Carrion flies are miniature wildlife census officials. Using simple fly traps in Africa and Madagascar to identify which species they have recently eaten, we can be alerted to disease outbreaks, rather than spending hundreds of hours trudging through dense vegetation trying to find rotting wildlife corpses.

Kissing bugs are not our only blood-sampling assistants. Ticks can be tested for Lyme disease carried by local white-tailed deer that have been made miserable with sore joints and limbs. Ticks can also help investigate if louping-ill, a sheep virus, is killing red grouse on Irish heather moors.

We may need to tell if animals live in an area, to plan special protection. This is difficult if they are small, shy, rare and nocturnal, such as the Truong Son muntjac. This small deer, recently discovered in a mountainous region of Vietnam, is impossible to spot. Even camera traps struggle, and taking samples is practically impossible. Leeches, unlovable as they are, come to the rescue here. Testing their gut content DNA tells us what they have fed on, and helps us establish where this elusive muntjac is living.

Sometimes we can use an animal itself as a living test, without any harm. High-frequency non-invasive valvometry involves gluing two tiny sensors and wires on the edge of oyster and wild clam shells to monitor how frequently, and for how long, they open their shells to feed. These animals are supremely sensitive to water changes, from toxin levels measured in parts per million of water, to microscopic changes in temperature or salinity, which affect the pattern and timing of shell openings. Using a network of clams with simple sensors over an area of ocean floor, we can monitor the health of an entire seabed region, picking up subtle water changes, or early developing toxic algal blooms. So we have a wild animal health test made out of live animals.

Occasionally, we need a more meaty sample without catching or anaesthetising our victim. We have special dartgun darts with a small sharp-edged metal tube, the size of a file hole punch, at the front instead of a needle. As we shoot the sable antelope to be sampled, the biopsy dart cuts a thin core of skin and underlying muscle that stays in the tube when the dart falls out. This is not pleasant for the selected individual, but still less stressful than being captured and anaesthetised. Biopsy darting is useful in the most difficult large carnivores to catch. Orcas are the ocean's apex predators, and they accumulate all the toxins eaten by animals below them in the food chain, storing them in their blubber layer. Orca pods in some regions have also become small, fragmented populations and inbred genetics is becoming a problem. Wildlife vets helping to study these problems use biopsy darts shot from a powerful crossbow. To stop the precious sample sinking to the seabed when the Orca dives, darts have a bright yellow float attached.

Darts can also be used in a gentler manner. Instead of a needle, sticky duct tape can be attached. Shot at a pig-tailed macaque squabbling with a group mate, the annoyed monkey will simply pull the dart off in disgust, removing a handy hair sample. Even two or three hairs can be a bonanza for testing. Pulled out from the hair follicle, living hairs have a tiny bulb of cells at their base. A host of genetic tests and ultra-sensitive disease screening by polymerase chain reactions is then possible. This barely visible hair base swelling can also be used to generate one of the most valuable samples from endangered animals – stem cells. While freezing of sperm and eggs is more high profile, stem cells hold the potential to yield both, as well as other cells, to investigate genetics, immunity and disease susceptibility. Humble hair roots are all we need to make stem cells, while researchers work towards one day reliably making these into sperm and eggs. This would allow us to make new embryos of even extinct animals. For now we just need to collect the samples for storage, as many endangered animals are likely to disappear before we actually get the technology working properly. This is the absolutely last, still non-working, floodgate against the rising tide of wildlife extinctions.

While hands-off testing, and samples like feathers and droppings, can tell us a lot about wild animals' health, occasionally they are just not enough. Sometimes we need to get our hands on a wildlife patient to get a good idea of what is going on.

Examining the retina at the back of an owl's eye, there are no visible blood vessels, but instead a wavy black projection called the pectin, which contains the vessels.

4

How to squeeze a porcupine, and look an owl in the eye

How do you palpate the internal organs of a crested porcupine, when even the underside is covered in quills? Porcupine quills are sharp, with a barbed surface, and have a horrid habit of pieces breaking off under the skin. Even lions usually stay clear of porcupines. When carefully past their spikey forest under anaesthesia, you may detect a large, firm, internal lump near the pelvis. Feeling worryingly like a tumour, or an intestinal blockage, it is in fact the normal spleen. In contrast, the human spleen is tiny, and sits next to the stomach just below the ribs. Trying to find out why a wild animal is ill is challenging when it is difficult to even know what is normal.

The physical examination of any patient, whether a child, llama or stranded pilot whale, is the mainstay of medicine since prehistory. Modern diagnostic tests and X-rays have only been around for a little over a century. You observe the gait of a running blackbuck, or leaping Thomson's gazelle, for any signs of lameness. With a stethoscope you listen to the occasional faint click of a macaroni penguin with a fungal lung infection, or the gentle hiss of a leaking heart valve in a Gambian giant rat trained to sniff out landmines. You feel the grating movement of an arthritic knee joint in a geriatric South American bush dog under anaesthesia with your hands, and run your fingers through a barnacle goose's feathers, feeling for small shotgun pellet wounds, invisible under the sea of plumage. If you smell the breath of a klip-springer, a faint nail-polish odour indicates its metabolism is not coping with its pregnancy, whereas a l'Hoest's monkey's fruity breath hints at diabetes. The faint whiff of pears in a sitatunga's diarrhoea probably means a rotavirus infection, while a sickly-sweet stench to a black-handed spider monkey's droppings alerts you to a dreaded *Clostridium difficile* infection. All the senses, with the obvious sensible exception of taste, are needed, Sherlock Holmes like, to assess non-communicative wild patients.

Nowadays, with the explosion of laboratory blood tests, X-rays and MRI scans, fewer and fewer doctors and domestic animal vets even perform physical examinations, and the evidence is that when they do, their examinations are more cursory. The last time you visited your doctor, did he peer into your eyes with an ophthalmoscope in a dark room, look up your nose, listen to your heart and lungs, feel your abdomen, measure your blood pressure, and check your knee reflexes with his rubber mallet? Chances are he didn't. Many doctor's visits now involve no physical contact at all. Lack of time, ease of other tests, and the fear of being accused of inappropriate contact have all conspired to affect this. Even in pet dogs, the different tests we were taught to examine individual nerves are rarely performed. Rushed veterinarians instead just send wobbly patients for MRI scans.

The coronavirus pandemic continued the irreversible trend towards telemedicine, supposedly examining a patient when they are not even present, via video chat or phone call. The doctor examining you may not even be human. Apps like Ada process your symptoms by computer algorithm AI. None of this is necessarily bad, with affordable healthcare unavailable in so much of the world. Even in wealthy countries, face-to-face consultations are now, in some instances, limited to just five minutes, so these apps provide opportunities for basic health advice and screening cases.

At the start of the COVID-19 pandemic, I advised on an anorexic cheetah in East Africa, examined a confiscated lion with a spinal problem in Russia, and explained how to simply fix a chimpanzee's broken leg in West Africa, all from my home in Scotland in a single week. But none of this is new. Years earlier, I was already talking Indonesian vets through emergency abdominal surgery they were performing on an orangutan via phone at 3 a.m. while travelling on an overnight train.

But nothing can substitute for a real, hands-on examination. Despite best efforts, I have got things horribly wrong on phone calls or when examining just a few seconds of video. The opportunity to get our hands on our wild patients is rare, so we try never to take it for granted. The thoroughness of my physical examinations looks like something out of the Spanish Inquisition. Looking up the nostrils of a Mediterranean monk seal for nasal mites, or inserting a gloved finger to feel a mandrill's prostate, I prod and poke everything. Pet dogs and cats can't describe their symptoms, but patients like a red lechwe calf are prey animals, so stoically hide any signs of illness that could help a veterinarian. If a red-crowned Amazon parrot appears ill, a hungry Cooper's hawk will naturally single it out as an easier-to-catch meal.

Even if only captured briefly for a research project, a basic examination is vital. Bird ringers are not vets, but still record bird weights and body measurements. Without realising it, this too is a physical health examination of sorts. Abnormally small or light birds may be ill or battling to cope in a region. Bird ringing helps us learn how long birds live, and where they go. We can analyse this data for the probable effects of climate change, heavy-metal contamination from a local factory, or how farming changes are affecting birds. We use all these individual measurements as a health examination for the population, and its environment. No wonder some vets like my friend Liam Reid are also keen bird ringers. He is not just checking one swallow's health, but that of the whole population over time.

If rushed, we tend to focus our examination on the obvious

problem, which is a mistake. Prey animal species are masters at hiding symptoms, which is extremely frustrating. I remember attending to a nyala calf one autumn morning. It was eating slightly less food than usual but looked completely normal from a distance. I caught him to check his stomach movements, but he slumped dead in my arms only seconds after catching him. On autopsy, half his entire chest was a massive abscess. Unbelievably, he had still been alive, let alone looking fine. Even if not expecting anything disastrous, we try to follow the same emergency ABC triage in humans and animals, as soon as we lay hands on a patient. A is for airways. Is the Seychelles tortoise able to breathe, or are the windpipe and nostrils blocked with mucus? B is for breathing. Is the grey seal breathing smoothly and regularly like a person or a dog would? If so, this alerts you to a problem, as seals normally breathe in short bursts, living in the water, and this could mean a heavy lungworm infection. C is for circulation. Has the bearded vulture got a pulse underneath its wing to match a regular heartbeat, with no burbles or whooshing murmurs down the stethoscope? Is blood reaching all parts of the body, or are the wing tips cool and pale, showing something preventing blood flow, and the wing tissue dying?

Once we're happy that our patient is not at immediate risk of shuffling off its mortal coil, we can get down to our examination. Perhaps our crested porcupine has red skin on the tops of his back feet. But instead of just focusing on the skin, checking for fungi, bacteria or crocodile-shaped hair follicle mites, we need to check the entire body thoroughly. Perhaps a spinal injury causes the feet to drag, or a kidney infection means he is scalding his feet in an uncomfortable posture when urinating. Perhaps cataracts are causing him to stumble. An initial unbiased examination is essential, otherwise you risk treating what is just a symptom or the wrong problem entirely.

Before touching a patient, it is worth considering that there may not actually be a medical problem at all. Over the years,

I have had many conversations with frustrated young vets who have run all manner of blood and stool tests, X-rays and ultrasounds on patients, for example when examining a brown capuchin that is losing weight and has a poor coat, which has carers concerned. Yet test results are all normal, and they ask advice about further tests for everything from tsutsugamushi fever to Epstein–Barr virus. A quick probing of staff reveals the capuchin is a member of a bachelor group of five boys, all the others being dominant. Although their diet was carefully calculated by a nutritionist, there is no food left over each day. The others are simply bullying him, getting fat on his share. The solution isn't a new test or medication, but simply increasing the food, or moving him to another group, and the problem disappears.

Eye examinations

Once you actually have your patient in hand, an examination could start anywhere, from the left foot to the navel, but we often start with the part associated with personality: the face. And while eyes are claimed as the windows of our soul, they are also a window into assessing a patient's health.

A tawny owl's eye is possibly the easiest to examine of any animal. While ostriches have the largest eyes of any land animal, almost 5 centimetres in diameter and far larger than their brain, an owl's eyes with their massive pupils are a beauty to peer into. Not only is a tawny owl's eye massive to gather the faint moonlight it hunts by, but like most owls it isn't even vaguely round. They have mushroom-shaped eyes. The large, beautiful eye front is actually the smallest portion, like the stalk of a button mushroom. The rear chamber is the largest part. Cramming huge eyes into the skull makes them so close together that shinning a bright light in one eye will actually cause the other eye's pupil to contract as light actually passes through one eye into the other.

Forces on a large eye swooping down on a mouse or landing on a perch would cause a soft eyeball to deform, wobbling in and out of focus and not useful for a golden eagle diving at 240 kilometres per hour. Birds solve this by having paper-thin bones, called scleral ossicles, embedded in the white of the eye, making the eyeball rigid. Eyeball bones are the only way a great horned owl can manage the weird mushroom-shaped eye that enables its superb nocturnal vision.

But like many adaptations perfectly evolved over tens of thousands of years, recent human changes throw up distinct problems. A massive eye supported by thin bones is superb for focus during the rigours of flight, but a rigid eye is also easily damaged. Colliding with your living-room window on a sunny day is enough to render a blackbird blind. This is no surprise when you realise that birds such as rock doves can fly faster than a cheetah can run, even faster than you can drive your car. A collision at these speeds would be fatal for a human. Yet a tawny owl bouncing off your car windscreen late at night appears fine, flying away a minute after being stunned. But of the thousand-plus injured tawny owls I have personally examined during the last two decades, more than 40 per cent of adults had serious internal eye damage, such as retinal detachment, and were so visually impaired as to starve to death if mistakenly released. Collision eye injuries are now possibly the most common cause of owls to be admitted to wildlife rehabilitation centres worldwide. We check the eyes even before looking to see if an owl has a broken wing. While I can fix a broken bone quickly in many cases, and have a bird flying again in just two weeks, a detached retina waving back at me through the ophthalmoscope is unfixable, and a death sentence for the owl.

If we look inside its eye with an ophthalmoscope, an owl's retina, like that of most birds, is different to ours. Instead of oxygen-carrying blood vessels snaking across the retina surface in gorillas or gerenuks, a bird's retina is a uniform pink colour, with no vessels in sight. Instead, there is what appears to be a scrunched-up black slug protruding from the retina's surface. This pecten oculi is a clump of blood vessels, which some reptiles, for example blue iguanas, also have.

While originally held up as proof of divine creation, scientists later used the eye's anatomy to help support the theory of evolution, as no designer would run the blood vessels and nerves over the retina's surface, where they interfere with vision. This is how mammals' eyes are set up. Elderly moon bears in sanctuaries often have tiny brown spots near the retinal vessels, small bleeds that alert you to their high blood pressure and risk of kidney failure or blindness if not treated. At first glance, a fennec fox retina seems bizarrely to have more large blood vessels for its small size than other tissues, especially since they interfere with the eye's purpose of vision. But blood vessels aren't mainly there for nutrition and oxygen. They are actually the retina's cooling system. High-energy light photons striking a fennec fox retina could quickly burn the delicate layer of cells, just like the desert sun burns my neck. Blood vessels help absorb this heat and remove it from the retina, like a mini-radiator inside the eye. But this also means bacteria in the bloodstream are more easily carried to the retina, and we occasionally detect this in eye exams.

Eliminating interfering vessels partly explains some birds' fantastic eyesight compared to ours. They also have much larger eyes for their body size, and their photoreceptor cells are more densely packed. A common buzzard has five times as many cells packed into an area of retina compared to our eyes. This helps explain how an American kestrel can spot a tiny 2-millimetre-long insect from 20 metres: far too small for us to see. At a distance we can barely read a truck's number plate; a wedge-tailed eagle flying above could easily detect the words on this page. Yet if you place the book in front of a grey wolf's face it can't even detect the letters, just as it is impossible for your pet dog to do so. Wolves, like most mammals, don't have a fovea, the patch of dense receptors that allows humans to see fine details. You may not realise it, but you can only read using a tiny part of your vision: try reading a book from the corner of your eye while looking ahead. That low resolution is how wolves, and most mammals, see everything. Visual acuity in wolves is only a quarter of a human's or bonobo's. Perfectly fine for chasing down caribou calves, rather than reading a thesis in Times New Roman 10 point font. A wolf needs to be four times closer to see the same detail as we do. But a wolf's lower-resolution vision makes its eye more robust than the high-definition but delicate eye of a steppe eagle. A kick in the face from fleeing caribou may hurt, but is unlikely to render the pursuing wolf blind.

Among mammals, only great apes and some monkeys have foveas. The fovea is a tiny region, less than 2 millimetres in diameter and only a thousandth of the retinal surface. But nerves from this region make up half of all optic nerve fibres and account for the majority of the brain's visual processing work. There is a tiny 0.3-millimetre area in the fovea that accounts for your best vision, where there are no nerves or blood vessels running over the surface, making things as high resolution as possible. The larger your fovea the more brain processing needed, so the eye is a compromise between a tiny amount of terrific detail for a bonobo to be able to peel a seed, while still having sufficient low-resolution vision around this to detect a leopard trying to creep closer. People are similarly limited, which explains why, if you try to read your phone while driving, you only notice the massive lorry as it is just about to hit you. If you were a blue-winged kookaburra, however, you could happily text on a mobile device while driving (if only they had learned that particular skill!), as kingfishers have two separate foveas. Some birds even have asymmetrical eyes to keep both the horizon and the ground in focus – something we can only do with bifocal lenses.

When I was a young vet I used to laugh if people recommended leaving the TV on for lonely pet African grey parrots. Birds can detect rapid movements far better than us, and while just 24 frames a second is enough to fool the human eye into seeing separate pictures as movement on a TV, the parrot would simply see the series of pictures, in a weird flashing slide show. It is no wonder parrots stared at the old cathode-ray TV screens. It wasn't the programme they were interested in, as owners thought, but the weird flashing zigzags of the cathode-ray tube, and perhaps they also wondered why the hell humans spent hours watching it. Budgerigars are even able to see the annoying flicker of fluorescent bulbs sixty times a second, imperceptible to us humans, with our far slower vision. No wonder some pet birds pluck their feathers out in frustration.

Birds like Sri Lankan hill mynas have four colour photo-receptor cell types, while we only have three. They can see into the ultraviolet spectrum, which is invisible to us. While to us these birds appear a boring black bird with small yellow wattles, with ultraviolet vision they are far more colourful, with large patches of green, purple and blue feathers, upon which they assess the suitability of potential mates. White-cheeked turacos recognise ripe berries by specific ultraviolet colours. Lake Victoria cichlid fish can instead see in infrared, to navigate murky waters. To them, your TV remote would resemble a couch-potato's lightsaber. Carp, like the humble goldfish (which belongs to the carp family), are possibly the only animals able to see in both ultraviolet and infrared.

Humans, orangutans and Sulawesi crested macaques are still lucky. Many South American primates, such as ornate spider monkeys and black capuchins, only have two colour photoreceptor types, as do black-backed jackals and ocelots. Searching for ocelots at night, you can spot them by their blue-green eye shine in torchlight. A reflective layer inside the eye boosts light collection, so an ocelot needs only a quarter of the light we do to see at night. Many animals, from Egyptian fruit bats to bull sharks, have this reflective tapetum lucidum, for seeing in the dark or in murky waters.

Tracking black-backed jackals at night by torch, sometimes you only see one eye shining back at you briefly, before disappearing. Some jackals are clever enough to close one eye when looking at the bright torch, then opening the other eye when running away, so they can still see clearly, instead of having to wait several minutes for their eyes to readapt to the dark. It's a useful trick I often copy. Interestingly, despite their fantastic night vision, owls don't have this reflective layer in their eyes.

An opaque white eye in an aardvark could indicate a superficial eye infection, cataracts due to a nutritional problem when it was a baby, or it could simply be the normal third eyelid or nictitating membrane across its eye. This extra eyelid helps protect the eye, and not just in lizards but in many species, including blue sharks and black cranes. While snakes like black desert cobras don't have a nictitating membrane, their eyelids are fused together, forming a transparent protective spectacle that prevents sand getting in their eyes when they burrow into the soil. They shed this spectacle with the rest of their skin. A boa constrictor could never have winked at Harry Potter, as they simply don't have eyelids. The tuatara has gone further, and has a tiny third eye on the top of its head, complete with a small lens and light receptor cells. You can see it clearly through transparent skin scales when newly hatched, but it becomes invisible after a few months. The Madagascar swift lizard even has a white ring surrounding its third eye, giving it a similar appearance to its other two eyes.

There are many nuances to remember when examining different species. Caracal cats have slit-like pupils with front-facing eyes, good for seeing the tiny movements of a bush rat, or judging the pouncing distance to a small duiker antelope. The duiker instead has rectangular pupils and eyes on either side of its head, to see the horizon 330 degrees around itself and to spot predators like the caracal trying to sneak up on it. Leaf gecko pupils are shaped like two guitars, while undulated rays have the most beautiful, tasselled pupils. We need to know what is normal to notice a problem's subtle clues. I've diagnosed an astrocytoma brain tumour in an elderly jaguar, from carefully examining the eye. Increased brain pressure caused the optic nerve to bulge slightly, which you could tell by the changes in angle of tiny blood vessels running towards it. We can tell from the rings of wet fur around a grey seal pup's eyes, no matter how sorrowful it may look, that it isn't dehydrated. Living in water, seal tear ducts are small, and most of their tears simply flow over their face. A seal with dry fur around its eyes alerts you to it being so dehydrated that its body has stopped making tears to try to conserve water, and you need to do something about it.

These differences are not interesting trivia, but essential knowledge when examining a wild patient, whose eyesight is an essential sense for survival. No wonder there are veterinarians just specialising in eyes, like my friend Claudia Hartley, who removes cataracts in everything from bears to sea lions. And this is only one tiny part of a physical examination, just one small organ. We haven't even started to open the mouth to check the teeth, or look at the ears, or examine the skin on the face.

A detailed examination takes time if you want to look at everything properly. But sometimes we only have seconds to absorb as much information as possible, holding a struggling pied avocet, or glimpsing a De Brazza's monkey bounding away through the branches. A limping bison wearily observes you briefly before galloping off into the distance. Prey animals, which are another's food, are good at hiding signs of illness so predators don't single them out. A veterinarian staring at you intently is also apparently cause for concern, and the majority of my patients, from Gila monsters to gorillas, hide their symptoms as soon as they see me.

Pondering over photos, one might only manage a best guess. Looking at the earliest known photographs of a wild animal, daguerreotypes from 1847 of Jacob Driesbach, a performer, and his jaguar, I can't help trying to assess the long-dead patient. In one image, lying melodramatically on the ground in strongman shorts with gold trim, and biblical sandals like Samson's, Driesbach is pretending to be savaged by the jaguar. The jaguar is lounging on Driesbach's chest, its mouth hidden, possibly licking his neck. No wonder, as photo exposures took several minutes at that time. The jaguar is small, despite the distinctive square head, and almost certainly a female. But my eyes are drawn to the front paw. It's almost imperceptible, but the toes are slightly rounder, with the toe pad edges just visible. Jaguars have sheathed claws, but this jaguar has had her claws pulled out, likely when a cub, as general anaesthesia had only been invented less than a year before. I can sadly recognise the subtle signs, still seeing them in confiscated circus lions.

I frequently have little more to go on than a blurred photo or a few seconds of video from the other side of the world, with a single line of someone's attempted English translation, upon which to try and base my advice. With experience, pattern recognition alerts to subtle clues with a glance. Watching a crowned sifaka jump clumsily between trees reveals an invisible injury at the tail base, probably from another lemur's bite. Its tail is vital for balance. Glimpsing an old red ruffed lemur, looking scruffy in the rain, makes you wonder if toe arthritis is preventing him using the special grooming nail on his second toe to keep his fur water-resistant. Pattern recognition relies on knowing what is most common, but sometimes that isn't the problem, and you will be wrong. Asked for advice on a photo and a few sentences about an ill cheetah a continent away during the pandemic, I plumped for a possible spiral bacteria stomach infection, and I recommended some blood tests that instead showed a kidney problem, something strong breath and irritated gums, or different-looking pee, would have alerted me to in person. For a vet, nothing beats prodding and poking a patient yourself.

The very first two photographs of elephants ever taken are still revealing, despite the distance of time. They are of two male Asian elephants in Italy: the one in the first photo looks a youngster until you see his metre-long tusks, and realise he is at least a teenager, but is barely taller than his handler. With thin shoulders, baggy skin and hardly any muscles, he is stunted and clearly malnourished. An adult elephant eats over 100 kilograms of food a day in the wild.

The photos were taken in the mid-nineteenth century just after the First Italian War of Independence, Garibaldi was in exile, and food was scarce even for people, let alone a hungry travelling elephant with a large appetite. What happened to him is unknown, but this elephant certainly didn't reach a ripe old age.

The other elephant, photographed the same year, couldn't be more different. A huge Asian elephant bull named Fritz, he towers over the tall, ornately dressed guard next to him, in front of the Stupinigi Palace, shoving food in his blurred mouth. He is obese but is standing in a strange half-sitting posture. Most of an elephant's weight is carried on its front legs, so I suspect his obesity is making the arthritis in his front legs worse, and he is trying to cope by shifting weight onto his back legs in this weird posture. A gift from the Viceroy of Egypt to the King of Sardinia thirty years earlier, Fritz danced to music when he first arrived, to amuse the hunting-lodge guests who came to blast wild animals in the surrounding forest. Sadly, like many captive male elephants, he eventually killed someone, and was shot dead in punishment, his stuffed body still displayed in the Palace museum. His moth-eaten straw-stuffed body has a more normal posture, with his arthritic bones now unburdened and placed in a more natural position. Unlike the stunted, starving, travelling elephant, Fritz belonged to wealthy aristocrats, and was daily fed 50 loaves of bread, 16 pounds of cooked rice, 5 pounds of sugar, a pint of wine and 2 pounds of tobacco, despite the human food shortages. It is no wonder his legs buckled under his own weight.

Male or female?

We can't ask wild patients any information, as your physician would ask you if you smoke, go to the gym, or if your parents had high blood pressure. Even determining the patient's age or gender can be difficult. A geriatric male pied tamarin with blood in his urine could have a prostate tumour, while a young female tamarin could instead be suffering a miscarriage with exactly the same signs.

Large external testicles or female swellings in olive baboons make identifying gender simple. But lowland streaked tenrecs have a single cloaca, like birds and reptiles, with no separate anus and genital opening to help distinguish their sex. Even watching elephants at a distance, it isn't obvious if an individual is male or female. Males have no scrotum, their testicles are inside their abdomen, and females have a vulva opening underneath, between their legs, which can resemble a male's prepuce. Dropping a new-born elephant three metres onto the ground wouldn't be a great strategy, so females have a birth canal, or vestibulum, that runs down to the underside of the belly, so the baby has the smallest fall possible. Male and female savanna elephants have different head shapes, and females form herds with babies while adult males are solitary or in groups of two or three, and these traits help you to identify which sex you are dealing with.

Spotted hyaena are confusing. The female is the larger, stronger, and dominant sex, which makes sense if defending your baby against a rival lion. A female's genitalia look very similar to a male's. There is no external vagina, the labia have fused to look like a scrotum, and the large clitoris resembles a penis, and can even have erections. I feel a voyeur looking at their genitalia in fascination every time I have one anaesthetised in East Africa, although having to sterilise one can get interesting.

Even a black-capped squirrel monkey female can be mistaken for a male, with a prominent clitoris, sometimes mistaken for a small penis. Telling the sex of a newly caught beaver is more smelly. Bundled in a hessian sack to keep it calm, its bum is squeezed to express the anal glands it uses to mark its territories. An adult female's glands have a thick grey content, while the male's glands contain a translucent oily fluid. They also have a different smell, if you did feel like sticking your nose so close to a beaver's butt.

Many birds have very different plumages. A male crimson sunbird has a bright red head, while the female is a drab brown. Even more distinctive are eclectus parrots, with males being green with an orange beak and females a bright red and purple with a black beak. Early Europeans didn't realise they were even the same species. For some birds, bright feathers are essential for attracting females. For a Congo peafowl hen incubating her eggs, it is best to have drab colours so as not to attract attention. But being a conspicuous male and not getting eaten is all part of proving you are a strong mate, whose genes are worth passing on.

Sometimes the only gender clue is size. Male peregrine falcons, like many birds of prey, are smaller than females, which need to defend the nest and chicks. This also means males can catch smaller, faster and more manoeuvrable birds, while stronger females can catch larger birds, maximising the variety of food they can hunt to feed their chicks.

Some birds look identical. But putting two male blue-fronted Amazon parrots together by mistake can mean finding one has killed the other the next morning. As a young vet, back in the day my only option was to anaesthetise birds like these, make a 3-millimetre incision and insert an endoscope, a small surgical telescope, to see inside the bird to check if it had an ovary or testicles. Thankfully, we no longer need to do this. Simple genetic tests on feathers exist to tell if there are two Z chromosomes, meaning the bird is a male, or both Z and W chromosomes, characteristic of females.

To identify the sex of reticulated pythons, thin metal probes with rounded ends are needed. Inserted into small pits on either side of their cloaca, towards the tail, the length tells us a snake's gender. Females have shallow scent glands, while males have a long thin cavity, their inside-out penis, or hemipenis. Lizards are the same as snakes, but not tortoises and turtles. Female elongated tortoises have a wider tail, with an opening closer to their body to lay eggs; males have longer tails, the cloaca opening further away from the body, which, when mating, they wrap around the females. Kangaroo and wallaby females have a pouch in which their joeys develop, but in seahorses and leafy seadragons a swollen pouch signifies a male. Like king and emperor penguins, it is the male of the species that carries the young. Gender isn't even fixed in clownfish, which all start off male, before the largest becomes a female. When Nemo lost his mum, in real life his dad would simply have changed into his mum – the ultimate parental replacement strategy.

Identifying wild animals' ages can also be confusing. We often rely on experience, and a best guess when, for instance, looking at the state of a smooth-coated otter's teeth. Young otters will have open growth plates visible if we X-ray them, while elderly animals may have arthritis that we can feel if we palpate their joints. Knowing the age can help guide you to whether vomiting is due to kidney stones in a geriatric otter, or intestinal parasites in a youngster. You can age elephant seals and sperm whales precisely by counting the growth rings inside a tooth, but this is not much use in a live animal. Young common buzzards have a pale yellow iris that becomes dark brown as they mature, but a honey buzzard iris instead turns bright yellow as it gets older. Birds replace their feathers as they become worn, usually at least yearly. Most, like bald eagles, need to keep flying while they moult their wing feathers in a variety of sequences. These help tell you an eagle's age, when combined with the gradual changes in tail feather colour patterns over their first five years of life.

Feathers also tell us about a bird's overall health. Feather lice are not a problem in themselves, but large numbers are a symptom that a bird is not preening normally. A black swan may have a hook lodged unseen in the base of its tongue making preening painful, or a wood duck may be too weak from lead poisoning to preen properly. Frayed feather edges on a turtle dove hint that it has a viral brain infection, affecting its coordination so it damages its own feathers trying to preen. Young ravens sometimes get transparent lines on their feathers, called fret marks. These show a chick was ill, or its parents couldn't feed it enough while the feathers were growing, and these weakened feathers tend to break easily. Broken feathers can thankfully be repaired by transplanting another feather into the broken one, a process called imping, using a toothpick as a splint inside the hollow shaft, until a new feather grows to replace it at the next moult.

The cornerstone of individual patient medicine, whether people, pets or pandas, is the physical examination. So annual health examinations are beloved by half of the zoo veterinary community, while reviled by the other half. Each discovered health problem is hailed as proof of its benefit, but the risks of catching, anaesthetising, examining and testing all a zoo's animals every year also add up, as does treating animals for erroneously diagnosed problems from unclear blood test results. Vital as it is to assess and treat ill patients, all the scientific evidence shows that, as far as human beings are concerned, there is absolutely no benefit to the annual physical examination, so beloved in many Western countries. Annual health checks in humans, with CT scans and blood tests fishing for any possible problems, have been shown by the Cochrane organisation, the international gold standard in medical evidence, to have no effect in reducing the risks of death from cancer, heart disease or most other common causes. It doesn't even reduce a patient's chance of hospital admission, missing work, or becoming disabled. But repeated unnecessary CT scans actually increase your lifetime risk of developing cancer, which is hardly good preventative medicine.

With wild animals, even in zoos, we don't know what is the ideal level of assessment or treatment. It is important to assess ill animals, but prey animals like Visayan spotted deer are also masters at hiding signs of illness. Yet to examine one we also risk breaking its leg catching it, or killing it under anaesthesia, which is tragic if there is actually nothing wrong with it. Examinations of apparently healthy wild animals also regularly find minor differences from what we presume is normal, and we can do real harm testing for and trying to treat these non-existent problems.

Encyclopaedic as physical examinations aim to be, they don't always give us the answer as to why a patient is ill. You have squeezed, listened to and peered deep into your unconscious prickly porcupine patient's eyes. You may know it is an adult male, or a young female, but you can't tell *why* it is ill. We now need other ways of starting to figure out what is actually going wrong inside our patient. And drawing a blood sample is usually where it starts.

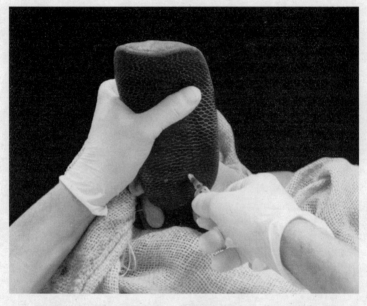

Bundled into a sack, a beaver has a blood sample drawn from its tail vein. With most of its body covered in thick waterproof fur, the tail is one of the few places a beaver can potentially lose body heat. Plucked from a cold river, the vein is small and constricted. Placing the tail on a hot water bottle for several minutes before drawing blood always helps.

5

Getting blood from a stone is easier than from a killer

You really do need to draw blood, and a sample via a kissing bug just isn't possible. Your patient is a half-tonne sleek killing machine, called a leopard seal. Eating other seals, and throwing back 10 kilogram king penguins as snacks, an adult human would be fair game as food. Thankfully, your ferocious patient is lying safely under anaesthesia on the ice, blissfully oblivious to your appetising presence. It's lying beautifully still, so taking blood from a vein should be easy, shouldn't it? Living in cold Antarctic waters, leopard seals have thick blubber, despite their sleek appearance. I have little hope of raising a vein anywhere, seeing it and inserting a needle. I am going to have to blindly stab my needle in, to find a vein, and where I am going to stick it appears even more worrying.

We normally use a tourniquet, elastic band, or just a finger pressed down on a vein. Veins have thin walls, unlike arteries, so blocking the flow of blood returning to the heart fills the bulging vein, raising it so we can see or feel it, and carefully insert our needle. Seeing a raised vein in your arm is easy, but the thick insulating fur of a Japanese snow macaque obscures everything. A small patch of fur can be clipped or shaved for us to see what we are doing, and take a blood sample safely. But animals with thick fur getting in our way have this for a reason. Clipping a patch from an Arctic fox's leg in winter to take your sample will make that skin cold and prone to frostbite.

Sea otters have the densest fur of any animal, with 150,000 hairs per square centimetre. These largest of all otters can spend their entire life at sea, even mating and giving birth in the cold ocean waters. Unlike seals and dolphins, they have no insulating blubber, but rely entirely on their dense waterproof coat to keep them warm. Even more valuable to fur trappers than sable, over a million sea otters were killed for fur, until the population plummeted to just a thousand otters and was threatened with extinction. The species is very vulnerable to oil spills. To give just one example, the *Exxon Valdez* tanker spill in 1989 killed thousands off the coast of Alaska, and it took a quarter of a century for their numbers to recover. Crude oil destroys the fur's waterproofing, and otters freeze to death, or die from swallowing the toxic oil, desperately trying to groom their fur. Clipping fur from a wild sea otter would be disastrous. Water seeps into the undercoat from the edges of the clipped patch of fur, soaking and chilling the otter. A marine animal that lives and feeds at sea, and which cannot swim or remain waterproof, won't survive long. So we have to take blood blindly, from the jugular vein.

Taking blood blindly can resemble an alien abduction science fiction scene. A long needle is inserted, guessing where the blood vessel is, based on the specific species' anatomy. The location of a sea otter's jugular vein can be guessed quite well, and we cheat by wetting the fur with alcohol to see the anatomy of the surrounding muscles slightly more easily. In leopard seals, our blood-sampling site is invisible, lying just above the spinal cord. We guess the location from feeling the pelvic bones, before inserting a very long needle to the vertebral bones protecting the spinal cord. Then, against our natural instincts, we gently move the needle forward, until reaching a space between the vertebral bones, and we plunge the needle into the depths of the spinal canal. Sitting just above the delicate spinal cord is a big vein, or rather a venous plexus, a big, dilated network of veins, which we are aiming for. While surface blood vessels constrict in cold weather to reduce heat loss, even in a blizzard these vessels, deep in the warm body, remain wide, and, once reached, the precious red draught foams into the syringe in a few seconds.

One wouldn't be so foolhardy to try to sample an awake wild leopard seal in this way, but some zoo seals have been trained to allow it, as it isn't any more uncomfortable for the seal than taking any other blood sample, no matter how nerve-racking for a vet performing this procedure for the very first time. Even after taking hundreds of samples from various seal species, I still pause for reflection every time. Orinoco croco-diles are similarly bled from just above their spine, but just behind their thick skull, from the post-occipital sinus, where the spinal cord runs into the brain.

Blood sampling a small, uncooperative Chinese box turtle, peeping out from deep within its shell, is still thankfully possible without waiting for hours for the nervous patient to emerge, only to immediately disappear again on first sight. There is a sinus sitting just beneath the top-shell carapace, and with care we can slide a thin needle under the shell just above the tortoise's head and draw blood from our unco-operative patient.

If blindly probing near a leopard seal's spine seems bad, in snakes we occasionally can't avoid drawing blood directly from the heart, like a scene from *Pulp Fiction*. In large snakes, we draw blood from the vein running below the tail – handy with a venomous monocled cobra, its front half shoved down a Perspex tube to keep us safe. Again, we can't actually see the vein. Piercing between the scales underneath the tail, until we gently touch the middle of the bone, we then edge the needle back a millimetre or two until the blood starts to slowly flow. But drawing blood from a large reticulated python, as it thrashes around trying to coil its tail around everything, still makes sampling very trying.

Male snakes have hemipenes, a couple of inside-out penises, complicating matters. Inside the tail, behind the cloaca, these have assorted spikes and hooks on their surface. For a snake that slithers, climbs branches or buries itself in sand, an external penis would just get injured. Evolution has given snakes and lizards a backup just in case one is injured. They are hidden in the base of the tail, so sticking a needle through a hemipenis while trying to get blood is unpleasant for the snake. It also risks transferring any bacteria from the needle to the vein, to circulate disastrously in the blood stream, and so really is best avoided.

In a tiny male eyelash viper, the remaining tail-tip vein is just too small, no matter how keen you are to avoid getting closer towards its impressive folding fangs. Hence the heart stab. With its head safely stuffed down a tube, we turn our patient upside down and look a third of the way along its body for the slow rhythmic pulsing that shows the heart's location. A snake's ribs run from their head to their vent. These prevent organs moving sideways, but organs slide back and forth in their tubular body. Putting a finger in front of and behind the slowly pulsing heart to prevent it moving, you slip your needle beneath the edge of one of the large scales on the underside, called a gastrostege, and then ever so gently advance the needle into the heart, with gentle suction on the syringe. The blood flows into the syringe in slow rhythmic red waves, synchronised with the snake's slow heartbeats. Despite research showing that snakes are unlikely to be harmed by this, it always feels inherently wrong to shove a needle into a beating heart.

Blood sampling small mammals like a Patagonian weasel is hardly any better. With the creature safely anaesthetised, we aim blindly for the vena cava, the main vein in front of the heart. Lying the weasel on its back, we blindly stab the needle into the entrance of the chest next to the collar bone, aiming for a large invisible vessel returning to the heart. This is a good and reliable site, but I can't help visualising the heart and lungs perilously close.

There is even one wild animal that is actually farmed just for its blood: the horseshoe crab. These bizarre ancient creatures evolved 450 million years ago, the same time as their relatives, the long-extinct trilobites. They watched dinosaurs evolve and go extinct quite recently in their species history, and human evolution and extinction will probably also be just the briefest blink in their long evolutionary journey. A similar size and shape to a World War I helmet, they swim upside down, coming to shallow waters to lay their eggs in mud. Difficult to captive breed, half a million wild Atlantic horseshoe crabs are caught every year off New Jersey, Delaware and Virginia. Taken to labs, they are held contorted in metal clamps for three days while a third of their bright blue blood is drained. Imagine long rows of metal lab benches with clamped prehistoric crabs, the massive needles that puncture their heart jutting out from their back, while the valuable turquoise liquid drips into glass milk bottles, attended by humans in masks and sterile suits. It is a hellish vision of alien abduction in reverse. Those that survive are dumped at sea, or sold as fish bait.

Their blood is blue from haemocyanin, an oxygen-carrying protein, also found in arthropods like centipedes and molluscs like snails. Horseshoe crab blood is worth up to £12,000 a litre, and a single large female can have a third of a litre taken. It contains a unique clotting ability in the presence of even minute quantities of bacterial endotoxin. Bacterial endotoxins are long thin molecules that in some infections contribute to serious problems, such as septic shock and meningitis in people. Horseshoe crab blood was until a decade ago the best available solution. Thankfully, a synthetic compound is gradually replacing the need for this annual mass abduction.

This isn't the most unusual commercial use of animal blood. Blood was an egg substitute for German cake baking in World War II, while the Allies used blood in aircraft glues, and blood is still used to make Japanese surimi fish sticks. The strangest use can be attributed to the Romans, however. Blood was added to the concrete mix used to make structures from amphitheatres to aqueducts. Roman concrete structures are fabulously durable, partly because including animal blood formed small bubbles, making the concrete lighter and stronger. Blood, which carries vital oxygen around the body, also adds air to building materials.

Some blood vessel sites are more worrying for the vet than the patient. I remember an ill pygmy hippo collapsing in an awkward position after anaesthesia, leaving no access to its tail, the usual site for intravenous access. Its thick fat hid everything, and the tiny blood vessels in its ears were collapsed. The only option was the veins on the underside of its tongue. Tongue muscles need a good blood supply, and these vessels are large in many animals. There is no surrounding tissue supporting the vessels, unlike most other veins, making it easier to rupture the large thin vessels when inserting a needle. Another hurdle is working inside the mouth. Wildlife anaesthesia depth can be difficult to judge, and inserting a needle can occasionally cause a twitch. If the needle prick in the sub-lingual vein causes the hippo to twitch its jaws closed, your arms will be mashed. On that occasion, I got away with wedging a wooden log in the corner of its mouth to delay any possible arm-chomping.

Blood sampling most animals is not so difficult or bizarre. Some are easy patients. Elephant ears have a network of large blood vessels, acting like a car radiator in hot weather and making blood sampling easy. Rhino ear veins are similarly easy to see and draw blood from. Tails are a convenient site for taking blood, with the added convenience of acting as a handle. Just like dairy cows, gaur, lowland anoa and European bison are all easily bled from the underside of their tail. Fish can also be bled from a vein deep underneath their tail. This works well for venomous stonefish, with spines and venom glands running over their back. Canadian beavers' flat tails have a large vein on their underside in the middle that could not be better designed for blood sampling. Tail blood sampling is our choice in many animals, from Nile monitor lizards to bandicoot rats.

Giraffes are easy patients, with large, clearly visible jugular veins in their long neck. The jugular is an easy site from which to draw blood in many species. We can use it even in small birds without needing anaesthesia. Holding a Java sparrow in my left hand, its neck between my index and middle finger, and thumb gently raising the jugular, I can take a blood sample in a few seconds from an awake bird, releasing it immediately afterwards. The neck feathers conveniently grow in long symmetrical rows, called pterylae. A gentle puff of breath parts the feathers, letting me see the vein clearly. I personally like to bend the needle in its cap beforehand, so the needle is parallel to the vein. In most birds, the right jugular is larger and so easiest to take blood from.

Chinstrap penguins don't have feathers in neat pterylae rows, but instead have densely packed feathers. They don't just need to be water resistant, like most birds, but truly waterproof for diving. Penguin waterproofing is put to the test daily in life-or-death struggles to avoid leopard seals and orcas, to avoid freezing, and to catch enough krill to eat. Aside from their beak, only their short ankle and foot aren't covered in dense feathers, so this is where we draw blood. A blood vessel runs on the inside of the ankle, but unfortunately is tightly constricted when on the ice, or swimming in the sub-zero sea water, to save vital body heat. The solution is to hold a hot water bottle or hand warmer on the ankle for a few minutes, until the vessel dilates enough for us to get our sample.

Some animals even try giving you their blood themselves. Well, almost. Short-horned lizards can build up their blood pressure enough to actually squirt blood from their eyes at threatening predators like coyotes. They are not unique in this skill. West Indian wood snakes and grass snakes can also expel blood from their mouth and nose during thanatosis – playing dead to deter predators. They seem to be saying, 'Look, I am dead, oozing blood, and probably rotten and so not at all safe to eat. Leave me alone.' Grass snakes also expel their foul-smelling anal gland contents to enhance the effect – the ultimate method actors. None can be used to collect blood for testing, so taunting vets frustrated by their futile efforts to collect blood from difficult patients.

101

Blood sampling is not the only reason to insert a needle or catheter into a vein. Intravenous access can help administer various drugs, from anaesthesia to fast-acting painkillers. Intravenous access is also important for humanely euthanasing severely injured and dying animals, to limit their suffering. Like some anaesthetised patients, ill animals may have low blood pressure, making access difficult. Finding a dolphin's tail fluke vein can be difficult at the best of times, but a seizuring and stranded striped dolphin surrounded by 30 onlookers asking questions just adds to the pressure of an already difficult procedure.

We can administer intravenous fluids to improve blood pressure and circulation, and even give blood transfusions to try to save an animal's life. In some countries, blood banks already exist for pet dogs. No blood banks exist for any wild animals. For a few years, we had a fluid made from cow haemoglobin that carried oxygen, which helped anaemic animals or wildlife patients that had lost large amounts of blood. As with much biotech, the planned move to the human health market proved more complicated and arduous than anticipated, and the company that pioneered the product went bankrupt.

In an emergency, vets occasionally resort to giving a xenotransfusion – a blood transfusion from a different species. An anaemic San Clemente Island fox can be given a life-saving blood transfusion from a pet dog. While xenotransfusion can be life-saving, it also risks killing your ill patient. There is huge variation in animal blood groups, and most are poorly investigated, if at all. Bison and Asian buffalo have more than 50 blood groups, while tigers and lions only have two blood groups. Cat species have a high risk of fatal blood transfusion reactions, even from the same species, while blue wildebeest and foxes tolerate transfusions well, even from other species. Rather than blood types, the best test for transfusion reactions is cross-matching. The quickest and easiest way to do this is, for example, to mix a drop of serum from an Iriomote cat (the patient) with a drop of red blood cells from a donor, such as a Siberian tiger from a local zoo. If the cells clump together or 'agglutinate', the blood is not safe to give. If the cells all remain separate, you have a much smaller risk of a fatal reaction. Still, you can only use a transfusion from a different species once. An anaemic Andean condor can be transfused with bald eagle blood, but if another transfusion is later needed, blood from a Steller's sea eagle or yet another species has to be used.

Even if cross-matched, transfused red blood cells are still broken down rapidly. Pigeon red blood cells transfused into another pigeon survive about a week, but if transfused into an anaemic red-tailed hawk the cells only survive about half a day. Xenotransfusion has been used in many bird species. Thanks to their fast metabolism, even 12 hours can help a critically ill avian patient recover.

Zoo vets have the benefit of being able to train animals, making blood sampling easier, but also less stressful for the patient. A diabetic drill monkey can be trained to present its finger for a prick test, to measure its blood glucose levels and administer the correct amount of insulin. Gorillas and giant pandas can be trained to put their arm into a special chute to allow blood to be drawn, and a Persian leopard can be trained to allow vets to draw blood from its tail, between the bars of its cage, for a food reward.

Easy or difficult to get, the warm vial of blood is now safely in your hand. Next, we need to try to figure out if we can diagnose the problem from it.

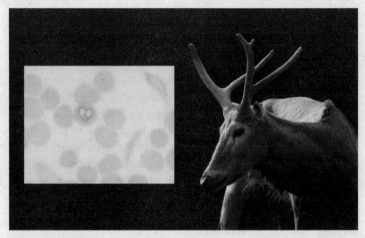

Milu deer's red blood cells seen down the microscope appear to be afflicted by sickle-cell anaemia, although the deer are completely healthy. We think there is some evolutionary genetic advantage behind this, such as resistance to blood parasites, like the small purple teardrop-shaped Babesia parasites shown here.

6

Why deer don't die of
sickle-cell anaemia

A blood smear slide from a Chinese milu looks the same down a microscope as one from a person dying of sickle-cell anaemia. Also named Père David's deer after the French missionary who sent the first dead specimens to Europe, the milu's red blood cells, or erythrocytes, are a bizarre assortment of long, thin crescent moons and spikes, instead of the normal round doughnut shapes. In a person this would indicate certain death, yet these deer are all perfectly healthy.

Milu are extinct in the wild. Large and ungainly, their hooves make a soft clicking sound when walking. I first saw them in the 1990s at the Woburn deer park, the place that saved them from extinction. By the time of their discovery by Westerners, they were already extinct in the wild, only clinging on in the imperial hunting grounds outside Beijing. A century ago, a flood toppled one of the walls and most of the deer escaped, to be swiftly eaten by starving villagers. Only thirty milu remained, until the Boxer Rebellion when European troops occupying the hunting grounds shot and ate the last deer, making them extinct in their native land. A small number had thankfully been illegally smuggled out to Europe as scientific curiosities and survived scattered among a handful of zoos and parks. The Duke of Bedford acquired as many as he could to bolster his Woburn Abbey herd. With the outbreak of World War I, the remaining deer outside Woburn were eaten, in what seems to be the sad life-story of these deer. Thankfully they thrived in Woburn, and in the 1980s some were returned to China.

The red blood cells of deer and other hooved animals are often strange. Mouse deer, or chevrotain, the smallest hoofed animal, have tiny red blood cells. Camels have long, oval erythrocytes. This shape may help prevent cells from sludging in the blood when camels are dehydrated and also perhaps protects the cells from bursting as they expand when the animal guzzles water to rehydrate itself. Several deer, from North American white-tailed deer to European roe deer, often have sickle cells. The first drawings describing them were made by George Gulliver, who published his illustrations in 1840, although his travels were not particularly exciting. Most specimens were simply procured from London Zoo.

Why do deer stay healthy, yet humans get sick with sickle cells? Despite copious research in the 1980s, we simply didn't have the right tools for the job. Only recently has genetics come to our aid. The genes causing sickle cells in deer are very old, and so there must be some advantage to maintaining this anomaly. The protein involved, beta globulin, is the same in humans and deer, but the genes involved appear different. There is a high rate of sickle-cell anaemia in sub-Saharan African people where I grew up, and having one copy of the gene makes people more resistant to malaria. It is only when a person has two copies that they become ill. In deer there must be some similar evolutionary advantage, probably also against blood parasites, although we still don't know for sure.

Yet deer red blood cells are probably one of the more boring erythrocytes out there. Capybaras have red blood cells five times larger than those of a mouflon; but mouflon have four times as many red blood cells as a capybara. This has probably evolved so mouflon blood doesn't sludge, and risk forming deadly clots causing strokes at cold high altitudes, when blood vessels constrict to limit heat loss. Mammalian red blood cells themselves are strange. Having no nucleus, they are little more than flattened bags of haemoglobin pumped around the body to deliver oxygen. These zombie cells are alive, but only last roughly a hundred days before being recycled, and their components used to manufacture new cells. Dried on a glass slide and stained, the cells have a doughnut appearance, with a thin central region where they have lost their nucleus.

This flattened, biconcave shape lets them distort and squeeze through capillaries slightly smaller than their diameter. This allows efficient oxygen exchange by bringing their oxygen-carrying haemoglobin contents as close as possible to the blood vessel wall, and to the oxygen-hungry cells beneath it. Humans have large red blood cells, compared to deer of the same size, supposedly as our large brains have high oxygen requirements. This is perhaps an evolutionary advantage for sitting through hours of television repeats and scrolling social media kitten videos!

African elephants have large, thin red blood cells, while minke whales have big, fat red blood cells. Whales live in water, with relatively stable temperatures, but elephants in the Namibian desert are subjected to furiously hot days and freezing nights. To cope, elephants' ears and all body surface blood vessels vacillate between tightly constricted to prevent heat loss at night, and widely dilated to lose excess heat during the day. Large cells are efficient in transmitting oxygen by being close to dilated blood vessel walls, while being thin makes the cells flexible, so they can contort to squeeze through constricted vessels at night, something whale blood cells don't have to do. Whale cells are instead optimised to carry the maximum oxygen through their fixed-diameter blood vessels, and so are much thicker.

Moving away from mammals, things get more interesting. There is even one animal, the crocodile icefish, that has no red blood cells at all. It doesn't even have haemoglobin. Oxygen simply dissolves in its colourless blood and is transported without those apparently essential components. It only copes because oxygen concentrations are high in Antarctic waters. Living in such cold water makes its metabolism very slow, and so it needs less oxygen. But icefish still had to evolve a larger heart and big blood vessels to cope.

The giants of the erythrocyte world belong to the olm, an aquatic salamander, with cells 50 times larger than a musk deer's. Olms are weird. Only living in deep caves under Central European mountains, the occasional ones washed out by storms in the Middle Ages were believed to be baby dragons. Also called the human fish, they are pale, fleshy, and resemble a giant worm, with small, shrivelled legs. Completely blind, they eat, sleep and breed entirely under water. Their large size is not the only interesting thing about their erythrocytes. Like other amphibians, birds and reptiles, their red blood cells still have their nuclei.

The Methuselah of erythrocytes belongs to the South American cane toad, and some other amphibians, and these giant blood cells can survive in circulation for more than three years. But then these largest of all toads can after all live more than three decades. Reptilian red blood cells, such as those of the Indian star tortoise, are also long-lived, circulating for over two years, in contrast to those of a Bornean orangutan that only last a paltry three months. Do red blood cells with functional nuclei always live longer than our zombie mammal erythrocytes? Well, no. Pygmy tyrant flycatchers, like all birds, have nucleated red blood cells, but with their frenetic metabolism their erythrocytes live life in the fast lane, and often don't survive even 30 days in circulation. Fish cover both extremes: while kissing gourami erythrocytes last as little as 13 days, crucian carp cells can survive a year and a half in circulation.

By booting out the nucleus, almost no oxygen is used by zombie mammalian erythrocytes themselves. Cells can be stuffed even fuller of the oxygen needed by faraway tissues. Cells can also be smaller and more flexible, to fit down smaller blood vessels, getting closer to the tissues needing oxygen. The nucleated erythrocytes of bar-headed geese are much larger, but then so too are their blood vessels, so erythrocytes pass down them just fine. They also have more muscle capillaries, useful for a bird that flies over the Himalayan mountains.

Humans can barely stumble up Everest, let alone perform prolonged athletic feats there. Efficiency in birds is also improved by having haemoglobin with a stronger affinity for oxygen, and a more efficiently designed breathing system than in any mammal, even the athletic pronghorn antelope. Birds' lungs have no alveoli, but instead their lungs are faveolar, or sponge-like in structure. Mammalian alveoli are like little balloons, with thick walls of elastic tissue. Inflating and deflating slightly with breathing, they would otherwise pop. Yet oxygen diffuses down to the alveoli. Breathing mainly involves moving air back and forth in your airways, with the breath itself never really reaching anywhere near alveoli. This isn't particularly efficient. In a needle-tailed swift, the fastest horizontally flying bird, the rigid sponge lung has a much thinner interface between blood and air that is more efficient. Birds also breathe in a circular motion, using a series of air sacs, and with no diaphragm.

Birds' nucleated red blood cells are not an inefficient design, offset by a better breathing system. Having nuclei means cells can repair damage, even to DNA, and also divide. If a Himalayan tahr gets wounded by a snow leopard and loses blood, the new blood cells have to be slowly produced by the bone marrow, even throwing immature nucleated cells into circulation to try to cope. But a Congo peafowl can lose a third of its blood, and yet have normal circulating erythrocyte numbers again in less than three days. A mallard duck can even lose almost two-thirds of its blood volume and still survive, while a rock pigeon can not only survive losing two-thirds of its blood, but will have completely normal circulating erythrocyte numbers again in less than seven days. This is all without any treatment, intravenous fluids, or transfusions. We frequently encounter this amazing ability of birds to survive blood loss when treating blackbirds or wood pigeon caught by a cat but which then managed to escape. With a couple of days of food and rest they will have completely recovered from their blood loss, although they may still have a bald butt, where the cat grabbed a mouthful of feathers.

In contrast, a chimpanzee or human can only lose about 15 per cent of their blood before showing symptoms, 20 per cent before shock sets in. Loss of a third of circulating blood is enough to cause a loss of consciousness. Sudden loss of more than 40 per cent is enough to be fatal, with people rarely surviving losing half their blood in a traumatic accident, even if treated promptly with a blood transfusion. After donating blood, which is only a small amount of your total volume, it takes one to two months for your body to replace all your donated red blood cells, somewhat longer than the three days it takes a peafowl.

The lack of red blood cell nuclei probably originates from mammals emerging in the Triassic period, when the air oxygen level was half what it is now. Mammals evolved small erythrocytes and capillaries to cope, and so the nucleus had to go. Birds are more modern than mammals, evolving in the Jurassic period when oxygen levels were more similar to today's, with no need for this adaptation, which is now partly redundant. Reptiles like the ancient tuatara emerged at a similar time to dinosaurs, and instead evolved tolerance to low oxygen levels, with a slower metabolism, never needing to change their blood cell design either.

Nucleated erythrocytes make a vet's life just a little more difficult, as modern blood cell counting machines, designed for humans and domestic animals, won't work for birds, reptiles, amphibians or fish. They can't differentiate between red and white blood cells, as they all have nuclei. In addition, the most common blood preservative, sodium edetate, ruptures the erythrocytes of birds like black-crowned cranes, laughing kookaburra and ostriches, as well as some reptiles, such as Hermann's tortoise. The resulting small vial of jam is then useless for any diagnostic purpose. Frustratingly for many bird and reptile species, sometimes erythrocytes rupture, and sometimes they don't, making it a bit of a lottery. Using different preservatives like heparin also changes how cells stain, which can make white blood cell identification difficult. Animals like Canadian beavers have such good clotting abilities, their blood often sets in a solid lump even when using plenty of anticoagulant. While this is frustrating for me as I stare at a useless clotted sample, it makes sense, for an animal living in water, to have excellent clotting if injured.

We need to make, dry, and stain a blood smear, then squint down the microscope and count a large number of the cells before performing calculations to work out how many of the different types of cells there are in circulation. If you live in a developed country where you can simply send blood to a commercial lab, a technician may be inexperienced and find identifying the different types of a rainbow boa's cells difficult. Then the sheet of numbers you receive back isn't just meaningless, but dangerous, leading you to misdiagnose conditions. There was even a scandal years ago, when a small lab didn't have the equipment needed, and simply started making up results. Despite a long day wrestling with uncooperative patients, squinting down the microscope yourself is often the best way to be sure of what you see. At least this way, any mistakes are just your own.

Erythrocytes are only one of the circulating blood cells, and the others also have their own quirks in the variety of creatures we deal with. Platelets, also called thrombocytes, are responsible for clotting. In mammals they are not cells at all, but simply small circulating sheared-off pieces of giant megakaryocyte cells hiding in the bone marrow. In birds, they have a nucleus, and can look similar to small white blood cells called lymphocytes. Examining a blood smear from an ill tree sparrow, you may not only see clumps of thrombocytes clotting on your slide, but also that the thrombocytes have swallowed bacteria, just like the white blood cells in other animals do.

The various white blood cells, leukocytes, are an essential part of the immune system. They help us diagnose health problems on a blood smear, as their numbers and appearance change in response to diseases or injury. But just catching or darting animals releases adrenaline, which almost instantly boosts the numbers of circulating leukocytes, which can be mistaken for a viral infection. However, prolonged stress in a wild Taita falcon being treated before release to the wild actually results in lower numbers of lymphocytes and eosinophils from the circulating stress hormone cortisol – a response called a stress leukogram, which can also be mistaken for an infection. Unnecessary handling and treatment only make immunosuppression worse, and the poor falcon risks ending up with a fatal Aspergillus fungal respiratory infection.

Neutrophils are the most common leukocyte in bobcats, and most mammals, but in Princess parakeets, and indeed in many birds, lymphocytes predominate instead. Birds and reptiles don't even have neutrophils, but instead have heterophils, a speckled cell under the microscope. A key difference is that heterophils don't have the same enzymes to break down dead infected tissue, so an abscess in a reticulated python is solid, and resembles a rubber ball, and abscesses in black-necked swans look more like an onion with solid layers. Pus is liquid in bobcats, and their abscesses can dramatically burst, spurting smelly yellow pus (which is simply dead neutrophils) everywhere.

Eosinophils are large cells with round pink granules, which hint at parasite infections when seen in large numbers. In an American marten this may be due to toxoplasma, or in a raccoon to *Baylisascaris* roundworms. In raccoons this worm causes little trouble, living in the intestines. But if the eggs are accidentally eaten by another animal, a deer, a person, or a bobwhite quail, the confused hatching worms can end up anywhere in the body, even inside the brain, causing all sorts of serious damage. As with everything, things can get complicated to remember. Gopher tortoises have higher eosinophil numbers in spring than in summer, while kelp gulls have higher numbers in winter than in autumn. Migrating loggerhead turtles also have lower circulating eosinophil numbers than turtles happily staying in one area, as do many birds after flying, especially migrating species like snow geese. Male and female Asian yellow pond turtles and mugger crocodiles will have quite different eosinophil numbers, while different-age Californian condors instead have varying numbers. Normal, healthy black lemurs in captivity also have quite different circulating numbers from those in the wild.

I could keep going on for each type of white cell for many more pages, but will only mention a few more. Elephants have a bizarre large white blood cell with a double nucleus. Originally called elephant cells, we now believe these are just a form of monocyte that is only seen in elephants. Snakes like puff adders have a strange, large pink-white blood cell, called an azurophil. Some vets believe this is just a strange monocyte, but others believe it is an entirely different cell. Even exactly the same type of cell, a heterophil, doesn't look the same in different species, such as steppe eagles and white-rumped vultures. The former's cells have small pink round granules, while the latter has purple cigar-shaped granules, with a clear spot at the end. Interpreting the actual meaning of what you see down the microscope can be a real challenge.

Parasites in wild patients

Peering down a microscope can resemble a trip to a microscopic zoo. On a blood smear from a single, tiny white-eye bird I have seen Plasmodium and Hemoproteus, two different types of bird malaria. There was also Leukocytozoon, a parasite that distorts white blood cells until they look like ancient aurochs heads with long horns. Joining them were some Trypanosoma, corkscrew-shaped protozoa whose relatives caused sleeping sickness and Chagas disease, which some people believed plagued Charles Darwin later in his life. And lastly, a large lazy filarial worm, that had been happily swimming inside the blood vessels, until I rudely drew it up into my syringe with my blood sample. There is a multitude of parasites we find in our wild patient's blood, all with complex life cycles. Some spend half their life developing in biting insects, before entering the patient. Trypanosoma prefer biting flies, or bed bugs, while malaria prefers mosquitoes, and Babesia and Ehrlichia parasites need ticks.

Despite our modern veterinary training, where all parasites of pet dogs and farmed pigs are to be ruthlessly eliminated, parasites are a natural component of wild animal lives. Most of the time, they don't cause illness in their hosts, unless there is some other problem that suppresses the immune system, or, as with zoo penguins, their unnatural surroundings make them susceptible to the avian malaria species carried by local birds. Getting rid of blood parasites in truly wild animals often doesn't help, as they will simply catch them again as soon as they return to the wild. Many have co-evolved for millions of years, and getting rid of them can sometimes harm our patients. Moving valuable African buffalo back from a European zoo to Southern Africa can result in them dying of blood parasites, as they have not grown up with these parasites or developed a normal protective immunity. Even buffalo from one region may not have immunity to blood parasites found in another region, and will quickly become ill. Theileria parasites in the blood of African buffalo may not cause their hosts any problem, but if brown ear ticks drop off and bite cattle in neighbouring farms, the cows will rapidly die of Corridor disease.

To explore the microscopic world of blood cells and parasites, we need to stain the dry smear of blood on a glass slide, to see the cells under a microscope. Without stains, cells are transparent ghosts with none of their details apparent. Blood stains have interesting tales involving Nazi supporters, Van Gogh's paints, malaria, and even Jacques Cousteau.

Some stains are better for viewing cell nuclei details, which is especially important in cancer detection. The most famous is the Papanicolaou stain. George Papanicolaou was a Greek doctor, who after years practising medicine decided to go back to university and get a zoology doctorate by studying water fleas. He then ended up working at the Monaco Oceanographic Institute, later run by Jacques Cousteau, the inventor of the aqua-lung, before moving to the USA. There he worked in medical pathology, developed his stain, and the 'Pap smear' test for cervical cancer. Perhaps an attraction to dolphins was his midlife crisis, and thankfully didn't diminish his contribution to human health. Papanicolaou developed another test using his stain, of importance to vets rather than doctors. He discovered that as female mammals of many species progress through their reproductive cycle, the cells lining the vagina change to protect themselves for impending mating, with a microscopic lining of cornified cells. Whether dealing with an Asiatic cheetah, African hunting dog, Scottish wildcat, or giant panda, looking at a stained smear of vaginal cells helps confirm the timing for mating or artificial insemination. If the smear contains only large flat blue cells, most without any nucleus, then we are good to go. But if the smear has smaller round cells with nuclei, we know we have missed the fertile period and the patient has already ovulated.

As mammals don't have nucleated red cells, we need stains that colour the cytoplasm, to tell the different blood cells apart and detect blood parasites. Most are called Romanovsky stains, after the Russian physician who developed the first decent stain for finding malaria in blood smears. We now use many improved versions, such as one named after Gustav Giemsa while he worked as a pharmacist in East Africa to find a better way to detect malaria. Less laudably, he was also a keen Nazi Party member. His stain is particularly good at highlighting the STDs chlamydia and trichomonas, and for diagnosing the typical safety-pin appearance of plague bacteria in Mexican prairie dogs.

Most of these stains contain eosin, sometimes used as a dye in the red paints that Van Gogh used. Unfortunately, it fades over time, and not just in blood smears. Looking at Van Gogh's still life painting of roses, the originally pink petals have almost completely faded to white. Blood stains also typically contain methylene blue, a bright industrial dye. This not only stains malaria on blood smears, but can kill malaria in patients too, and was used as a treatment until World War II. Soldiers hated it as the temporary side-effect was that it turned the whites of their eyes blue, and made bright blue urine too. It is now making a comeback in regions with drug-resistant malaria, and can treat some blood parasites in wildlife. Babesia is a parasite similar to malaria, only spread by ticks. Sometimes, for example when you're examining blood from a maned wolf, two teardrop-shaped parasites in a red blood cell seem to stare back at you through the microscope like sad little eyes. Treating babesia with methylene blue works well, but turns the wolf's tongue and gums bright blue, just like those of a Shar Pei dog.

We count different types of blood cells down the microscope, then compare this to the normal numbers we expect. We imagine that we are like Sherlock Homes, trying to determine what has caused subtle changes. But when squinting at rows of numbers at the end of a difficult day and trying to decide what they actually mean, I feel much more like an incompetent Inspector Clouseau, as you will see.

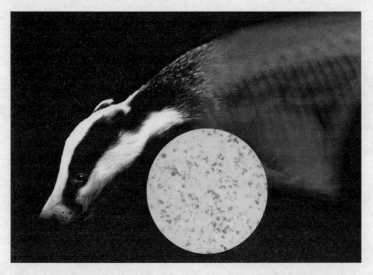

Cattle tuberculosis in badgers is a perfect example of the difficulty facing vets when trying to interpret a diagnostic test's results. The fewer badgers are infected with the pink-staining tuberculosis bacteria, the less likely it is that an individual badger's positive test result is correct.

7

Lies, damn lies, and test results

Everyone imagines the wildlife vet, clad in khaki, alongside a weather-beaten Land Rover in the African savanna, dartgun in hand. Coverage in the media, and even in video games, reinforces this nonsensical image. You never see a TV wildlife vet scratching their head while staring at sheets of numbers. Whether a mandrill, a mountain lion, or a speckled mousebird, the long columns of figures are mind-numbingly similar. Yet test results are sometimes the most important tool we have. The more glamorous darting of desert bighorn sheep out of a helicopter, or wrestling to get blood from an uncooperative monk seal, is often only so we can run a specific test. But test results are a minefield. Their interpretation can be more challenging than most surgical operations.

There is a dazzling array not only of things we can test for, but also types of tests. Some tests try to detect something, such as a herpes virus in American bison, by mixing the sample with fluorescent markers, to give us a positive or negative result. Sometimes these markers bind to a different virus, or even mistakenly bind to completely the wrong thing. This is particularly a risk when we are using a test developed for humans or livestock in something so different as a Sunda pangolin. Polymerase chain reaction (PCR) tests, beloved of crime writers and television dramas, amplify a tiny fragment of DNA. But PCR tests cannot really tell us if what we have detected was actually causing the problem. Even finding anti-bodies to a disease in the blood of our patient is not clear-cut. A giant panda with antibodies to distemper virus may simply have been vaccinated as a cub. Or perhaps it survived an infection years ago, and has antibodies because it is now immune. Similarly, finding antibodies to chicken viruses in Antarctic Adélie penguins doesn't mean they are ill, or even that the virus can make them ill. It may simply reflect visiting cruise ship tourists' love of fried chicken, and poor waste disposal habits.

Other tests measure a quantity of a substance, whether calcium, vitamin K, or a liver tissue enzyme like alanine transaminase. Just because a liver enzyme is diagnostic in humans or pet dogs, doesn't mean it will help to tell if a Chinese red goral has liver damage due to an infection with liver fluke (a parasite). Even different liver enzymes, such as gamma-glutamyl transferase, that are more diagnostic in domestic goats, may still not mean much in a distantly related wild cousin.

Now that we have done a test, and the result is 367 units per litre, what does that actually mean? We flip open a book, or search the internet for papers in scientific journals. If we are lucky, we are working with a common wild animal like a Burchell's zebra, and it is easy to see what has been reported as normal. If the test is unusual, or the species rare, then we try to compare it to something related. A Malayan tapir could be compared to a domestic horse, or a reticulated giraffe to a beef cow. We have to be careful about the normal value ranges printed in books and journals. Reference ranges for human and veterinary tests usually comprise a 95 per cent normal range. That means there is only a one in twenty chance a normal animal will have a result outside this range – a small chance. Sometimes a different range is published, as when looking at Malayan flying foxes recently, where a standard deviation was used. This only includes about three-quarters of normal values. A test result from a normal, healthy flying fox has a one in four chance of being outside the apparently normal range. Books frequently don't even explain how the range was calculated. Looking at Western long-beaked echidna ranges, I simply can't tell. If I get an abnormal result, it is clearly important to know if I have a one-in-four or a one-in-twenty chance of the result actually being OK.

And what animals were tested to determine that range? In humans, tens of thousands of individuals are included, with separate accurate ranges for men, women and children. This is impossible for endangered species. Sometimes the range has been calculated from only a handful of captive individuals, or perhaps only based on males. Our Western long-beaked echidna's values, it turns out, were calculated from 14 zoo animals. No matter how well they are kept, it is impossible to replicate their wild diet of termites and ants. In captivity they are fed various mixed diets including minced beef, eggs, wheat bran and olive oil. Even carefully balanced for major nutrients like protein, micronutrients will never be the same. Diet has a real effect on health, but also on many blood sample parameters like vitamin D. Gender and age also affect levels of calcium, hormones and enzymes, and not just when females are pregnant or laying eggs. How does this affect your patient, and was this a factor in the small group used to calculate the normal range?

Even season and temperature affect results. Bears about to hibernate have different normal values versus those in summer for several tests. Most extreme are reptiles. All their metabolism and body processes depend on external temperatures, as they don't generate their own body heat. A Hispaniolan ground iguana will have different results depending on the temperature where it is. Even wild iguana individuals can be quite different. In captivity, replicating the true range and complexity of temperatures and habitat is impossible in a glass vivarium, which will always influence results.

All these factors complicate interpreting results, making it difficult trying to explain gut feelings based on experience to a conservation biologist or zoo curator, when they have rows of numbers, unhelpfully marked as normal or abnormal, analysed at a laboratory.

When I first qualified, we really had to ponder after examining a lethargic Choco toucan, consider its symptoms carefully, and decide which few expensive blood tests would confirm our diagnostic hunch of liver iron overload. In those days, laboratories went further than supermarket buy-one-get-one-free offers, with cheap pre-packaged test panels. Suddenly, a panel of 20 organ function enzymes and electrolytes cost the same as three single tests, and everyone started running large panels on all their hairy or feathered patients, irrespective of symptoms. Labs then added haematology, with 20 or more blood parameters for almost no additional cost, and suddenly it didn't seem worth spending 10 minutes peering down the microscope at a blood smear when the lab would run it cheaply through a machine for you. Desktop machines quickly arrived, running all this for you in your own practice or wildlife hospital, generating a sheet of almost 50 results in five minutes, while very helpfully adding asterisks to highlight any abnormal numbers.

Cheap and easy diagnostic testing spawned a different way of examining wildlife sanctuary and zoo patients, which are not alway cooperative. Peering over the fence at a Southern serow in a Cambodian rescue centre, I couldn't tell if it was ill because, like so many animals, it was good at hiding its symptoms. As I've already mentioned, if you are potentially another animal's lunch, you don't want them to be able to detect that you are unwell and therefore easier to catch. Even with experience we are still caught out occasionally by animals suddenly keeling over dead, despite looking perfectly normal.

How great it would be to detect diseases and health problems early, say in a sloth bear, when we could treat it and before it started to show symptoms. Many vets anaesthetise and perform yearly health tests on zoo and rescue centre animals. But anaesthesia is not without risks, from breaking a dhole's leg during darting, to a gorilla dying during recovery. Even drawing blood holds risks. I have seen even big birds like a red-legged seriema bleed to death after blood sampling. But in most cases the risks are felt to be worth the potential benefit.

Yet all too often we forget the boring statistical basis underpinning tests. Even a 95 per cent normal range means one in 20 results is likely to appear abnormal in a completely healthy animal. In a report sheet of 50 test results, two or three could come up as false positive, supposedly indicating a problem that doesn't exist. But random processes don't work evenly, and you don't get two abnormal tests in every wild patient's test results sheet. They cluster and clump, often in unfortunate ways. Then our brains tragically find imaginary patterns that don't actually exist. After several patients with completely normal results, a critically endangered blue-eyed black lemur will have eight abnormal results, with several of them liver enzymes. None are sky-high, but all are outside the normal range. The end result is that a month later at autopsy, the lemur actually turns out to have a completely normal liver, but has instead died from the stress of multiple anaesthetics, tests, and invasive liver biopsy surgery. There is a movement in modern human medicine to lower risks from 'overdiagnosis', but this has barely been recognised in the veterinary profession, let alone the small branch of wildlife medicine. It's little wonder that Gerald Durrell commented that one of the two most dangerous animals to let loose in a zoo was a vet.

The other dangerous creatures, according to Durrell, were architects. Understandable considering the number of people climbing or falling into dangerous animals' enclosures in zoos. Even in Durrell's own Jersey Zoo, a five-year-old fell into the gorilla enclosure. Thankfully, the silver-backed male, the first male gorilla ever born in captivity, actually protected the unconscious boy from the other gorillas, until he could be rescued by keepers. It is always a balance between enclosures that are safe for both animals and people; they need to be functional but should also allow people to feel close to the animals. Getting it wrong can have deadly consequences. As vets, it is good to know we are not the only profession to make mistakes.

Sometimes a blood sample is not enough. Testing a red-ruffed lemur for kidney disease, we usually draw blood for urea, creatine and electrolytes. The mammalian kidney has a lot of inbuilt spare capacity, so tests will often only become abnormal if more than two-thirds of the kidney is already damaged. If the lemur, mainly a fruit eater, decided to snack on a dead leaf tail gecko it found earlier, giving it a quick protein boost, the results can appear elevated even if the kidneys are actually functioning well. We need to compare urine taken at the same time, to actually evaluate our blood results. Kidney testing in a seriema or a ground iguana is complicated by birds and reptiles excreting uric acid rather than urea, and also inconveniently voiding urine and faeces together from the cloaca. So does a red-legged seriema with annoyingly elevated uric acid levels have serious kidney disease, or is it simply happily digesting a mouse it caught earlier? Urine from our ruffed lemur patient can also provide us with other useful information. High protein levels could help confirm kidney disease, as protein is leaking into the urine. White blood cells in urine may hint at an infection, while clumps of cells, called casts, seen under the microscope highlight different causes of kidney injury. We often need multiple different tests, as well as our essential clinical judgement of our patient's symptoms, to come to any meaningful conclusion.

Examining urine is recorded on 6,000-year-old Babylonian clay tablets, while Sanskrit texts from 100 BCE recognised diabetics' sweet-tasting urine, which attracted black ants. Thankfully, I don't have to taste a saki monkey's urine, or wait for ants to appear. I simply put a few drops on a paper test strip. Yet, drinking urine is a surprisingly popular alternative therapy. Even the Indian Prime Minister Morarji Desai and British actress Sarah Miles admitted to it. Bengal tigers and Burchell's zebra may appear to drink urine, but are actually detecting pheromones, drawing scents across their vomeronasal organ to tell if urine is from a female in season.

Yet, even sipping urine would probably give us less of a headache than test results frequently do. A Bali myna may be dying of an Atoxoplasma liver parasite, but we can't detect the guilty organism with our test. Sometimes there is no test, or just experimental work kindly run in a university several countries away. But the six weeks needed for a result, even without worrying what a result actually means, is hardly practical when screening a European beaver from a Scottish loch you have just trapped for *Echinococcus multilocularis*. This nasty parasite of the liver can also infect humans, destroying your liver. You need to make a decision within hours whether to euthanise the patient, or release it back to the wild, knowing it is now wise enough for you to never be able to trap it again. In desperation, I developed a combination testing protocol including actually examining the liver via keyhole surgery to improve our limited ability to diagnose the disease. Surgical disease testing is probably the most extreme technique for wild patients.

Getting it wrong can have tragic consequences. When two endangered Asiatic lions were moved overseas to improve captive breeding genetics as a backup against extinction, they had comprehensive examinations and diagnostic testing under anaesthesia. As lions are affected by tuberculosis, vets used a new procedure for the first time. An award-winning test developed for cows, it used a bacteriophage, a virus of bacteria, to detect the mycobacterium bacteria causing the disease. Both lions tested strongly positive, and so with great sadness were euthanised. The tragedy was that at autopsy no actual tuberculosis infection could be found anywhere in their bodies.

Mycobacteria cause tuberculosis, leprosy, and are even implicated in Crohn's disease. They are a nightmare to diagnose, causing a number of diseases in various animals, from diarrhoea in Mishmi takin and deaths in field voles, to leprosy in red squirrels, liver abscesses in white-winged wood ducks, and skin ulcers in edible bullfrogs. Mycobacterium tuberculosis is mainly a disease of people, rarely affecting animals. Unfortunately, other mycobacterium species can infect humans or spread between different species. *Mycobacterium bovis* found in cattle is the main reason for pasteurising milk, to prevent people getting TB from infected milk cows. Unfortunately, the disease is now also common in European badgers, brushtail possums, white-tailed deer, and even carnivores like coyotes and African lions, spreading between people, cattle and wildlife. Mycobacteria are the most important infectious cause of human deaths in the world, killing one and a half million people yearly – more than HIV. But the World Health Organization estimates that a staggering quarter of the whole planet's human population has a latent infection – where someone carries the bacteria, but is not ill or shedding the bacteria yet. We are always on the alert to wildlife patients being infected, and the risk they pose to other wildlife, people and domestic animals. Zoo vets have night-mares about seemingly healthy elephants, chimpanzees or sea lions breathing out infectious mycobacteria droplets into the faces of visiting children.

An ancient disease, TB was known as consumption. It ran a slow course, the patient gradually wasting away. It literally consumed its victims, who quietly coughed blood into hand-kerchiefs for years, all the while spreading the airborne disease. Just as the infection progresses slowly in patients, it is also unusually slow at multiplying for a bacteria, when we try to grow it. In the lab it may only divide once in a day, unlike those bacteria that double in number every 20 minutes. Trying to culture it on agar plates, as for most bacterial infections, takes months instead of days. Many tests have hence been developed to detect mycobacterial species faster, but none are without problems.

Even the best tests – and none for mycobacteria are fantastic – have an error rate, which is critically important. We refer to how sensitive and specific tests are at detecting a disease. But what does a result actually mean for an individual wild animal? This is where the nightmare really begins. What a positive or negative result actually indicates for an individual patient can change, depending on how common or rare the disease is in the population. If only one in a hundred badgers is infected with TB, the majority of the badgers testing posi-tive will actually not have TB; you will sadly discover false positives during autopsy. We refer to this problem as a poor positive predictive value of the test. Well, at least most of the badgers testing negative don't have the disease, you say. Tests may indeed have a very good negative predictive value. But even if as high as 99 per cent, this still hides the fact that one in every few hundred badgers testing negative actually does have a TB infection. Disease screening, especially when animals are culled on the basis of the results, is complicated. If your head is starting to hurt, then you know just how we often feel. I have spared you all the actual complex mathematics, statistics and disease modelling we often need in wildlife disease scenarios. If only wildlife veterinary work were as simple as I thought it was as a child, dreaming of tracking gemsbok on foot in the Kalahari desert.

If only diagnostic tests were a yes or no answer; where yes actually meant yes, and no definitely meant no. While sample testing can give us useful clues and information, it may not yield a definitive answer, and widespread testing carries its own risks. For some health conditions in individual animals, nothing beats peering inside the living body itself, in an attempt to figure out what is actually going on.

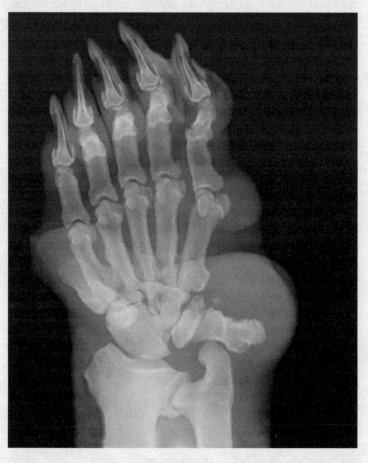

An X-ray shows that, with all five front foot toes pointing forwards,
what appears to be a giant panda's thumb is in actual fact an elongated
wrist bone, to perform the same function.

8

Turtle migraines and the six-fingered woodpecker

Looking at an X-ray picture of a giant panda paw reminds me of the very first X-ray photo. Unlike other brave medical pioneers who first tried their discoveries on themselves, Wilhelm Roentgen decided that his wife was a preferable guinea pig. Twenty minutes' radiation yielded a blurred image of her hand bones, complete with wedding ring. Seeing the snapshot, she exclaimed that she had seen her own death. Prescient words, considering the yet unknown risk posed by ionising radiation.

Are hands more important for our species' success than our brains? No matter how intelligent a bottlenose dolphin, it can hardly use a keyboard to search Wikipedia, or dial for take-away anchovy pizza. Yet, dexterous hands enabling me to perform microsurgery are far from unique. A giant panda precisely rolling bamboo leaves, to rival Havana cigar makers, appears to have a hand. All five nails point forward, as in other bears. But watching a panda eat, it also appears to have a thumb, helping grip its food. On an X-ray, all becomes clear. One of the panda's wrist bones, the radial sesamoid, has become a sixth finger – the panda's thumb. A giant panda's hairy hand may look clumsy but is essential for its survival. I once undertook some research with human hand surgeon friends and found that wild pandas losing a front paw were less likely to survive than other Asian bears with the same injury. An injured hand is more catastrophic for a panda than for a professional tennis player or a neurosurgeon.

Radiographs

An X-ray photo, or more correctly a radiograph, works on simple principles. Radiation particles travel through the body and hit the photographic plate, which turns black after developing. To keep physicists happy, I should mention that strictly speaking X-rays are both waves and particles, or wave-like particles. But because I am not clever enough to really comprehend quantum mechanics, I will pretend they are just particles. Dense materials like bone and metal absorb the most particles, and so appear whiter on a radiograph. Air absorbs no particles, so results in black on the picture. Less-dense soft tissues allow some particles to pass through, and appear as varying shades of grey. To penetrate denser tissues or a larger animal part, such as an Indian rhino's foot, we can either use more particles, give greater energy to the same particles to make them move further through tissues before stopping, or release X-ray particles for longer, although never anything resembling Roentgen's long exposures.

X-rays show us the invisible. I can use X-rays to see a broken wing bone in a striated caracara, view a harbour seal's pneumonia due to wriggling lung worms, or discover a leopard tortoise's bladder stone. X-rays were even taken of Californian condor eggs, to aid chicks slow to hatch. Californian condors were extinct in the wild, and with only 27 left on the planet, every egg was precious. Vets carefully opened eggs and rescued chicks in twisted positions before they could die of exhaustion. Radiographs poorly differentiate tissues of the same density, but fluid is the ultimate enemy, painting everything a homogeneous grey. A fist-sized bladder tumour in a fallow deer that is eating too much bracken fern will be invisible inside the urine on an X-ray.

Some surprisingly subtle changes can be detected. Ferruginous hawks with an infection may have an enlarged marble-sized spleen on X-rays. With experience, a spotted paca's liver abscess can be guessed at from the organ's distorted shape. Even a swallowed string can be discovered. While the string itself may be invisible inside the Indochinese tiger, the bizarre concertinaed intestines are very distinctive on a radiograph.

A relative of ours has even stranger hands on X-rays than a panda. The aye-aye lemur is truly weird. Although a primate, it has continuously growing front teeth like a squirrel and nipples in its groin. Resembling an alcoholic gremlin, it was first believed to be a rodent by scientists, not a primate at all. Its hands are its true marvels. Similar to a giant panda's, a small moveable wrist bone with three muscle connections makes an almost invisible extra thumb. Unnoticed by scientists until recently, it adds a tiny amount of extra grip – vital for tree climbing at night when your other hand is occupied. But an extra thumb is actually the boring part of its hand. Its third finger looks like a long, thin, dried twig. Any novice vet would immediately worry that this finger is dead, shrivelled, and needing urgent amputation. Yet X-rays will show the finger bones to be perfectly healthy. This finger is its woodpecker's beak. It taps on wood, listening for any sound of a grub wriggling away deep beneath the bark. Faint sounds are reflected by ear ridges, focusing sound like a lighthouse lens. After chewing at the wood, the aye-aye uses this twig-like finger to prise the grub from its tunnel, as a meal. It also has a longer and thicker muscular fourth finger for other holes. While aye-ayes would be rubbish typists, their hands are a Swiss Army Knife of fingers for different purposes. In the wild their survival depends on each performing its specific role, and so it's essential to consider this when peering at an X-ray photo.

Only weeks after Roentgen's discovery, the very first wildlife X-rays were taken. Unblurred half-hour exposures of patients were still impossible with the weak X-ray sources in 1896, so these were only of dead animals. But it is still fascinating what we can tell of these victims' health from the radiographs. The crested chameleon is particularly interesting. His leg bones have no breaks or deformities, but the front leg bones have a faintly moth-eaten appearance, and a kink in one of the vertebrae indicates a fracture. His gut contains small stones, and despite being thin, he has a swollen section of intestine distended with food. This chameleon, plundered from West Africa, must have been in Europe for months, and was not coping. He was lacking sufficient ultraviolet from sunlight, needed for him to synthesise vitamin D; essential for absorbing calcium from his intestines. The moth-eaten bones and spinal fracture show metabolic bone disease, or secondary nutritional hyperparathyroidism to give it its full name. His body was cannibalising its own bones for calcium to run vital body functions. The chameleon swallowed the small pebbles in a desperate attempt to get calcium from anything. Emaciated, the lump of food in his intestines shows he had become anorexic, but despite being force-fed he had died within a day or two. Not bad diagnostically for a century-old radiograph. Although we now better understand a captive chameleon's needs, we sadly still see this condition today. Chameleons destined for the pet trade continue to be trapped in the wild, with as few as 1 per cent actually surviving to reach pet shops.

Like the ring on Roentgen's wife's finger, X-rays are perfect for seeing metallic objects, which are denser than bone or stones in a chameleon's stomach. X-rays are the best way to find a bullet; its tiny entry hole hidden between the dense feathers of a bean goose. I have X-rayed dead eagles for the police, and rotten badgers found at the roadside; illegally shot animals are dumped to appear as if hit by a car. Other radiographic favourites are swallowed fishing hooks, whether in the throat of a cormorant, or in the spiral stomach valve of tiger sharks, although a shark is decidedly more difficult to X-ray. Gentoo penguins in some zoos swallow coins so frequently, jangling in my hand like an old lady's purse, that we actually use a metal detector to screen them weekly, before subjecting any silly suspects to X-rays yet again. Perhaps the coins remind them of the silver shimmer of small fish.

Bullets and coins highlight a disadvantage of radiography. X-ray photos are flat, two-dimensional representations of the body. I may see a bullet on a bearded vulture's X-ray, but it isn't always clear where it is. Appearing to be in the leg muscle, perhaps it is actually in the stomach beneath this. These are very different medical problems. One needs painkillers and a police search for someone illegally taking shots at a protected bird. The other needs urgent treatment for lead poisoning, after a vulture has scavenged a shot ibex carcass. There are horror stories of patients like a Canadian lynx having been operated on after supposedly swallowing some coins, but after being X-rayed it was discovered that the coins had simply been left on the blanket beneath the lynx! Even a hair stuck to the old silver photographic plates could be mistaken for a swallowed wire in a young Komodo dragon. To prevent these diagnostic cock-ups, we aim to take at least two perpendicular radiographs to figure out exactly where an object such as a bullet or coin or wire sits in three-dimensional space.

Despite the disappointing reality of the 99 pence X-ray spectacles advertised in my childhood comic books, some animals can actually see X-rays. Frogs can see X-rays, as can the houseflies they eat. And while peacocks and jungle fowl can't see X-rays, owls can. It isn't clear exactly how some animals are able to see X-rays. It could be by the usual light excitation of the rhodopsin molecules in the retina, or perhaps by an effect on the retina nerves. Or perhaps something else entirely. However, the ability of a Western screech owl to actually see a distant neutron bomb straight through a wooden trunk is evolutionarily pointless. The owl would still be doomed.

Today, we are cautious about balancing the diagnostic benefits from X-ray imaging against potential radiation harms such as cancer. Not just to ourselves, but also our patients, considering, for example, that an Aldabra giant tortoise can live more than 200 years. Birds like Andean condors, greater flamingos, and Major Mitchell's cockatoos can all live more than 80 years, a good human-length lifespan. Supposedly geriatric animals may even still breed – a 111-year-old tuatara named Henry fathered 11 youngsters with an 80-year-old female. Tumour development in animals, however, has an interesting paradox. While an African elephant has 100,000 times as many cells, and lives 50 times longer than a striped grass mouse, there is no difference in their lifetime risk of developing a tumour. This is bizarre. While tumour suppressor genes have been found in elephants, this doesn't explain why, across the range of wild animals, body size and longevity don't change the risk of dying with cancer. Understanding this fully could perhaps help reduce human cancers. But radiation still increases health risks, despite the elephant cancer paradox. Airport X-ray scanners can damage frozen semen (from endangered species like fishing cats, transported for conservation projects), posing a risk even before conception.

Yet despite the increased radiation, fluoroscopy, or X-ray video, can sometimes be useful in wildlife veterinary practice, quickly replacing multiple separate images. We can check if a confiscated Lear's macaw has normal stomach movements and emptying, before being returned to the wild. If the gut movement is abnormal and slow, it may have caught bornavirus when smuggled with other birds, and can sadly never be released. Doing so would risk spreading the dreaded wasting disease to the remnant wild population. One of my earliest operations two decades ago was on one of these confiscated rare birds. Without fluoroscopy or other tests, we still had to take surgical biopsies of crop tissue, to make the diagnosis. These beautiful bright-blue macaws were named in honour of Edward Lear, one of the best natural history illustrators of his time, who amusingly introduced himself later in life as Mr Abebika Kratoponko Prizzikalo Ablegorabalus Ableborinto Phashyph. He is best known as the author of the poem 'The Owl and the Pussy-Cat'. My friend Jonathan Cracknell still has the regular pleasure of looking at Lear's illustrations housed at Knowsley Hall where Cracknell is the safari park director.

Fluoroscopy helped us understand the unusual blood flow to tortoise kidneys, the renal portal system, affecting the drugs we can safely give our shelled patients. The system diverts some blood returning from the back legs to flow through the kidneys on its way back to the heart. This anatomy helps prevent kidney failure in desert tortoises going for months without drinking. But this ingenious anatomy complicates which medications we can safely inject in a back leg, and which could damage our tortoise patient's kidneys fatally, a problem we never face when injecting a pronghorn antelope. Fluoroscopy can also be useful in joint problems, so we can see exactly how a joint is moving, to understand pain in our lame cheetah's knee, or why a lar gibbon's wrist is stiff.

Ignoring a lar gibbon's long fingers, the real secret to swinging through rainforest trees faster than we can run, is its wrist. Real gripping strength comes from the wrist, as one morbid French doctor proved. In a series of gruesome experiments, Pierre Barbet showed that, unlike in classical crucifixion paintings, only the wrist was strong enough to hold human corpses nailed to a wooden cross. A carpal tunnel wrist injury is a pain for a typist, but far more serious for a gibbon. Its mobile wrists are usually described as ball and socket joints, but looking at an X-ray this is clearly nonsense, although even Wikipedia makes this mistake. The anatomy of a gibbon's wrist is actually similar to ours. Two rows of small squarish bones are all connected by the same ligaments and tendons that we have. Gibbons do have a small extra bone in the wrist that we can see on X-rays. In humans, this has fused to another small wrist bone. But this has little to do with their amazing movements. These are all due to subtle, easily missed differences. The styloid process of the ulnar, a bony spike of the forearm bone that connects to the wrist, is slightly smaller than ours. More importantly, each little bone in the two rows of the wrist is slightly rounded, and the ligaments allow just a millimetre or two more movement. The wrist bone rows are also more curved, making a cup shape at their bottom where they join the forearm, allowing a little more twisting ability. Together, these tiny changes makes the gibbon's wrist supremely flexible.

X-ray pictures of a lar gibbon's wrist will only show the bones, and not the multitude of small connecting ligaments. A slight gap between bones can hint that a ligament has burst, while a faint fluffy bone edge suggests a ligament has torn loose. But X-rays cannot always demonstrate what is injured in a joint. Critical cartilage joint surfaces are invisible on X-rays. A white-tailed eagle with a drooping wing may have nothing visible on initial X-rays. But after failing to improve for a month, repeating the X-rays will show the shoulder joint has become dense and fuzzy. This delayed change testifies that the bird dislocated its shoulder when colliding with a power-line, damaging the vital joint cartilage. Sadly, it will never again fly well enough to survive in the wild. This was immensely frustrating, but we could only have seen this initial damage by surgically inserting a tiny telescope, called an arthroscope, into the joint.

X-rays are, however, fantastic for broken bones. Understanding the shape and position of fragments helps me when planning how to fix the broken hind leg of an African hunting dog, or a young gorilla's broken pelvis after falling from a tree. Seeing a broken bone on X-rays is actually the best news, when treating an injured peregrine falcon that has collided with a pylon. Joint injuries have such a poor prognosis that I am always elated to see a fractured coracoid bone. This larger bone behind the wishbone clavicle acts like an airplane's wing strut, supporting a bird's wings in flight. Buried deep under chest muscles, it is challenging to even reach for surgery. Yet even if horrendously shattered, it usually heals on its own. This bone actually heals better without surgery, despite all modern technologies. Most birds will be flying within two weeks, and can return to the wild after only three weeks. Birds do heal amazingly rapidly. More amazingly still, bone is the only tissue healing without any scar tissue in most animals. Once healed, it is just as strong as before. But steel or titanium plates and screws can block your view of broken bone healing beneath them on an X-ray; frustrating if trying to decide if the bone is strong enough to remove your implants.

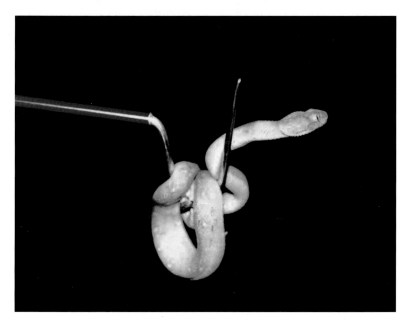

Hooks can be used to move snakes without handling them at all,
and this is always the safest option.

To maintain a small snake on gas anaesthesia, we can improvise an
endotracheal tube from a human intravenous catheter. As snakes have
no eyelids, they can at first glance appear to be wide awake under anaesthesia.

A leopard caught in a snare will usually remain very quiet, so as not to attract attention from larger predators, even if very stressed. In contrast, a tiger will thrash around loudly if caught.

Plastic waste has garnered much recent media attention, but the insidious long-term detrimental effects of chemical pollution on apex predators like polar bears is more difficult to investigate. Without something easy to show in photos and videos, it can be difficult to get the public engaged in this problem.

Palpating a porcupine's organs is usually impossible without anaesthesia, but even then, as each species has different anatomy, it can be difficult to know if what you are feeling is normal.

A barn owl's face is mainly feathers. The eyes are not round, but mushroom-shaped, as seen on an X-ray taken from above. Thin bones (in yellow) help maintain the eyes' unusual shape, and prevent the large eyes wobbling in and out of focus during flight. The ears are also asymmetrical, helping an owl to pinpoint the sounds of the small rodents it hunts with maximum accuracy.

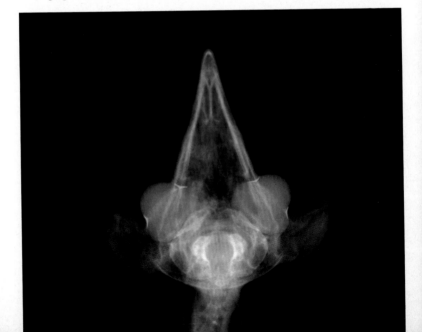

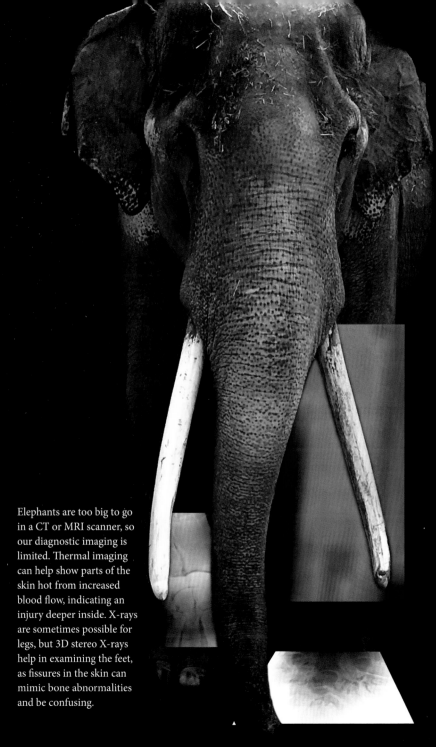

Elephants are too big to go in a CT or MRI scanner, so our diagnostic imaging is limited. Thermal imaging can help show parts of the skin hot from increased blood flow, indicating an injury deeper inside. X-rays are sometimes possible for legs, but 3D stereo X-rays help in examining the feet, as fissures in the skin can mimic bone abnormalities and be confusing.

Gentoo penguins in some zoos swallow coins so frequently, we use a metal detector to screen them weekly, instead of needing X-rays. Their stomachs conveniently extend almost to their tails, making this easy while they stand on land. Perhaps the coins remind them of the silver shimmer of small fish. Decades of stomach-pumping of wild penguins to try to discover what they naturally eat failed to reveal that they commonly eat jellyfish, something we now know from genetic analysis of their droppings.

Brain ultrasound in young fox cubs is possible as the skull is thin and allows ultrasound through at the large coronal suture crack. This can help detect hydrocephalus, or water on the brain, before a cub starts to show signs of illness.

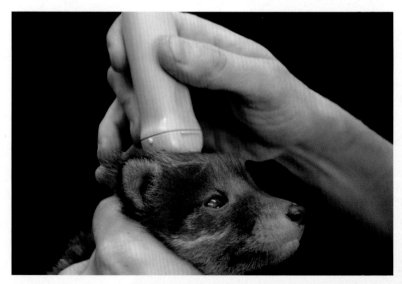

Despite erroneous descriptions in books, documentaries and on the internet, a gibbon's wrists are not ball-and-socket joints at all, but very similar to our own wrists. Their incredible flexibility is just due to very subtle differences in the shapes of the small block-like bones and ligaments

We can only view the heart as a lump between the lungs in the chest of an animal on X-ray photos. To actually see inside the heart, and to judge how it is functioning as an active blood pump, ultrasound is essential.

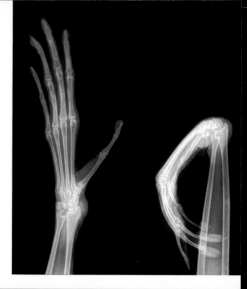

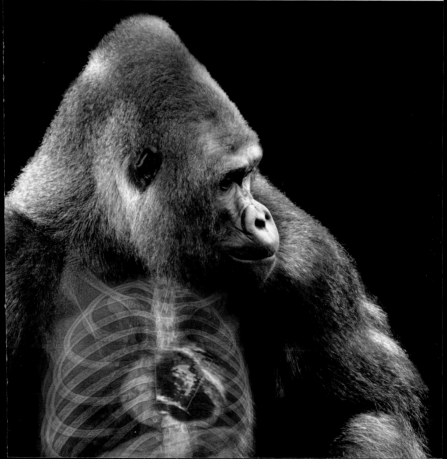

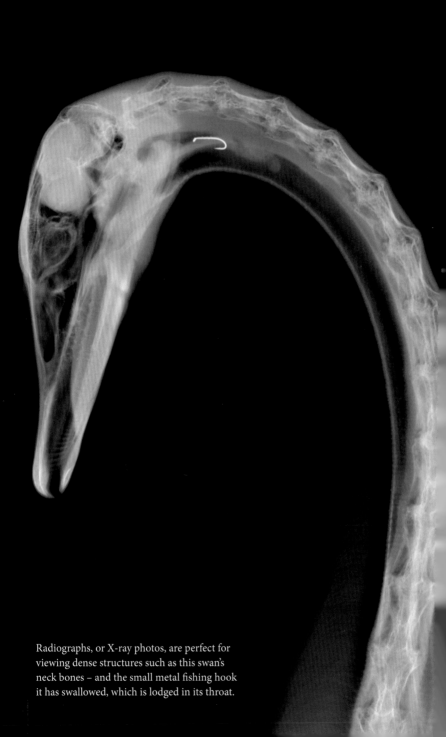

Radiographs, or X-ray photos, are perfect for viewing dense structures such as this swan's neck bones – and the small metal fishing hook it has swallowed, which is lodged in its throat.

My worst nightmare would be a Visayan spotted deer taking only a few bounds before its leg crumples beneath it, after removing the bone's surgical scaffolding.

There is one bone we never insert metalwork in. Humans don't have one, and neither do elephants, duck-billed platypus or manatees. But most mammals, including our close relatives chimpanzees and bonobos, do. The baculum. Better known as the penis bone. Helpfully revealing the gender of an anaesthetised Azara's agouti, or a Canadian beaver bundled in a sack, the size will even tell us a male raccoon's age when X-rayed. Anthropologists appear infinitely fascinated with why humans lost their penile bones, with assorted theories to choose from. Perhaps a blood-engorged erection indicates fitness and health, and hence a good genetic partner, the human equivalent of a peacock's tail. Covered by clothing, some men try to signal the same value with a red sports car – essentially a giant metallic pseudo-erection. Others believe it is because humans are more monogamous than other great apes. Or perhaps you prefer the biblical interpretation that when God removed Adam's rib to create Eve, this was actually a polite reference to the baculum. Missing one themselves, some collectors bizarrely pay thousands for desirable half-metre-long walrus oosik penis bones.

Eurasian otters not only have a baculum, but their females also have a tiny os clitoridis. Otters also have an even stranger bone, which you can sometimes glimpse on X-rays. Inside the heart, a ring of bone, the os cordis, reinforces the base of the heart valves. Yaks and wapiti, while too big for good chest X-rays, also have this bone reinforcing their big hearts, yet strangely elephants don't.

X-rays are not ideal for examining the heart, which just appears as a large blob in the chest. Some heart diseases result in fluid in the surrounding lungs. We can see this pulmonary oedema as a cloudy appearance in the lungs on the X-rays of a douroucouli short of breath with congestive heart failure. Pneumonia instead looks like cottonwool patches in the lung of an ill orangutan. But only mammal lungs have alveoli.

Pneumonia in an Indian star tortoise looks very different. Tortoise lungs are balloons, with a lining of spongy tissue. With no diaphragm, they can't cough, so fluid pools in the lungs with pneumonia. Only horizontal X-rays will show this fluid. Their thick bone shell poses an obstacle for X-rays to penetrate, as do the bones in a giant armadillo's armour or in the scales of an African plated lizard. These make confusing patterns overlying lung X-rays. Fluid isn't the strangest thing to be seen in reptile lungs. Occasionally, you spot the spiral shapes of *Pentastomida* parasites in the lungs of a Boelen's python. Called tongue worms, they are crustaceans, so actually related to lobsters and woodlice.

Lung X-rays are also essential before considering operating on an elderly orangutan with a mammary tumour. Fluffy 'cannonballs' on the X-rays reveals that surgery is pointless. The malignancy has already spread to the lungs and other organs, even if the orangutan shows no signs of coughing. Which brings us to John Lennon's contribution to wheezing orangutans.

An orangutan with sinusitis doesn't sound severe. That congested feeling in your face is not a great sympathy-play if trying to shirk work. In orangutans, things are different. While chimpanzees and humans are social, orangutans in their rainforest are largely solitary. Better at problem solving than chimps, perhaps even more intelligent, orangutans have to figure out everything on their own. Chimpanzees instead learn from watching others in their social group. But being solitary, orangutans have not evolved the same immunity to respiratory infections. Humans live in very high densities and have evolved resistance to many cough- and sneeze-borne viruses. Mountain gorillas living in small family groups are less able to cope with these viruses; hence the precautions for visiting tourists. But orangutans are most vulnerable. Whether in an Indonesian rescue centre or an air-conditioned zoo building, a person sneezing in the vicinity can make an orangutan severely ill.

Orangutans have a unique anatomy, making even mild

infections serious. Large balloon-like air sacs extend over the neck and chest, and under their armpits. These are normally collapsed and you wouldn't be aware of them, connecting via a tiny opening to the windpipe near the voice box. Unfortunately, with a minor cold, any mucus we would simply cough or sneeze up instead drains into these air sacs, where it accumulates. This becomes a soup-kitchen for any stray bacteria to multiply, until the orangutan has large bags full of pus sloshing around under its skin. A concoction of toxins is absorbed, and movements splash and spray the deadly brew down the windpipe into the lungs. Being able to examine the sinuses and air sacs is difficult but crucial. Normal radiographs won't work for this.

CT scans

CT, short for computed tomography, is a moving X-ray machine. The beam and detectors circle around the patient, taking images in slices. Clever software then builds us a three-dimensional picture of the inside of the body. The CT scanner was developed at EMI, the Beatles record label, in a lab just outside Heathrow. While most of the research funding came from the Government Department for Health, some probably did come from the millions of records sold by the Beatles. I can't imagine one of today's hip-hop labels researching cures for prostate cancer.

CT has been used to find parasitic tapeworm brain cysts for surgical removal in Nubian ibex before returning them to the wild, and to treat a lung abscess in a US Navy bottlenose dolphin, so it could return to military work. We can diagnose abnormal livers in red-footed tortoises, find a nerve sheath tumour in a wild toco toucan that can't fly, or a fungal infection in the brain of a swell shark that swims in circles. It has even been used on fairy penguins, standing patiently in a box, to check their lungs for nasty fungal infections. Like normal X-ray photos, CT is particularly good for examining bone. Spadefoot toads and boa constrictors can have their bone density assessed before weak bones actually break. Elderly red-necked wallabies with complex dental abscesses in their long mouths can be managed, or a zoo Komodo dragon with a neck bone dislocation treated.

But CT is only available to the wealthiest Western zoos, and exotic pets taken to a university or human hospital. The thousand-plus wild orangutans currently in rescue centres throughout Indonesia do not have this privilege. Love them or hate them, the health care for animals in Western zoos can be unlike anything possible for rescued wild animals, and good zoos take their animal welfare and conservation obligations seriously. Good zoos will spare no expense to keep their animals healthy, the equivalent of the best private medical insurance. Even if highly skilled, wildlife vets never have the resources to treat 600 orangutans in a rescue centre the same way as in a wealthy zoo. I remember it taking me five days just to get to one forest orangutan centre to perform operations. Transporting orangutans to a distant human hospital, prohibitive costs aside, was clearly impossible. So cheap low-tech alternatives were needed. This is where elephants come in.

No matter how wealthy a zoo, you cannot CT scan an elephant. There is just no way to get a 10 tonne animal near a machine sitting in a hospital, let alone fit it inside the CT machine's ring. This is a pity, as CT would be really useful. These massive animals have a weak spot. Their feet. Bearing such a heavy body, anything afflicting the foot bones is extremely serious. An elephant that cannot walk cannot survive. Elephant foot X-rays are notoriously difficult to interpret. With thick wrinkled skin, and a sole with fissures and cracks, the lines overlying the bones on an X-ray make it difficult to tell what is actually going on. Is that a small fissure in the bone, or a skin wrinkle?

With my friend, Jon Cracknell, I invented a simple solution – a 'poor-man's CT'. The idea came from Victorian parlour games, a toy, and a research method for measuring microscopic movements in bone implants. Growing up, one of my favourite toys was a red plastic View-Master, with its cardboard discs that let you see paired photos in 3D. I wondered if we couldn't X-ray elephants' feet in the same way. With a cheap wooden X-ray plate holder, we take an X-ray of the elephant's foot, replace the X-ray plate and move our portable X-ray machine a few centimetres for the second view. Putting the two X-rays together, we can use our uncool red-blue paper glasses to see the X-rays in 3D out in the field. It isn't a CT, but with depth perception we can now tell whether a fissure is just a skin groove, or a fuzzy patch is actually in the bone and worth worrying about. Pretty damn nifty for the cost of a wooden box and a pair of paper glasses.

It's useful in other awkward animals that can't fit through a CT scanner, whether a giraffe with an injured knee, or a walrus with a tusk root abscess; or to treat a Sulawesi babirusa shot through the face by a poacher in a remote location. I have used my poor-man's CT on everything from sea eagles' injured beaks, to otters with kidney stones. And even in orangutans with air sac infections.

Sometimes, things go the opposite way. One journal paper describes a pet leopard gecko CT scan just to diagnose constipation, something normally easily diagnosed and solved with a bath or enema. Another describes using CT just to check where a zoo porcupine's testicle was before castration, something equally baffling. As in humans, CT can be a luxury. While it makes understanding complex 3D structures easier, it is often far from essential; perhaps overkill when planning knee surgery on a zoo's snow leopard, when normal X-rays would be sufficient. It is easy to pop an ill golden monkey through a CT scanner, but without a diagnostic plan it often tells you nothing, despite the big bill. Young vets, now reliant on CT to repair even a simple broken bone, are horrified that I frequently need to fix a brown wood owl's fracture in Sri Lanka, or a chimpanzee's broken leg in Sierra Leone, without any X-rays at all. Just because we can CT scan an animal, it doesn't mean we should. It is after all a huge dose of radiation compared to normal radiographs.

Yet CTs of dead animals can be useful. Accurate Callimico

kidney sizes from CT allow us to check that simple ultrasound measurements are normal, and the male aardvark's reproductive anatomy is better understood thanks to CT. Scans of decapitated dead rhinos have also helped us treat rhinos with their horns hacked off by a poacher's chainsaw, by understanding their complex underlying nasal anatomy. Yet while CT is excellent for the bones of the skull, if it is the brain inside you want to view, you would really be better off with something completely different.

MRI

MRI was originally called nuclear magnetic resonance imaging, but nuclear was dropped from the name due to the Cold War connotations of atomic bombs and Dr Strangelove. It is a superb way to view the brain. MRI uses giant magnets and radio waves to map tissues of the body in 3D, by influencing the spin of hydrogen nuclei. Living bodies contain large quantities of hydrogen, mainly in water, but also in fats and other molecules. Being no nuclear physicist, I will have to leave my explanation at that. MRI is better than CT for examining soft tissues like the brain or spinal cord, as these mushy organs contain copious water and hence many hydrogen atoms. Encased in bone, these cannot be easily examined by ultrasound, as can the liver.

A young African lion staggering around may have nothing abnormal on a CT scan of his skull. But an MRI will show the cerebellum section of the brain bulging out the back of his skull, squashing the spinal cord and causing his problems. Once diagnosed, we can relieve the pressure by surgery, and correct the cause; usually a vitamin A deficiency when a cash-strapped rescue centre provides an unbalanced diet. MRI may also be the only way to diagnose a stroke in a chimpanzee with a paralysed hand, or an astrocytoma brain tumour in a jaguar that has suddenly gone blind.

The very first live MRI was of a wild animal, although much smaller and less charismatic. A 4-millimetre long clam, which

American chemist Paul Lauterbur's daughter had collected, with its small soft body, was ideal. His Nobel prize co-recipient Peter Mansfield performed the first human MRI scan, in typical medical tradition, by using himself as a guinea pig. He wasn't completely sure if it wouldn't stop his heart when he first tried it.

When I have gone through an MRI scanner, I have felt nothing besides annoyance from the noise. But going through an MRI scanner appears so painful for a loggerhead sea turtle, they can even feel it when unconscious under anaesthesia. Loggerheads move and writhe about despite being at a depth of anaesthesia sufficient for major surgery. So what is going on in the turtles?

Loggerhead turtles navigate the vast oceans using the Earth's weak magnetic fields, returning to the same beach for decades to lay their eggs. We still don't really understand how, but one theory is that microscopic magnetite crystals in their brains play a role, detecting the planet's tiny magnetic fields. But an MRI machine's magnetic field is more than twenty thousand times stronger. Could well-meaning attempts to help treat loggerhead turtles injured by boats actually do more harm than good? MRI may more accurately diagnose a lung injury or help surgical planning to fix a broken bone, but are we actually damaging their magnetic sense, which is essential for navigating the world's oceans? Some turtles can live to over a hundred years, so this could be extremely serious. We still don't really understand how they sense magnetic fields, or if the supermagnets in MRI scanners damage their navigation abilities, or for how long. So is an MRI painful for a turtle? It is difficult to understand, but perhaps a comparison would be our staring into a football stadium light from just a metre away, or being blasted by music as loud as a jet engine. My friend Daniel Garcia at Valencia's Oceanographic Institute is studying this to try to understand what is going on. The little Arctic tern I am treating today, entangled in some carelessly discarded fishing line, would be fine in an MRI scanner, if I could afford this. This unassuming little bird, that we joke has no feet, has the longest migratory route of any bird, from pole to pole, an astounding 64,000 kilometre trip. We know that they too navigate using the Earth's magnetic field. Yet Daniel's work appears to show that birds' navigation is not affected by MRI magnetic fields. They don't react under anaesthesia, and homing pigeons also don't appear to take longer to fly home if they have been through an MRI.

One theory is that birds rely on entirely different methods to navigate. Perhaps birds can actually see the Earth's magnetic field with a magnetically sensitive protein in the eye, called cryptochrome. Blue light causes electrons in the protein to produce pairs of radicals, whose electron spins respond to magnetic fields. But quite how they see it, as lines or graduations or at all, we have no idea. While MRI scans don't appear to be painful, or affect their 'magnetic sight', birds are still disturbed by all the electromagnetic pollution we create. AM radio can confuse urban birds when they can't see the sky, and while old experiments showed captive European robins accumulate at the south side of their wooden cages when the time came for them to move south, I have never seen this in rescue centres, with all our mobile phones and electronic equipment around. Perhaps this is why, when releasing birds, I often see them fly high in the sky, before they appear to orientate themselves and fly off strongly in their intended direction. Are they escaping all the man-made electromagnetic haze around them, so they can detect the Earth's magnetic field clearly?

The most unusual animals I have ever put through an MRI scanner were Chilean rose tarantulas. We were studying their heart function, and I was responsible for the anaesthesia. But despite high levels of anaesthetic gas, some tarantulas moved slightly during their MRIs. Looking back at the scientific paper now, I do wonder if it wasn't my incompetence as an anaesthetist after all, but perhaps something else. Monarch butterflies have a backup magnetic field navigation system, when overcast days prevent them using the sun, and painted lady butterflies fly an amazing 4,000 kilometre round trip between Europe and sub-Saharan Africa and back. Considering their size, and how easily wind-blown they are, their navigation is extraordinary.

Like CT, MRI can also be useful after death. The high resolution of organs can save one hacking open a body, sparing parents of stillborn babies the trauma of an autopsy, and I have examined MRI scans rather than damage a rare monkey needed for anatomy research. MRI can sometimes help understand things that are impossible to see well normally. A man-eating lion may not yield its secrets on autopsy, until an MRI shows the migrating fragments of porcupine quills in its front legs, the disability that led to its human-munching ways.

While a CT scan is equivalent to radiation exposure from hundreds of individual X-rays, MRI has no ionising radiation. Multiple CT scans during a person's life increase the risk of developing cancer, and probably pose a similar risk to loggerhead turtles, which often live into their sixties. MRI doesn't have the risk of inadvertently causing a tumour decades later. And while a zoo's spotted hyaena with an anal gland tumour doesn't really need an MRI for its diagnosis, MRI can still usefully check the lungs and liver for any tumour spread, before putting the hyaena through a pointless operation.

MRI is also safe in pregnancy. Yet MRIs are rarely run in wildlife patients. They are expensive, and thanks to giant supercooled magnets, need patients to be transported to a big hospital, pretty difficult in the middle of the Pantanal wetlands. The risk of a jaguar with a suspected brain tumour escaping in a city hospital, can also make getting permission tricky. The world-leading giant panda centre in Dujiangyan, China, now has its own dedicated MRI scanner, and in wealthy countries there are portable MRI scanners, which come to you housed in their own huge dedicated articulated lorry. This mini-hospital needs good flat roads, and is tremendously expensive, as you would expect. So wildlife MRIs are only really performed on valuable zoo animals, such as tigers with a spinal cord injury, or a Western lowland gorilla with a pituitary gland tumour deep in its brain.

The massive supercooled magnet, which limits scanners from becoming smaller or cheaper, also carries the only real risks. MRI rooms must be free of metal. Stories of MRIs fatally ripping pacemakers out of chests, or steel replacement hips exploding out of patients' thighs, are highly exaggerated, but wild animals carry a different invisible risk. Lead is not ferro-magnetic, but bullets often have a copper jacket, or other metal impurities within the lead. Inserting an animal hiding an old lodged bullet may not only shoot the patient again, but the bullet hurtling out, torn towards the powerful magnet, could also kill you as the vet. Less dramatically, an unjacketed lead bullet may simply be heated up by magnetism, burning through any nearby vital structure, such as the carotid artery.

Ultrasound

MRI is sadly not practical in the middle of the jungle in a developing country. We need other ways to achieve the same sort of thing. How do I try to examine an Asiatic black bear in the jungle in Laos needing brain surgery, when there isn't even a human MRI machine in the whole country? In fact, when you don't even have access to an X-ray machine? Faced with a bear suspected to be suffering from hydrocephalus a decade ago, I needed to find a different solution. Hydrocephalus, or water on the brain, is where the ventricle spaces in the brain bulge with excess fluid, crushing the brain tissues inside the rigid skull. It can be very painful. While I could solve the problem by surgically inserting a special valve and tube called a ventriculoperitoneal catheter into the brain and burying this under the skin to drain excess fluid harmlessly away into the abdomen, I still needed to be sure this really was the problem. Otherwise, I risked surgically kebabbing a brain with an entirely different problem. Hardly amenable to improving the poor bear's life, it would quite possibly kill her.

The solution was to sterilise an old ultrasound probe in a rubble bag, using gas for fumigating chicken houses. Starting the surgery, I drilled a hole in the skull just smaller than a pencil's diameter, and using sterile gel, applied the ultrasound probe, to view the brain beneath. We could only see a thin sliver of the brain at a time but carefully pieced together an idea of the inside of the brain. The ventricles were very dilated with excess fluid, confirming she had hydrocephalus. I then used my small hole to continue the surgery. Proceeding was also far less routine than in a human hospital. With the rainforest's high humidity, one of the electrical appliances blew up and almost electrocuted me mid-surgery, and I ended up having to use a mattress pump to finish the operation. The rest went OK, and she did well for the next seven years. I must admit we broke military curfew that night to go drink beer in celebration.

Medical ultrasound is so logically simple that it is one of the most understated of modern medical inventions. Sound waves bounce back from organs, like sonar on ships, or bats with echolocation, to give us a picture inside the body. I can use ultrasound to examine everything from a Brazilian tapir's ovaries to a Moloch gibbon's retina. It is the ultimate non-invasive, portable, and low-cost diagnostic imaging machine. Yet its small size, simple premise and low cost doesn't necessarily make it easy to interpret. Squinting at the speckled image of a sloth bear's liver, I feel I am looking at a shaken snow-globe, hoping for a plastic Eiffel tower to suddenly appear, rather than the liver tumour I am expecting.

Watching a bottlenose dolphin foetus swimming inside her mother, I can't help wondering if the dolphin foetus is old enough to also see my friend Kerstin Ternes' hands and scanner in the water via her own echolocation, right from inside her mother. Water is the perfect medium to transmit sound waves, and dolphins can see unborn human babies inside their swimming pregnant mothers. Medical ultrasound is inaudible; it's a far higher frequency than bats or dolphins can detect, and so doesn't disturb them at all. Being just low-powered sound, ultrasound is the safest way of looking inside a living body. But veterinary ultrasound didn't start with patients at all. While doctors started to use ultrasound to check babies in the womb, vets instead first used it in breeding cows to evaluate their rib-eye steak sizes!

Then zoo vets and researchers used ultrasound to help understand the hugely varying reproduction cycles in the animal kingdom. Vets tried to understand why cheetahs almost never bred in zoos, or why jaguar artificial insemination was so difficult, work that continues today, with the added urgency of increasingly critically endangered species. Slowly, clinical cases in zoos, whether tuberculosis in a Siberian tiger, or kidney disease in a chimpanzee, proved how useful diagnostic ultrasound was. But these first vending machine sized units were not mobile. Today, you can buy a simple unit the same size as a laptop for a similar cost. Wireless machines the size of a chocolate bar can now connect to a mobile phone, quickly helping check if a shot orangutan is pregnant. In contrast, even a supposedly portable MRI machine still needs an enormous truck.

Pregnancy examination on an elephant? No problem. After a quick warm water enema with a hosepipe, you can insert the ultrasound probe per rectum with your arm to see the uterus and young foetus. Or you can pregnancy scan a 30 tonne wild whale shark, the same size as a T-rex, while it's happily swimming normally in the sea. A waterproof ultrasound scanner is all you need. And a vet who is an experienced scuba diver, of course. Water is the perfect medium for transmitting ultrasound. It is easier to see through a submerged whale shark's skin than an Indian rhino's with air trapped in its wrinkled crevices.

Fur and feathers trap a layer of insulating air, through which ultrasound cannot travel. Applying ultrasound gel to fur just makes a mess. The microscopic bubbles of air trapped by hair in the gel are an impenetrable ultrasound barrier, a medical version of a hunting humpback whale's bubble nets. Yet, as already mentioned, clipping fur from a sea otter has serious consequences. Having the densest coats in the animal kingdom is essential to sea otters' waterproof protection from the freezing Arctic sea. Our love of this beautiful insulating fur led to over a million sea otters being killed, to the point where only a thousand otters were left at the beginning of the last century. Clipping any wild otter's fur will usually do more harm than the benefit from an ultrasound examination. Thankfully, I discovered soaking a small patch of fur with surgical spirits will give you a temporary window. At a pinch, even whisky will do. It also works for a bearded seal on the beach, or beavers in the Scottish highlands. It even works for Vietnamese black bears rescued from illegal bile farms, when examining their liver for signs of damage. It saves clipping all their fur, and leaving them with an irritated bald belly afterwards. Yet it doesn't work at all on their cousins, giant pandas, or on badgers with their bristly fur, or on civet cats or sun bears.

Trying to examine the uterus and ovaries of confiscated sun bears in Cambodia a decade ago was challenging. The world's largest group of rescued sun bears sat in a rescue centre run by Free the Bears, and my friend Matt Hunt wanted to know if they could act as a genetic ark against extinction. Even if I had clipped all their coarse hair, gas in their intestines wouldn't let ultrasound reach the ovaries, deep in the abdomen. So we taped the ultrasound probe to a plastic plumbing pipe, and, with plenty of lubricating ultrasound gel, popped this up their bums under anaesthesia, to scan the ovaries from the inside. Human patients should be grateful for hairless abdomens!

Ultrasound is really good for visualising fluid and soft tissues, which X-rays are poor for. In contrast, ultrasound cannot look through bone or air, which X-ray photos are ideally suited to. X-rays can be used to diagnose pregnancy, but only very late, once the foetal skeleton becomes visible. But they are also not ideal, as growing cells are the most sensitive to ionising radiation damage. Taking X-rays of aquatic animals needs them to be removed from water, far from easy when your patient is a bluefin tuna or a shark. Ultrasound, like sonar, loves water. As a child I collected mermaid's purses, shark egg capsules, and tried my best to return them to the sea. But not all sharks produce eggs. Some, like the tawny nurse shark, have eggs that hatch inside them.

These threatened sharks lie in a pile on top of each other hiding under rock ledges, and at night come out to suck octopuses, sea snakes and small fish out of crevices and holes, like a powerful seafood vacuum cleaner. They are quite placid, but will defend themselves by spitting water in your face if you catch them. Mother sharks have two wombs, unlike us, but baby nurse sharks are even more interesting. Once hatched, and still in their mother's womb, they suffer a bad combination of boredom and the munchies, and solve this by eating each other. Despite numerous eggs hatching in the womb, only a small number of bigger baby sharks eventually emerge to the outside world – evolution's way of selecting the strongest next generation. On ultrasound, you can watch baby sharks squeezing out of one uterus to swim up the other looking for more brothers and sisters to snack on, or poking their head through the cervix to peek outside before wriggling back to swim around in the womb again. One can only imagine how difficult an expectant human mother's life would be if her baby occasionally stuck its head out while in the supermarket, to see if anything interesting was happening in the frozen food aisle.

Some problems can be diagnosed by either ultrasound or X-rays. A red kangaroo's bladder stone can be detected on ultrasound in a full bladder just as sonar detects a submarine's reflection, but is also visible on X-rays, containing dense minerals like calcium, just like bones do. Mineral imbalances cause different types of stones to form. Some, like small cystine stones in a serval cat, a long-legged supermodel of the small cat world, will cause a blockage but be almost invisible on X-rays, hidden in the urine, making ultrasound diagnosis best. Decades ago, when expensive Dalek-sized ultrasound machines were limited to hospitals, finding cystine stones was more difficult. They were invisible in a maned wolf's urine-filled bladder, so we would need to drain the urine, then fill the bladder with air like a little balloon inside our hairy strong-smelling patient. The air would then make it possible to see these otherwise invisible stones with X-rays.

Kidney stones are also easy to find with ultrasound, although you do need to know anatomy to make sense of what you are seeing. The rare and endangered hairy-nosed otter has kidneys that look like two bunches of grapes on ultrasound. Each grape-like lobule functions as its own mini-kidney. Stones causing pain and infection look like tiny, scattered pips, and so are easily missed. Kidney stones appear common in all otter species, across continents, no matter whether in the wild, in a zoo, or in a sanctuary. Thankfully, if I find a single stone in just one mini-kidney lobule, I can simply remove the offending lobule with keyhole surgery, leaving most of the kidney intact, something that is impossible in most other animals.

There are other less obvious applications. Ultrasound is really useful for examining eyes. Before contemplating a long, nerve-racking anaesthetic for complex cataract surgery in a lesser mouse lemur weighing as little as a 9 volt battery, it is essential to know that he can actually still see. Otherwise, surgery would be useless. The opaque crystalline lens not only blocks the mouse lemur's sight, it also prevents us examining the retina with an ophthalmoscope. Thankfully, ultrasound allows us to check the retina is still attached. I may need anaesthesia for a wriggly mouse lemur, but it is simple to scan a hooded seal pup's painful eye when it's awake. Pouring a jug of salt water over its head provides enough contact to scan the entire eye through the skin of the tightly clenched eyelids. This is certainly the quickest way to differentiate between a minor ulcer that will heal in a week, and a ruptured eye that needs surgical removal.

Encased in bone, supposedly impenetrable to ultrasound, the brain is another surprising organ we can sometimes examine. Water on the brain, hydrocephalus, is a common problem in orphaned red fox cubs in Scotland. Voles infected by the Ljungan virus eaten by a pregnant vixen can affect the foetus's brain. Small ventricle spaces inside the brain contain cerebrospinal fluid that must be formed and drained at precisely the same rate, or the brain will swell and be catastrophically crushed inside the unyielding skull. While a fox mother can tell subtle differences in the behaviour of a cub just a few days old, we humans can't. Over the last decade, I used brain ultrasound in young, orphaned cubs, measuring the ventricles to detect affected foxes as soon as they are admitted, and weeks before they would show us any signs. At this early age their skull is thin and flexible, allowing ultrasound through at the coronal suture, a large crack between the front and back parts of the skull. Occasionally, I see a small cub running around apparently completely normal, but on ultrasound it has a fluid-filled skull containing just a few millimetres of surrounding brain tissue. But I guess some politicians appear to function with even fewer neurons.

Aside from jungle brain surgery, ultrasound can be useful during other operations, such as looking inside the liver to view a tumour's location, to avoid removing too much healthy tissue during surgery. Ultrasound can also find where the testicles are hiding when castrating a common hippopotamus. Even under anaesthesia, hippos are able to yo-yo their testicles up to their body, thanks to a retractor muscle, making them impossible to find under the thick blubber, even when elbow-deep in the large surgical incision.

Ultrasound can help you take biopsies without needing full surgery. Tissue may look abnormal on ultrasound, but you still need a sample to make a diagnosis. Ultrasound helps you insert a needle into the exact place you want to sample in an African fur seal with a swelling on its back, as you watch the needle tip on your ultrasound screen. Examining the cells down the microscope gives us an answer. Dead neutrophil white blood cells show us that the swelling is a blubber abscess that will heal well. But clumps of different-sized cells with large purple nuclei would mean we are instead dealing with a tumour.

Wanting to avoid major surgery, sometimes a few cells sucked up with a thin needle just isn't enough for a diagnosis. We can use a special biopsy needle that cuts a small core of tissue. Perhaps an ill and critically endangered variegated spider monkey has a lump just in front of the left kidney. Is this a benign adrenal gland tumour that can be treated with medication? Or a malignant lymphoma about to invade other organs and needing major surgery? Or could it just be a swollen lymph node from a chronic entamoeba parasite infection? Without ultrasound to guide the tip of the needle very precisely, you could damage the kidney, or puncture the vena cava right next to the adrenal. The vena cava is the main vein returning blood to the heart, so accidentally biopsing this would be fatal, the spider monkey bleeding out in the abdomen in less than a minute.

Ultrasound-guided biopsies are not easy to teach safely to other wildlife vets on my travels. One doesn't want a baby black-shanked douc langur ending up like a voodoo doll, while colleagues try learn the technique. Differences in wildlife anatomy make learning particularly difficult. A brown howler monkey has a solid wedge-shaped liver, while an Asian golden cat liver has six fat leaf-like lobes, attached at their base, sliding over each other in the abdomen like leaves in a breeze. With baggage space at a premium to avoid attracting customs officials looking to extort a bribe, I make my ultrasound training models in lunchbox containers with a secret mix of powdered laxatives, food colouring and ground seaweed, the organs moulded from condoms, tubing and other miscellanea. I mix the small packet of powder with water, and the fresh models help young wildlife vets safely practise ultrasound-guided biopsies before needing to use them on an endangered patient. To avoid carrying kilograms of ultrasound gel that is just 95 per cent water, I have also invented a non-toxic ultrasound gel powder that weighs next to nothing and is biodegradable. This was precipitated after an incident where customs officials in West Africa thought I was smuggling plastic explosives. Invention is the daughter of necessity. Yet there is a greater ultrasound challenge than taking biopsies.

No organ is as difficult to understand as the heart. In death, this flabby sac of muscle, with a few white tubes protruding, is rather unimpressive. But in life this meat machine is astounding, pumping non-stop for over two hundred years in Greenland sharks, giant tortoises and bowhead whales. In comparison, the internal combustion engine has been in existence for less than that. On X-rays we can sometimes recognise heart disease in an African golden wolf when the heart is failing and has dilated massively in size. But at this stage the heart is so bad there is little we can do. Trying to detect heart disease earlier, we will measure the golden wolf's heart's size and compare this to the spinal vertebrae, a crude internal anatomy ruler. We can try to use this in different species of varying sizes, as an African golden wolf should have a similar vertebral heart measurement to a small Panamanian bush dog.

Gorillas frequently die from heart disease, despite eating a high-fibre plant diet and getting plenty of exercise. Yet chest X-rays will show us nothing, the heart and lungs looking normal. To understand what is happening, we have to see inside a gorilla's beating heart, watching how the heart muscles contract and pump blood. X-rays can't do this. We need ultrasound.

My long-suffering wife Yolanda is a specialist veterinary cardiologist, and is far more intelligent than I am. Many a time I have phoned her from the other side of the world for advice on a cheetah with a heart murmur, or an orangutan with poor pulses. As I watch her perform a detailed heart ultrasound examination, called echocardiography, on an anaesthetised African painted wolf, or giant panda, she deftly finds the tiny invisible window between the air-filled lungs that block any ultrasound transmission. Just trying to view this constantly squirming organ is difficult enough, without needing to understand how it is functioning as a pump. I may understand the principles, but can only admire how she speedily measures and interprets the rapidly wriggling snow-globe images on the screen before her.

Ultrasound can watch the beating heart, see how much each chamber contracts, measure the thickness of the different muscle walls, and measure the speed of blood being pumped out of the heart, with an armoury of different modes available to help. Brightness or B-mode is the most familiar, giving a view that is a slice through the body. Motion or M-mode measures exactly how much a structure is moving, to calculate how sections of the heart muscle are contracting. Doppler ultrasound measures blood flow towards or away from the ultrasound probe; coloured red and blue to make it easier to understand. In the same way you hear the pitch of a ranger's pick-up engine rise as its speeds towards you on a dirt road, or drop in pitch as it speeds away into the distance chasing poachers, the simplest doppler ultrasound machines don't even have a screen. Inexpensive handheld foetal monitors detect a baby's heartbeat in the womb, with loud whooshing sounds everyone in the room can hear. As wildlife vets we can also use this to monitor a tuatara's slow heart during anaesthesia, or hear the frenetic fluttering of an Ovambo sparrowhawk's heart while hidden under surgery drapes.

Echocardiography ultrasound of the heart can help us detect heart failure in a pregnant zoo okapi; help screen for early heart disease in Tonkin's leaf monkeys to exclude detrimental genes from a captive breeding programme; or diagnose a hole-in-the-heart of a young, coughing maikong crab-eating fox. Sadly, there are scores of invariably fatal congenital heart abnormalities wild animals can be born with, thanks to the complicated origami evolution has forced on what was once a simple tube. As the pathologist at London Zoo two decades ago, I came across all sorts of occasional mishaps with the heart's development, such as a young Komodo dragon, being bullied by its siblings after hatching, that had a hole in the heart between the ventricles, called a ventricular septal defect. These abnormalities are not more common in zoos, but most afflicted animals in the wild would die shortly after birth before we could ever be aware of their problem. More than 1 per cent of births may have a heart abnormality, and that's also true for humans, but we detect far fewer even in pet animals. In zoo or wild animals, we may not recognise the signs, or even see the young before they die. Asiatic lions are sometimes blamed as bad mothers, neglecting or eating cubs.

But finally managing to examine some dead cubs before they were eaten, we discovered they had a severe heart abnormality. We had unfairly blamed the mothers for eating cubs that had died after birth from heart abnormalities. The lionesses wouldn't sue us for libel, but it was important knowledge to keep the gene pool healthy for conservation breeding.

The heart has evolved from a single tube, a pump serving one circuit in a tiny clown fish as well as in a massive 2 tonne sunfish. Blood just flows through the gills to pick up oxygen before continuing on to the rest of the body. Zebrafish can even regenerate up to 20 per cent of their heart muscles if damaged. If only this were the case in humans, heart attacks wouldn't be fatal so often. The mammalian heart has instead become a complex double pump, running different pressures, coordinated by a network of nerves. The right heart pumps low-pressure blood to the lungs to collect oxygen, before blood returns to the left side of the heart. This then pumps the oxygen-rich high-pressure blood to the body, all the time balancing pressures and volumes of blood going out and returning, changing with exercise, eating, sleeping, or the outside temperatures that cause blood vessels to dilate or contract. Mammals from the edible dormouse to northern elephant seals all change their original embryonic heart tube as the foetus grows. It folds in on itself, forming new connections, some parts fusing, to form the four chambers and two separate pumps, the sides wrapping around each other like entwined lovers' hands. Any folding mistake in the origami, and the heart can be catastrophically malformed.

Any placental mammal in the womb is not only temporarily plumbed into its mother's blood supply via its navel, but also has an inbuilt heart bypass called the ductus arteriosus, to shunt blood away from the collapsed lungs, while swimming in amniotic fluid before birth. After birth, when the lungs inflate, this tube needs to close. Otherwise a new-born red wolf literally suffocates, despite breathing air, as the blood mixes from both sides of the heart and can't carry enough oxygen for the body. An affected wolf cub will have bluish gums, as a hint that the blood has little oxygen. Blood going the wrong way down the unclosed or patent ductus arteriosus also causes turbulence that we can hear as a loud continuous heart murmur. We can see the bright-red jets of blood going in the wrong direction on our ultrasound screen. Yet this murmur is common in new-born grey seal pups, sometimes taking weeks to close. They appear just fine, unlike a wolf cub. But lying on a beach sleeping when not suckling high-fat milk, and rapidly morphing into small round balls of blubber, this is hardly taxing to the heart for those first few weeks.

Occasionally, a thin channel remains inside the ductus, and a small amount of blood leaks back the wrong way. We may find this by chance in an adult amur leopard that has been living a sedate life in a zoo and that otherwise appears healthy, being anaesthetised for something entirely different. But in a wild leopard chasing prey in the harsh Russian winter this would be a major handicap, and likely fatal. Keyhole heart surgery is my favourite type of surgery, but I rarely undertake it in wild animals. While you can perform heroic heart surgery on young snow leopards and pumas, or even in a giraffe born with a heart deformity, this can be problematic. Many congenital heart problems have a genetic component. Saving one animal may not simply be delaying problems for their future offspring, but actually harm the gene pool of a critically endangered species such as the amur leopard.

Evolution of the heart as we can see it on ultrasound is fascinating. While fish have a tube-like one-sided heart and mammals four chambers split into two separate sides, these are pretty boring. Cuttlefish have two hearts to pump blood to their gills, which are completely separate from their main heart that pumps oxygenated blood around the body. Hagfish have accessory hearts near their liver that help pump blood around their long body, and this hasn't changed for over 300 million years. Bird hearts are similar to mammal hearts, which is surprising, considering they evolved from dinosaurs. This is an elegant example of convergent evolution, where high activity resulted in the same heart design, just by different embryonic folds. Flying needs high performance from the heart. A saker falcon's right atrioventricular heart valve is actually made of a flap of muscle, rather than a thin membrane as in mammals. This extra muscle boosts the heart's pumping during the high-speed chase of a fast-flying duck. But an ill falcon loses muscle from this valve as from other muscles, and on ultrasound we will see the flabby valve leaking. The avian heart is much larger for its body size than a mammal's. A sapphire-bellied hummingbird's heart is 2.5 per cent of its whole body weight, five times larger than a human's measly 0.5 per cent. The bigger the patient, the smaller the heart usually is. A European bison heart is only 0.3 per cent of its weight. An exception is the giraffe, with a heart weighing almost 1 per cent of its weight, thanks to the special demands its long neck places on blood pressure and flow.

Bird organs are suspended between inflated air sacs, keeping the body light for flight. Even flightless king penguins have these air sacs. As ultrasound can't pass through air, echocardiography on birds can be challenging. In a lesser rhea, the air sacs are small and the large flat liver makes a window we can scan the heart through. We can sometimes scan a Sichuan partridge when its full stomach squashes the liver into a helpful position for ultrasound. But this is no use for a penguin, with its dense, waterproof feathers. My solution to ultrasound a king penguin's heart is similar to viewing ovaries in a sun bear. Inserting a small ultrasound probe up its bottom, you can examine the heart by scanning it through the internal organs.

But bird hearts are boring compared to those of reptiles and amphibians. Argentinian horned frogs have two atria but confusingly only a large single ventricle. Deep grooves, separated by trabeculae ridges, fill with blood from one atrium first, before the central cavity fills with blood from the other atrium, ingeniously making one ventricle act as if two. Reptiles like the perentie goanna lizard also have a single ventricle, but with three interconnected compartments. The ventricle contracts with a squeezing motion, emptying the compartments separately, so most blood doesn't mix. At first glance a crocodile's heart appears similar to our own, with four separate atria and ventricles. But there is a connection between the outflows of the two ventricles, exotically named after the bushy-sideburned Italian surgeon Bartolomeo Panizza, who was secretly in love with his sister-in-law.

These different heart models all result in some mixing of blood returning from the body with that coming from the lungs. This melange of oxygenated and deoxygenated blood at first glance appears massively inefficient. This led taxonomists and Victorian zoologists to classify reptiles and amphibians as lower vertebrates, presuming man as the pinnacle of evolutionary perfection. But this supposedly primitive heart model is anything but. Superbly adapted to their lifestyles, reptiles and amphibians have some major advantages over us and other mammals. Despite only one pumping ventricle, there is actually less mixing of oxygenated and un-oxygenated blood than the old scientists presumed. But it is when underwater that the advantages become obvious. Submerged, a Congo dwarf clawed frog's lungs are doing nothing. Instead, oxygen can still be absorbed by its skin and the lining of its mouth. Shifting most of your blood flow away from uselessly perfusing your lungs, helps transport oxygen from the skin to the rest of the body, allowing you to stay underwater much longer, and away from pesky predators in the trees above. It is the same in a Chinese sea snake, or a New Guinea crocodile. A spiny softshell turtle can even breathe underwater via respiratory epithelium in their cloaca – yes, they can breathe through their bottom! When combined with other adaptations and a slow metabolism, a loggerhead sea turtle can hold its breath underwater for more than 10 hours. Not even the record-holding mammal, the deep diving Cuvier's beaked whale, can come close to this, holding its breath for a meagre two hours. And while a Canadian beaver can hold its breath underwater for 15 minutes, a New Guinea crocodile can hide motionless underwater for more than an hour, awaiting the approach of its unsuspecting meal. But while we can diagnose bacterial heart valve infections from their cauliflower-like appearance in large snakes like an Argentinian boa, these weird and wonderful variations in reptile and amphibian hearts make ultrasound diagnostics of most heart disease extremely difficult.

Returning to more familiar heart anatomy, there is tremendous medical interest in the heart diseases of great apes like chimpanzees, bonobos, orangutans and gorillas. But it is not clear that a zoo gorilla with heart disease is any more natural to study than an obese middle-aged smoking man, even if it does provide a nice day out from the hospital for medical researchers. Cardiovascular disease is the leading cause of human deaths worldwide. The most common human heart disease is caused by cholesterol plaques forming inside the critical coronary arteries. Despite the heart being constantly filled with blood, the heart muscle is dependent on these thin vessels to supply its own oxygen and nutrition needs. Ultrasound can show the clogged arteries and pathetic blood flow, before a complete and catastrophic blockage causes a heart attack; a chunk of heart muscle dying when its blood supply is blocked off, known as a myocardial infarction. Cholesterol plaques sound medically detached, unless you think of your arteries like a London sewer blocked by a massive fatberg. A real fatberg is also similar to what is clogging your arteries. While most fat from your food is absorbed, the remnants go down the toilet to clog the sewers.

The effect of a major myocardial infarction on the heart is like your car engine being hit by a bazooka. Neither will work very well afterwards. Yet wild gorillas don't usually get clogged arteries, being unable to subsist completely on double cheeseburgers in the Congo rainforest. Even in zoos they eat a vegetable-based diet. Yet they still drop dead from heart disease, and ultrasound battles to detect their impending doom. Gorillas appear to suffer from a condition called interstitial myocardial fibrosis. Very gradually and imperceptibly, heart muscle fibres are replaced by fibrous scar tissue, leading to a streaked and rigid heart that battles to pump. Any sudden exertion, even just trying to pass a motion, and the gorilla just drops dead. Much like how Elvis Presley died on the toilet – his battling heart, dulled by a brew of drugs, just couldn't cope.

Gorilla heart disease poses two problems. Firstly, we have no idea why they develop it, even with the healthiest vegetable zoo diets. One theory is they are missing some vital protective wild plant in their diet, such as melegueta peppers. Perhaps a hepatitis virus, or other infectious agent, is the cause. Hypertension or chronic inflammation have also been proposed. And yet another theory is that the problem arises from an unbalanced gut microflora, never the same without the balance of plants they eat in the wild. Nutritional deficiencies can cause heart disease in other wild animals. Giant anteaters develop a flabby heart if deficient in an amino acid called taurine. This is hardly surprising, as feeding an animal that normally only eats termites and ants, and up to 30,000 in a single day, is a challenge in captivity. But with gorilla heart disease, we simply don't know. To complicate things, we occasionally also see it in other primates, from orangutans to white-handed gibbons. One stressful day a young adult chimpanzee dropped dead only five minutes after I darted him with anaesthetic drugs, to everyone's consternation. He had been rescued from a medical research facility and an autopsy showed that his heart was a hard, white mass of scar tissue. The only consolation was that the condition is not painful. It possibly just feels like one is fainting, only never to awake. So I am not sure how relevant this comparative research work actually is to human heart disease.

The second problem with gorilla heart disease applies to most wild animal cardiology. As the heart is a pump, what matters to diagnostic evaluation is how well it is functioning. But while humans and pet dogs will allow you half an hour to make a detailed assessment of their heart's function, this is usually impossible in our far less cooperative wild patients. If our gorilla requires anaesthesia, this makes the heart sluggish and contract differently, with blood vessels dilated and blood pressures altered. Perhaps a Diana monkey can be grabbed and held for its echocardiography awake, but stress hormones change the blood pressure and heart rate and alter how the heart contracts, thanks to the infusion of adrenaline. Heart disease so severe the patient is about to drop dead can be detected under anaesthesia, but subtle early changes amenable to treatment sometimes cannot. Advanced myocardial fibrosis can be completely invisible on an anaesthetised gorilla's ultrasound. Challenging even in people, sometimes ultrasound needs to be performed on a treadmill to detect the problem, and this is something I have yet to convince any gorillas to do.

Anaesthesia, by changing how the heart contracts, altering blood pressure and blood flow speeds, can also make it appear there is a problem when there is none. When starting to re-introduce European beavers after 600 years of extinction in Britain, we found that, under anaesthesia, most beavers had loud heart murmurs. As man's long history with beavers was mainly trapping and shooting them, rather than diagnosis of heart disease, we didn't know how to interpret this. A heart murmur is simply an abnormal sound, caused by turbulent blood flow – much like a small stream burbles and sings over rocks, while the smooth-flowing Rhine is silent. Turbulent heart flow is not normal in the heart, and usually hints that something is wrong. But after scanning large numbers of wild beavers in great detail, my expert cardiologist friend Craig Devine had to conclude that the heart murmurs were a normal artefact of anaesthesia in beavers.

Despite its questionable value, determining normal echo-cardiographic measurements of anaesthetised wild animals remains a popular research topic for conferences. Scanning the odd bonobo or cheetah is after all an enjoyable break from seeing hundreds of sick patients in a darkened hospital room every day. Similarly, researchers recently succeeded in briefly attaching a heart rate monitor to a blue whale, and reported, with much media fanfare, that its heart beats just twice a minute. Yet what value this brings to the conservation of whales, or any individual whale's health, is not really clear.

So we can see inside our wild patients' bodies in myriad ways. We can examine a giant panda's wrist with radiographs, or a loggerhead turtle's brain with MRI. The mysteries inside a gorilla's beating heart are revealed by ultrasound, while, thanks to the Beatles, we can understand an orangutan's sinusitis with computed tomography. But, occasionally, all we need is to take our patient's temperature.

While zebras radiate heat from their dark stripes during a hot day, at night it is the white stripes that glow warm on thermography, emitting more heat as they have less insulating fat beneath them than the black stripes.

9

How sidewinder missiles help
a black rhino

Aside from the stethoscope, nothing typifies vets and doctors more than a thermometer. Toxic mercury-filled glass thermometers are a distant memory from my early vet years, but animal patients will still bite the digital versions. So they are inserted per rectum – just as when children we were reminded would be our fate if uncooperative when visiting the doctor. A thermometer is however pretty useless when looking down the binoculars at a critically endangered black rhino that a ranger has told us is acting erratically.

A grumpy patient, with poor eyesight, and living in dense bushveld, a rhino is prone to charge anything unexpected, even termite mounds, when in a bad mood. With the highest mortal combat death rate of any large mammal, almost half of all wild adult male black rhinos die from fighting. They are much more nimble than their larger lumbering, placid, white rhino cousins, so getting closer on foot for a better look is not a sensible option.

A century ago, black rhinos were the most common rhinos on the planet, with several hundred thousand roaming southern Africa. Now they are critically endangered, with little over two thousand left. Every individual wild black rhino matters.

Could the ill rhino have been shot, but we can't see the small festering bullet hole? Or dying from rabies thanks to a tiny mongoose bite? Has she been speared by a rival rhino underneath? Or is she simply about to give birth? The last thing a pregnant mother needs is to be chased and darted from a helicopter. It could kill her and her unborn calf. Taking its temperature could give us an answer, but how to get it?

Illness and injury cause blood vessels to dilate, bringing more white blood cells to the battlefield, which we call inflammation. If severe, the whole body's temperature increases, which we can detect with a thermometer up the bum. But if an injury is small, such as an infected gunshot wound, sometimes only that area is hot. Using the same technology in heat-seeking missiles, monitoring nuclear reactor cracks, and evaluating your home insulation, thermal cameras allow us to see heat in the form of infrared radiation. Two and a half thousand years ago, Hippocrates sometimes covered patients in mud. By noting where it dried quickest, he identified where disease was located. Hippocrates detected heat transferred through the skin from the blood flow. A thermal camera made of mud – I guess we could use this on warthogs, but a thermal camera is less messy.

A black rhino is a perfect patient for pregnancy diagnosis via thermography. Its tough dry skin is practically hairless and doesn't stretch easily during pregnancy, so the placenta and foetus lie close to the body surface, and the increased blood flow and heat are easily detected. A gunshot wound, or infected mongoose bite, will instead glow as a bright white spot when seen on the thermal camera. While an African elephant appears similar, with its baggy skin trousers, thermography will only pick up pregnancy so late the fact is obvious anyway. However, a hot elephant vulva is instead useful, highlighting the fertile oestrus period when mating and conception can occur. Female chimpanzees, despite huge pink butts, don't have any detectable temperature difference in their intumescence swellings when fertile, infertile, or pregnant. Female chimps have evolved to hide their fertility, to stop randy males desperate for sex from killing their infants. Like bonobos, female chimpanzees use sex strategically – to convince males to treat them well all the time, and not just on the day they are ovulating.

Thermal imaging is versatile. I can see if an angry elephant has an abscess at the base of its tusk, or instead ankle arthritis from years chained up at a logging camp. I can detect an infection deep inside the hoof of a lame Rothschild's giraffe or in a Javan mouse-deer's tiny foot. I can diagnose a sprain in a limping sarus crane, or even compare stress levels in blue tits as they leave their nests.

Many animals, most inconveniently, have fur or feathers. Just like clothing, these trap an insulating layer of air. Thermography of a maned three-toed sloth is useless. You will just see the temperature of its lush fur surface, gently heated by the sun on a warm day. But even a rectal temperature can be pretty useless in sloths. Sloths are weird. Slow, and with a small brain to survive on their low-energy leaf diet, they look as though they are smiling, thanks to their mouth shape. With a metabolism so slow it takes weeks to digest their food, there seems no reason to grin. They save further energy with a body temperature much lower than other mammals, which can vary by as much as 10 degrees Celsius. A human can barely survive a few degrees change before the effects are fatal. So how do you know if a sloth has a fever? You don't. But if their temperature drops too low, the microbes in their stomach stop being able to digest their food. They can't even generate warmth by shivering. At least temperatures can show if a sloth is too cold and at risk of dying, even it can't tell us if it has an infection. Hummingbirds are the opposite extreme. They burn energy at a frantic rate, with a heart rate over a thousand beats a minute in flight. Their normal body temperature can be more than 41 degrees Celsius. But spending every waking minute finding high-energy nectar as fuel, how does a purple-throated carib survive the night without eating? They go into torpor overnight, stalling their metabolism, and dropping their body temperature by more than 20 degrees. These tiny birds literally have to hibernate every night just to survive until morning.

167

In reptiles, amphibians and fish any body temperature measurement is almost meaningless. Poikilothermic, they regulate their body temperature by choosing their environment. A Nile crocodile that is too cold to digest the chunk of zebra thigh in its stomach, will bask in the sun; and a sidewinder snake in the Namibian desert will burrow under the sand, to prevent it basting in the sun. Rather than being primitive, not generating your own body heat has huge evolutionary advantages. Imagine being able to get away with just one or two large meals in a year, as a large saltwater crocodile can. No dinner for me, I ate a few months ago, thanks. Reptiles live at amazing extremes, from tuataras active at as low as 5 degrees Celsius in New Zealand, to desert tortoises that cope with temperatures more than ten times that in the Mojave desert.

Observing a reptile with thermography is little use. Its entire body is usually the same temperature as where it has been hanging out. A Greek tortoise will be hot above, where the sun has shone on it; a blue-tongued skink warmer beneath, after lying on a warm rock. Yet a yellow anaconda needs a cooler spot to breed than to digest food, and different species need different temperatures for different body processes. So we can use a thermal camera to examine a rhino iguana's zoo enclosure, checking there are hotter and cooler areas it can choose from, and this is essential for its health.

While cold-blooded patients are out, thermography can still detect illness in one of the best insulated animals on the planet. Penguins have the densest layer of feathers of any bird. Emperor penguins can dive more than half a kilometre deep, where water pressure and freezing temperatures tax any waterproofing insulation to its limit. Penguins' feet aren't covered in feathers, but are still almost useless for thermal examination, as they have an ingenious blood vessel heat exchange system, to save losing valuable warmth on the ice or in freezing water. But there is one location a penguin cannot control heat loss: their eyes, which act as a window into their interior thermal world. We can reliably diagnose penguins ill with fungal pneumonia just from their eye surface temperature, without having to catch them. Ill birds have a higher internal body temperature, and radiate more heat from their cornea surface than healthy penguins. But ocular temperatures only work in animals with large eyes, such as ostriches, tawny owls and tarsiers. Squirrel monkey eyes are too small for us to detect if they are ill. There is only so much heat the small surface can radiate, and a fever can't increase this.

Sarus cranes and greater flamingos have long thin legs devoid of feathers; perfect for spotting small increases in blood flow that mean a sprain or infection. Examining a Cape griffon vulture that has collided with an electricity pylon injuring its wing, we can part the feathers to use thermography. By comparing the two wings we can judge if the blood supply is viable, before we put the unlucky bird through any surgery. Similarly, we can monitor a skin graft's healing in a timber wolf in a zoo after its surgery, as the insulating fur has been shaved off.

Not all fur is an insulating hurdle for thermal imaging. Many antelope have short dense hair. A nilgai striding across a dry Rajasthani plain on a cool early morning is a perfect thermography patient. Any important wound or joint injury is visible. But hair gets interesting when patterns are involved. The sun heats up a Rothschild's giraffe's darker skin patches, and they glow brightly on a thermal image. Confusingly, at night these dark patches also glow. While there is no difference in blood flow, the skin is thinner and the fur over the patches sparser, helping them radiate more body heat. Chapman zebra also radiate heat from their dark stripes during a hot day; the difference between the black and white stripes can be as much as 20 degrees Celsius. Bizarrely, at night it is the zebra's white stripes that glow on thermography, emitting more heat as they have less insulating fat beneath them than the black stripes.

Aside from fur pattern quirks, there are other obfuscating ingredients. Dawn is the best time for thermal imaging, with the cool air helping you see subtle temperature differences. A buffalo with a hot butt at midday was probably avoiding the sun's glare, just before you saw it. Lying down, or leaning against a tree, also affects blood flow, which you risk mis-interpreting. A Malayan tapir sitting near a heater in a Scottish zoo can mimic a multitude of non-existent problems. A Bornean bearded pig with cold skin patches on thermography may be an early sign of diamond skin disease, a nasty bacteria causing clots in surface blood vessels – mini skin strokes. Before panicking, however, it could just be evaporating water droplets.

Water, like sunlight, muddles thermography diagnosis. Excess heat dissipates if the patient has been swimming, and evaporation can be uneven, making thermal pictures confusing. We can't strand a beluga whale just for thermo-graph, but a trained aquarium beluga can lift its head for vets to check for any early tooth infections radiating heat. But we do actually prefer it if one animal patient bathes before a thermal exam. Common hippopotamuses have thick skin peppered with perforations by minuscule blood vessels, a confusing thermal acne of spots and patches. Wet skin blends the confusing jigsaw into something we can actually interpret.

Sea lions and seals are not hippos, and need to be dry for us to examine properly. Observing orphaned grey seal pups, otherwise invisible bite marks glow brightly on thermography. The rows of teeth are clearly visible for a week or two, where tissue has been bruised and damaged, even if the skin has no wounds. These bites come from over-protective seal mums when the pup strayed too close to their own baby. Even in related species there are confounding differences. Northern elephant and harbour seals tend to radiate most heat from flipper skin, while Californian sea lions radiate heat evenly over their entire bodies.

We can use thermography not just to examine hippopota-muses, but also find them. It may seem difficult to lose animals so big, but that is precisely the situation in Colombia. Escapees from the richest criminal in history's private zoo, Pablo Escobar's original four hippos were very fruitful after escaping and have multiplied to more than a hundred, ranging over more than two thousand square kilometres. Just as military drones and snipers use thermography to find targets, we can find vagabond hippos, monitor elephants, or catch poachers sneaking about at night. Thermal cameras can also help census nocturnal animals, from rock wallabies in the Flinders ranges, to bilbies and bettongs in the desert of South Australia.

Some patients can observe me with thermography. Pit vipers have two hollows on either side of their head which are sensitive to temperature differences as small as a thousandth of a degree; far better than any machine I can buy. The curved pit surfaces detect the direction of heat, like eyes, to see in 3D infrared. Without a lens the picture resolution is not highly focused, but still perfect to strike a small mouse on a dark moonless night. Vampire bats instead have their infrared detection in their nose. So do they smell heat rather than see it, I wonder? This is only sensitive over a hands-breadth distance, and is useless in finding a victim, but it locates a patch of skin with good blood flow to bite.

While airport thermal cameras detect passengers with Ebola virus before they can cause an outbreak, vets use thermography to look for foot and mouth disease in mule deer; their hot feet a give-away. Thermography can help find everything from desert bighorn sheep with nasal bot fly sinusitis, to bufflehead ducks with fungal bone infections. Thermography can help select the freshest giant panda poop to submit to a lab, or detect raccoons infected with the dreaded rabies virus, despite a thick fur coat, thanks to their distinctly hot noses. Nose temperatures can be life-saving for a wildlife vet. An anaesthetised Asiatic lion's nose becomes much warmer just before it wakes up from anaesthesia; its blood pressure rising as the drugs wear off. This is very useful for ensuring that your carnivorous patient doesn't unexpectedly awake and mistake you for a convenient hospital meal.

So we can monitor our black rhino, simply going into labour, from a distance. At night on the thermal camera we see the distant red blob has been joined by another smaller warm blob. The birth a success, we watch the heat patterns of the mum and her suckling calf wander out of thermal sight.

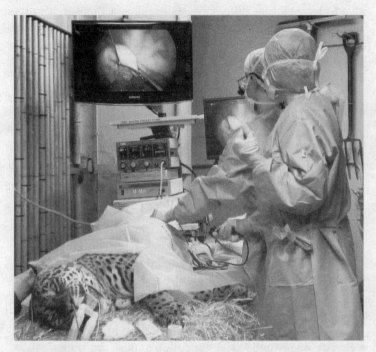

Keyhole surgery results in very small wounds, and so is well suited to operating in
less than ideal surroundings, without risking post-operative infections.

10

Surgery and the secret police

Placating secret police with drunken karaoke; building brain surgery equipment in the jungle from a beer keg and mattress pump the night before an operation; smuggling a battered suitcase containing everything normally occupying an entire operating theatre to avoid corrupt customs officials; or spending five days travelling on boats through the rainforest to get to a makeshift theatre with a stone operating table. And all before I even put a scalpel to my unusual patients. My specialist work as an international wildlife surgeon is somewhat different to that of my human surgeon friends.

Surgery is legalised violence. Stab a baby gorilla with a knife, and you will be prosecuted for animal cruelty. Yet do the same in a blue robe and gloves and it is called surgery and perfectly acceptable, even if the victim still dies. While surgeons are seen as brave warriors battling illness, and lauded when the patient recovers, we take far more credit than we deserve. It is the patient that bears all the risks. Operate on a dead dugong, and no healing occurs. A living body heals itself. As surgeons we are just meat mechanics, placing tissues in the correct positions for healing, something occasionally forgotten by those of us on the handle side of the scalpel.

Healing in animal patients

The spectrum of weird and wonderful animal anatomy you need to know for surgery is only rivalled by the different ways in which our wildlife patients heal. Purple-naped sunbirds are in the fast lane of healing, making them great surgical patients. While a human needs skin stitches for two weeks after an operation, a sunbird's skin heals so fast you can remove sutures in just five days. A broken arm in an orangutan takes three months to heal even with a metal plate and screws, yet the same bone in an Ovambo sparrowhawk heals so fast that even without surgery it will be flying again in two weeks. But while reptiles like saltwater crocodiles are closely related to birds and dinosaurs, their healing is somewhat different. Their slow metabolism means a crocodile can survive without food for half a year, or a slider turtle can brumate, hibernating underwater, for several months. Yet healing is painfully slow. Skin sutures may need to remain in place for two months for even a small wound in a reticulated python, and it can take over a year for an Aldabra giant tortoise's broken leg to heal.

Nevertheless, despite slow healing, there are surprises. During the months after surgery, a green tree python will shed its skin, often including the surgical scar complete with the sutures: convenient if you don't feel like handling a grumpy snake again. Sawtail lizards have another novelty if a hungry African wildcat grabs them. They shake their neon blue tail off. Twitching on its own, it distracts the cat while the lizard escapes into a crevice. Many lizards and geckos use their tail as a fat store, so it is still a loss. Thankfully, most can simply regrow a tail bitten off, or one amputated by the vet. It isn't perfect; the spinal cord and tendons don't regrow. But it does grow back to function as an inbuilt larder for lean times.

Japanese giant salamanders can do more. Even when 50 years old, they can regrow an entire amputated leg. All the tissues, from skin to bone, even nerves, will regrow entirely, and with no scar tissue. Costa Rican zebra tarantulas are the most extreme. Not just regrowing a leg over the next few moults, they act as their own surgeon to perform the amputation. You can assist in the same way as an angry female who's latched her fangs into a male's leg after an inappropriate advance. Grabbing the upper leg firmly with forceps, the tarantula jerks his leg's base, and the limb severs off naturally. Small muscle attachments close the joint membranes over the wound so there is no blue haemolymph bleeding. Anaesthesia is not needed, as the spider has to be conscious to perform this autotomy. Imagine if when you broke your arm or developed knee arthritis, instead of needing a knee replacement or arm full of metal screws your limb could simply be pulled off, to grow back as good as new. Orthopaedic surgeons would be out of a job.

If our cars repaired themselves after a collision, that would amaze us, yet we take healing for granted. A sword-tailed newt takes a month for their surgical wound to heal, while a golden starfrontlet hummingbird's skin heals so fast that a blob of surgical superglue rather than sutures is perfectly fine for the few days needed. But when the newt's skin heals there will be no scar at all, in contrast to the hummingbird. A scar forms when cells are replaced by fibrous tissue. This repair is not nearly as strong or as flexible as the original tissue. So in most patients, from black caiman to gelada baboons, surgery always has a price to pay. The scar never works as well as the original tissue. Yet there is one tissue that surprisingly always heals without any scar. Bone.

Broken bones

Orthopaedic surgery has uncharitably been compared to carpentry. Looking at my battered array of saws, drills and screws, it can be rough-and-tumble surgery. Separating and cutting through bruised and oozing muscles just to reach the broken bone in a brown howler monkey that has plummeted from the forest canopy is messy, even before you start drilling, or fire-up a whining bone saw that splatters a fine mist of blood and bone powder everywhere. Brutal as my bone repair with gleaming metalwork may appear, this tissue heals better than almost anything else in an animal's body. A year after surgery bone will be as strong as before breaking, but the muscles and skin, despite healing much faster, will never again be the same for the monkey's remaining life. Bone constantly reshapes itself, so even if my repair is bent, the bone will slowly remodel, responding to forces pulling and pushing cells in its structure. X-raying the leg after a few years, it will be impossible to see it was ever broken.

I can't prescribe bed-rest after my patients' operations. Even if a howler monkey would be cooperative and rest after I have fixed her broken arm (they never do), she really needs to return to her group as soon as she is awake. Otherwise she risks being attacked, thrown out of the group, or even killed. Watching one dangle from its freshly shaved arm, while her friend hangs from her legs just hours after surgery, is a nerve-racking test of your surgical repair. I usually use special bone plates that lock the screw heads firmly and act as a rigid internal scaffold. Although more expensive than those commonly used in dogs and cats, they are sturdier and better survive the abuse a running cheetah, hopping kangaroo or swinging monkey will put my bone repair through, and I have even had a custom set made for extreme patients like giraffes and rhinos.

Unplanned fracture surgery in remote locations may need simpler materials. I've repaired a Sri Lankan wood owl's broken wing using pins and car body repair putty, and during the pandemic I talked West African colleagues through repairing a chimpanzee's broken leg with bicycle spokes and a wood drill. Even before COVID-19 I have talked young Indonesian vets through emergency surgery in a Bornean orangutan, whispering on my phone at 3 a.m. while on a sleeper train. I find trying to explain how to amputate a snare-mangled limb via internet video call more stressful than any operation I ever undertake myself. Even repairing a beating heart accidentally punctured by a trainee was relatively relaxing in comparison. It is probably the illusion of control; just as one feels safer driving a car than being a plane passenger, despite the opposite being true.

Bones vary tremendously. A whooper swan has a similar-length humerus bone in its wing to that in an American black bear's upper front leg. Yet an X-ray shows that the bear's bone has thick dense walls, while the swan's bone is paper-thin and hollow, with internal struts to reinforce the lightweight bone. This all makes sense, as weight is critical for flight. The swan's skeleton is only 5 per cent of its body weight, while an elephant's skeleton is 17 per cent of its body, to support its massive weight. These structural bone peculiarities are important for surgery. Drilling into elephant bone needs long hardened bits, taxing my drill's power to its limits. Yet swan bones pose their own challenges. Thin and brittle, they are prone to shatter from pressure while drilling, like a dropped champagne glass. Screws are useless, as the bone walls are too thin for the screw threads to hold a plate to the bone. Its best to use an external fixator. This scaffolding, a combination of pins going through the limb joined together on the outside, makes the repair resemble knitting-needle voodoo combined with Meccano. And if you mistakenly flush blood from the bone during surgery, to your horror the bird will splutter and drown, as many hollow limb bones connect directly to a bird's lungs.

When repairing a Siberian musk deer's broken leg, the bones are strong, holding screws and metal implants well. But their long legs have almost nothing between bone and covering skin. Even the thinnest metal plate makes it difficult to suture the thick rigid skin over your repair. It can be a slow-motion race between bone healing and the skin breaking open over the plate, forcing you to remove the screws and implant much sooner than you would like. In one young wild deer with a horrible open break just above her foot, I had to remove my metal work after just two weeks, although thankfully she was fine, and returned to the wild a few weeks later.

Keyhole surgery

Most soft tissues heal faster than bone. But the price is a weaker scar for the remainder of an animal's life, one reason keyhole surgery is so valuable in wild patients. It may take years to become skilled operating with chopsticks, but the tiny wounds heal with far less damage than the massive slash needed to shuffle a siamang gibbon's intestines between your hands while looking for a blockage. Also far less painful, minimally invasive surgery lets us view minute structures magnified on our screen more clearly than is ever possible with our eyes.

Dexterous patients like gelada baboons with their dainty grass-plucking fingers can unpick the finest suture material and open their wound. Rummaging around in their own innards or chomping on their intestines is hardly therapeutic. Despite their lumbering appearance, giant pandas can also open even small wounds, the fine points of their claws acting like precision tools, making cancer surgery planning even more challenging. And while chimpanzee fingers are thick sausages in comparison, their mastery of tools leads them to inquisitively poke twigs, even if caked in poo, into the smallest wounds to investigate pain. Keyhole wounds just one centimetre thick, while normal in humans, are not ideal. While 5 millimetre wounds thinner than a pencil are fine for a 200 kilogram Amur tiger, for the most difficult of customers I use keyhole surgery instruments only 3 millimetres in diameter. For the first-ever great ape keyhole appendectomy, deep in the Bornean rainforest, I left wounds only the size of a microchip needle puncture. Even an intellectually gifted orangutan couldn't interfere with those.

Still, operating on a fur seal, which immediately after surgery dives into the water, makes me nervous. Despite my apprehension they are always fine, but human surgery colleagues are horrified. A human abdominal surgery patient jumping in the pool an hour after anaesthesia and swimming a few laps is simply unthinkable. While I can keep a capybara out of water for a few days after operating, this isn't possible for beavers. A beaver's dense fur is also essential for their waterproofing, insulating them from freezing winter waters, so I can't even clip their fur. Instead I painstakingly shampoo their belly, before careful parting the fur with a comb, in readiness for my tiny incisions. Wildlife patients test our surgical techniques in strange ways. No wonder when the Association of Laporoscopic Surgeons of Great Britain kindly awarded me honorary life membership, they called me surgery's crash-test-dummy.

Keyhole surgery on a Western lowland gorilla or a black squirrel monkey results in identically sized wounds. In a squirrel monkey it requires small precise movements of the instrument tips, but operating in larger animals is not necessarily more spacious. Thanks to their habit of arguing by biting each other, chimpanzees often have extensive adhesions; patches of scar tissue weld the intestines and body wall together. Navigating an old male chimp's abdomen is a bleeding obstacle course. Even peaceful gorillas, with their large vegetation-filled bowels, pose a challenge to keyhole operating. Yet navigating a one-tonne gaur's innards is more taxing. Aside from the need for long instruments to have any hope of reaching anything, their massive four-chambered stomach takes up most of the abdomen. An internal fermentation tank of fibrous food, liquid and microbes, fasting has no effect. Once the animal is anaesthetised, the bowels inflate with fermenting gases that the gaur would normally constantly fart and belch out when awake. Searching for a cancerous internal testicle feels as difficult as looking for your dropped hat in a collapsed circus tent full of elephants.

Keyhole operations need more equipment than traditional open slash-and-hack surgery. Inside the abdomen, there is naturally no light or space to see anything. We have to inflate it with an inert gas like carbon dioxide; no one wants internal combustion and an exploding patient from a flammable gas like oxygen. The pressure needs to be carefully maintained. Just enough to make a space for operating, but not so much to suffocate the victim by squashing the diaphragm, or stopping blood returning to the heart. Capybaras and Luzon giant cloud rats blow up like party balloons with little pressure, while trying to inflate pygmy hippos and Malayan tapirs will often give you little operating space, even at the limit of safe pressures.

Endoscopes are thin surgical telescopes, and to see anything we must shine a powerful light via a glass fibre cable into our inflated operating space. Four times brighter than a car headlight, this light gets hot enough to set fire to the operating drapes. Electrosurgical instruments to coagulate bleeding or cut tissue also pose a risk if you inadvertently brush a hot tip against a spectacled leaf monkey's intestine. A small blanched white spot appears, with no hint of how serious this is. The tiny injury appears innocuous, but a piece of intestine has been cooked by your carelessness. While the monkey may appear fine, a few days later this will burst open, oozing faeces and bacteria into the abdomen with fatal consequences. The cure is to immediately place a single stitch across the white spot. Then, when the tissue breaks down in a few days, it has actually already been repaired in advance. Suturing in keyhole surgery at first feels like trying to stitch a torn car seat – but having to do it via the exhaust pipe. It is something I still have to practise regularly. The most challenging keyhole sutures I had to place were inside a huge Galapagos giant tortoise with a large bowel tear, propped on her side on the floor between two chairs. She is still fine half a decade later, hopefully with another one to two centuries' lifespan ahead of her.

There are many things to consider before operating on a wild animal. A technique to repair dogs' torn knee ligaments seems reasonable in a fossa, until you watch it running along branches and jumping between trees, like the lemurs it hunts. It clearly needs a completely different operation. Suturing a large gash in a Grévy's zebra is simple, until realising you need to match the stripe pattern, or the zoo's passport documents won't be valid. Yet surgical decisions in wildlife are often based on gut feelings with a pinch of guidance from human or pet research. There is very little published information to base realistic expectations on, or guess how likely complications are. And there is another hurdle.

Surgery can be enjoyable, intellectually challenging, even quietly thrilling, so how do we know we are genuinely performing it for the patient's benefit? Surgery can appear a cure for almost anything. It is a messy, imprecise science, with training much like an auto-repair apprenticeship. No wonder we are disparagingly called meat mechanics. I may perform a perfect operation on a spotted hyaena, but the patient dies because of other problems. Or I could make a mess of a fracture repair in an ornate tree-kangaroo, yet the patient heals beautifully, despite my actual incompetence. Nothing can really be judged on a single case. It is the invisible rate of successes, failures and complications that matters.

Expectation versus reality

When I did my doctorate on wildlife surgery, I read every single scientific article ever written on any surgery involving a wild animal I could find. I read more than 20,000 research papers, consuming every scrap of information. I even looked at reports from zoo animals, pet parrots and snakes, and trained falconry birds. As some papers focusing on anaesthesia included surgery, I read those too. Then I reviewed the previous quarter of a century's records from leading zoos, to see how reality matched published research.

Most papers were just personal opinion, or only about a single operation. Overall, only 5 per cent of operations reported any complications. But this statistic seemed unlikely to reflect the reality of operating on a howler monkey under a tarpaulin in the rainforest. Actual zoo operations had complications almost a quarter of the time – almost one complication for every four patients. This is understandable, considering how uncooperative a leopard or hamadryas baboon may be. But leading zoos have well-trained specialist vets, good equipment and operating theatres, far beyond anything available in a rescue centre, or when operating in the jungle. In primates, from marmosets to gorillas, the published data only gave a ridiculously low complication rate of 1.8 per cent – less than one out of every 50 operations. This is better than many top human surgeons achieve. But real complications in zoos were more than 10 times higher. While orthopaedic surgery articles only reported a complication for about one in eight wildlife patients, in zoo animals more than half of all orthopaedic cases had complications, with more than one in three zoo bone surgery patients suffering a major life-threatening complication.

These mismatches between expectations and actual outcomes can have catastrophic consequences. A young Indonesian veterinarian may get her dream job in a wildlife rescue centre. Soon after starting, she is presented with a young proboscis monkey with a broken arm. She diligently reads everything about any similar cases in other monkeys, made difficult by most journal articles being locked behind expensive internet paywalls. She reads some pet dog surgery books, the only ones available, and looks at human arm fracture repairs on YouTube. The likelihood of success seems good, she explains to the sceptical manager, who reluctantly agrees to let her operate. The surgery is more difficult than she anticipated, but she does her best, and it all looks good at the end. But within days, the monkey chews at the wound and it becomes infected. She battles to get him to take the daily medications, hidden in food. Frantic to get away from her, he swings on the arm, and the metal pin snaps. She then tries a splint after another long anaesthetic, but a week later he is depressed, stops eating, and dies of sepsis. The manager is upset. Despondent, the vet blames herself for being useless at her work. She leaves her job. Confidence shattered and disheartened, she resigns herself to a life of selling farm animal feeds, rather than saving threatened wildlife. A few weeks later, the rescue centre's new, enthusiastic, replacement young vet is presented with a gibbon, its hand injured from a snare, and the whole cycle risks repeating itself.

Unrealistic expectations can seriously harm wild patients, causing more pain and suffering for conditions that may even be untreatable. It is far easier to operate than to hold one's nerve and recommend against it, treating a case conservatively. Any surgeon knows how to operate, but good surgeons know when *not* to operate. I have done numerous supposed world-first wildlife operations, from a keyhole appendix removal in a great ape, to brain surgery in a bear, and am consulted daily by wildlife vet colleagues around the world for surgical advice on cases from dolphins to giant snails. Yet, I am also an extremely cautious surgeon. I advise against surgery in far more cases than I suggest it. Resisting the urge to operate is more difficult than learning any surgical technicalities. And I am paranoid whenever I may be the first one to attempt any new operation. History reveals one would be wise to be cautious.

Media hype and the ultimate spectator sport

Growing up in South Africa, Chris Barnard was a national hero, the first surgeon in the world to perform a successful human heart transplant. As a young vet student I even spent a few days at his original research centre, volunteering to help anaesthetise a pet Jack Russell dog for open heart surgery. I wasn't prepared for the cages full of forlorn chacma baboons, trapped from the surrounding hills, awaiting experimental open-heart surgery. Chris Barnard was tall, charismatic and good with the media. He was the world's first superstar celebrity surgeon. He dated models, slept with actresses, and endorsed dodgy anti-ageing creams later in life. Yet his patient, Louis Washkansky, died after only 18 days.

The *South African Medical Journal* issue dedicated to the operation had Barnard's article proclaiming 'Successful human heart transplant', while the cover ironically proclaimed the patient's death. While Washkansky's condition deteriorated, as many predicted, Barnard was flying around the world on a rockstar-style publicity tour. Hardly good patient care.

Technically, heart transplant wasn't that difficult. Barnard had made a quick grab for fame, aware that donor heart rejection was nowhere near being solved, even in lab animals. Yet he had misleadingly promised the patient and his wife an 80 per cent chance of success. Within days, other surgeons were attempting the surgery. More than a hundred heart transplants were tried the following year, yet less than a third survived even three months. It took another 15 years for better anti-rejection drugs to improve things. And the greatest irony was that Chris Barnard hadn't actually performed the first human heart transplant at all.

While Barnard courted the media, with wildlife surgery it is usually the media that courts vets, being desperate for a furry, feelgood news-filler. No one is interested in reading about yet another human operation, even if it's the world's second face transplant. But even the simplest operation in a zoo lion never appears to lose its appeal. Operating keyhole on a chimpanzee hernia in West Africa, performing brain surgery on a moon bear in Laos, and doing the first robotic-assisted surgery on a tiger, I soon discovered that large TV crews were eager to fly over and film them. Yet, despite spending a hundred times what it cost me to operate in one case, there was depressingly little interest in filming the patients' actual recoveries. The TV crews were only interested in the drama of the operation. All the animals did well; the chimp even went on to give birth to a beautiful baby the next year. But she could equally have died three days later. You would never know. Newspapers happily report operations on an emperor penguin or brain surgery in a rare kakapo, but it is almost impossible to find out later if the patients' lives actually improved. After our moon bear brain surgery escapade, we conscientiously monitored her progress for five years before we felt it finally reasonable to publish her case in a scientific journal.

When friends of mine were filmed during a lion operation in South Africa, routine work did not make for exciting television. When the lion briefly coughed as the anaesthetic tube was moved, it was edited to appear as if the lion was about to wake up and kill everyone. The sound of a defibrillator, nowhere to be seen, was even added artificially to heighten the supposed drama. Little wonder none of us want to be filmed. TV coverage can be harmful. As failures are invisible, the public and young vets get unrealistic expectations, and go on to harm patients with overly heroic surgery attempts.

Some effects of media attention can be unexpected. A decade ago, a company donated a load of keyhole surgery instruments I could never otherwise afford, in return for recording an operation. It happened to be a reindeer surgery in November, and a clever press release before Christmas saw the company's share price rise over half a million pounds in 24 hours. I wish I had owned a few shares! I do my best to avoid being filmed, although it isn't usually up to me. And much as I prefer surgical solitude, it is only fair to carers, who rescued a cheetah or need to look after her for life, to let them watch my fumbling efforts to help. Surgery can risk descending into showmanship. Historically, operating theatres were just small amphitheatres for doctors and voyeurs. One of the oldest of all operations was the ultimate surgical spectator sport.

After trepanning (drilling holes in skulls) and circumcision, lithotomies are one of the oldest operations. Even Hippocrates urged not to 'cut for the stone', the first recorded distinction between physicians and surgeons. For over a thousand years, lithotomists travelled from town to town performing surgery and making more of a living from the crowd of spectators than from the patients themselves. The pain would have been excruciating to endure, being trussed up, naked butt on display, and slashed between scrotum and anus while the lithotomist poked around with a dirty finger to retrieve the stone. Some surgeons kept a stone up their sleeve, which they could produce with a flourish for the crowd, if unable to retrieve the actual bladder stone. Many victims died, but so did those without surgery. Even fortunate survivors were incontinent through their new opening for the rest of their lives. One Dutch blacksmith found the whole experience so horrid, he cut his stone out himself. Patients have long been aware that their surgeon may not have their best interests at heart. Thankfully, with modern endoscopes I can often manage to retrieve bladder stones, from Greek tortoises to maned wolves, without needing surgery, or a stone hidden up my sleeve.

The forgotten story of the true first human heart transplant is no less dubious than medieval lithotomists' tricks, or Chris Barnard's operation. Four years earlier, James Hardy in Mississippi transplanted the first heart into a living human, but it didn't even last two hours. Yet scientific criticism wasn't because the patient was an elderly deaf-mute, or that there was almost no chance of success. It was because he used a chimpanzee's heart, unbeknown to the patient's family. It wasn't Hardy's first rash operation. The year before, performing the first human lung transplant, he used a dead human donor's lung, and chose a convicted murderer serving a life sentence as the first patient. Misrepresented to his victim's wife and three children as something to improve his shortness of breath, on opening his patient's chest Hardy found tumours that had spread. So surgery could never cure him. But deciding this was beside the point, Hardy performed the transplant anyway. His victim survived only 18 days, the same length of time Chris Barnard's first heart transplant patient would survive four years later. Mis-sold to unsuitable patients with unrealistic expectations, these operations were little more than human vivisection. Yet some surgeons kept trying to implant sheep, chimpanzee, and baboon hearts into people unsuccessfully for another two decades.

Chris Barnard's famous heart transplant had another dark secret, later revealed by his brother Marius. Brain dead after being hit by a car, the donor's heart still beat strongly, and so by legal definitions of the time she was still alive and the heart could not be removed. Barnard injected the heart with potassium to stop it. Most countries would later change their definitions of death to facilitate organ transplants, but at the time it was ethically dubious, and legally possibly murder.

Barnard's younger brother Marius is virtually unknown, yet seeing the financial hardship of many patients, he invented critical illness insurance; something that has now saved far more lives than heart transplants ever have.

Ambitious surgeons still strive to be the first to pioneer new operations, even if all risk is borne by the patient. The media is complicit, blazoning the first partial face transplant in headlines a decade ago, when surgeons reconstructed a dog-mauled patient's face. But less heralded was the fact that sadly she died just ten years later at 49 from cancer many claimed was caused by the anti-rejection drug cocktail.

It's not that surgeons ever wish ill on their patients, be it your mother, a race horse or a cheetah. Surgeons perform surgery – but perhaps even when this is not what is best for the patient. The fact that I love surgery – the absolute focus, the clarity of mind, getting lost in a bubble of absolute mindfulness, while using my hands to perform microscopic technical movements – makes me, like other surgeons, a danger to my patients. We have had to find ways to protect patients, with one of the best derived from the plight of a World War II bomber 80 years ago.

The surgeon's checklist

The Boeing B-17 Flying Fortress was superior to competitors' planes as it auditioned for a lucrative contract approaching World War II. But on a demonstration flight, the highly experienced pilots forgot to disengage a crucial flight control lock, and the aircraft fatally plummeted to the ground. Boeing lost the contract. Aircraft had become incredibly complex in the thirty years since the first flights at Kitty Hawk. There was simply too much for pilots to reliably remember. As a result of the accident, Boeing developed a pre-flight checklist to prevent mistakes, and the B-17 went on to be the second most produced American bomber of all time. Checklists became an essential component of the safe air travel we have today.

Surgery was very slow in trying to protect patients from

doctors. It was only a little over a decade ago that the World Health Organization started to tackle unsafe surgery using a checklist that was far simpler than those pilots used. It was initially ridiculed, as it was claimed surgery was more complex than flying an airplane. Yet even when staff didn't believe in it, the death rate halved, and complications decreased by a third; a massive improvement. I have used checklists for a decade, for keyhole surgery in a bale monkey in Ethiopia, a bear with a paralysed tongue in Myanmar, and a chimpanzee needing a leg fracture repair in Sierra Leone. The checklist runs through discussing things that may go wrong, how long the operation is expected to last, concerns from the anaesthetist, who is giving the painkillers, and, most importantly of all, the list gets everyone to introduce themselves. Unfortunately, there is usually a hierarchy in an operating theatre, with the surgeon traditionally at the top of this. But for a good outcome everyone has different roles to play, and needs to act as a team. Since I am constantly travelling to new places, the introduction is perhaps the most important part of my whole checklist. In many developing countries, staff would otherwise never dare raise concerns with someone they feel is senior. Yet telling jokes during introductions can later be life-saving, when a worker in Sierra Leone has the courage to point out I am inadvertently leaning on the infant chimpanzee's chest beneath the drapes and hindering its breathing, while I am drilling screws into a broken bone. Without this vital all-eyes-on-deck approach, the patient risks becoming a preventable fatality. A single sheet of paper, with a few ticks, can improve surgical outcomes far more than any fancy new instruments or wonder drugs.

Ethical reviews

Yet checklists can't protect against surgeons performing unnecessary operations. There are operations performed at a lower rate in surgeons' families than the public. So human surgeons perform operations they would never have done on themselves. I can't compare the rate of surgery in my kids to macaque monkeys, no matter how badly behaved my children, but wildlife surgery also carries risks the checklist can't mitigate. A surgical checklist could not have prevented the most catastrophic operation of modern times. Started on two chimpanzees named Becky and Lucy, it won a Nobel prize, and was even performed on US President John F Kennedy's sister. But before its demise, the lobotomy ended up being performed just using ice-picks hammered into the corner of a patient's eyelids without any anaesthesia. Hundreds of thousands suffered this brutal operation, designed to sever connections in the brain's frontal lobes and in theory make life better for the mentally unstable. Even small children were victims for as little reason as being noisy and hyperactive; as normal kids are.

Ethical review committees now try to protect patients from dangerous mavericks, getting non-surgeons to review proposals. My doctorate research demonstrated that many published wildlife surgery papers were centred on some novelty, whether a new procedure, instrument, or approach, and the reported complication rate of only 2 per cent is highly unlikely to represent any surgical reality I am aware of. Just as surgeons have been said to bury our failures, we also don't tend to publish them. This is human nature, but in the tiny field of wildlife surgery it has horribly biased the published literature. I have a group of human surgeons and other non-surgical colleagues to review some of my difficult cases, to ensure I am not putting patients at risk from any misplaced enthusiasm.

Ethical review may help prevent you inadvertently harming an eagle with an unproven prosthetic leg implant, but it can't help you improve your own operation outcomes as an individual surgeon. During my research I questioned young vet students, before any of them had ever undertaken any hands-on surgery. Asked to predict what they thought their surgical skills would be like compared to their classmates five years after graduating, almost all thought they would be above

189

average surgeons, with less than 4 per cent thinking they may not be. The laws of statistics make this impossible. Other studies have shown that 80 per cent of drivers believe they are better than average, which probably goes some way towards explaining many traffic accidents. We all tend to think we are better at things than we are.

Asked what would most improve their own surgical results, most vet students chose being mentored by an experienced surgeon, attending workshops, reading books or watching surgery videos. Yet this misses something crucial. Being able to perform more technically challenging operations doesn't necessarily mean you are a better surgeon. You may simply have found new and more complicated ways to maim and injure more patients, whether squirrel monkeys or people.

The only way to improve your own surgery is to audit your own surgery cases. Sitting down and calculating the percentage of your operations that had complications is always depressing. It is humbling to realise just how many cases hadn't gone as well as hoped or expected. But realising that you have had more infections after operating on orphaned grey seal pup eyes this year, or that your fracture repair in a short-clawed otter didn't work, means you can try to find out why, and make changes to continually improve what you do. It makes you hesitate before considering any potentially reckless intervention. It keeps it real. Surgical results are a pot of gold at the end of the rainbow you can never reach, but whatever your starting level as a surgeon you can always improve. Not only for yourself, but for your patients.

When, and when not, to operate

Yet the more experienced we get the less likely we are to feel we need to audit, use checklists, or ask colleagues on an ethics committee. One surprising finding of my research, was that most highly experienced specialist surgeons, even human surgeons, often achieved no better results with wildlife patients than anyone else. Specialist dog or horse surgeons have sometimes operated on wolves or zebras in zoos with disappointing results. When one giant panda started rolling around the floor with severe pain, top human surgeons were called in to look inside via keyhole surgery. They explained the gallbladder looked inflamed, a common problem in humans, and they meticulously dissected the gallbladder without a single drop of blood. But the panda died two days later. As with many giant panda cases, there was a twisted gut, which, unrecognised, had killed the panda. No matter how technically brilliant, the wrong operation can't cure any patient. The most valuable skill is not technical ability. It is decision-making that is most crucial to how a patient will do. While almost any surgeon knows how to operate, good surgeons know when to operate, and most importantly, when not to lift a scalpel at all.

When I was asked as a last resort to operate on a wild Sumatran orangutan who had undergone six failed previous operations, I hesitated. Shot 66 times, and blind in one eye, after falling from a high tree in the forest he had developed a rectal prolapse that had resisted all previous surgical attempts at repair by highly skilled veterinarians. We all agreed this would be the last operation he would be put through. If it didn't work he sadly couldn't be returned to the wild, but would have to spend the remaining decades of his life being cared for in the sanctuary. Discussing the case with experienced human surgeons, including my friend Peter Sedman who was the president of the Association of Laparoscopic Surgeons, we thought previous failures may have been from approaching this in light of the fact that most animals walk on four legs. An orangutan in the trees was actually more like an upright human, with different pressures and strains. We discussed different procedures and risks, before settling on a simple operation called the Delorme's procedure. Least invasive, as only performed on the prolapse rather than needing abdominal surgery, it had the lowest likely complication rate. Simple as the procedure was, and keen as I was to help the orangutan, I wasn't the person for the job. Peter, having done hundreds before, did the surgery. Head vet Yenny sent us a video months later of the orangutan's return to the wild, racing up a tall tree before blowing loud raspberries of disgust at those who had so selflessly cared for him. A most unappreciative patient, but all worthwhile.

There is a learning curve to wildlife surgery. When I started performing keyhole surgical gallbladder removals in rescued moon bears in Vietnam, about 7 per cent, or one in 13 patients, would get a minor complication, such as a small gap developing in one of the tiny wounds. Considering I was performing surgery on a stone table with few resources or equipment, I was happy with this. I realised this was mainly in cases just before winter, when bears were fattest before hibernating, and was able to improve this over the next few years. Encouraged, I believed with this low complication rate I could teach the wildlife vets in Vietnam and Cambodia to do the operation themselves. I started by teaching a much simpler operation, just taking a tiny liver biopsy from rescued bile farm bears with liver disease via keyhole surgery. But despite the procedure's simplicity we had a 28 per cent complication rate, affecting more than one in four bears. We now know it takes more than 80 operations for vets to become competent and safe in even one simple keyhole operation in dogs. Sadly, my expectations had been unrealistic.

Difficult as it is to get vets to use patient protection measures, I despair that loads of wildlife surgery is still not even performed by vets at all. And not from some desperate goodwill to save an animal in a remote location in an emergency. No, most non-vet wildlife surgery is pre-meditated months in advance, by research biologists. Reading yet another newspaper article on biologists inserting radio transmitters into the abdomens of everything from rattlesnakes to polar bears is depressing. Some genuinely believe a two-day course has adequately prepared them, yet concede they wouldn't want the hospital's IT manager doing their wife's caesarean section after similar training. Opening a polar bear or a rattlesnake and inserting a radio tracker may appear a simple procedure, when taught in a day. But knowing how to handle a bleeding slash in the snake's liver or punctured hole in the bear's intestine you have inadvertently made, is not. In these cases, the patient is doomed to die. Incredibly, as part of their studies, some biologists are happy catching flat-backed turtles on a boat, and performing surgery to identify their sex without any anaesthesia before releasing them back into the ocean. Their claims of the turtles appearing to be fine are ludicrous, as we simply don't know whether or not this is the case.

Surgical speed

Before the advent of modern surgery and anaesthesia, surgeons went straight from autopsies in the morning to operating on ill patients in the afternoon, without changing clothes or even washing their hands. Yet sheer speed could overcome some of the infection risk. The Victorian surgeon Robert Liston, the fastest knife in the West End, had far superior surgical survival rates than other surgeons of his time despite no hygiene or anaesthesia, simply because he could amputate a leg in only two minutes, gripping the surgical knife in his teeth as he went. Liston was the pinnacle that 10,000 years of surgical expertise could reach without anaesthesia or sterility. Self-confidently, he would quip to spectators to time him, when about to start operating. Abrasive and argumentative with other surgeons, he was also deeply principled and kind and caring to even the poorest patients. His famous surgical speed was a genuine effort to make surgery safer and less painful for desperate patients. Sadly, he is now best known for supposedly performing the only operation with a 300 per cent death rate. Operating at haste, he not only amputated the patient's limb, but also several fingers of one of the assistants, and slashed the coat of a spectator. The patient and assistant died of sepsis, and the spectator supposedly of fright. Despite the story's appeal, it is highly unlikely actually to be true. Liston was also open-minded and progressive. In the last year of his life, he became the first surgeon in Europe to operate under anaesthesia, just two months after the very first anaesthetic demonstration by William Morton.

Today, anaesthesia means I have once been able to operate for almost eight hours. Yet Liston was right. Speed still makes a huge difference. Even in the cleanest theatre, the longer we operate the more bacteria are able to settle from the air and invade our hairy patient's wounds. When operating on a jaguar on a table made of straw bales, or on a capybara in a shed next to a tractor, speed definitely reduces the chances of infection. As do tiny wounds, another reason why I love endoscopic keyhole surgery for wildlife patients, with wounds smaller than a bite by a vervet monkey. It is as near to the body still being sealed closed as possible, and a hurdle to bacteria starting an infection.

Minimally invasive surgery gets even smaller than endoscopic surgery. Sometimes an entire operation can be completed via the tiny intravenous catheter normally used for a drip. We can insert a balloon to stretch a lethargic cheetah's constricted heart valve; expand a mesh stent from a catheter to help a zoo baboon with endometriosis adhesions pass urine; or screw a pacemaker lead into an ill Western lowland gorilla's heart via a vein, burying the attached small watch-sized pacemaker under the skin. Only a few problems can be treated this way. It is expensive, needing a large video X-ray fluoroscopy machine in a radiation-shielded room, with surgeons wearing lead gowns. This is not possible in the field, but sometimes an option for valuable animals in a city zoo. My cardiologist wife Yolanda specialises in interventional radiology surgery: putting pacemakers in dying Dobermans, and blocking abnormal liver vessels in jaundiced Yorkshire terriers. Yet procedures are very rare in wildlife patients, because most of these conditions are heritable birth defects.

Fixing a cleft palate in an orphaned grey seal pup is a simple procedure, little different to the operation in a pet puppy or a young child. But perhaps not sensible in a wild seal. Healed, and returned to the wild, the seal would appear fine, but you would have missed the big picture. Your surgically altered seal will breed and pass on its genes. Its babies will have a cleft palate, or pass the hidden genes around the population. Most seal pups born with a cleft palate would never be found by people. Living in the sea, a cleft palate is a death sentence. A seal could swim and dive, but on opening its mouth, sea water would rush through the cleft into the windpipe, drowning it. It is also impossible to catch fish, so a wild seal with a cleft palate would be destined to starve.

While an operation can harm more than the individual patient, an apparent surgical success may still not actually help the patient. Amputee elephants are a slow-motion disaster, playing out over decades. A landmine, a snare, or a collision with a truck will mangle even these behemoth limbs beyond repair. Vets can perform heroic surgery to heal the huge, mutilated stump but can miss the bigger picture. No wild elephant can survive a missing limb. Being so colossal, elephants can't jump. They can't even really limp, making it difficult to know when they are in pain. Perhaps rescued as an infant, with a leg blown off by a landmine, caring people will build him new prosthetic legs every six months while he grows, and the staff must change his prosthesis twice a day, to prevent a pressure sore on the stump. But when puberty arrives, his testosterone will surge to 50 times normal during musth. An intelligent, sexually frustrated patient weighing several tonnes is extremely dangerous. Eventually, he will likely kill one of his carers while they try to change his prosthesis. Or if everyone is afraid to change his peg leg regularly, he will eventually get an infected pressure sore and die of sepsis. Sadly, this may take decades to play out. So, even if the initial surgical wounds healed perfectly, was that operation a success?

When is a life worth living? It is a question human and veterinary surgeons all too frequently forget to ask. Are an extra few weeks for a gorilla with terminal cancer really worth the pain a torturous operation will provide? While I have removed tumours from mousedeer as well as giant pandas, there is always a risk despite one's best efforts that the cancer has already spread invisibly. But I would never put a patient through surgery unless there was a very high likelihood of a complete cure. An endangered Hainan gibbon swinging through the trees is not contemplating the sad state of the world, or his species' looming extinction. He lives in the moment, something modern humans strive for with expensive yoga retreats, mindfulness meditation, or Mandala colouring books. Whether he lives another month or another decade doesn't concern him now. But however long my hairy patient has to live, if I mistakenly choose to fight time, unasked, on his behalf, I can risk just filling his entire existence in the 'now' with pain he cannot understand. It is a responsibility to decide when to fight battles our patients have never chosen, on their behalf.

It can also be surprising what can heal without any surgery. Tawny owls hitting car windscreens, or a pink-footed goose colliding with a wind turbine, often break their coracoid. Not a bone us humans have, it acts like an aircraft strut, propping up the wing when flying. This is a difficult bone to operate on, wide but thin on one end, and buried deep beneath the flight muscles. Even in the best surgeon's hands, less than half heal well enough for a feathered patient ever to fly again. Yet if you instead simply rest birds in a small cage for two weeks with painkillers, three-quarters will be flying perfectly three weeks later, and can return to the wild. Surgery actually yields far worse results than doing nothing. We even successfully healed broken arms and legs in rescued orangutans and chimpanzees early in the coronavirus pandemic, when no surgery was possible. Surgery can reduce pain and speed healing, but as thousands of years of evolution has ensured, this is not always necessary, despite what we may think. In one case, even an adult bull elephant's open thigh bone fracture healed on its own. But as it took over a year, we could possibly have done better. I was working with my friend Sam Miller at Braun to re-engineer a forgotten system used to fix a few elephant fractures in Uganda when Idi Amin was in power; elephant fractures that have no hope of healing on their own. But we can't forget that the body is designed to heal itself, and we are only helping. We should only interfere surgically when sure we will make a meaningful difference and save the patient from pain.

While sticks and stones may break even an elephant's bones, we can thankfully fix fractures in patients from sparrows to giraffes using the latest locking plates, or just bicycle spokes and car repair putty. And sometimes things heal without any surgery at all. Amazingly, a few years after removing the metal work there will be no difference at all in the bone's strength from before it was broken. Yet if bone is a surgeon's favourite tissue, healing with no scars or weakness, there is an even harder tissue in the body. But this tissue often has no healing capacity, and its treatment is a real pain, as we will see next.

Big cats are prone to breaking the tips of their teeth, leading to painful exposed tooth pulp cavities. Root canal treatments clean out and seal the canal, stopping pain and infection, and protect the remaining tooth, so it can continue to function in the mouth for eating.

11

Hippopotamus dentistry with an angle grinder

A hippopotamus with toothache is not a great patient. The third-largest land mammal, with a notoriously grumpy disposition, they kill more people every year in Africa than crocodiles, lions or elephants. Toothache can make a snow leopard starve, or reduce even hardened mercenaries to tears. I remember little of one rainforest expedition, when on cracking a tooth I could only focus on getting to the end of the trip, despite frequently applying clove oil as local anaesthetic. Little wonder that a common hippopotamus is a nightmarish dental appointment.

In our privileged ignorance of widely available dental treatment, we can forget how seriously ill an animal can become with a painful tooth. Wolves with periodontitis, inflammation of their gums, which sounds minor and is easily overlooked, are at increased risk of kidney disease and deadly heart valve problems. The low-grade inflammation and occasional circulating bacteria can have disastrous consequences for the heart. Little cauliflower bacterial growths distort the thin smooth valves, which no longer meet and close properly. If these valves become sufficiently leaky, the wolf develops heart failure: all from what simply appears to be slightly redder gums. There are also reports of this in chimpanzees, a reminder that not brushing your teeth can be more serious than just causing repulsive breath.

In 1832, well before the advent of general anaesthesia, an adult lion and a tiger-lion hybrid in a private menagerie each had a tooth extracted by a Mr C S Rowlands, a dentist. The article reported keepers having such good control of the animals, they were not even tied down for the extractions. This is almost certainly nonsense. The poor cats were likely extremely ill, septic with circulating bacteria and toxins from infected teeth, and close to death, rather than being mastered by the men. No one alive today would ever contemplate extracting an adult lion's tooth without any anaesthesia, considering they can weigh more than four times the average man. Mr Rowlands must have been made of stern stuff indeed.

Teeth are not similar structures in all animals, just with different shapes. Our species' strategy of just one lifelong set of adult teeth appears a poor evolutionary choice, considering our frequent visits to the dentist. But then grey seals actually shed their milk teeth while still in the womb. By the time they are born they already have their only set of adult teeth for their whole life ahead. Not ideal, but then, unlike us, they don't subsist on jam doughnuts. How much better if your teeth grew continuously like a hairy-nosed wombat's, perhaps? Even teeth erupting into the mouth is not the only strategy. Golden babirusa, or deer-pigs from Indonesia, have long upper canine tusks that bizarrely erupt vertically, through their long nose, and penetrate the skin over their snout, before curling backwards over their face – the ultimate piercings – making them resemble some bizarre pig-rhino-unicorn hybrid.

You may imagine at least all teeth have enamel on the outside and dentine inside. But elephants' back teeth not only erupt forwards from the back corner of their mouths, but also consist of upright plates of enamel and dentine. Wearing at different rates makes a rough abrasive surface for grinding the huge quantities of fibrous plant food they consume. Plates flake off at the front of the mouth, aided by the teeth erupting forwards. Even more strangely, while mammoths had six sets of teeth, just like elephants, mastodons, which seem very similar, had a single set of adult teeth, with large cusps, just like those of pigs, hence their name means 'nipple-tooth'. Patagonian mara, rodents resembling a strange cross between a rabbit, a wallaby and a guinea pig, also have back teeth with ridges of enamel and dentine to grind their grass diet before swallowing. As rhinos are also a large grass-grazing herbivore, do they have the same teeth as elephants? Not at all. Their teeth instead look like bigger versions of horses' teeth.

In the Victorian era there was an explosion in the number of zoos and private menageries, and in the keeping of exotic pets, and hence animals to study. Combined with advances in human medicine and dentistry, this fostered an interest in comparative dentition. A major book on comparative tooth anatomy was published in 1845 by Sir Richard Owen, the director of the Natural History Museum, which is still useful reading today.

Different animal teeth determine the type of problem, and which treatments will work. Dolphins, orcas, and crocodiles have teeth that are basically all the same shape. But if your feeding is very rough, replacing them is a good strategy. Crocodiles spin around to rip pieces off their drowned prey. While their teeth all have the same basic design, they are constantly replaced through the tooth socket vertically. Human dentistry would never have evolved if we had similar dentition.

Constantly laying down calcium and minerals in these ever-forming teeth can give us health clues we would never get in other animals. We occasionally see crocodiles with pale blue-green teeth, letting us know it has swallowed something copper, which it is now laying down in the newly forming teeth. The culprit is often coins. In zoos, this is from visitors throwing money into the pool. I have yet to encounter a crocodile pool resembling the Trevi Fountain or ye olde wishing well, but to some, wishing upon a crocodile apparently appears a viable alternative to Pinocchio's star. Crocodiles losing teeth more rapidly than normal can also alert us to vitamin A and E deficiencies before other symptoms develop.

While crocodiles' teeth erupt vertically from beneath an

old tooth, a Komodo dragon's teeth come in sideways, from behind the old tooth. The most extreme tooth replacement strategy belongs to sharks, which shed teeth so frequently they constantly have numerous rows of replacement teeth on the go, and an extremely toothy smile.

Many animals have differently shaped teeth that evolved for different purposes. Humans are a pretty poor example, but chacma baboons have long canines, impressive enough weapons to chase a leopard away if they catch it trying to creep up on the troop. As a child I watched the big males repeatedly yawn, to display their status to other baboons. Some animals have sequential erupting teeth, such as manatees, and elephants, whose teeth erupt from the back of the mouth to the front. Red kangaroos are similar. Their teeth also erupt from the back of their jaw to slowly drift forwards in the mouth, eventually to be shed from the front row of back teeth. It is bizarre that a kangaroo tooth is strong and stable enough to take the huge forces of grinding dried grasses, yet float like a cork in the bones of the jaw over months in ultraslow motion. This results in some unique problems. Kangaroos are prone to a condition called lumpy jaw, where soil bacteria growing where there is no oxygen invade the jaw bone via the tiny gaps between the teeth. Unlike when humans get a tooth infection via a cavity, in kangaroos this happens in reverse. The jaw infection invades the roots of the teeth, making them infected and loose. While extracting a kangaroo's tooth is not difficult, it causes problems. With a sudden gap in the jaw, the neighbouring teeth drift and change position. The opposite tooth, with nothing to wear it down, starts to form a sharp spike that can lacerate a kangaroo's tongue until it is simply too painful to eat, and the unfortunate kangaroo starves to death.

Animals eating large quantities of abrasive food, whether a plains zebra or a banteng, need strong ridges of enamel and dentine to grind their food, and their teeth are long, gradually wearing down over their lifespan. How much better if you have continuously growing teeth, constantly replacing the worn away surface. Beavers are the ultimate gnawing machines, and use their front incisors like a Swiss army knife for all sorts of purposes beside eating. Cheek pads fit behind the incisors, preventing chewed wood entering the mouth while constructing their dams. These front teeth grow throughout their lives. To keep a sharp chisel edge, they have thick enamel only on the front, which wears away more slowly than the back portions of the teeth. Some animals only have back teeth that continuously grow, such as the aardvark, to grind up its diet of ants. Although ants are tiny, they have abrasive exoskeletons of chitin that wear down teeth. Perhaps this is a subtle defence mechanism, waging a slow war against its predator's teeth and shortening their lives. Other ant-consumers like tamandua have solved the problem differently. They have got rid of teeth entirely, relying on their stomachs to digest and grind up ants and termites. A small number of animals have both front and back teeth that grow lifelong. Northern hairy-nosed wombats have constantly growing incisors, as do beavers, but their back teeth also grow lifelong, replacing any worn-away parts. Endangered short-tailed chinchillas also need constantly growing teeth to cope with their dry grass diet. Plants growing in the silica soils of the Andes wear down teeth somewhat like chewing on sandpaper. Despite their diminutive size, chinchillas can live for almost two decades. If their food is not abrasive enough in captivity they develop serious dental problems, with overgrown teeth painfully cutting into their tongue and cheeks.

The different dental problems are not just related to tooth structure, but also animals' lifestyle and behaviour. Elephants use their tusks as crowbars, so it is of no surprise that they are prone to break or crack. Many rampaging killer elephants have been discovered suffering from long-term dental pain, so their bad temper then makes much more sense. Ten tonnes of bad mood and tooth pain is a tremendous force of destruction.

Walruses are another unique patient. Their tusks are easily damaged in captivity, because in the wild their behaviour is to dredge up the soft sediment on the seafloor looking for clams with their sensitive beard of highly innervated vibrissae whiskers. In a concrete pool, they simply wear through the enamel on their tusks. Unfortunately, their dentine is full of fine channels for nerve endings, as they use their sensitive teeth when feeding on the ocean floor. Once the thin protective enamel layer is breeched, bacteria easily invade through the porous dentine and set up an infection in their sensitive pulp. Because root canal treatment won't work in constantly growing tusks, if the pulp becomes infected and dies, the tusk usually has to be extracted. This would be nerve-racking enough without the horrible risks of the long anaesthetic needed. There is a pretty high risk of a dead walrus by about halfway through a tusk extraction. To try and prevent this, zoo walrus tusks are often capped with titanium or cobalt chrome metal tips to protect them, making them look like an obese hip-hop artist wearing metal tooth grills.

Walruses use their tusks to keep breathing holes open in the ice, as well as to help haul out their huge flabby bodies. Males also use tusks for status display, a marine mammal version of peacock tails, deer antlers, or the human equivalent of a convertible sports cars. Walrus tusks are their elongated canine teeth, just like warthog tusks. Elephant tusks instead are actually their incisors – the most extreme 'rabbit-teeth' in the animal kingdom.

Although prehistoric sabre-toothed cats no longer exist, the closest present-day equivalent is the clouded leopard. A medium-sized Asian cat, they have the longest upper canines for their skull size of any living carnivore. Despite their size, these massive canines are surprisingly delicate, and easily broken. Annoyingly, their pulp cavity is very close to the tooth tip, so even a tiny chip is more serious than for many other carnivores, and usually needs root canal treatment. Why on earth have huge canines for killing prey, but then have sensitive nerves close to the tip, making the tooth more fragile? A strong bite is enough to snap a tooth entirely, and so by having sensitive teeth, clouded leopards can apply just the right amount of force to a victim's neck, without inadvertently breaking a tooth.

Big cats, whether Amur leopards, jaguars or Bengal tigers, are frequently afflicted with broken teeth when kept in captivity. This happens in even relatively tame individuals. Cats often communicate displeasure by giving a warning bite to another cat. Their teeth are designed by evolution for biting soft tissue, which yields. When a puma gives a brief warning bite to tell someone to back off from their food, but is behind metal bars, things go wrong. The biting force these predators can generate will easily break a tooth when striking a hard, unyielding steel cage bar. One in five critically endangered Amur leopards kept in zoos for conservation breeding has dental problems, and dental disease is the most common illness in captive jaguars. Modern enclosures may appear to have no metal bars, but the night quarters where keepers work in proximity to dangerous animals always have some form of steel bars or rigid mesh, and this is usually where tooth smashing occurs. There isn't an easy solution, unless someone invents soft spongy bars that can still keep an angry jaguar in an enclosure, which seems unlikely anytime soon.

Most Asian black bears rescued from bile farms in Vietnam and Laos that I treat also have numerous damaged teeth. Their damage comes from years of frustrated biting at the tiny coffin-like crates they live in, rather than the furious defensive bites we see in leopards. Wild foxes, coyotes and jackals also break their teeth trying to escape snares or horrendous foot-hold traps. Even cage traps, used to fit satellite collars on lynx, or relocate African painted wolves, can result in broken teeth as the trapped animals try to chew their way to freedom. Living a completely wild life isn't protective of dental disease. A fifth of wild Swedish lynx have complex canine fractures, not that dissimilar to those in captivity, while over 80 per cent of wild endangered Iberian lynx are affected by periodontal disease.

If a clouded leopard in a Western zoo has only broken the tip of one of its impressive canines, a specialist dentist can try to save the remaining part of the tooth by performing a root canal. A root canal, or endodontic treatment, removes the tooth's pulp, filled with nerves and blood vessels, which is invariably infected in the animals we deal with. The empty space is then sterilised and filled. It is less traumatic than removing an entire tooth, with the benefit of keeping the tooth for the patient to use. But endodontics can be complicated, require long anaesthetics, and need monitoring. They may need repeated repairs or develop problems, and so are not always the solution for a lynx returning to the wild, never to be seen again. If most of the tooth has snapped off, extracting the tooth may be best.

Human dentistry appeared almost 14,000 years ago, yet Neanderthals had already been using rudimentary dental tools over 100,000 years earlier. Despite dentistry's long history, there are still few ways of healing teeth. Japanese scientists have actually recently managed to grow a replacement mouse tooth from stem cells in a mould, and successfully re-implant it back in a mouse. It does raise the exciting possibility of one day replacing a clouded leopard's smashed tooth with a new one grown from stem cells in a mould. But for now, much dentistry in wildlife patients simply involves removing the offending tooth.

Extracting a tooth can be far from easy. An elderly African golden wolf's periodontal ligament, attaching the tooth root to the jaw bone socket, can become calcified; the tooth root and jaw bone fuse into one solid mass. Elderly animals may have osteoporotic jaw bones, so just when a tooth is the most difficult to remove, the jaw is weakest and easily broken. Dental instruments for humans or pets are also too flimsy to remove a sun bear's broken canine. The smallest and most hyperactive bear species, resembling a cross between a chimpanzee and a large rottweiler, sun bears have larger stronger canine teeth than polar bears weighing almost ten times as much. Together with their huge claws, they rip apart wood looking for grubs and honey, which they love. Bears, like big cats, pose a dental challenge. To support their large canines, the root is larger than the tooth. It is impossible to simply extract one of these teeth, as the root is wider than the tooth you can see in the mouth, and so cannot exit the socket. You have to actually remove bone surrounding the tooth.

In a Western zoo, with anaesthetists, time and specialist high-speed diamond burrs, we can cut a flap in the gum and remove the bone over the side covering the tooth, before lifting the tooth out sideways. But a decade ago, when I was helping Cambodian wildlife vets treat confiscated sun bears with teeth broken and painful for years, something more basic but robust was needed. Making the gum flap by the light of a wind-up torch, we would use a small wood chisel from the local market to carefully remove the overlying bone instead. Over the last decade, those vets have become far faster at removing rotten bear teeth than I can ever be, at what is now the largest sun bear rescue centre in the world.

You may imagine a lion's bite to be stronger than a bear's, but if you try to remove a tooth in the same way you can easily break a lion's jaw. While only eating grubs, a sun bear's jaw needs to rip through thick wood to get to them. A lion's teeth appear impressive, but the main way they kill most prey is actually by suffocation, and you don't need nearly as strong a jaw bone for that.

The most dangerous and challenging wild dental patient isn't a tiger with toothache, a crocodile with a cracked tooth, or even a venomous Gaboon viper needing an extraction. It is probably the common hippopotamus. And the first hippo dental extraction was on the most famous hippo that ever lived.

Obaysch was the first hippopotamus seen in Europe since ancient Rome, and the first hippo in Britain since prehistory. Captured as a young calf on an island in the Nile, from which he took his name, he was bizarrely swapped by the Viceroy of Egypt with some other 'exotic' animals, to the British Consul General, for two deerhounds and four greyhounds. He was sent down the Nile by boat with a herd of cows to provide fresh milk, then shipped by steamer to Britain, arriving at London Zoo on 25 May 1850.

The Zoological Society of London Zoo had been in financial crisis for years, and the council felt a spectacular beast was needed to attract crowds. The society's president, the Earl of Derby, had his own exotic animal collection at Knowsley, now a famous safari park, but it still took years of planning to finally secure a hippo. Obaysch was a sensation, considering how little attention hippos now warrant during a zoo visit, and London Zoo's visitor numbers doubled. Even Queen Victoria came to see him. Obaysch was the giant panda of his day.

He was so valuable, that when he escaped his enclosure after chewing through a gate post, the zoo superintendent asked the elephant keeper, whom Obaysch hated, to act as bait to lure him back into the hippo house. The keeper happily ran in front of the angry 1.5 tonne charging hippo, taunting him, to get him back in the house. The same keeper would a few years later look after the most famous animal ever at London Zoo, Jumbo the Elephant. I can't imagine what a zoo health and safety officer would think of this technique if suggested now.

The zoo superintendent, Abraham Dee Bartlett, did not particularly liked the hippo, which he referred to as an 'uncouth and powerful amphibious monster'. However, he performed the first recorded hippo tooth extraction, in another equally dangerous situation. Obaysch, now massive and 24 years old, had broken a tooth, and Bartlett had 60 centimetre long iron forceps specially made. After a few attempts at grasping the tooth, performed while Obaysch charged open-jawed and tried to mash him through the bars, Bartlett finally succeeded. The hippo was so angry that he smashed the brickwork holding the steel gate, and Bartlett just about escaped without being killed. While gas anaesthesia had recently been discovered and even used in a few bears at the zoo, no attempt was made to anaesthetise Obaysch. He was just too strong and dangerous to try restraining and administering any foul-smelling anaesthetic gas. Even today, hippo anaesthesia is a stressful job. Their thick blubber makes darted drug absorption unpredictable, with the fluctuating worry of them either waking and trying to kill everyone, or stopping breathing and you having to jump up and down on their chest, which is the only way resuscitation can be performed in such a large animal.

Bartlett can also lay claim to the other most dangerous dental procedure ever undertaken without anaesthesia. While at London Zoo, the celebrity elephant Jumbo developed two painful impacted tusks. The stumps had started growing into his cheeks instead of out of his mouth, forming large painful swellings. Bartlett used a long metal pole with a big sharp hook to lance the swelling on one side of Jumbo's face, while he was chained up. It is incredible that Bartlett wasn't trampled to death. He then proceeded to repeat the stunt on the other side of the elephant's face two weeks later. Examining Jumbo's back teeth after his death, researchers found them distorted from his soft food diet. Unrecognised tooth pain caused the grumpy periods the elephant was known for during his time at London Zoo. The zoo authorities, who feared he would kill someone, were forced to sell him to P T Barnum despite public outrage.

Dentistry can be cruelly misused. For decades, wild macaques and baboons caught for laboratory experiments were 'disarmed' by having their canines cut off. This cruel practice is still widespread in illegally caught and endangered slow lorises sold as exotic pets. These small nocturnal primates are appealing with their large eyes. As terrified wild-caught lorises will bite, their tiny front teeth are cut off with nail clippers. The open pulp cavities are painful, and often become infected. Lorises frequently die of sepsis as a consequence. A tiny, slow-moving creature weighing under a kilogram hardly seems a threat. But slow lorises are uniquely the only venomous primates. Secretions from a gland on their arms combined with saliva makes their venom. Besides acting as an insect repellent on their fur, the venom causes painful, slow-healing wounds. Only in a single recorded case has someone died, likely due to an allergic reaction. While fear is sufficient to cause their dental mutilation, it is not sufficient to stop their rampant illegal trade, which has decimated populations.

Things are worse if you are a venomous snake. Cutting, breaking, or ripping off venom-injecting teeth won't work, as replacement teeth can erupt just days later. Sipping mint tea in Morocco, I watched snake charmers trying to fleece tourists who were happy to pay for a novel holiday photo. Unbeknown to them, the poor snakes had their mouths sewn shut. After dying of starvation, they were simply replaced with another wild trapped snake. Venom gland removal surgery has been performed by researchers, some zoos, and even by snake-keeping hobbyists, who may like the idea of owning a venomous snake but not the actual reality of it being venomous. Some veterinarians will still perform this large painful surgery, but in many countries it is simply the snake-keepers themselves who do it, happy to perform kitchen table surgery without anaesthesia. Sadly, this cruel practice is still legal in some countries.

No teeth? No problem

What about dentistry in animals that don't have any teeth? A blue-and-gold macaw's beak is strong enough to open a can, although it prefers the huge woody fruit of Brazil nut trees, whose seeds we mistakenly call nuts. If it breaks its upper beak, it can starve. The same can happen with the beak-like mouth of an alligator snapping turtle. Like their namesake, they have been known to eat young alligators, not to mention removing veterinarians' fingers. Beaks present their own challenges. A broken beak is just as painful as a fractured tooth. Birds have many nerves in their beaks: to feel what they are holding, and apply sufficient pressure to open a nut, but not so much as to damage their beak. Sacred ibis and little spotted kiwi have especially sensitive nerves at their beak tips that can sense underground movements of small animals they aren't even touching. But losing the tip of their beak is like going blind, and they can starve.

Beaks consist of keratin overlying bone. In snapping turtles the bone is solid and thick, while in toucans and most birds, to keep it lightweight for flight, the underlying bone is more like a scaffolding of thin bone struts. A toco toucan's beak is featherlight, paper thin, and so delicate it could be crushed with two fingers. They are a nightmare to repair. Most attempts to repair toucan beaks using small screws, wires, fibreglass, or 3D-printed prosthetic beaks invariably fail, as there is little underlying bone to attach it to. Lacking nerves, the bird can't control the force it applies to the prosthesis, making it likely to snap off. Even those that do succeed are never robust enough to be used in the wild, so affected toucans need to remain in captivity for the rest of their lives. Repairing a turtle's beak is perhaps easier, as the hard underlying bone is better able to hold metal pins and screws, and once healed the bone is as strong as before. However, the considerable force they apply when biting is still a challenge. Tortoise and turtle beaks are bone overlaid with keratin plates, very similar to their shell, and we use the same techniques to repair them both.

One condition that predisposes turtles, from alligator snappers to common mud turtles a hundred times smaller, to mouth problems is metabolic bone disease. If a turtle does not get enough calcium in its diet, or insufficient ultraviolet light exposure for its skin to make vitamin D to help absorb the calcium from its diet, then its bones gradually become soft and rubbery. Rare in nature, it is a common problem in captive turtles. Then muscles that normally open the beak slowly distort the pliable jaw. The lower jaw becomes shorter than the top jaw, and the upper beak then keeps overgrowing if not trimmed. In severe cases, the jaw can completely crumple. Because the bones are so weak, metal implants are useless initially, and it can take many months of feeding, vitamin D and calcium treatment, via a feeding tube in the neck, before the bones are sturdy enough for any surgical repair with screws or pins, if this is even possible.

Wires are not just useful for parrots or turtles with damaged beaks; they can also be used for giraffes. Wires are ideal to fix the most serious dental problem a giraffe can get: a broken jaw. A zoo giraffe startled while eating from a hay rack can snap its lower jaw on both sides by rapidly moving its head sideways while its mouth is still between the metal bars of the hay rack. Seeing a distressed giraffe, lower jaw dangling, and tongue lolling out pouring saliva in pain, is horrible. Using strong metal plates and screws, as we would for a broken leg, is not an option. Drilling screws through the jaw would destroy the tooth roots, nerves and vessels. We use wire inside the mouth, twisted carefully between the teeth and tightening it with pliers, similar to tightening a fence, to hold the broken jaw bones tightly together. It is pretty fulfilling to watch a giraffe awaken from anaesthesia to explore its mouth with its tongue and realise it can eat again.

Sadly, sometimes there is simply nothing we can do, no matter how endangered or valuable an animal is. An elephant with no teeth remaining is just not compatible with life. Teeth seem like an innate biological clock in many species, reminding us we have a finite lifespan.

Dental problems frequently pose a quandary for vets rehabilitating injured animals for return to the wild. A Bengal fox has the tips of two canines missing. Hardly noticeable, but probing with a fine needle, the root canal is open. Now you are stuck. The teeth's nerves and blood vessels are exposed, painful, and risk infection. Root canals, even if they didn't need a specialist dentist, hours of anaesthesia and expense, may not be sturdy enough to last for several years. Once back in the wild, it is impossible to know if a problem occurs. Root canals are usually only possible in zoos and sanctuaries, where animals can be monitored. Yet if you extract the fox's two teeth to solve that problem, it may not be able to kill prey, or defend itself against another fox. It is frustrating that such small structures are so vital yet so problematic. I must admit I am happier to see a broken leg, as I can usually fix this with no future problems, rather than a broken tooth, which I can never fix as well.

The biggest dental challenge

So what remains the ultimate wild dental challenge? It would have to be treating the tusk of a narwhal. The real source of the fabled unicorn's horn, its purpose was long uncertain. It was guessed to be for fighting, breaking breathing holes in the sea ice, or even to harpoon fish.

The narwhal tusk is actually its elongated left upper canine tooth. Occasionally a right canine is found, and about one in 500 narwhals have two tusks. While males all have tusks, only one in seven females will grow a tusk. The tusk always spirals to the left, even in the rare cases of double tusks. It is a truly impressive tooth, reaching over two and a half metres in length. Like other species' tusks, it is not covered in enamel. Uniquely in narwhals, the dentine is covered over the whole tooth's length by cementum, which is softer than dentine or enamel, and normally covers the roots of other animals' teeth, joining them to the jaw bone. No-one has managed to keep narwhals alive in captivity. There were attempts in the 1960s and 70s by aquaria, but unlike their closest relatives beluga whales, the narwhals all quickly died. So why would a narwhal's tusk be the ultimate dental challenge?

Sandie Black, a friend in Canada, is probably the world's only specialist narwhal vet. For decades she has travelled to the Arctic Circle, dropped off by helicopter with a small team of researchers for a month with no outside contact, while they study wild narwhals' health. Her normal job as a head zoo vet appears challenging enough, without spending holidays in cold Arctic waters. Her team discovered that the narwhal's tusk is truly unlike any other tooth on the planet. If we have a cavity, or our enamel thins, our tooth becomes supersensitive to a cold ice cream. Even in animals, much of what we do in dentistry is to prevent the exposure of nerves in the vital tooth pulp, as this is extremely painful, and liable to cause an infection in the middle of the tooth. But, once you have cleaned algae off a narwhal's tooth, the spiral surface is finely pitted, giving the tusk a rough feel in my hands. These holes are the

213

openings for nerve endings. The narwhal, unlike every other animal, actually chooses to have its sensitive dental nerves exposed. So why do such a crazy thing? Because the narwhal's tusk is possibly more important than its eyes. While the narwhal sees its world through sonar like other whales and dolphins, it also seems to see, smell and taste its world through its unicorn horn.

The main natural risk to narwhals, like their cousin beluga whales, is being trapped by sea ice. Being salt water, the sea freezes at temperatures lower than zero degrees Celsius. But there are widely varying salinity concentrations in different patches of sea water. This poses real risks to the narwhal being caught out. We now believe that the narwhal's tusk can detect the sea water's salinity, telling them how close to the freezing point the surrounding water is. The tusk-rubbing behaviour, which even ancient Arctic mariners saw, probably has little to do with fighting most of the time. Narwhals are likely cleaning the surface of their special tooth, so essential for their survival, just as we brush ours.

We still don't know the whole picture. But some behaviours hint that the narwhal's tusk is perhaps even more interesting. Female narwhals, when they do grow a tusk, have one that is slightly different microscopically, and appears to sense things differently. Male narwhals wave their tusks in the air or under the water. We think perhaps they can detect other chemicals and molecules, perhaps food, or fertile females. Perhaps the tusk can also detect water currents. Five hundred years ago, it was postulated that the tusk was an acoustic probe, and it hasn't been disproven that it may somehow help their sonar detection. Or smell things in their surroundings. We really don't know. The fact that not all narwhals have a tusk is equally bizarre. But it is clear that the tusk is an essential sensory organ for narwhals' survival, and a broken tusk has to be the greatest challenge a dentist could face. Being a constantly growing tooth, the tusk can regrow over time. Thankfully, narwhals live in small social groups, so a narwhal with a broken tusk can rely on its friends for help in the meantime.

The narwhal is an animal more wondrous than the fabled unicorn, but with heavy metal pollution and climate change, sadly we could lose narwhals without ever truly understanding how they experience the world. They might be the planet's only animal with tooth-vision; but for animals who use their teeth for grinding their food, eating doesn't stop in the mouth. It only starts there.

Hand rearing a lion is simple, using a kitten milk replacement. Other species can be more difficult. A hooded seal's milk may have no lactose, but has as much fat as double cream, while a black rhino's milk has almost no fat compared to that of humans and domestic animals. These differences make hand rearing many wildlife species difficult.

12

Manatee junk food

For a manatee, eating lettuce is like having a double cheese-burger. This seems bizarre, as lettuce conjures visions of salads, weight-loss diets and lean healthy figures, yet for a manatee romaine lettuce is the ultimate junk food.

Florida manatees, nursed back to health in rehabilitation centres after being ripped up by boat propellers, are difficult to feed. Lettuce can encourage them to start eating. Manatees eat sea grass, but lettuce actually contains two and a half times as many calories as sea grass. I am not trying to promote sea grass as a new human health food, rather that a lettuce-based diet for manatees is actually very unhealthy. Manatees even get diabetes and heart disease if kept on lettuce for long periods. It takes over a week for food to move through a manatee's gut, so they can get every bit of nutrition from their natural diet of low-energy sea grass. Manatee metabolism is very slow, five times slower than that of most mammals, and so healing is equally slow. It can take two years of care before a Florida manatee is ready to return to the wild, and sometimes up to five years for an even slower-healing Amazonian manatee.

Feeding ill patients well is essential. Injured wild animals have much higher nutritional requirements than normal to repair their bodies and fight off infections. Things are easier if animals are living in countries where their normal food sources occur. Animals in captive breeding programmes or zoos can be more challenging to feed adequately, and even more so when we occasionally need to hide medication in their food.

Some animals are easy to bribe to start eating once they arrive at a rehabilitation centre. Badgers have a sweet tooth, and if all else fails they like nothing more than a custard cream. Once interested in those, it is easier to wean them onto a healthier, more natural mixed diet of nuts, berries and cat food while treating them. Similarly, many beavers are particularly partial to apples, orangutans to durian fruit, giant pandas to honey, and brown bears to tinned sardines, when we need to convince them to start eating, or if hiding medicines in their food.

For any possible food source there is usually an animal that has evolved to eat it. This poses a real challenge to caring for some of them. Many species, like manatees, have gradually evolved to eat poorer food sources ignored by other animals, in order to survive. Eventually, after millions of years of evolution, they become perfectly adapted. Specialist feeders depend on their diets and are very vulnerable to changes in the climate and environment that alter their niche food sources.

Omnivorous generalists like rats, pigs, macaques and humans have instead gone in the opposite direction, broadening the range of things they can eat. Feeding Bornean bearded pigs, Gambian pouched rats or Barbary macaques in captivity is relatively easy, for they will eat almost anything available. Even domestic dogs are generalist feeders. I regularly catch our rescued street dog in the compost heap, eating everything from woodlice to potato peelings before later stealing a bowl of pumpkin soup.

Specialist animals, evolved to eat niche foods neglected by other species, are much more difficult to feed. Giant pandas are bamboo eaters, consuming almost nothing else, since splitting from other bears several million years ago. They are notoriously fussy, preferring certain bamboo species' leaves, other bamboo species' stems, and to complicate matters preferring different species and plant parts in different seasons, different weather, or before the breeding season. Small changes in diet can cause dramatic abdominal cramps, or colic. Cramps can be difficult to tell apart from a twisted gut, a dramatic emergency that will be fatal in less than a day unless surgery is performed. Colic is unfortunately common in giant pandas, and stressful for those of us working with them. There is nothing worse than nervously watching a cramping giant panda, and having to decide whether painkillers are enough, or if emergency surgery may be needed. Despite insurance values similar to prize-winning race horses, unlike our equine vet colleagues we can't simply listen to their gurgling guts with our stethoscope or take their temperature easily.

Walking through a forest of giant bamboo stems, you need to remind yourself it is actually grass, not trees. Bamboos are the fastest-growing plants, able to grow centimetres in an hour, but contain few calories. Raw bamboo contains cyanide precursors, making it toxic if not cooked. Hardly an ideal food source. Biting through thick woody bamboo stems takes phenomenal chewing power, hence the massive masseter and temporal muscles that give giant pandas their appealing round faces. Bamboo species very rarely flower, sometimes taking over a hundred years to do so. When they do, there is a huge die-off of all plants of that species at the same time, no matter where on the planet they grow. It is bizarre that pandas evolved to only eat bamboo, putting themselves at dramatic risk of starvation every few generations. Yet these long flowering intervals have little to do with animals. European oak and beech trees have mast years, producing large numbers of nuts or acorns, and other years with few, usually but perhaps erroneously explained as helping control the numbers of animals eating their seeds. But bamboo, and likely oaks and beeches too, do it for a different reason. Producing fruit or seeds requires tremendous energy. If only producing seeds every few years, saving its energy for a bumper crop, it has a chance to swamp the lower number of seeds of its rivals, and is more likely to pass its genes to a new generation. Over time, this seed war selected bamboo with long periods between dramatic flowering events. Bamboo isn't trying to starve pandas; this is just a side-effect of competing with other bamboo plants for millennia.

Feeding giant pandas outside China can be complex, with cooled transport trucks from nurseries and walk-in fridges with water misters to keep bamboo fresh, all adding to the cost. Zoo curators despair at seeing pandas discard most of their bamboo uneaten when not quite to their liking. It is easier in the breeding centres in Sichuan, where fresh bamboo is cut every morning in the misty mountains above the centres and simply carried down to the hungry pandas.

Other animals, in other parts of the world, have also evolved to eat this abundant giant grass. Golden gentle lemurs are also specialist bamboo eaters. We still don't know how they daily consume what for other animals would be ten times the deadly dose of cyanide present in the fresh shoots of Madagascan giant bamboo that they eat. Watching Bale mountain monkeys on misty mornings in the Harenna Forest, to me they appear similar to their vervet and green monkey relatives common throughout Africa. But living on a single, small, isolated mountain in Ethiopia, they too have evolved into a separate species eating a diet of over 80 per cent bamboo. Seeing African forest elephants and mountain gorillas occasionally eat some bamboo, it is easy to imagine how some African green monkeys evolved to take advantage of a food others were not using in this unique site, until this small population became an entirely new species.

Specialising can also occur with a food type, rather than a specific plant. Mountain gorillas eat leaves and shoots in their home range's lush vegetation. Less than 2 per cent of their diet is fruit, but they only have to travel a few hundred metres most days to get all the nutrients they need. Eastern lowland gorillas have a more diverse diet, with fruit making up to a quarter of their diet in season. But they travel several kilometres daily to gather enough to eat. It is a fine balance between the increased energy density of fruit and the amount of energy spent to collect it.

Fruits contain energy-rich sugars, a prize for wild animals that seek them out. Over half a wild orangutan's diet is fruit, but other fruit consumers are less obvious. When I was a young vet, maned wolves in zoos were commonly afflicted by bladder stones. These always consisted of cystine. In humans, cystinuria is usually genetic, so this was investigated, and different medications tried to alter the urine pH to prevent bladder stones forming. This was all without success, until we realised that half a wild maned wolf's diet actually consisted of fruit. We were giving them way too much meat, which was causing the problem. Changing zoo diets made the problem almost completely disappear. Half a maned wolf's diet in the Brazilian Cerrado consists of lobeira, or fruta-do-lobo, meaning wolf's fruit. This tomato-like wild fruit contains low levels of alkaloid toxins: too low to affect wolves, but enough to protect them from giant kidney worm infections, which can cause fatal kidney failure.

While maned wolves turned out to mainly be fruit eaters, brown woolly monkeys need their fruit consumption restricted. There has been a strong move away from feeding much fruit to most primates in sanctuaries and zoos. While you can buy raspberries and pineapples year-round in supermarkets, even when it is snowing, wild fruit are seasonal, and only available for a few weeks a year. Two-thirds of a wild Sumatran orangutan's diet may be fruit, but they will eat over a hundred different items, also consuming everything from ants and eggs to leaves and bark. Farmed fruit is entirely different to what black-headed douroucouli would find in the wild. We have domesticated only a handful of fruit types, selectively bred to be large, full of sugar and water, and often with quite poor nutritional value. We buy fruit based on its appearance in shops, but animals naturally judge fruit by the taste and how they feel after eating it. Wild strawberries are tiny, deep crimson, soft and deliciously tart, compared to huge hard pink sugary commercial strawberries, twenty times their size.

Feeding a Sumatran orangutan patient two-thirds of its diet as fruit in a sanctuary or zoo may appear natural, but quickly results in obesity, compounded by them never being as active as in the wild. Limiting fruit to a quarter of their diet, with more vegetables, results in far healthier orangutans. Woolly monkeys, despite mainly eating fruit in the wild, can develop diabetes in a zoo on a commercial fruit diet. Even omnivorous guinea baboons that eat limited fruit in the wild will still binge on fruit if they can, like a child let loose in Willy Wonka's factory.

Diets and supplements in animals

Humans have ingeniously solved the difficult balance of eating appealing, unhealthy foods like chocolate cake, with healthier, higher fibre, less appealing fruit and vegetables. We have simply made our fruit more like cake to make everyone feel better about the situation. Even vegetables are selected to be sweeter and less bitter, which is proven to be at the expense of nutritional content.

With limited variety of fresh produce available, and their markedly altered nutritional content, it can be difficult to ensure a diet is balanced. So primates, from white-lipped tamarins to howler monkeys, are often given a pelleted diet with vitamins and minerals, supplemented by some fresh produce. But even this is difficult. While stump-tailed macaques and Guinea baboons are adaptable omnivores eating almost anything, white-bellied spider monkeys eat mainly fruit, gelada baboons are specialist grass eaters, and pygmy marmosets specialise in eating gum and nectar. One pellet cannot be balanced for them all. Pellets aim to ensure basic levels of protein, vitamins and minerals. Like humans and fruit bats, primates from lowland gorillas to pygmy tarsiers need vitamin C in their diet, or they develop scurvy. Thankfully, the rare cases I have seen, of squirrel monkeys with loose teeth and bleeding gums, were all confiscated pets eating human food; their symptoms were the same as described in old mariners' journals.

Other vitamins can be more problematic. South American

yellow-breasted capuchins and bald urakaris need more vitamin D than red colobus monkeys from Africa or golden snub-nosed monkeys from Asia. Vitamin D is essential for absorbing calcium from food for strong and healthy bones. Humans and most animals make this in skin from exposure to the ultraviolet rays in sunlight, and vitamin D in the diet is less important. But a squirrel monkey indoors in Scotland, a white-faced saki monkey in northern China, or a variegated spider monkey in Canada doesn't get enough sunlight, so supplementing their diets is essential. Vitamin C is water soluble and in excess simply results in orange pee, but vitamin D isn't, so any excess can cause calcium being deposited in the kidneys and large blood vessels of the heart, damaging organs, which you can see on X-rays.

A compromise between taste and nutrition would appear to be a balance of pellets and some fruit. But most primates are social, living in groups, further complicating matters. I remember a male red-faced spider monkey that broke both his legs after a small fall. On X-rays his bones were pale and looked moth-eaten, distinctive for metabolic bone disease from a lack of calcium. Yet he was on a perfectly balanced diet of pellets and a small amount of fruit, as formulated by a specialist nutritionist. As he was the dominant male, it turned out he was grabbing all the group's fruit, and eating no pellets, while the rest were stuck eating the boring but nutritionally balanced pellets. After all this, he ended up with rickets.

What animals are offered is not always what they eat. Beautiful, naturalistic enclosures, with a mix of different species living together, are appealing to zoo visitors, and the animals have more interesting lives and mental stimulation. But just like children, someone else's meal always looks more interesting, and some animals prefer to steal each other's food. A toco toucan may die from liver failure due to iron toxicity, despite its low iron diet, as it persistently steals the emperor tamarin's orange pieces. Rich in vitamin C, they prevent scurvy in the tamarins, but fatally boost iron absorption in the toucan.

This is even presuming the diets given are correct. In the

early days of the Zoological Society of Ireland a hundred and fifty years ago, a young Indian one-horned rhino arrived at great expense, to help attract zoo visitors. When the poor rhino arrived, he was sickly and never did well. Prescribed a diet of hay, cabbage, boiled rice and bran, with milk and tonic powders, when he got ill the cabbage was replaced with potato: not ideal from what we now know. Despite the four medical physicians and veterinarians looking after his health, he slowly deteriorated, developed a prolapse and died. As usual in those days, the body was auctioned to the highest bidder, to help the zoo recover some of its costs. When dissected by the winner at Trinity College, he found its stomach and intestines completely filled with fermented corn, not something on the diet sheet at all. In punishment, the angry zoo council cut the responsible zoo keeper's wages for a year.

Dietary drift is still a frequent problem in zoo and sanctuary animals I see today. Feeling sorry for a Brazilian tapir that doesn't like his hay one week, his carer just adds a few more apples to his food, as the poor animal appears very hungry. Then lettuce is missing for a few weeks and replaced by extra carrots and bananas, but it gets forgotten when the lettuce is again available. A few months later the sanctuary has had a load of cabbages donated. Staying in the diet, cabbage gradually increases over the months. As staff change, gradually the original diet is forgotten and the tapir ends up on a completely different diet to the one originally prescribed, now sitting gathering dust in a folder somewhere in an office. Eventually, the poor tapir unexpectedly collapses dead with blocked and twisted intestines, and the dietary drift is finally tragically discovered.

While our farmed fruit is not as healthy as we fool ourselves into thinking, just feeding chimpanzees vegetables and dry pellets is extremely boring. Giving regular scatterings of nuts, seeds and some berries to help keep intelligent animals mentally occupied is also essential, if we don't want them to fight and supplement their diet with each other's fingers and toes.

Wild animals foraging for food

Most behavioural problems in captive wild animals are related to food. Most of their lives, whether a bee hummingbird or a bowhead whale, are completely consumed with finding and eating enough food to survive, while keeping a watchful eye out for other animals trying to eat them too. Driven by hunger, most animals spend almost all their waking hours searching for food. Polar bears can swim non-stop for a week, travelling hundreds of kilometres. On land they cover enormous distances, always on the move looking for places to hunt ringed seals. In human care they can eat a week's nutrition in just minutes. While humans may blossom on the sofa, happily watching hours of television, animals like polar bears simply cannot cope with this.

While apparently lazing on a branch in the sun, being territorial in nature, leopards can still walk over 50 kilometres in a night patrolling their territory. I have watched Indian leopards catch sambar deer, wild pigs and silver langur, but also seen African leopards eat termites, eggs and mice when times are lean. It is no surprise that gulping down their meat ration in captivity, thousands of years of evolution doesn't allow them to relax and do Sudoku. Without care this leads to zombie-like repetitive pacing, which we call stereotypical behaviour.

Despite their predisposition to pacing, most carnivores easily become fat in care. Posters of tigers, with their full round faces and distinctive saggy skin on their undersides, show trained animals from photography farms in North America. No wild animal looks like that. Obesity in animals holds the same risks as in people. Large carnivores like lions need regular fast days, to mimic not catching buffalo every day. This has some effect on obesity, similar to the methods used by yogis and intermittent fasting dieters. But if pushed too far, lions become tetchy and prone to squabbles. If caring for Asian black bears rescued from bile farms in Vietnam who share large sanctuary enclosures, with pools to swim in and trees to climb, you are still always stuck with chubby bears. If you keep your bears lean, they become mean, and will invariably eat each other.

We are fortunate with social primates like lion-tailed macaques. Although highly intelligent, and they eat all the nutrition they need quickly, they are much more rarely afflicted with behavioural problems. They are happy to instead turn their available time to local politics, bitching, bickering, and watching each other, which keeps them fully mentally occupied.

Keeping an animal patient's brain engaged and healthy can be a real challenge. The term 'behavioural problem' is horribly disingenuous, implying the behaviour is a problem for people, rather than a symptom of mental distress in an animal. Zoo visitors don't like seeing zombie polar bears endlessly pacing their concrete enclosure, hence this behaviour is a problem. But it is the animal's mental health we should be focusing on. Zoo keepers have come up with enrichment; ways to increase captive animals' mental stimulation and encouraging natural behaviours. While it's a good concept, I hate the term 'enrichment', as it can imply that keeping animals badly is OK, if you then toss in a few toilet rolls stuffed with straw and treats a few times a week. If you keep animals well enough, with different routines, changing feeding devices and other ways to keep them stimulated, you don't need to enrich their environment. You just look after them well.

Watching wild galah cockatoos spend all day digging up and eating grass roots, having the odd squabble and preening session with flock mates, highlights why a single pet parrot in a cage with a bowl of sunflower seeds, containing all the fat and energy it needs for weeks in the wild, is such a sad state of affairs. There are sadly millions of lonely, mentally tortured yet obese pet parrots, tens of thousands still tragically trapped from the wild for clueless owners every year. Little wonder there are specialist animal shrinks who only deal with pet parrots.

Wild animals so easily become obese, yet food-directed frustration causes most mental health difficulties. So how to improve their environments without using even more food? Part of their ration can be finely chopped fruit or nuts, scattered in the grass, so yellow-breasted capuchins have to spend hours looking for their food, closer to what they would do in the wild. Tigers can be fed from the top of wooden poles they have to climb, encouraging exercise, and ensuring they only eat when they are actually hungry.

Even ultra-intelligent chimpanzees will spend hours with grass stems getting a tiny amount of honey from an artificial termite mound, even though the actual nutritional value is minimal. Simply rubbing items with food scents is enough to encourage exploratory behaviour, as anyone accosted with fresh smells when passing a bakery well knows. And it's even better if it benefits different animals. Once a month, my friend Douglas Richardson would lock the snow leopards in their zoo house and let markhors graze their enclosure. The markhors enjoyed the fresh grass and exploring the different enclosure, while the markhor scents and droppings, the snow leopard's natural prey, captivated the leopards for ages after a visit. A simple but effective non-fattening way of keeping animals mentally active, while also saving gardening costs.

Humans are not the only species to have problems with high cholesterol. I was once asked to perform keyhole surgery on a Sumatran orangutan, rescued after supposedly being kept by a princess. After decades of human food he was obese, but also had a large gallstone causing him pain. Gallstones in people are usually rock-hard lumps of cholesterol due to our predilection to eat things like chips, and I only rarely see them in other primates. When I finally made it to the orangutan sanctuary a few months later to see a number of surgery cases, we found on ultrasound that the gallstone had completely gone now he was back on a natural diet. It had simply broken up and passed, and no surgery was needed. In meerkats, instead of gallstones, heart attacks and strokes, the manifestation of high cholesterol is more dramatic. A meerkat staggering

about like a drunkard hints at the problem. A lump of cholesterol in the meningeal membranes around the brain, surrounded
by angry white blood cells, results in a hard marble squashing
the brain beneath it. This is no wonder, considering how badly
we still get things wrong with our own nutrition.

Even what we regard as healthy natural food is not what
we are designed for. A bowl of muesli and orange juice for
breakfast is full of problems. We are actually a very young
species, nothing like *Homo erectus*, which was around for about
two million years. Modern humans have only existed for a
few hundred thousand years, and we have been farming for
only around ten thousand years. Despite how slowly natural
selection works, we have started evolving to parts of our
unnatural farmed diets. The most highly-selected-for gene in
humans over the last ten thousand years is our ability to drink
milk.

Milk in all its forms

Lactase persistence, the ability of adults to digest the lactose
in milk, has a stronger genetic selection pressure than any
other known human gene. This may be disappointing to those
who believe we are being selected to be more intelligent. Our
brain size is not increasing, and it appears likely we have
reached peak intelligence for our species. It is our stomachs
that are ruling our evolution. There are various theories; those
with the gene were less likely to get osteoporosis, survive
living in deserts better, or were less likely to die from dehydration from cholera or malnutrition during famines. Yet the
gene is still currently being selected for, even in modern times.

There are fascinating regional differences. Almost all Irish
people have lactase persistence, followed by almost all Swedes
and Danes, while only about one in six Greek adults do, and
less than one in twenty Native Americans. Mongolia has high
levels of lactase persistence, yet nearby Chinese ethnic groups
have low levels. East African tribes like the Kikuyu in Kenya
tolerate dairy foods well as adults, but other African tribes

like the Akans in Ghana don't. Lactase persistence to adulthood is a uniquely human phenomenon. All other mammals lose their ability to digest lactose, or milk sugar, once weaned. Some animals never even tolerate it as new-born babies. Hooded seals, like other seals, sea lions and walruses, have no lactose in their milk, so I can't use normal milk replacers to rear a wild orphan. Despite this, their milk is full of energy and nutrition. It can be two-thirds fat, twenty times what is in human milk, and far more than in the richest ice cream. Drinking hooded seal milk is like drinking double cream. With such a super-milk, hooded seal pups double in weight and are weaned in less than a week. Instead, feeding a diet of fish soup with added oils takes us months to achieve the same in a rehabilitation centre. It's the exact opposite with rhinos. Black rhino milk has only a tenth of human milk fat. No wonder it takes two years to wean their slow-growing calves.

Tammar wallaby milk has high energy, but not from fat. Wallaby milk has almost no lactose, but is packed with about 15 per cent oligosaccharide sugars, making it more sugary than a fizzy drink. African elephant and giant panda mothers change their milk's composition dramatically as youngsters grow. Tammar wallabies not only change the composition of their milk as a joey grows but can also produce two very different types of milk at the same time. A very young joey on one nipple gets more sugars in its milk, while an older joey on another nipple gets less sugar but much more protein. All this conspires to make hand-rearing orphaned wild animals challenging. Every year healthy deer fawns are unnecessarily 'rescued' from the wild by walkers incorrectly presuming them to be abandoned. Tragically, they often arrive with a stomach full of their mother's milk. She naturally hid them in the grass, staying away to protect them from predators. Despite our best efforts, many of these fawns can't adapt to bottle-fed milk replacers and sadly die.

No matter how well formulated, milk replacers, even if specifically made for African elephants or giant pandas, are always a poor compromise, just as in humans. The milk in the first day or so for many mammals, called colostrum, contains a host of antibodies to protect a baby for the first few weeks of life from the diseases to which the mother has immunity. Without this, hand-reared infants are more prone to dying from infections. The same happens at weaning, when cotton-tail rabbits and Arctic hares normally get the complex mix of bacteria needed to digest their food from their mother, by eating her soft night faeces. This is almost impossible to replicate when hand-rearing, and so some hand-reared leverets and rabbits don't survive weaning.

Sucking on a bottle teat is very different to the kneading action that naturally stimulates milk release through a nipple. Domestic cows milked by machines are more prone to teat damage and mastitis than those hand-milked, which is closer to natural suckling. Milk sucked from a teat and bottle more easily goes down the windpipe into the lungs, driving a horrible reaction that kills an orphaned suckling moose a few days later. Bottle-rearing male moose also risks them becoming species-confused. Later in life, as testosterone-filled adults rut, they are more likely to attack people, seeing them as rivals.

Treating Western chimpanzees in Sierra Leone, I watched the small infants drinking human milk replacer from a bottle, their large brown eyes observing you and the world. Human milk replacers work well with our closest relatives, but it is easy to forget that for each confiscated baby there are another ten dead chimpanzees in the forest. To get a chimpanzee baby to sell as a pet, or to smuggle overseas, not only must the mother be killed, but usually the entire group that desperately try to come to their rescue. Even the best milk replacers, made of cow's milk and soya proteins, don't contain the myriad hormones, antibodies, and amino acid ratios found in natural milk. Bottle-fed chimpanzees usually sleep peacefully the whole night, like human babies on formula, as they don't get the same amount of glutamate in artificial milk. An amino acid that is also a neurotransmitter, glutamate helps tell the infant's brain when it has had enough milk. Without this and other natural compounds in chimpanzee milk, infants drink much more, distending their stomach until stretch receptors tell the brain to stop. This may seem appealing to a sleep-deprived mother but contributes to higher infant death rates, with excessive milk poorly digested, the lack of milk anti-bodies, and lack of clean water to reconstitute milk powder, making chimpanzees and human babies in developing coun-tries prone to fatal enteritis. We suspect milk replacers may even increase a chimpanzee's lifetime risk of developing obesity and diabetes, as has been shown in people.

Invasive species and acclimatisation

No discussion of wildlife nutrition would be complete without mentioning the surgeon Francis Buckland, and the acclimati-sation movement. Wildlife nutrition was his obsession, but not in a way similar to wildlife veterinarians. He was a pioneer of zoophagy, obsessed with eating his way through the animal kingdom. Even at school at Winchester College he trapped and ate mice and rats, to his classmates' disgust, who also complained of the smell from a half-eaten cat stashed under his bed. While studying at Oxford, he learned that a leopard at Surrey Zoo had died and been buried. He made a hurried trip to dig it up, cook and eat it, but claimed it didn't taste particularly good. Considering it had been dead for some time, and probably pretty rotten, this was a massive gastro-nomic understatement.

Studying surgery at St George's Hospital, he was taught by Henry Gray, famous for his anatomy textbook, which gave its name to a hospital soap opera series. He was sent dead animals from London Zoo for anatomy research, but also culinary testing. At his dinners he served everything from cooked dolphin heads and rhino pies to stewed moles and boiled elephant trunk. He wasn't pleased when Darwin quoted some of his work, as he fervently opposed the concept of evolution. His mistaken belief that adaptations during an animal's life could be passed on to future generations led to the formation of acclimatisation societies. Proponents believed that exotic species could be useful for agriculture. After potatoes from Peru, maize from Mexico and silkworms from Asia, it was felt that other species could adapt to the cold, wet European climate for man's benefit. In the shadow of the Napoleonic wars, industrial revolution, and years of poor harvests and potato blights, meat was expensive and, for most people, only eaten occasionally. Today, we realise the harms that non-native species can wreak in unique environments, from the rabbits, red deer and common brushtailed possums in New Zealand, to the North American grey squirrel that has largely displaced the native red squirrel in England. Introduced rabbits became a nuisance in New Zealand, and weasels and stoats were then introduced in a further blunder in an attempt to control them. There are now 30 million possums in New Zealand, eating their way through endemic birds' chicks and eggs, and over a million red deer have been shot in official control programmes on the two islands. In the northern hemisphere, a hundred starlings introduced in North America have multiplied to more than 200 million today.

At the first meeting of the British Acclimatisation Society in the London Tavern in 1859, attendees dined on eland, American partridge and bean goose, and the future appeared bright; these future problems far from sight. Acclimatisation was far from just one weird man's folly. Professor Richard Owen, famous for coming up with the name 'dinosaur', was the host of the first meeting, with backing from Angela Burdett-Coutts, the wealthiest woman in Britain, and supporting noblemen such as the Earl of Derby. Even the Duke of Bedford, president of the Zoological Society of London, was responsible for releasing Himalayan tahr to New Zealand, that tragic country for non-native species experiments. Today, almost 1 per cent of New Zealand's entire gross national product has since been spent on invasive species control.

Francis Buckland and his friends envisaged herds of eland and other exotic antelope roaming the Sussex countryside as food sources. A laudable aim, perhaps. But he also once vowed to eat a piece of every member of the animal kingdom, and not all the Buckland family's eating habits were scientifically minded. His father William is even rumoured to have gobbled down the embalmed heart of Louis XIV during a dinner party.

Disastrous and misguided as these attempts were, wild rabbits, introduced to Britain by the Normans, often form part of many zoo carnivores' diets in Britain and Australia. Fallow deer, originally from Asia, but likely introduced by ancient Phoenicians three thousand years ago, are hunted for meat, raw pet foods, and zoo animal feed in England. While I and many others who work with animals are vegetarians or vegans, we still need to feed meat to many of our animal charges. Neither snow leopards nor pet cats can produce the essential amino acid taurine, so unlike wolves and domestic dogs must take it in from a meat-based diet. With insufficient taurine, cats from African lions to Persian moggies can go irreversibly blind from retinal degeneration, or fatally develop a dilated heart muscle condition. Strangely, two-toed sloths are also prone to taurine deficiency, as are many songbirds. Blue tits specifically seek out taurine-rich spiders to feed to their chicks. Thanks to parents' attentive feeding, these fledglings develop better spatial perception, vital for small birds constantly darting in and out of vegetation.

Meat is expensive, making large carnivores costly to keep. Even the royal menagerie at the Tower of London had problems feeding its assorted carnivores, most given as royal gifts but not always appreciated. George III, upon receiving a massive grizzly bear from the Hudson Bay Company in 1811, remarked that he would have much preferred a new tie or pair of socks. Six hundred years earlier, the tower's animal keepers solved their problem feeding a polar bear gifted from the King of Norway, by letting him catch fish in the Thames while tethered by a long chain to the shore. By the eighteenth century, the situation had deteriorated to the stage that the menagerie was opened to the public to help cover the food costs. Admission cost a penny halfpenny, but was free if you brought a dog or cat to be fed to the lions. Thankfully, today zoos only ask for Christmas trees to be donated as animal feed.

Meat is still expensive today, and has environmental impacts with its farming. It is tempting to use other sources of protein. Feeding dead zoo animals to zoo lions and cheetahs twenty years ago resulted in cases of feline spongiform encephalopathy, the cat equivalent of mad cow disease. One low-cost source of meat for feeding zoo animals is fallen stock; cows and horses which have died on farms, and cannot be used for human consumption. A cheap source of zoo carnivores' food, very rarely a euthanased animal mistakenly enters the system. The barbiturates used to put an animal down affect any animal that eats its meat. I have seen African lions simply a little quieter for a day or two afterwards. Other animals can be very badly affected. I remember being called into a zoo as an emergency for an African painted wolf that had suddenly started staggering around like a zombie. By the time I arrived at the zoo fifteen minutes later, the wolf had collapsed and was unconscious and two others were now staggering around. I spent most of the rest of the day with my tireless nurse Donna Brown, running intravenous fluids into three unconscious wolves, all the while wondering when they might wake up and try to kill us. Thankfully, we managed to protect their kidneys and flush the drugs out and they all recovered. A tiger I saw at another park was not so lucky. He never became unconscious, but stayed in his outside enclosure, too weak to walk, but still too dangerous for anyone to go in with. By the time he had recovered, he had sustained irreversible kidney damage from dehydration. Yet it isn't economically viable for most zoos to feed human-quality meat to the large number of large carnivores they look after, and so the tiny risk of poisoning is ever present no matter how careful they are.

Some zoos are surrounded by farms with wild rabbits damaging their crops and use these as a food source for animals ranging from leopards to golden eagles. These too are not without risk. The hunter will try to shoot a rabbit in the head, and remove this before feeding, but sometimes a shot rabbit has had a previous lucky escape and has a bullet lodged invisibly in a leg. A weak, collapsed, golden eagle, with black-green diarrhoea, makes one immediately suspect this, and removal of the swallowed bullet from the stomach and medication to bind lead in the blood stream are essential to save its life.

If someone unsuccessfully shoots a mute swan, whether a bored teenager with a pellet gun, or someone after a cheaper Christmas roast, the swan will not be poisoned and simply wall off the bullet in its muscle. But if the swan swallows an old lead fishing weight, then it will be poisoned. It is the acid in the stomach that allows lead to be absorbed. I am sure medical doctors also can't help laughing when action movie heroes need a bullet removed after a swig of whisky to save their life. The bullet itself is no risk, although the dirt and clothing sucked into the hole could kill later from an infection. I guess it is better filming an attractive actress removing a bullet, dousing the wound with whisky, than the more important removal of shirt fragments before cleaning the wound with soap.

Animals feeding animals

Meat is a very poor source of calcium, so it is essential that carnivores also consume bones. In the wild, most do this by eating a variety of smaller and larger prey. A leopard may not get much calcium from a large bushbuck, leaving bones intact, but it does get its calcium from cane rats and the odd genet. This can be a challenge for zoo and sanctuary carnivores fed beef and venison with large bones. Smashing bones with a sledgehammer is a simple solution, but won't help an African sand cat. They need smaller bones, or a calcium supplement. Not just carnivores are dependent on calcium. While most herbivores get enough from the plants they eat, in the poor soil on the Scottish island of Rum, red deer find this difficult, especially when growing antlers. Their solution is gruesome. They have taken to biting the heads off flightless Manx shearwater chicks on the island, occasionally also biting their legs off, as these are the most calcium-rich parts of the young chicks' bodies. With this island the breeding ground for a quarter of the world's population, there are plenty of victims.

One major food source for everything from fossa and Komodo dragons in zoos, to orphaned barn owls, and snared otters being rehabilitated for return to the wild, is day-old chickens. Traditionally cockerels were kept for the pot, and hens for laying. But this ceased in the 1920s and birds were selected to be as efficient and economical mini food-factories as possible. Now hens can lay 300 eggs a year for their two-year working life, compared to half that before. A wild red jungle fowl, the chicken's ancestor, will only lay a clutch of eggs up to 12 then stop, but instead they now live up to a decade. Meat broiler chickens now reach a 1.5 to 2 kilogram slaughter weight in a month, while before the 1920s this took four months. Today, 7 billion hens lay 80 million tonnes of eggs a year, with many Western countries consuming almost 300 eggs a year per person. While having specially selected chicks is much more efficient and economical, keeping meat and eggs cheap, it comes with a variety of ethical and animal welfare costs.

The problem is that, until recently, eggs couldn't be sexed before hatching, and cockerels are no longer economically viable to raise for meat. Seven billion male day-old chicks are killed annually, a sizeable proportion of the 50 billion chickens raised annually across the world, the most common bird on the planet. Day-old male chicks are killed in North America by dropping them into a massive grinder, or in much of Europe by being gassed with carbon dioxide. Similarly, 40 million female ducklings are killed annually in foie gras production, as males are preferred for their rapid weight gain. These chicks and ducklings are used to fertilise growing crops like corn, that then feed chickens. It's somewhat ironic that small yellow chicks are a symbol of new life at Easter. Day-old chicks are also used in dog and cat foods listing chicken as an ingredient. And they are a mainstay diet item for animals from pet Argentinian tegu lizards to falconry red-tailed hawks; from

Scottish wildcats in conservation breeding programmes to maned wolves in zoos. They are such an integral part of zoo diets that their nutritional composition is included in software for creating balanced diets. And no wonder, as they cost a tenth of the price of minced meat.

Day-old chicks differ in nutrient content to naturally caught wild birds. Being hatchlings, their soft bones are low in calcium, which needs to be supplemented. Metabolic bone disease is common in animals fed mainly chicks, with young Goliath herons growing with deformed twisted legs, or crocodile monitor lizards getting leg fractures for no reason. Chicks contain a yolk sac, a source of cholesterol, which is problematic for meerkats and some other species. Farmed beef and mutton is also very different nutritionally to what wild animals would eat. Leopards would catch prey ranging from termites and lizards, to birds, rodents and antelope. They would consume the small bones for their fatty marrow and calcium, and the entrails for their vitamin B, iron and other minerals. Even the fur and feathers of wild prey items are an important part of a natural diet, needed to prevent constipation, as well as providing some amino acids. Scientists are working on commercial ways of sexing eggs before hatching to solve the ethical and animal welfare problems that male day-old chicks pose. For zoos and other animal facilities this will pose a challenge in adapting, and they will likely need to buy more rats and mice specifically bred as animal food.

The ultimate animal protein consumers are the most specialised. Conjuring images of Dracula, the three vampire bat species are unique. Other animals will eat blood occasionally to supplement their diet, like vampire ground finches in the Galapagos. When prickly pear nectar is scarce, they boost their protein intake by pecking the feet of blue-footed boobies until they draw blood to drink. Surprisingly, boobies don't resist this. They seem to confuse the behaviour with beneficial pecking to remove parasites. Vampire bats are the only mammals living entirely on blood, specialising in this diet for over 26 million years: so long, in fact, that we don't know how they evolved to do this. Perhaps they switched from eating parasites like ticks that contain blood, or evolved from having sharp teeth to pierce fruit, or even from eating small birds and mammals like large spectral bats do. Unlike Dracula, they don't use their razor-sharp teeth to suck blood, but to make a small cut before lapping up blood with their tongue. Because they drink blood they can transmit the dreaded rabies virus, and so are vaccinated in zoos. Indeed, in some countries like Britain they would need to spend their entire life in a rabies quarantine level enclosure if anyone chose to keep them, in contrast to fruit bats that can live in walk-through enclosures. Common vampire bats are actually easy to feed in captivity, just relying daily on fresh blood from an abattoir, with a little citric acid to slow clotting. They are perfectly happy with cold blood, despite using heat detection to find warm animals to feed on at night. While many are horrified at the thought of blood-drinking animals, common vampire bats are kind to each other. A bat won't survive for more than two days without food, so they feed each other if they haven't had any luck finding food.

Raw diets

As a wildlife vet, I am usually spared getting cornered in a supermarket or at family gatherings to be asked questions about a dog dragging its bum on the carpet, or an elderly cat's toilet habits, unlike my wife and most veterinary colleagues. Yet there is one thing dog and cat owners do specifically ask me about. Raw diets. After all, wild grey wolves don't eat soft food from a can, or African wildcats dry biscuits, do they? Feeding your pet a raw meat diet has the same instinctive appeal as following a Palaeolithic diet yourself. But a Pekinese looks nothing like a wolf, its short, deformed skull and jaws incapable of the function of its wild ancestors. Even a more wolf-like Alsatian is still a very different creature, prone to a host of conditions that wild wolves rarely suffer, due to its selection and inbreeding.

Wild relatives will eat everything from earthworms and voles to small birds, deer, and even rotting seal carcasses on the beach, a variety impossible to replicate in your house. Pet owners are highly unlikely to buy a bag of frozen rats, worms and birds as pet food, so deer or beef is the mainstay of raw diets. The large bones are difficult for dogs to eat well to reliably get sufficient calcium. If a dog does gulp a large chunk of bone down, there is a risk of this lodging in the intestines, and proving fatal without surgery. Sourcing affordable safe venison is challenging for raw food manufacturers. Cooking not only improves digestibility, lowering our pet's environmental impact, it importantly helps eliminate infectious diseases which people can get. Outbreaks of salmonella and tuberculosis sometimes occur with raw diets, not only risking a pet's life, but owners too, as dogs live so closely with us. This is a particular risk for those with weaker immune systems such as children, the elderly, and those undergoing cancer treatment or on immunosuppressive medication after organ transplants. Safety is the main problem with raw diets. In a group of wild wolves, one will occasionally die from an intestinal blockage or infection, even though they are supremely adapted to this way of life, but the group overall does well. While commercial pet diets may not appear ideal, they are safe. Few owners want to play Russian roulette with their pets' lives, who are less able to cope with raw diets. Yet if a Pekinese has tiny dysfunctional teeth, there are wild patients that go one better.

Pangolins have no teeth. Secretive, nocturnal mammals that walk on two legs, with scales like a lizard, rolling up into a hard ball safe even from lions, and eating only ants and termites, are always going to be a nutritional challenge. Pangolins are the most trafficked wild animals on the planet, with millions illegally caught every year. They are notoriously difficult to keep alive once confiscated, and this is not helped by the smuggler's habit of force-feeding them via tube with a large volume of water, gruel, or even mud, to increase their weight, and so price. Seized shipments can be large, and it is essential to quickly assess a truck-full of dehydrated, stressed and squashed pangolins, if you are to save as many as possible. While I was helping to run a training exercise for wildlife and customs officers in Laos with Free the Bears, we comically used pumpkins in hessian sacs to simulate how to handle, move and assess a large, confiscated shipment of animals while minimising stress. And each officer then got to take a pumpkin home for their family as a reward.

Feeding any animal naturally that subsists entirely on ants, is close to impossible. Even if you dig up termite nests, you will quickly exhaust your local supply. Rescuing a Sunda pangolin in Vietnam, you have the advantage of finding bags of frozen ant eggs in the markets, even if expensive. However, if rescuing an African tree pangolin, there is no farming or traditional collecting of small insects for human food in their range. You face the same problem in Patagonia with rehabilitating giant anteaters, another toothless animal that eats only ants and termites. Despite their impressive size, and sabretooth-like claws for ripping into rock-hard termite mounds, they have evolved lower energy needs by minimising the size of the most energy-demanding organ. Their brain is only walnut sized, and a third is taken up by nerves used to process their sensitive sense of smell. They switch between different species of ant and termite, depending on season, as these have different nutritional content, and can sniff out and select different worker ants or breeder termites to consume. Tiny silky anteaters are even fussier, eating only certain tree ants.

All sorts of diets have been tried in captivity, containing combinations of boiled eggs, ox heart, shrimps, mincemeat, cat food, sunflower oil, yeast, fruit and yoghurt, blended in a mixer. Giant anteaters lick them up with their long thin tongue, but if even a tiny sinew or muscle fibre survives blending, it can wrap around the tongue, strangulating it and causing the tongue to fall off. An anteater with no tongue cannot eat, and even with the best care, they fade away and die.

Just like inbred aristocrats, anteaters on artificial diets suffer from bleeding, seeming unable to clot properly, and needing daily vitamin K in their diet to counteract this. In busy Western zoos, these complex diets have been replaced with a powdered formula that can be used to feed everything from tamandua to armadillos, which would normally eat ants or termites. Convenient, but expensive, many rescue centres in developing countries still rely on their own recipes. Even powdered diets are not perfect. Several anteaters died recently, when just one ingredient was inadvertently changed by a manufacturer.

Another captive patient prone to bleeding is the black rhino, and this seems strange in so combative a species. Their white rhino cousins are basically placid hippo-sized unicorn lawn-mowers, as easy to feed as cows. In contrast, black rhinos have a number of health problems, such as liver and skin conditions only seen in captivity, and likely due to the difficulty in replacing their natural diet. While they eat leaves from over a hundred African bushes and trees, only three or four make up the bulk of their wild diet. These plants, from the acacia or wattle tree family, are only found in Africa.

The wood-wide web

It can be hard being an acacia tree in the African savanna, when so many different animals are keen to eat your leaves. Humans too use acacia trees heavily, and not just for firewood. Gum Arabic is in everything from Turner's watercolour paintings to marshmallows and shoe polish. Even acacia bark can be used to make environmentally friendly wood glues without using petrochemicals, something my father spent his chemistry career developing. Acacias have long thorns between their small leaves to discourage animals eating them, and tannins in their leaves. Used for tanning leather from which they take their name, these compounds bind proteins in animal hides, making everything from shoes to saddles resistant to decomposition. Making your mouth dry after a glass of Cabernet Sauvignon, or peaty Scottish whisky, they are made by plants to make leaves difficult to digest, interfere with digestive enzymes in herbivores' digestive tracts, and have a bitter taste that many animals avoid.

It isn't just animals that can taste plants. Some plants appear able to taste the animal eating them. When roe deer nibble on young beech and maple trees, they react differently to when twigs are broken off by wind, or a human snaps a twig off. Trees normally produce hormones to encourage healing. But when a deer takes a nibble, saplings appear to taste the deer's saliva, and they instead release salicylic acid. The first pain-killer anti-inflammatory drug used by ancient humans, it is still found in aspirin, acne creams and heartburn medicines. But if released by the nibbled plant, it stimulates tannin production. This interferes with digestion, but also tastes bitter, and so after only a few bites the deer will have to find something else to eat. Plants can do the equivalent of a scream when eaten, although this is completely inaudible and invisible to us and other animals. Acacia trees browsed by giraffes release volatile chemicals in the air, letting other acacias know they are being eaten, and surrounding trees increase their tannins too, so the giraffes need to move further away, upwind, to find unaware acacias, out of tree earshot so to speak. Giraffes are a nightmare for acacias. Specialised to reach higher than other animals, they eat the young growing tips that the tree tries its best to keep out of reach. After the giraffes have had a good meal, an acacia may be unable to grow any taller for over a year. It is no wonder they put so much into their defences.

In European forests, instead of shouting via chemicals in the air, many trees communicate underground, via the wood-wide-web. This invisible mass of fine fungal threads connecting all the roots allows beeches to warn their neighbours they are being eaten by a deer or attacked by bark beetles. Beech appear particularly chatty trees, as most neighbours are relatives. They also appear kinder than many human communities. Walking in a forest, you may see an old tree stump that is alive, years after the tree broke off in a storm, or was hacked off by a chainsaw. Without photosynthesis, survival is normally impossible, but the old tree stump has been kept alive by its surrounding relatives, feeding it via their interconnected roots, sometimes for decades.

When I was a teenager in South Africa, hundreds of greater kudu antelopes were found dead every year, despite stomachs full of leaves. Kept in game farms, they didn't move over large areas, and acacia trees built up formidable amounts of defensive tannins, enough to kill the kudu. In contrast, giraffes were fine. They ate heartily then moved a reasonable distance away up-wind before starting to eat on naïve trees again, and it could be many months before they again returned to a tree.

Black rhinos appear completely oblivious to the bitter tannin taste, eating leaves more bitter than most other herbivores can tolerate. They have co-evolved for so long with the trees trying to fight them off, they have become dependent on these compounds that are toxic to most other animals. Tannins can have beneficial functions. The ancient Egyptians used tannin ointments to treat haemorrhoids, and tannins in red wine may hold health benefits, aside from the alcohol reducing one's stress levels after work. Zoo black rhinos frequently accumulate too much iron in their liver, suddenly dropping dead from liver failure. Tannins in acacia leaves bind iron, causing iron deficiency in goats not adapted to eating acacia. But black rhinos have evolved to now actually need these tannins to protect their livers. Tannins may also act as antioxidants, binding free radicals, similar to vitamin E's function in other animals. Adding tannins, but just in the right amounts, may help us maintain the health of black rhinos in zoo captive breeding programmes.

Being vegan and not eating my patients, it is disconcerting to remember that plants can live thousands of years, care for their elderly, be kind, taste, scream, and even learn and have memories, even if in very different ways to us animals. Even if completely indifferent to the lives of plants, all this can impact the nutrition of wild animals we look after. Plants repeatedly mechanically harvested are slightly different to those naturally grazed, and so don't contain the same compounds. While we are pleased with ourselves when simply replicating protein, carbohydrates, and a few vitamins and minerals in our patients' diets, there are layers of complexity in natural nutrition which we can never replicate.

Poison or medicine?

What will kill a kudu is actually vital for a black rhino's health. The line between poison and medicine is hazy, and shifts depending on species and how something is ingested. Sometimes food doesn't contain beneficial nutrients. Reindeer search out and eat *Amanita muscaria* toadstools just to get high, and even fight over these magic mushrooms. Sami herders can get high without being poisoned by drinking the tripping reindeers' urine, which concentrates the psychedelic compounds, without the nasty side-effects. Wild bighorn sheep in the Canadian Rockies navigate long arduous ledges to eat a psychoactive lichen high in the mountains, with no nutritional benefit. Even carnivores are not above doping themselves. Jaguars like chewing hallucinogenic yage vine bark, just like Peruvian shamans.

Sometimes getting stoned is inadvertent, as with not-so-mysterious crop circles in Tasmania when red-necked wallabies bumble into medical opium poppy-growing fields. Most famous are stories of African elephants getting drunk on fermenting marula tree fruit, then charging around trumpeting loudly and falling over. Sadly, this is impossible, because of how much alcohol an elephant would actually need to consume. However, it is possible that something else in the marula fruit may instead affect elephants' brains, which are four times as large as ours. Baboons and vervet monkeys also appear drunk eating fermenting marula fruit, although this is probably a side-effect rather than their aim. Fruit flies, a species that has actually domesticated itself to adapt to humans and our constant fruit supplies, have an extremely high tolerance for alcohol in fermenting fruit, and their wild ancestors actually specialised on fermenting marula fruit. Plants even intentionally intoxicate animals. Some orchids make male solitary bees drinking their nectar so drunk that they try mating with the flowers in their inebriated state, helping to pollinate them. Bees can also intoxicate us with their honey if feeding on poppy flowers; revenge for agricultural pesticides decimating their numbers, perhaps.

The line between nutrition, recreational drug and poison is a blurry one. Poisoning can arise because exotic plants are introduced to a country and wild animals have not evolved to avoid it. Red kangaroos can get liver failure if they eat lantana, a garden plant from Central America, that has gone rogue from gardens in many countries. Early in my career, I treated an African spurred tortoise. One of the biggest tortoise species, it was easy to forget that the 13 kilogram four-year-old was really only a toddler. In a garden one morning, the ravenous tortoise made the mistake of eating a stomach full of Japanese andromeda, not something it would normally encounter in the wild. It grunted, groaned, and salivated with severe stomach pain. Thankfully it recovered, and I suspect learned its lesson. But wild animals can't learn to avoid all toxic plants. If a swamp wallaby eats foxglove in a zoo, it simply drops dead from heart failure.

Food may be healthy or toxic, depending on who eats it, and how much they consume. Avocados are delicious, driving crime cartels and extortion rackets in Mexico. But although a yellow-headed Amazon parrot finds avocado just as delectable as you, pigging out will result in the parrot dropping dead from heart failure. If you took a sufficient amount of the toxin persin, you would also damage your heart muscle. Domesticated avocados have lower quantities than their ancestors, and none of us is likely to eat enough to be poisoned. Avocados have evolved to being farmed for their survival, as their original seed dispersal disappeared with giant ground sloths, eaten to extinction in the early Anthropocene.

Just as anteaters select different ants for their nutritional content, gentoo penguins swimming at high speed actually select between male and female Antarctic krill to eat, as these have differing fat and protein contents. Astonishing, as krill are only a couple of centimetres long. Krill are even more abundant on the planet than ants, and everything seems to eat krill, from blue whales to tiny squid. Even the bird with the largest wingspan in the world, the wandering albatross, eats Antarctic krill. The whole Antarctic food chain depends on phytoplankton and the krill that eats it. Crabeater seals are the planet's most abundant seal, thanks to their krill diet, with a population twenty times that of the northern hemisphere's common seal. I can immediately recognise a washed-up skull in Tierra del Fuego, thanks to their wavy teeth, used to strain the tiny krill from the water. Their teeth seem to be trying to evolve into the baleen plates of minke whales that I see back in Scotland. The crabeater seals' main predator, the fearsome leopard seal, despite documentaries only showing it gruesomely ripping up penguins, also eats krill. Young leopard seals eat almost entirely krill diets, and even half-tonne adults, despite their penguin-chomping image, also have a diet that can be half krill, as revealed by their trident-shaped back teeth, similar to those of the crabeater seals they also eat.

Antarctic krill are one of the most abundant animals by weight, and despite everything from whales to birds frantically consuming them, are still one of the most successful animal species on the planet; with 300 million tonnes in the southern oceans, they weigh just slightly less than humans' total biomass on the planet. Despite this, looking into their nutritional content when trying to optimise the diet of one of the largest gentoo penguin zoo colonies in the world two decades ago, I could find almost nothing published in scientific journals or on the internet. Penguin diets were simply based on inexpensive available northern hemisphere fish, while wild gentoo penguins eat mainly krill, some squid and jellyfish, and only small amounts of fish. The nutritional guidelines were based on guesswork from the metabolic needs of farmed chickens and pet cats, which seemed nothing like a penguin. The zoo birds were not doing well, with adults often ill, and poor chick survival, which we suspected could be related to their diet.

I made a trip to the offices of the British Antarctic Survey, who kindly allowed me to read faded brown, typewritten Russian and Japanese fishing reports from half a century earlier. I managed to find some detailed nutritional analysis, when krill was investigated for human and livestock feeds. A hundred thousand tonnes of Antarctic krill is fished yearly now, mainly for farmed fish food, ironically. The main hurdle to krill fishing is how rapidly it spoils. This has so far spared all the Antarctic wildlife that depends on krill, but researchers are working to solve this problem using factory ships. If krill fishing dramatically increases, the distinctive Antarctic wildlife populations will be decimated on a far more dramatic scale than portrayed by tap-dancing penguins, or has occurred with global warming.

Using the krill fishing data, we tried to select affordable available fish with vitamin supplements to get as close as possible to the natural diet. My findings hinted that the fat in the fish the zoo was feeding to the penguins was too high, and the supplements provided too much vitamin A and E. In excess, these fat-soluble vitamins can cause problems, something health store aficionados seem unaware of. Researchers discovered that, contrary to expectations, supplementing these antioxidant vitamins to human smokers on poor diets actually resulted in higher numbers of strokes and heart attacks – not what they were expecting, and studies had to be stopped early to protect the patients. There is simply no pill to solve an unhealthy diet.

Putting the penguins on a new diet of a different fish with only thiamine supplemented, as this B vitamin is destroyed by freezing, I waited nervously for a year for data to know if I had made things better or worse. The fish selected was not ideal, but had to be reliably available, affordable, and a suitable shape and size for penguins to comfortably swallow. Feeding by hand is unnatural, but the only way to be able to check each individual penguin daily, or sneak medication in their fish if ill. Time-saving as throwing fish in the pool would be, these would become impossible. The improvements were dramatic. Chick survival doubled, and adult penguin deaths were quartered, and we saw far fewer ill birds. It didn't change any specific illness, whether fungal respiratory tract infections or diarrhoea; the birds' immune systems and health just improved overall. Yet the fish species causing the original problem is still safely fed to gentoo penguins in other zoos in North America and Japan with good results. But the same fish species hides a multitude of differences. Winter-caught and summer-caught fish contain vastly different nutrients, as do fish feeding on different foods, or different ages and sizes from different parts of the world's oceans.

A good diet is medicine in itself, not only providing nutrients, but also essential to mental wellbeing. Food may actually not contain any nutrition even if not toxic. Food can act as an animal's recreational drug, or have medicinal effects. The ancient Greeks believed that everything was medicine, from how you lived your life to the clothes you wore. But most important of all was food. While their theory of illness arising from bad air was way off, their holistic attitude still has lessons for our care of wild animals such as penguins. Modern medicine, however, set about isolating compounds in food, wild herbs and barks that may have had beneficial effects, putting them in pills, and calling this medicine; something to be administered for specific illnesses. And medication of our uncooperative wild patients is where we turn to next.

Asian vultures went from populations of several million birds in India to almost extinct in just a decade. We eventually discovered that the common painkiller diclofenac used in cows was uniquely toxic to vultures. Even the tiny quantities found in the muscles of dead cattle were enough to fatally poison them.

13

A spoonful of ants makes the medicine go down

How on earth do you give a spoonful of syrup to a spitting cobra, a tablet to a tamandua, or an injection to an Indian elephant? While you can hide a tablet inside a fish you offer to a zoo penguin, hiding medication in mealworms for a scarlet ibis is more difficult. Most medications are for humans, with only relatively few modified or manufactured for livestock and pets. Yet white-nosed monkeys hate the taste of veterinary tablets manufactured for dogs, as they are meat flavoured. Once suspicious, they carefully search their food for anything they don't recognise; so completing a week-long course of antibiotics, even when it's a small, tasteless pink tablet, can be difficult. Sometimes we resort to human infant syrups with a sweet fruit flavour. Yet with raccoons even this doesn't help, as they wash their food in water, quickly getting rid of most medications.

While tablets can be crushed up between two spoons and mixed in food, emptying the powder from a capsule into a purple-faced langur's food isn't always a better solution. Often capsule contents are particularly bitter, hence the reason for shielding them from the mouth. How do you mix medication into the food of a langur when their diet mainly consists of fresh leaves? Sometimes we choose a medication not because

251

it is the best, but simply because it is the only drug we can get a fussy chimpanzee to reliably eat. Even then there is almost always another greedy chimp all too eager to steal whatever treat we try to hide medication in.

Thankfully many birds have little sense of taste, but with their ability to see ultraviolet and so extra colours compared to us, they can sometimes see crushed-up tablets or syrups mixed in their food that are invisible to our eyes, similar to how airport customs officers search for drug traces using UV lights. Some wildlife patients, however, can be slightly easier to medicate. Even though the Chinese giant salamander can unbelievably weigh more than an adult grey wolf, we can simply administer many medications by pouring them on their skin or dissolving them in the water they live in, and they will simply absorb it. No need to wrestle with these patients at all. Other amphibians, like the Sagalla caecilian, which looks more like a large worm than its frog and newt relatives, also absorb substances across their skin, despite the ancient Greeks mistakenly naming these amphibians 'naked snakes'. Unfortunately, most infections, even tuberculosis, also enter amphibians' bodies through their skin. This method is useful for a small golden poison arrow frog, coated in enough toxins to kill twenty people. Poison arrow frogs accumulate most of their toxins from their wild diet, so zoo bred frogs are not dangerous, but getting a patient weighing less than an ounce to open its mouth for medicine is pretty much impossible.

The earliest tablets found were on board a Roman ship-wreck from over two thousand years ago. A massive 4 centimetres across and containing zinc salts and olive oil, they were actually meant to be pressed onto sore eyes, rather than being swallowed. While eyedrops are now much more convenient, getting them into my patients is still difficult. Grabbing a red-fronted macaw several times daily to admin-ister them is no fun for patient or vet, while avoiding the can-opener beak latching onto a finger. But there is no way I can grab an uncooperative adult Patagonian sea lion weighing a third of a tonne to carefully apply a drop to each eye. In captivity they are prone to getting ulcers on the surface of their eyes, as shallow water doesn't shield their eyes sufficiently from ultraviolet radiation. It is as if they are prone to sunburn of their eyeballs, a condition as painful as it sounds. And it is a serious problem, as bacteria can eat their way through the surface and rupture an eye in just a day or two, causing permanent blindness.

Training a sea lion is your only hope, but this has to start when the patient is well, to have any hope of working when needed. Months of zookeepers patiently getting a large sea lion with the attention span of a toddler to accept plain salt-water eyedrops all pays off when it is needed to save his eye. Electric eels in an aquarium can even be trained to patiently touch a metal plate and accept an injection without electro-cuting the veterinarian. An equal training challenge is getting an elderly Bornean orangutan to not only accept daily insulin injections to treat her diabetes, but also carefully urinate into a cup every morning so we can check that her dose is correct for the day. Golden lion tamarins just don't have the patience for this, and we resort to giving longer-acting injections once a month, even if this doesn't work nearly as well.

Injections are always our last resort for giving medication. Darting an ill but still angry mountain lion has a risk of causing an injury, and doing more harm than good. Despite their size, an unlucky shot with a dartgun can actually break their leg bone. Injecting a large quantity of a thick drug through a big needle into a rescued elephant's butt is unpleasant for the patient and dangerous for the vet. Even if trained to be on its best behaviour, it is difficult to get the poor animal to behave every day. Despite their intelligence, they and my other unusual patients never seem to realise we are trying to help them. Far better to insert 50 tablets into oranges. If you start to let the other elephants in before the patient has finished its treat, it will frantically guzzle down the last oranges with drugs hidden inside, and you may just get away with it. I have had stones thrown at me by elephants that I have injected, and poo flung at my head by chimpanzees I have darted, despite not having seen some of these patients for over a decade since their treatments: testimony that the traumatic experience is seared into their memories. The first modern needle and syringe for injections was invented in 1853 by Scottish doctor Alexander Wood. But Native Americans were already using small animal bladders and hollow bird bones for everything from flushing wounds and ears to administering enemas, and even giving injections, before Columbus ever landed. One can only imagine how one of those injections stung.

What drug?

Challenging as it is to administer drugs to some of our less cooperative patients, this is often the easiest part. More challenging is what drug and dose to choose. For a bonobo, we can use the same drugs and doses as for a person. For a coyote, we can use a similar dose to that for a pet German Shepherd. But what about choosing a drug dose in a hippo, an emu, or a sungazer lizard? While an African elephant bull weighs two million times that of an Etruscan shrew, the shrew will eat almost double its body weight every day, while the elephant only eats about a hundredth of its body weight. Larger animals have slower metabolisms, while smaller patients have much faster ones. The tiniest injection in a shrew would equal an injection of several litres in an elephant, something clearly impossible. Even using far more concentrated drugs in larger animals, we also scale their medication doses for their lower metabolic rates, using allometric formulas. Three decades ago we were still doing a lot of this, but thankfully now with more and more wildlife vets sharing their experiences, and more published research studies, we have many more doses to go on, without having to constantly resort to algebra.

And that is a good thing, because some drug effects just don't make any mathematical or logical sense. It isn't just the amount we have to give for an effect, but also how long the drug lasts in the body to do its work that is important. Cefovecin is an antibiotic that caused much excitement when it first came out a decade ago for pet dogs and cats. An injectable antibiotic that lasts for two weeks, it saved thousands of cat-lovers from mauled arms when struggling to give their cat a tablet twice a day. From a class of antibiotics first discovered from a fungus in a sewer in Sardinia, it is very useful to be able to give a single injection to a bobcat with an infected bullet wound, or a tiger freed from a snare, without having to worry about how to get further antibiotic doses into them. Sadly, it doesn't work the same for other animals. A single injection can last for six months in a Californian sea lion, and even just half the usual dose will still last two months in a walrus. While this at first sounds good, it is not great if it did happen to cause a side-effect like an upset stomach, which could then take months to settle down. And while in bottlenose dolphins this antibiotic lasts a more reasonable three weeks, in a whitespotted bamboo shark it only lasts four days. This is still better than once daily injections of other antibiotics. But in a Russian rat snake you would actually need to inject it three times a day for it to work, while it would only last two to three hours in a scarlet ibis, making it pretty useless for most birds.

Sometimes you are faced with needing a drug in an unusual patient where nothing has been written, and even phoning colleagues doesn't help. We can start by trying to find a dose in a related animal. While obvious that you can probably use the same dose in a Sumatran rhino that has been safely used in its white rhino cousin, the same dose is probably also safe in a woolly tapir from the Andes cloud forest on the other side of the planet. Tapirs and rhinos all belong to the taxonomic order Perissodactyla, containing all uneven-toed hoofed animals, which also includes all the equines from zebras to domestic horses. They conveniently all have similar digestion and metabolism, so their reactions to drugs and doses are also similar. Felidae from the tiny rusty-spotted cat to African lions a hundred times larger can usually have similar doses to those tolerated by pet cats. But there are no domestic relatives similar to pangolins, sloths or dugongs to help us base our drug doses on. We also sometimes naively hope that ten thousand different bird species all react to medicines in the same way as chickens, pet parrots and a few falcon species that have had some research carried out on them. Considering the differences between an emu, a kiwi and an Alpine swift, I am not sure that this is always a reasonable assumption. Many doses are just hearsay between wildlife vets, usually that a drug wasn't obviously toxic. This doesn't mean it actually works at all.

Reptiles pose perhaps the greatest challenge. We tend to think of them as a group, like mammals and birds, hoping for a single drug dose suitable for all of them. Yet if we look at their evolutionary family tree, things get more murky. Tortoises and terrapins split from the rest in the Triassic period 200 million years ago, before even the reign of Jurassic dinosaurs. Dinosaurs, crocodiles and birds are actually much more closely related to each other than any of them are to snakes and lizards, let alone the ancient and only distantly related tortoises and turtles. Snakes have only recently evolved from burrowing lizards less than 100 million years ago, with the remnants of what were once a lizard's hind legs still visible as small spurs next to the vent of massive green anacondas.

In a vet formulary, a book of medication doses for different animal species, the section on reptiles, over ten thousand species, is thinner than the section on pet rabbits. There is a two-hundred-fold difference between three doses of a painkiller, with no details of any specific species of reptile. Most doses are just anecdotal. Someone used the drug at that dose and the animal didn't immediately die and appeared to get better. Perhaps its recovery had to do with the medicine, but perhaps it had nothing to do with it at all. It ends up in a book and gets quoted forever, whether it makes sense or not. Most of us have our own doses we are familiar with and like to use in a similar way, more like medieval apothecaries than scientists. Even the handful of published research studies usually just measure the levels of a drug in the blood stream. We are presuming similar levels in a green iguana will provide the same effects, whether pain relief, fighting infection, or killing internal parasites, that would work in domestic animals like dogs or chickens. But this may not make much sense, as some species may not even have the specific enzyme a drug was designed to target. Reptiles seem to have similar pain receptors to us mammals, yet don't react to opioid drugs like morphine at all like us. Some opioids can have a sedative effect like in other animals, while others do nothing at hundreds of times the dose. Traditional tests for painkillers, such as putting an animal's foot on a hot plate, mainly don't work, and even pet bearded dragons will also show different behaviour if they know they are being watched. Just like other animals who know they could potentially be food, most hide their symptoms. Evidence-based medicine is the new buzzword in veterinary science, but is impossible to practise with many animals when there is such weak evidence. Does a single, simple study in a handful of corn snakes mean the same dose is best for a Seychelles giant tortoise? Despite our best attempts, aside from a handful of doses in reptiles, it is all horribly unscientific.

None of these problems are new. Reading the very first medical records from the world's first employed zoo veterinarian Charles Spooner who attended to patients at London Zoo most Tuesdays, Thursdays and Saturdays, I can't help noticing that his meticulous handwriting in the zoo journal, with pale brown ink, and its artistic curled embellishments is far more beautiful than the handwriting of Charlotte Brontë or William Turner from the same year. This is probably just as well; these notes were the main way of the new veterinary graduate justifying his expense to the zoo council. Veterinarians had a large armoury of medications, powders, drenches, tinctures and liniments, just as doctors did, but for most of the past ten thousand years medication probably did more harm than good in the majority of patients' cases.

Spooner's very first entry, beautifully written but brief,

prescribes the application of a mercurial ointment to a white llama with skin eruptions. It is impossible to be certain, but in the damp London conditions this was possibly an infection called rain scald caused by a bacteria with the colourful name of *Dermatophilus congolensis*, or perhaps a sheep parapoxvirus that sometimes causes lumps around the mouth or nose. A fascinating liquid metal, obsessed over by alchemists seeking to make gold from base metals, mercury has been used in ointments since ancient Greece. Mercury compounds can kill bacteria, and I remember the bright-red mercurochrome disinfectant painted on my grazed knees when I was a child. But it also risks poisoning the patient as the metal is extremely toxic. Getting the balance wrong can be disastrous. The very first emperor of China, Qin Shi Huang, two thousand years ago, died drinking an elixir meant to bring immortality, which consisted of powdered jade and mercury: possibly one of the most spectacular medical failures in history.

If this was a bacterial infection in the London Zoo llama, the ointment may have helped clear it, but at a cost to the llama's subsequent health. Ironically both *Dermatophilus* and parapox, which being a virus would not have been helped by the ointment at all, usually clear up on their own after a few weeks. So it would have appeared as if whatever medication the keepers had lathered on, it had worked. And that is the rub. Until the recent advent of clinical trials, experience fools even experts. A patient may die despite the best medicine for its condition, or get better despite being given completely the wrong drug. A handful of cases can lead even an expert in completely the wrong direction with their ideas.

The placebo effect

Humans today are no more sensible. Market research consistently shows that people believe medication in a capsule form to be more potent than a tablet. Hence the invention of the caplet, simply a capsule-shaped tablet as a way for painkiller manufacturers to make their products seem stronger. Red-coloured tablets have also been shown to have greater painkilling effects than the same medication in a blue-coloured tablet. We still waste billions of pounds a year buying branded medicine like ibuprofen from supermarkets, although generics containing the identical drug sitting next to them on a shelf may be less than a tenth of the price. None of these old medications, whose patents have long since expired, can be any more powerful than the others despite the manufacturer's packaging claims. Southern African sangoma witchdoctor remedies I tried as a teenager were foul-tasting, pungent, and made you feel like you had been kicked in the head. After all, what better way to feel you are getting your money's worth, and the traditional 'muti' is potent and powerful, than by its taste and your dizziness, more likely to be intoxicating than actually beneficial? Western research has shown that telling someone a painkiller is expensive actually gives them more pain relief than the identical pill if told it is cheap. Indeed, giving any medication, even if it's just a disguised sweet, usually causes an improvement. Welcome to the placebo effect.

The placebo effect also works in animals. Working as wildlife veterinarians, there is always another person involved, whether a carer hand-rearing a bear cub in a sanctuary, a concerned ranger watching a limping rhino through binoculars, or a zookeeper who has worked with an individual tiger for a decade. Similar to how we fool ourselves with a red versus a blue tablet, animal carers frequently believe their charges improve with treatment no matter what you give them to administer. But it isn't entirely their fault. The veterinarian is usually associated with bad things by most animals, as we are the culprit darting and injecting them, or grabbing them for an examination. If worried, you will normally pay your ill patient more attention. But the hated veterinarian checking on an ill Indian hog deer several times a day, when they normally don't see you for weeks or months, is stressful, and similar to being faced with a predatory leopard. It is no wonder that most animals will hide their symptoms, and everyone mistakenly thinks they are getting better. This regularly fools even the most experienced of us.

Even if my patients all hate me, a caring and attentive bedside manner is essential in the healing arts. It is no surprise that in the British National Health Service, despite its fantastic scientific evidence basis, patients don't get that feeling of being cared for, as doctors are sadly constantly overworked. So they turn to alternative therapies for the personal attention and feeling of individual care they crave. Throughout history patients have paid doctors handsomely to cup and bleed them to death, with no scientific basis, simply because they felt cared for. Alternative therapy is a misnomer, unless it is like an alternative reality where we heal unicorns with magic wands. Unproven therapies may be a better description, but some supposed treatments have consistently failed so many scientific research efforts to evaluate them that they should actually be called disproven therapies. Not such a useful advertising term for their proponents, though. All scientific attempts at demonstrating any real effect from homeopathy have failed. Choosing substances that cause the same problem in small amounts seems bizarre. Why would tiny amounts of arsenic cure a Japanese spotted deer of arsenic poisoning? While arsenic is not even used in pesticides anymore, homeopaths appear to know better. To make them safe, toxic homeopathic substances are diluted, and beaten to impress their 'memory on water'. If C represents a one-hundred-fold dilution – so a relatively concentrated remedy, at least in homeopathic terms – then 12C is the equivalent dilution of a pinch of salt being added to the Atlantic Ocean. While concentrations over 50C are commonly sold commercially, these dilutions are the equivalent of less than 1 molecule of substance in the entire known universe. Claiming that water keeps its memories of a tiny amount of a substance is also a little strange. Isn't it also then going to remember passing through a cow's bladder and sloshing around the local sewage pipes before it is administered to an ill patient? And if it is water that keeps the memories of substances, why are remedies then sold in convenient sugar pills, not even disguising their similarity to placebos? While the founder of homeopathy more than two centuries ago was undoubtedly correct that most medicine at that time did more harm than good, it is ironic he based the entire pseudoscience on his scepticism of Peruvian cinchona bark which was being used to treat malaria. This was actually one of the very few remedies of the time that actually worked, containing the antimalarial compound quinine, which you can still enjoy the taste of, in an Indian tonic. Still, homeopathy is widely used in animals, from Asian elephants to common grackle birds, as it is not limited to being prescribed by a veterinarian.

Those working with wildlife are not immune to other magical thinking either. I once sat biting my tongue until it almost bled in a wildlife rehabilitation meeting a few decades ago, where a couple described how they would attend wildlife casualties hit by cars and administer Bach flower remedy drops to them, then leave them at the side of the road to recover. Returning hours or days later, the animals were always gone, which they took as a sign of successful treatment. Of course, it was more likely that the poor creatures crawled off into the undergrowth to die, or were swiftly eaten by the next passing fox.

Humans are judge and jury

We have another problem with animals too. A stressed zoo gorilla may start to catastrophically chew her fingers down to the bone, or a polar bear pace on a concrete floor until his feet bleed, but curators immediately want drugs like haloperidol or amitriptyline to try to stop this behaviour, without trying to understand and address the underlying cause of their extreme mental distress in the first place. While these medications have a place, one has to take care not to simply dope animals, instead of improving their environment or separating individuals who simply don't get on.

Even as veterinarians who supposedly work with animals,

we are always stuck with the fact that it is the humans along-side that will judge your efforts. While Charles Spooner is often remembered as the world's first employed zoo vet, it is less widely known that he was also the first zoo vet to get fired. Perhaps being a new graduate he hadn't yet fully honed his client communication skills. For whatever reason. he became unpopular with the animal keepers, and the zoo council replaced him with the older and more experienced, yet unqualified, William Youatt after only a few years.

Reading Youatt's notes shows little difference in treatments, but he was actually much more expensive. Yet he would inspect animals together with the head keepers and issued joint reports with them to the zoo council for a decade. He clearly was skilled with people, becoming both an honorary vet for the RSPCA, and the Queen's veterinary surgeon. His book on selective breeding of cattle was even used by Darwin when formulating his theory of natural selection. He was a leading veterinary figure of his day, yet was unqualified and hated the new Royal College of Veterinary Surgeons that oversaw the profession, as it was still bizarrely run by human doctors, not vets at all. He eventually submitted himself to college examination at the age of seventy when it had finally reformed to consist of veterinarians. Tragically, he committed suicide only a year later due to depression. Working in any health care profession has a risk of emotional burnout and fatigue, but in England vets have a four times higher suicide rate than doctors. The trials and tribulations of working with both humans and animals sadly seem to take a heavy toll. Even if the ability to access controlled drugs doesn't have deadly consequences, vets and doctors still have higher levels of drug and alcohol addiction than the general public.

After a decade's work, and despite Youatt's popularity, the zoo finances were in a complete shambles, sadly a regular theme over the next hundred and fifty years, and the council dismissed him. While the council of the zoo liked the visibility of a vet being seen to do something, they possibly realised that despite the expense, the vets had made no real difference, as a third of all the zoo's animals would still die every year. From then on most treatment was simply undertaken by the keepers, with the zoo superintendent Abraham Dee Bartlett even performing surgery on patients as difficult as elephants.

I would love to think we have moved away from veterinary examinations, diagnostics and medications simply for show – to be seen to do something. It's a problem that can also afflict domestic animal veterinarians with demanding pet owners in commercial practice. Yet looking at different zoos of similar size today, some have numerous full-time vets on staff, while others have vets only visiting weekly; some vets have strings of qualifications behind their name, while others have none; some have worked in zoos for several decades, others are green and fresh out of vet school; some zoo vets insist on anaesthesia and annual health checks of every animal in the zoo, while others only treat animals when ill, or to vaccinate them; one zoo will have a CT scanner, while another may not even have a cheap, portable ultrasound machine. So what is best, as these different approaches can have more than a twenty-fold difference in cost?

More than a decade ago, I briefly researched this across a selection of zoos. Similar to the London Zoo council a hundred and fifty years ago, I found there was little statistical difference in overall death rates or breeding success between most systems, which was a little disconcerting to say the least. It is not that veterinarians accomplish nothing, but rather that so many other factors of animals' lives, such as their nutrition, activity, shelter and general care, just play bigger roles in their health. Not everything is solved with tests or tablets.

Amazingly, placebo effects can work in animals when no humans are involved, something most believe shouldn't be possible. If mice are given daily morphine injections to dull pain, and weeks later this is replaced with injections of water, the mice continue to still show the same effect as if they were actually receiving the morphine. Pain is all in the brain. Anticipation of pain relief, even if the injection is just a placebo, gets the pituitary gland to release its own opioid painkilling endorphins, that also cause the 'high' one gets from chocolate, exercise, sex or meditation, even if the mouse is not consciously aware this is happening. Yet, this can even work with drugs that have nothing to do with pain relief or natural endorphins. Giving animals cyclophosphamide, a chemotherapy drug syrup used for treating cancers like leukaemia, not only makes them feel nauseous, but also decreases the number of white blood cells they have circulating, making them more prone to infections: so not only of questionable benefit, but something that can be dangerous. Yet researchers found that after giving dogs the drug for several weeks, if they stopped and replaced it with the same-tasting syrup with no drug in, the body continues to produce the same effects, with dramatically low numbers of circulating white cells, just from giving a dose of sugar water. Placebos are so much more interesting than just being a control sugar pill with which to compare a new medicine on trial. We really understand very little of some of these effects, but they do hold tantalising possibilities of getting the benefits of some medications without actually having to give them continuously. Treating an elderly arthritic zoo elephant without actually having to use painkillers constantly for many months, which risks damaging the kidneys, but instead just in short courses interspersed with a similar placebo, is definitely an appealing prospect, and well worth investigating. It is certainly no worse than the homeopathy sometimes used.

Drugs are not the cure-all

In some wild animals, we can go one better than placebos, and actually medicate a patient without any drugs. Indeed, it may be essential. You may give the best antibiotic to a reticulated python, yet it has no effect on the painful mouth infection and the patient continues to deteriorate. You may diagnose osteoporosis in a Russian tortoise, yet despite months of calcium medication there is no improvement on X-rays, and the bones continue to weaken until they crumple and break just with the normal effort of the tortoise walking. For these,

It is possible to evaluate a king penguin's body temperature without needing to catch it or use a thermometer. The penguin's large eyes lose heat, and a thermal camera can alert you to early signs of a fungal infection or bird malaria that you would otherwise miss.

Bone healing in birds happens in the fast lane. Unlike a human or most mammals, whose bones can take months to heal, a bird can fly normally after a broken bone in as little as two weeks.

Repairing fractured bones in animals that cannot be rested after surgery poses a challenge. Locking plates and screws act like a type of internal scaffolding for broken bones and can be a more robust repair in patients like chimpanzees, which may swing from a repaired arm immediately after surgery.

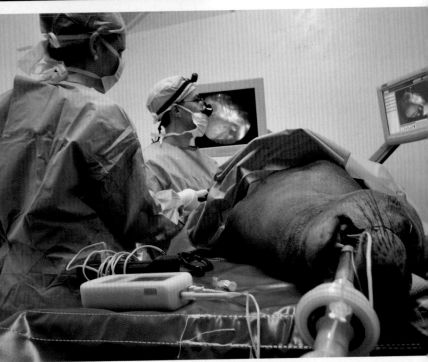

Complex operations can be completed with keyhole surgical instruments only 3 mm in diameter – the same thickness as a microchip needle or a pencil lead. This is a major advantage in making water-tight wounds in a patient such as a sea lion, which will start swimming in water just a few hours after its operation.

(Photograph by Jonathan Cracknell)

A Komodo dragon's replacement teeth come in sideways, from behind the old teeth. And in another unique trait, female dragons have the ability to produce clones of themselves in unfertilised eggs by parthenogenesis if no males are available.

Even though a white rhinoceros weighs two tonnes, darting is still an unpleasant experience. Modern carbon-dioxide-powered dart rifles and plastic darts now rarely cause wounds. Dart syringes can only carry a small volume, so concentrated anaesthetic drugs a thousand times as potent as morphine are needed. The red fluffy flight helps make an airtight seal to propel the dart down the rifle barrel. It also stabilises the dart in flight, and helps you to find the dart after it drops out of a galloping rhino.

The giant anteater has a tiny mouth and a long, thin tongue, which
it uses to lick up huge numbers of ants at lightning speed. If injured
anteaters are fed diets with blended meat, and if even a tiny sinew or
muscle fibre survives, this risks wrapping around the tongue,
strangulating it and causing the tongue to fall off.
An anteater with no tongue cannot eat.

Placing an endotracheal tube for anaesthesia
is also very difficult. The anteater's long, thin
mouth, which hardly opens, is a challenge.
Its windpipe entrance, the larynx, actually
sits in its chest, so a special half-metre-
long tube inserted with a thin,
flexible endoscope is needed.

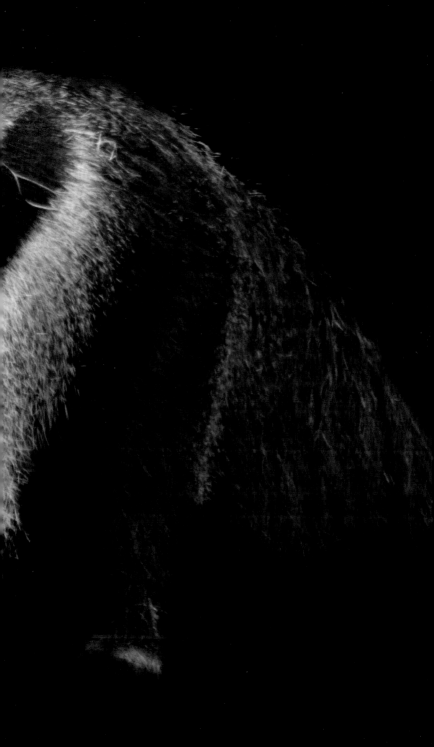

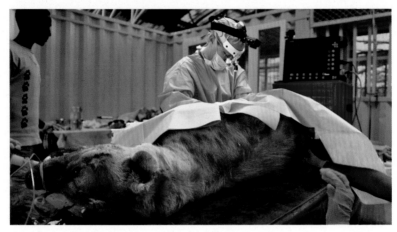

Female hyaenas have higher testosterone levels than males, and are larger and stronger to protect their youngsters. Surgery to sterilise a female is unlike the kind used for a domestic dog or cat. It is essential that the ovaries remain, so that normal hormones are produced to keep the group hierarchy intact. (Photograph by Jonathan Cracknell)

Collecting a tiny sample to make pluripotent cells, precursors to stem cells. The hope is to one day make eggs and sperm from stem cells of endangered species and help prevent extinction. However, despite much media hype, assisted reproductive techniques have made little impact on conservation thus far. (Photograph by Craig Devine))

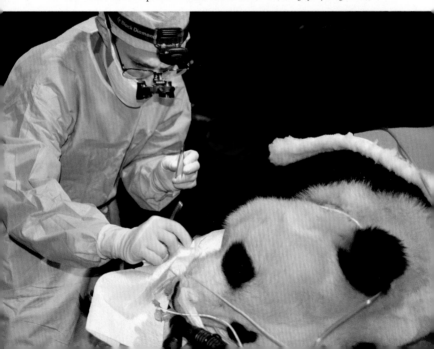

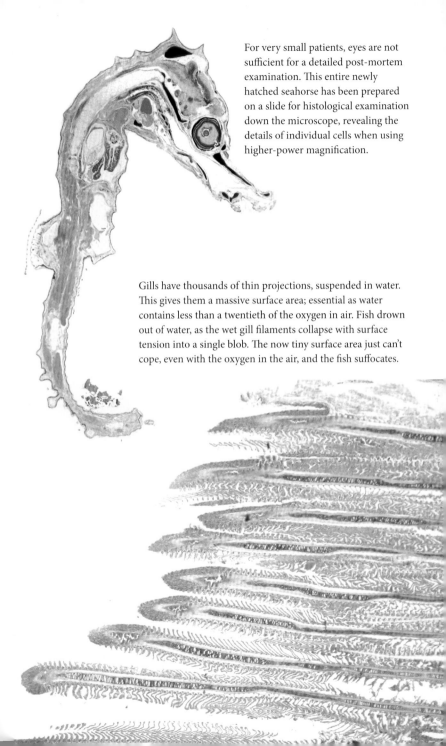

For very small patients, eyes are not sufficient for a detailed post-mortem examination. This entire newly hatched seahorse has been prepared on a slide for histological examination down the microscope, revealing the details of individual cells when using higher-power magnification.

Gills have thousands of thin projections, suspended in water. This gives them a massive surface area; essential as water contains less than a twentieth of the oxygen in air. Fish drown out of water, as the wet gill filaments collapse with surface tension into a single blob. The now tiny surface area just can't cope, even with the oxygen in the air, and the fish suffocates.

If you are close enough to a lion to examine its retina with an ophthalmoscope, you can see the small white circle that is the optic nerve. The blood vessels snaking out from its edges allow us to diagnose diet insufficiencies causing early retinal detachment, brain tumours causing the optic nerve to bulge, or high blood pressure and infections. The only part we can normally see from a distance is the yellow tapetum lucidum layer of the retina that reflects light to boost a lion's night vision, and also gives away its presence, reflected in our torchlight.

Radio-transmitters surgically implanted in a brown bear's abdomen may yield research information on their habits, but they also carry risks to the individual animal. Transmitter batteries can explode, leak acid, become infected and kill even these large animals.

and most reptiles, the greatest medicine is not a medication. It is their temperature. While a cold vervet monkey maintains its own body temperature by shivering if needing to generate extra heat, reptiles like a reticulated python or Russian tortoise can't do this. Reptiles are poikilothermic, or dependent on external temperatures. This inability to generate their own body temperature is actually an advantage, as mammals spend most of their energy simply maintaining their temperature. Instead reptiles save this energy, can eat less, and survive lean times that would kill a mammal. A saltwater crocodile can go for more than a year without eating, something a mammal could never do.

In the wild, a Russian tortoise can choose what temperature it likes. It may want to be warmer in the morning to become active, or to digest food, or cooler when it wants to rest, or when it wants to breed. While different body processes all work better at slightly different temperatures, this is simple for a reticulated python to achieve by roaming in the wild. But in captivity, whether in a zoo or a wildlife rehabilitation centre, we usually need to keep reptiles enclosed in vivaria, those glass-fronted enclosures with artificial heating. There may not be enough difference between the hot and cool ends of a tank for a patient to select the temperature they prefer. Ill animals seem to need warmer temperatures for good healing and a strong immune response, and they can't always achieve this if the vivarium doesn't get warm enough. Even with a good range of temperatures, reticulated python enclosures are frequently not even long enough for them to stretch out their whole body, being the world's longest snake species. If your immune system is not working because your temperature is wrong, you will be prone to infections that even antibiotics can do nothing for. Yet with warm enough temperatures and a big enough range of temperatures to select from, a python's mouth infection may actually resolve on its own, as the immune system kicks in, with no need for antibiotics.

Deprived of sunlight in the box-like vivarium, a Russian

tortoise is unable to make vitamin D in its skin and shell, and without that can simply not absorb the calcium you medicate it with to strengthen its bones. Just injecting vitamin D can actually result in calcification of the wrong tissues, like the main blood vessels exiting the heart, and cause different health problems. Far better to give the tortoise natural sunlight outside in summer months, and in winter and on rainy days provide special ultraviolet light bulbs hung low in the vivarium to help it synthesise vitamin D naturally. Often the best medicine is not a drug at all.

It is difficult to compress all the complexity of the natural world into a small box. Temperature and lighting issues cause most health problems in reptiles under human care, but can also treat them. Good nutrition also helps treat or prevent health problems from flaky skin to kidney stones in everything from otters to imperial eagles. It is no wonder the ancient Greeks saw everything as medicine. A holistic approach. We know keeping animals mentally stimulated is also a very good way of treating pain. A chimpanzee working for hours with a food puzzle to get raisins can be oblivious to the pain from a wound, just as you only feel the discomfort of an arthritic knee at night, after being mentally occupied all day at work. When we are already using all the painkillers we safely can in a geriatric elephant, this can help improve the patient's life.

Sadly, our modern societal consensus appears to be that medication is only stuff you can put in a pill, and every problem, from an unhappy marriage to obesity, can be solved with a tablet. What genius of modern marketing thought of that? Surely it is better to keep physically active, eat a healthy mix of vegetables and get enough sleep, making you less likely to get ill, than the alternative of constantly swallowing a selection of different cough and flu remedies when overworked, stressed, sleep deprived, and living on fast food while glued to your computer? But we have unrealistic expectations with our 24-hour lives and on-demand video. We forget it took a decade to become obese and are angry when a week's worth of diet tablets fail to transform us from blob to chiselled heart-throb. Who wouldn't prefer a tablet if it promised wisdom instead of years of studying at university, or instant perfect physique and fitness, instead of months of hard exercise and heathy eating every day? Or imagine if you could buy an expensive tablet that would let you master the clarinet – would you really instead choose to spend years learning, paying for lessons, and practising? I think not. But clever marketing seems to have fooled us all into some similarly unrealistic expectations with human and animal health. I am frequently asked why an orangutan, tiger or zebra is not better yet, just hours after starting on medication. As our lives have sped up, we fail to remember that healing today is at the same speed it was ten thousand and even ten million years ago, and simply takes time.

Natural plant remedies, stirring thoughts that everything natural must be healthy and good, are another marketing success. Many plants are full of cyanide or a wide range of other toxic substances and are anything but good for humans or animals. The good medicinal ones we know about have usually already been refined into safe medications. Yet we can't help wondering if there is still something to be learned from how free wild animals keep well, and treat themselves when ill in the wild.

Everyone loves tales of the wisdom of wild animals. Detached as we are from nature, we want to believe they have secrets for us to learn, whether it is predicting the weather or teaching us about new medicinal plants. Tales of elephants travelling miles to eat a specific tree's bark to help them give birth that is also brewed into tea for the same purpose by local Kenyan women, or chimpanzees choosing specific plants to help rid themselves of gut parasites, have been the subject of many articles, books and documentaries. Female orangutans carrying a heavy baby will rub the chewed-up leaves of the Dracaena plant with its natural anti-inflammatory properties on the muscles of their tired arms, while lemurs in Madagascar rub toxic millipedes on their fur as insect repellents. Scarlet macaws will eat mineral-rich clay after eating fruit with toxins in, and red colobus monkeys in Zanzibar eat charcoal to allow them to eat the leaves of farmed almond trees and mangoes, without the toxins upsetting their digestion, which hasn't evolved for this foreign food source. Zoopharmacognosy is the study of animals self-medicating – which even applies to your pet cat eating grass.

Yet I remain a little cautious about what we can really learn from all this. Over my career, I have also seen many free-ranging wild animals poison themselves by eating toxic plants their species has evolved around for millions of years, let alone swallowing everything from stones to plastic bags. Wild animals in care will also just as happily pig-out on unhealthy foods and get obese, just as their human carers do. Some good studies have clearly shown that butterfly larvae carrying para-sites eat plants containing toxins that while stunting their growth affect the parasite more, and fruit flies will also eat more rotting fruit containing toxic alcohol when carrying para-sites. But the evidence for the more exciting stories featuring in magazines is more tenuous than may be apparent. The scientific paper of the chimpanzees in East Africa that swal-lowed whole *Aspilia* leaves that then passed through whole, removing some parasitic intestinal worms, was based on obser-vation of just seven animals. Yet this is scientifically luxurious compared to self-medicating elephants in labour. This widely circulated story is based on just one sighting of the behaviour in a single elephant.

While I have spent plenty of time in my career dealing with wild animals that have eaten the most stupid things, I do believe that wild animals sometimes do perform some sort of self-medication by what they eat, but I am much less convinced this is actually a conscious decision we can learn great wisdom from. I suspect it must be more instinctive, much as when pregnant women develop insatiable cravings for the most bizarre foods. It is often theorised that these pregnancy crav-ings are to correct nutritional deficiencies, perhaps due to morning sickness. Hmong women in Laos believe that a baby will be born with deformities if the mother is not allowed to eat all the things she craves. However, the common craving for chocolate in pregnancy is probably more due to the presence of tryptophan, a precursor to serotonin, the neuro-transmitter affecting moods, than any nutritional deficiency. Some pregnant women will also eat soil, stones, chalk or hair, which clearly have no nutritional benefits, and can actually be harmful. Perhaps these cravings actually serve an entirely different purpose – to attract group members' attention to a woman's early pregnancy and alert them to her ongoing need for help and attention during her pregnancy.

Antibiotics

While modern drugs consist of just one active chemical, rather than the hundreds of compounds contained in a plant leaf, pure drugs still can have adverse side-effects. Indigo snakes are poisoned by what would be a normal dose of the antibiotic metronidazole in most other snakes. While injectable penicillin is a perfectly safe antibiotic to use in capybara, it will cause a fatal gut upset if mistakenly given by mouth, and even if the capybara just licks a spilt drop off its fur after an injection. Most wild cats, from margays to snow leopards, develop a serious anaemia if treated with paracetamol, and tortoises are paralysed by the wormer ivermectin, while snakes and lizards treated with it are fine even with a ten-fold overdose. It is no surprise that animal testing of human drugs cannot prevent disasters like thalidomide, when there is such variation between animal species.

We often have a good idea of what is toxic. It only takes news of one vet's unfortunate disaster to change all our prescribing habits: for example, a pour-on cattle wormer that somehow causes permanent blindness when used on some bongos, or a spray-on flea treatment for dogs that kills rabbits. This can quickly become gospel even if not truly the drug's fault. Sometimes it isn't the drug or dose, but where it is given, that could be a problem. It may seem bizarre that if you inject medication in the front leg of a rhinoceros iguana versus the back leg of the same iguana, you could end up with different drug levels circulating in the blood. Yet, this is possible thanks to a special bit of plumbing that these iguanas have. The renal portal system is a system of blood vessels that shunt a portion of blood returning from the back of the body through the kidneys before it reaches the heart. This ensures the kidneys get enough blood to keep them from failing, even if an iguana is dehydrated and not making any urine.

For decades we believed it essential to not inject antibiotics like gentamicin that could be toxic to the kidneys into the rear half of many reptiles, lest this caused kidney failure. However, we now know that the drug needs to be filtered via the glomerulus to be toxic, and this doesn't happen within the system, so our precautions weren't really necessary. Those first lizards that died probably did so just because they were already very ill and dehydrated and the gentamicin would have proved too much for their kidneys to cope with, no matter where it was injected.

Enrofloxacin, another popular antibiotic, can sometimes cause permanent blindness in pet cats if given at high doses. Yet looking back at zoo records, it never seems to have caused a problem in any lions or tigers. But it occasionally will cause permanent blindness in another random animal of a different species, just to make your life miserable. You may treat a whole group of guanaco, but one suddenly goes permanently blind, a disaster as the others will then use this as an opportunity to rip their competition up with their surprisingly sharp teeth. Domestic animal vets are always extremely careful to weigh pet cats, but this is something we are not always able to do with our wild patients. We frequently have to guess the weight of a nervous plain zebra galloping away into the distance, or a jaguarundi hiding in the shadows. I love quizzing vet students as to what they think different animals weigh from photos. They are frequently wildly wrong, reminding me to always check my 'guesstimates' when I finally do get the opportunity to weigh a patient. Even with decades of experience, you can easily be more than enough out for an antibiotic to be completely useless in fighting an infection, or err on the other side causing fatal intoxication with a heart medication.

Sometimes side-effects are real, but not in the species given the drug. Vets treating African elephants for parasites with ivermectin also inadvertently kill all the dung beetles that recycle their waste, disrupting the normal ecosystem function. More carelessly, veterinarians actually made the Californian condor lice extinct when they took the last few condors into captivity to save them with captive breeding, and unthinkingly dusted them with insecticide powder. While not as charismatic as its host, it did the condors no harm, and highlights the fact that not everything needs treatment, a mindset unfortunately drummed into us all during vet school to prepare us for commercial work, but not always applicable to conservation. My friend Andrew Routh, as head vet for the Durrell Wildlife Conservation Trust, is only too aware of this, working with the endangered pygmy hog in northern Assam. The International Union for the Conservation of Nature lists its unique louse as even more critically endangered, and they are careful to select drugs that won't harm the parasite, something pet owners with their paranoia of creepy crawlies may find bizarre.

The anti-inflammatory painkiller diclofenac, taken by people with gout after indulging in too much red wine and fatty food, is also used in arthritic camels and farmers' water buffalos in Asia. But it is so toxic to vultures, that simply scavenging off one of these dead animals that has small traces will be enough to kill a vulture from kidney failure. This medicine has been responsible for making the most common vultures in the world only a few decades ago, the white-rumped and Indian vultures, almost extinct. They are now both critically endangered. This has happened since I worked in India two decades ago trying to help discover the cause of their disappearance with Vibhu Prakash, the scientist at the Bombay Natural History Society who first discovered there was a problem. Safer painkiller drugs that we sometimes use to replace diclofenac also have their quirks. Meloxicam, a common painkiller given daily to people, pet dogs, horses, and, safely, in vultures, lasts five days in a bottlenose dolphin, essential knowledge if you don't want to fatally poison your aquatic patient. Yet, frustratingly in mountain hares, even ten times the dose used in other animals doesn't seem to work as well for pain as it does in many other species.

High doses of anti-inflammatory painkillers can cause stomach upsets, vomiting, and even ulcers in people. Collared peccaries are more sensitive, so we often give them anti-nausea medication. Hares and rabbits can also get stomach ulcers, but they can't vomit. So can the critically endangered riverine rabbit actually experience nausea? It would seem horrible for evolution to play this trick on you, but who knows? It may be possible for animals that can't vomit to still feel nauseous. So do you use anti-nausea medication, and at what dose? And even if you decide to do so, how on earth can you know if it is working or not?

With all these uncertainties, and almost as many side-effects as potential benefits for some medications, reaching for any drug requires careful consideration. Especially when it comes to antibiotics and long-term care. With exploding numbers of multi-drug resistant bacteria causing infections in people and species ranging from wild seals to zoo tigers, the veterinary and human medical community are all trying to protect antibiotics so we will still have medicines that work when we vitally need them. But doctors and vets are constantly under pressure from paying clients to dispense antibiotics. If you don't, your clients will simply abandon you for another more laissez-faire clinic. It is estimated that more than half of all antibiotics prescribed by human doctors are unnecessary, and at best a placebo. Yet vets have often been blamed by the medical community for increasing antibiotic resistance, despite only using a tiny quantity in comparison. Are the real culprits intensive livestock farms in some overseas countries, which actually account for three-quarters of the total global antibiotic consumption? These are not prescribed by vets, or indeed for sick animals at all, but simply because of their side-effects of acting as growth promoters. This seems crazy, as there are few new antibiotics being developed. For a few pence off the price of your sausages, humanity may be dooming itself to a future of untreatable antibiotic-resistant infections.

Being the best custodians of antibiotic use is just as important in sanctuaries and zoos as in a human hospital. Working with a group of chimpanzees living in a large forest enclosure in a sanctuary, you have to fight your initial tendency to want to prescribe antibiotics for the massive bite one got on its backside during an argument with his friend that morning. It is always best to wait. There may only be one or two types of tablets that the chimpanzees will be prepared to eat every day consistently for a course of treatment to work, already severely limiting your options. One has to remember that we have only had antibiotics for less than the last hundred years of our 10,000 years of human history. Healthy, happy chimpanzees heal unbelievably fast most of the time. Only very occasionally will one get an infection from a bite that really does need antibiotics. Perhaps their habit of settling arguments by biting each other has made them more robust and resistant to infection. I am not sure. But if you repeatedly reach for antibiotics for each case when it isn't needed, you store up a disaster for later. Many microbiologists believe that even a single week's course of antibiotics can change forever the normal balance and species of bacteria living in the gut. Chimpanzees are what they eat, and have more bacteria in their gastrointestinal tract than their own cells in their entire body. Like us, and most animals, they are their own walking mini-ecosystems. Chimpanzees, due to their largely plant-based diets, have more diverse and balanced gut microbiomes than most people. Antibiotics don't just kill bacteria causing infections, but also play havoc with beneficial gut bacteria. Gut bacteria produce a host of neurotransmitters, and more than 90 per cent of serotonin is produced in the gut, not the brain. So a depressed chimpanzee may need a good diet to re-establish the normal healthy gut bacteria, rather than us just reaching for the Prozac.

While antibiotics may be an essential compromise to save a life, if used unnecessarily for minor bites, the change in gut bacteria can actually change a chimpanzee's mental status and behaviour, and your antibiotics simply result in more fighting and more bite wounds in the troop. When possible, we always try to resort to disinfectants before antibiotics. These can kill bacteria in wounds before they attach and invade tissues, and are the reason your mum always told you to wash your cut finger with soap, a cheap disinfectant too. And the real beauty of disinfectants is that bacteria do not develop the same resistance to them, as they do to antibiotics.

But the most serious risk is that using antibiotics frequently, and even more disastrously chopping and changing the types of antibiotics you use between the different individual chimpanzees in the troop, means you are simply selecting for bacteria resistant to these antibiotics to colonise the gut and the chimpanzees' environment. So the one time there really is a bad infection, it will be due to these already antibiotic-resistant bacteria invading, and when you finally really need antibiotics, your medicine won't work.

The Scottish wildcat, or Highland tiger, is often heralded as the most endangered wild
animal in the British Isles. Yet it is only a subspecies. With all remaining wildcats
already heavily hybridised with feral domestic cats it is questioned by many whether
focusing on subspecies conservation in this case is meaningful.

14

To breed or not to breed?

Cheetahs were the giant pandas of my childhood. Growing up in South Africa, at school we learned that cheetahs really could become extinct. Their numbers had fallen as low as 700 in the country, and attempts to breed them in zoos were not going well. Zoos couldn't even sustain their captive population, let alone breed them for release into the wild. And it all came down to sex.

Animal sex can be fascinating, amusing and downright weird. The Victorians were embarrassed by the whole notion. Zoo animals were described as playing or wrestling as euphemisms for mating. This is not dissimilar to answers given to children watching hamadryas baboons vigorously mating, or a drill monkey happily masturbating in a large viewing window. Sex also often has nothing to do with reproduction. Bonobos often use sex to prevent fights, console a friend, or strategically forge alliances. While male chimpanzees mount other males to assert their dominance, bonobos frequently engage in lesbian activity simply for fun. Same-sex gentoo penguin couples build nests together, and are often excellent parents when given abandoned eggs to foster in zoos.

The fact that long-beaked echidnas have a four-headed penis but only use two heads at a time to mate, will enliven any dinner conversation. Equally bizarre, female echidnas lay an egg but keep it in a pouch, and after hatching the young puggle attaches to a nipple and stays in the pouch for three months. Long-nosed bandicoots have two separate vaginas; great hammerhead sharks have two spikey penis-like claspers, one of which they inflate with sea water as an anchor; sugar gliders have a forked penis; and electric blue geckos have two completely separate inside-out penises hidden in their tail, with the spare just in case one gets bitten off by an unhappy partner. Things get even more colourful when we try to convince endangered animals to cooperate in captive breeding.

Spermatozoa

Cheetahs are the supermodels of the cat world – beautiful, long-legged, and not overly bright. More importantly, their genetics are a mess. Ten thousand years ago, the species almost went extinct. Recovering from just a few animals, most of their genetic variation disappeared. We share about 80 per cent of our genetic information with any other human on the planet, but for cheetahs their genomes are all almost 99 per cent the same. It is as if every cheetah is a close cousin.

Variation in a population is vital for a species' survival. Some individuals are more resistant to a disease, while others can tolerate hotter temperatures, or cope with other environmental changes. Watching sparrows in a city park, it is clear that some are braver, quickly approaching crumbs thrown to them, and would survive when food is scarce. Others, being more cautious, will occasionally go hungry, but are less likely to be eaten by a cat lurking nearby. Variation underpins natural selection. With little genetic variation, harmful genes can also persist for thousands of years.

Cheetahs have unfortunately inherited genes for rubbish sperm. Compared to a zoo cheetah, a domestic Yorkshire pig can produce two thousand times as many sperm in an ejaculation. While the volume is over a hundred times greater, the semen concentration is also ten times more. That is before even looking at the spermatozoa themselves. How many are normal and swim in a straight line is equally important.

Cheetahs have many sperm with weird deformities, or kinked tails that can only swim in a circle: pretty useless for reaching the distant egg they are supposed to fertilise. Cheetahs also suffer from stage fright. Sperm quality is far superior in cheetahs kept away from people, compared to those on display in a zoo. Who can really blame them?

Spermatozoa vary. While a Cape porcupine's spermatozoa is half the length of a human's, that of a tiny honey possum is six times as long as ours. One fruit fly has sperm more than half a centimetre long when untangled from their coiled shape, many times longer than the fly's entire body. Massive sperm are costly to produce, and a fly only produces a small number during their life, similar to a female and her eggs. Larger animals don't have larger sperm. As one reproductive scientist put it, the larger the playing field the less important the player's size, but the more important the number. Large sperm in small creatures can crowd out or block a competitor male's sperm from the female's small reproductive tract.

Blobfish even produce two types of sperm: normal shaped fertile spermatozoa and flat infertile ones. Not every sperm is sacred, but this isn't a biological mistake. Silk moths' artificial insemination with just the fertile sperm doesn't result in fertile eggs; the infertile second type of sperm is also needed for fertilisation to occur. Common periwinkles, small sea snails, collected for food for ten thousand years in Scotland, produce three types of sperm. Besides normal fertile sperm, a larger, stronger infertile sperm type acts as transport, which fertile sperm latch onto to catch a ride – a sperm taxi. Another smaller infertile sperm type acts like a crowbar, helping open the protective outer layer of the egg. Wood mice have instead solved these problems with a single sperm type. Their sperm have a hook on their head. This lets them link up with other sperm, forming a sperm train to out-swim the competition. The hook also helps them enter the egg. Swimming sperm are not even unique to animals. Ferns and mosses also produce sperm cells with tails, and swim in water like a shark's sperm.

Females also have some tricks. Black-legged kittiwakes can

eject the sperm of males they don't want to fertilise their eggs, and store sperm of males they prefer. Tuatara females, besides choosing which males' sperm should fertilise their eggs, can store live sperm for months after mating. But the sperm storage record-holder is a Javan wart snake that stored viable sperm for over seven years after mating.

Cheetahs' breeding woes are not just due to male sperm problems. Female cheetahs ovulate less frequently when kept with other females, and are incredibly fussy about which males they like. And we have caused a second genetic bottleneck in the last two centuries, the population crashing from more than a hundred thousand to less than seven thousand today. Other species have survived genetic bottlenecks, without their sperm count self-destructing. Wisent, European bison, recovered from just 12 individuals, and all Chatham Island robins are descendants of a single female, when the population crashed to just five individuals forty years ago. One of our most common pets is the most extreme inbreeding example. All of the millions of golden hamsters, bred as pets every year, are the descendants of a single pregnant wild female caught near Aleppo in Syria in the 1930s. Sadly, in the wild it is now classed as vulnerable to extinction.

At an ex-chicken farm in De Wildt, South Africa, where my vet school classmate Peter Caldwell is the wildlife vet, they finally cracked captive cheetah breeding. 'Lovers' Lane' is a dating service for cheetahs, a feline Tinder. Males are brought into the lane, a long thin enclosure in front of the female enclosures. If a male and female hit it off when she is in season, the date has been a success and he is allowed into her enclosure. The result is fewer fights, and more pregnancies than from random partnering, or even artificial insemination.

Lovers' Lane was a game changer, with hundreds of cheetahs bred there and at other centres translocated back to the wild. As cheetahs live in many isolated pockets in the wild, re-introductions helped prevent further genetic deterioration. At the same time, vets also progressed zoo breeding with improved artificial insemination and other assisted reproductive techniques. Eventually this led to the cheetah being downgraded from endangered to vulnerable by the IUCN. This was a conservation success story recently replicated in giant pandas, due in part to captive breeding by centres in Bifengxia, Dujiangyan and Wolong, and work by my friends, Wang Chengdong and Wu Honglin.

Successful zoo management and genetics

Responsible zoos now rarely take animals from the wild, aiming to maintain self-sustaining populations. For critically endangered species like the addax, Visayan warty pig, European mink, and Bali mynah they try to act like modern-day Noah's arks, maintaining maximum genetic variation should wild populations be decimated. Zoos have re-introduced a few extinct species back to the wild, such as the Arabian oryx and Przewalski's horse, and boosted the falling golden lion tamarin population. Some zoos maintain species now completely extinct in the wild, like Spix's macaw, the scimitar-horned oryx, and the Socorro dove, the rarest species I have had to operate on so far.

But how do you maintain good population genetics when each zoo only houses a single pair of Amur leopards? No zoo can keep 300 leopards, so the whole zoo population across different countries is managed with a studbook, looking at how closely related leopards are, and which leopards have bred. Some may be too successful, and risk swamping the population with their genes, which is detrimental to maximising the genetic diversity we are aiming for. Individuals are moved between zoos to form new pairs, reshuffling the genetic card deck.

This works well in solitary species like Amur leopards that only come to together to mate. But as with cheetahs, mate choice is difficult to manage when dealing with intelligent highly social animals like chimpanzees. A particular male may be very genetically valuable on paper, but be low in the troop's hierarchy, and so never allowed to mate. Complex games with contracepting other dominant individuals can be a bit of a lottery. Laudable as conservation breeding is, the mental health and social life of individual animals can be forgotten. Imagine waking up with a groggy anaesthesia headache, in a different place alongside a stranger you have never met, to discover this is now your spouse for the next few decades. Imagine how a middle-aged female Western lowland gorilla must feel. It is no surprise that despite genetic matching, some partnered animals won't breed. They just don't like their internet-dating selected match.

Many days I am sure my wife wonders why on earth she married me. We speak different languages, have very different personalities, and besides both being vets, have almost nothing else in common. We are probably like raccoons. Raccoons choose their partners based on smell. But it isn't pheromones or an appealing scent that does the trick. Raccoons can judge each other's immune system by smell. Via their nose, they know how different another raccoon's major histocompatibility complex is from their own. Over 400 million years old, the complex is a section of DNA that codes for cell surface proteins critical in the immune system. Raccoons want a partner with immune system genes as different from theirs as possible, so their offspring have a good shuffle of disease resistance. This DNA complex also influences the volatile fatty acids in sweat, which potential partners can detect. The same thing happens in humans, shown in studies of students selecting different sweaty T-shirts. So the next time you're arguing with your partner, and wonder how such incompatible people could ever have linked up, blame your primitive brain for trying to sniff out a divergent immune system at the expense of everything else.

Even with computer programs analysing genetics, sometimes you are pointlessly looking for the holy grail. The European zoo population of endangered banteng, founded from a dozen animals, has bred and grown in size. Unfortunately, one of the original males only had one testicle. To be more scientific, he had cryptorchidism, where one testicle fails to descend into the scrotum. The problem is often hereditary. Banteng testicles are designed to hang outside the body to prevent them overheating. Inside the abdomen they are prone to malfunction, give off abnormal hormones, and sometimes develop tumours: not ideal in the captive breeding programme of an endangered species. Lying on the ground with an aching back as I remove an abnormal internal testicle in a half-tonne anaesthetised banteng by keyhole surgery is a reminder to me of how difficult inadvertent genetic problems can be to address.

Internal testicles have caused problems for a host of animals I have operated on, from a bullied reindeer with abnormal antlers, to Roloway monkeys with low libido. Yet some species have evolved with internal testicles. Elephant testicles remain deep in the abdomen, safe from being tusked by rival males, as do those of their relatives, the rock hyrax. In contrast, brush-tailed rock-wallaby scrotums are so pendulous it seems miraculous they don't kick them when jumping, or bash them on rocks. Tasmanian devil scrotums dangle so low it is a wonder they don't get tangled on vegetation, or have them bitten off by a screaming rival devil.

Assisted reproduction

When natural breeding is difficult, researchers often turn to assisted-reproductive technologies. This covers everything from artificial insemination of giant pandas, to cloning African wildcats, and even genetic engineering to resurrect mammoths. Touted widely for everything from bringing back the dodo to cloning the northern white rhino, the potential appears tremendous. But most techniques have had minimal real conservation impact, despite decades of funding, research and extensive media hype, due to their complexity and high cost. Most are difficult to apply in field conditions, and many are still more in the realms of science fiction than reality, despite decades of research work.

Twenty years after the first human births from artificial

insemination with frozen sperm in 1954, Kurt Benirschke a human pathologist, started the first frozen zoo in San Diego. He started keeping reproductive tissues from endangered species in the hope technology would eventually catch up, helping us save, or resurrect, extinct species. The idea was slow in taking off. Cryonics and freezing severed human heads was initially far more appealing to researchers, after James Lovelock, who later developed the Gaia hypothesis, found a way to resuscitate frozen hamsters with up to 60 per cent of the water in their brain crystallising, without any apparent ill effects. It is difficult to know if this was truly the case: you couldn't ask the hamsters to recall childhood memories, or ask where they had left their car keys.

Always on the edge of quackery, cryonics fell into further disrepute when one company, run by an ex-TV repair man with no scientific background, allowed several bodies to thaw and decompose, and was subsequently sued. Economically, it seems impossible for any of the currently frozen bodies to be salvaged, even if the technology does eventually prove possible. The current business model is simply not viable. The companies will long since have gone bankrupt and have had to thaw and dispose of the current frozen victims. Yet it still holds appeal. Humans just don't want to face the inevitability of death. Apparently the disgraced financier Jeffrey Epstein not only wanted his head cryogenically frozen, but ominously also his penis.

There are animals than can naturally survive being frozen. Spring peeper frogs contain natural cryoprotectants, and can survive their body temperature dropping below zero Celsius and freezing. The record goes to Siberian soil nematode worms, which, after being frozen in permafrost for over thirty thousand years, were thawed, and woke up, moved and ate. The most extreme survivors, as many people know, are tiny water bears, or tardigrades, that can survive freezing, complete dehydration, and even the vacuum of space, and come back to life unharmed even decades later. Not that we vets have to treat many water bears!

Freezing living cells sounds miraculous; pressing pause on all the complicated chemical reactions going on inside. This is particularly appealing with delicate short-lived cells like sperm and eggs: the latter, for example, from an elderly endangered Borneo bay cat in a rescue centre, that has never bred, and whose genetics are on the cusp of being lost forever. But freezing living cells is difficult. Sharp ice crystals form during freezing, fatally ripping cells apart from the inside. Slowing down freezing, causing smaller ice crystals and helping some water leave cells before freezing, helps protect cells from exploding. But many antifreeze compounds are unfortunately toxic. Ethylene glycol used in car antifreeze has a sweet taste but has poisoned everything from children and pet cats to Californian condors and cheetahs, drinking spilt antifreeze. It is a fine balance between enough antifreeze to protect cells during freezing but not enough to kill them. Different cells from different species all react slightly differently, so other substances, from sugars to egg yolk, are also added. There are hundreds of different concoctions, some jealously guarded, making the whole process somewhat more akin to alchemy than science. Done well, frozen stem cells are practically immortal, and semen can result in conception decades after freezing.

To avoid the hassles and risks of freezing, we can use fresh semen for artificial insemination, or even fertilise freshly ovulated eggs outside the body, in vitro fertilisation, before returning them to the uterus. Louise Brown was the first human born by IVF, in 1978 in Oldham, England, with Sir Robert Edwards receiving the Nobel prize for his part. Yet just two months later, another baby girl was born from IVF in India from completely independent work by Dr Subhash Mukhopadhyay, using little more than a household refrigerator and a few simple instruments. Coming second in the lottery of science, not only is he completely forgotten, but he was ostracised, bullied and stopped by the authorities from presenting his work at any scientific conferences. He committed suicide less than three years later in Kolkata.

One downside to avoiding freezing reproductive cells is

that you may need to anaesthetise both male and female in quick succession. More people running back and forth, means more room for error. You also need to know when the female will ovulate. With valuable zoo animals like Asian elephants and giant pandas, daily urine testing for months can help us calculate the few fateful hours when they are fertile. Someone has to watch them for hours until they pee, coax them into another enclosure with food, then rush in to suck up what little urine there is with a syringe, avoiding dirt, faeces and straw. Many hormones and metabolites used to figure out when a female may be fertile need specialist analysis, so daily motorcycle couriers to human hospital labs may also be needed. There is a plethora of hormones and compounds in different species, with their varying breeding cycles. For a solitary orangutan, a drop of urine on a cheap human pregnancy test from any supermarket works great. It is more tricky in chimpanzees that all hang out together.

In giant pandas and cheetahs these tests don't work at all. Both often become pseudo-pregnant after mating. A false pregnancy after ovulating means a panda will nest, sleep more and behave just as if pregnant, even if she isn't. She will even secrete the same pregnancy hormones in her urine. There is a host of scientific papers looking at different hormone metabolites or ratios that may possibly be slightly better for prediction; reminiscent of stock exchange charts for guessing when to buy shares, and often probably just as tenuous. Cheetah false pregnancies also make behaviour or urine testing unreliable, but some hormones detectable in poo work better for them. Feeding some glitter on meat to the female means we can recognise her droppings, and not test her boyfriend's stool by mistake. Even when collecting zoo samples first thing in the morning, by the time lab results arrive, you will often end up doing artificial insemination in the middle of the night. Missing ovulation in a cheetah is not the end of the world; they cycle roughly every month. Giant pandas, however, only ovulate once a year, with a fertile window of less than 24 hours, making giant panda breeding in zoos a somewhat stressful affair.

Polar bears, although related to pandas, have a three-month fertile period in spring. As with cheetahs, it is mating itself that induces ovulation. We can induce ovulation in a polar bear by hormone injections; essential for arranging a visiting reproduction specialist's travel, or planning a male's anaesthesia to collect semen. Usually a horse hormone is given, followed by pig luteinising hormone three to four days later. A variety of hormones and schedules can be used in different species. Vets sometimes even use a hormone from pregnant women's urine, called human chorionic gonadotropin. This can be injected to stimulate the ovaries of animals from gorillas to dolphins, although it is perhaps most often used in cats like caracals or cheetahs. The egg can be collected, or the ovulation timing used for artificial insemination. It even stimulates lake sturgeon to spawn, so eggs can be collected and the fish returned to the wild. Specific fish-spawning hormones are now also manufactured for fish farming. Vials of white powdered hormone from pregnant ladies' pee aren't just for females. They also get male Booroolong frogs to release sperm, fertilising spawn for captive breeding, when the female is not around to get the male excited.

Artificial insemination with fresh semen is closer to natural mating, but why bother, if female and male are both healthy, with normal eggs and sperm? Asian golden cat males can be twice the size of females. Biting her neck roughly when trying to mate can quickly get out of hand when she can't escape. Some captive males have killed numerous females, and simply can't be used for natural mating.

African elephants can be trained to ejaculate into an artificial vagina: the world's largest sex-toy. We puny humans must hold this through the enclosure bars if not to be inadvertently crushed. Most other species are less cooperative and need anaesthesia. For forty years, collecting semen has mainly been by electroejaculation. Probes are inserted in the rectum, above the prostate, of donors from black rhinos to ring-tailed lemurs, and increasing cycles of voltage applied until the 'shock of life' occurs. Anaesthetic drug combinations need careful selection, as some can cause ejaculation into the bladder, or the unconscious victim to urinate, ruining the sample.

Electroejaculation has been used in farmed blue crabs, paralysed men, and even to collect and freeze sperm from dead husbands, but isn't without risk, at least to the living. Without care, probe electrodes can fatally burn a hole through the rectum. In ring-tailed lemurs and some primates, semen in the urethra can form a cement-like blockage. Preventing urination, this rapidly results in kidney failure and death. Anyone who has struggled to hold their bladder while sitting through a long boring lecture can imagine what a horrible way this must be to go.

More recently, a less shocking approach has been yielding good results. Simply inserting a catheter up a male lion's penis to the prostate's level will collect a small semen sample by capillary action. No shock therapy or prostate massage needed. Samples are microscopic, but unlike from electroejaculation are not diluted by prostatic fluid and so are far more concentrated. My colleague Imke Lueders uses this to get golden cats pregnant without them becoming the male's dinner. Under anaesthesia, she positions females on their chest like they would be if naturally mated. All cats have induced ovulation, so grasping the female's neck firmly, as if bitten by the male, and stimulating the vagina with a cotton bud also helps conception, even under anaesthesia. While all closely related, there is a bewildering variety even among cats. Clouded leopards, fishing cats and margays can also spontaneously ovulate, but this is rare in cheetahs and ocelots. Like egg-laying chickens, Pallas's cat breeding cycles are very sensitive to light levels, while lions, leopards and ocelots are not influenced by light at all. And while cheetahs cycle all year round, clouded leopards only ovulate seasonally. It can all get a little confusing.

A large Spix's macaw parrot can be held on his back with a tiny electroejaculation probe and glass capillary tube to collect semen, but some birds are more cooperative. North American peregrine falcon numbers plummeted when DDT thinned their eggshells, until Rachel Carson's book *Silent Spring* rewrote the script. One recovery solution came from falconers. Imprinted falcons get species confused, and may try to mate with their owner. This might be amusing if a merlin perches on your head – markedly less so if it is an African crowned eagle. Wearing a rubber matting hat with little depressions, and making falcon come-hither sounds, you can collect semen for artificial insemination once your head has been mated with. This technique helped boost peregrine numbers for return to the wild. I once helped train a king penguin keen on mating with zookeepers' shoes, to allow us to collect semen. True to his species, he was only attracted to the tallest keepers. Rockhopper penguins that we trained were far less fussy, happily mating with anyone's gloved hand. Many parrot owners don't even realise their beloved bird, bobbing on their shoulder, is actually using this as a sex toy.

Semen is not designed to survive outside the body, and is easily killed. The collected vial must be kept dark and warm. This may mean wrapping it in a sock and keeping it in your pocket. Volumes vary from as much as a can of beer from a European wild boar to only a drop or two from an Asian golden cat. We usually extend its life with combinations of protective agents and antibiotics until using it for insemination, or we freeze it in liquid nitrogen for future resurrection. Different research groups have their own semen-saving cookbooks, sometimes jealously guarded. A single liquid nitrogen canister can house thousands of semen samples: an entire male zoo in a jar. It is easier to fly a few tiny frozen tubes across the world than a bull elephant or adult giant panda. But airport X-ray scanners actually give off enough radiation to damage some frozen semen samples. Sometimes there may be no alternative than a long drive across North America with a large canister of semen in the trunk.

Delivering the semen may appear simple, but females have an ingenious gatekeeper. While tamandua don't have a cervix, most other mammals do. The ultimate biological high-security door, with rings, folds and sometimes spirals, it is essential in keeping a foetus safely locked away from the outside world, preventing any infections entering. This also makes inserting semen difficult. Aardvarks, tree hyrax and rabbits actually have two cervices, side by side. Even when ovulating, there is only the smallest of spaces, and plenty of protective mucus. Placing feeble defrosted semen into the uterus directly can make all the difference between success and failure. We can use a thin surgical endoscope, to see what we are doing magnified on a screen. It is especially helpful with a watching crowd around the rear end of a giant panda. This ensures that everyone sees you have done your job properly, even if, as is so often the case, no pregnancy results.

For all one's cajoling and twirling of long thin insemination catheters, some species stubbornly resist passage through the cervix, so surgical insemination is sometimes used. When I started keyhole surgical insemination on jaguars, we placed semen directly into the uterus. Now we get better results from the opposite end, placing semen down the fallopian tube near the ovary in clouded leopards and the other cats. Performing surgery to make babies is a last resort. Which brings us to making endangered animals without semen at all.

Cloning

The first cloned animal was not Dolly the sheep, but actually an African clawed toad, or platanna, back in 1958 for which John Gurdon eventually got a Nobel prize. However, cloning mammals proved more difficult, and most scientists had long given up by the time my friend Bill Ritchie made Dolly the sheep 38 years later. The embryologist who actually transferred the nucleus into the empty cell, sadly Bill was unbelievably omitted as an author from the scientific paper.

Cloning can potentially make multiple copies of rare animals, just like in *Star Wars*. The problem is that they would all be identical. There is no benefit for the genetics of endangered species. Clones could potentially perhaps still help salvage something like the northern white rhino from the cusp of extinction. While banteng were the second endangered species to be cloned, they claim the title of first to survive past infancy; the first endangered species to be cloned, a gaur named Noah, died after only two days. The banteng scarcely did better, as only one of twins survived. Gaur and banteng are closely related to domestic cattle, whose reproduction has been very highly researched, and cows provide an easy surrogate mother for a cloned calf. The cloned banteng calf that died after birth suffered the same problem we often see in zoo banteng calves born normally: it only had one testicle. The surviving banteng lived another seven years at the San Diego Zoo, only half the normal lifespan we can manage in captivity. Cloning endangered species may be a newsworthy novelty, but it has not yet had any real conservation impact.

Banteng highlight some of the quandaries in conservation breeding. There are fewer of these endangered wild cattle in their native Cambodia, than feral in the Australian Northern Territory from a failed outpost a hundred and fifty years ago. Expensive efforts to protect native banteng in Cambodian forests contrast with the identical species being shot as an introduced pest in Australia, and with zoos working to breed them in captivity. It would be more efficient keeping a wild population in Australia as the backup, rather than in zoos for the same purpose.

In modern cloning, unlike with Dolly the sheep, we no longer need to inject a nucleus from one cell into another with steady hands, big microscopes and minuscule tools. No fragile egg cells are needed. Stem cells can now be cajoled into any cell we desire, whether to help repair a broken bone or make an entire new animal. Stem cells are more robust when frozen, and once thawed can divide to make their own replacement cells.

I ended up as co-author with Bill Ritchie of a scientific paper on giant panda multipotent progenitor cells, a step away from stem cells. This wouldn't let us clone pandas, but was progress in how to make stem cells from adult pandas. The fact it was giant pandas and Bill Ritchie created a media frenzy. Even

National Geographic mistakenly reported we were trying to clone pandas. Despite many patient explanations to numerous journalists about the more boring reality, the story that we were trying to clone pandas with Dolly's creator was just too appealing, and was what newspapers ran with that week. In one way, they were correct. What cloning could achieve is remarkable. One extinct wild animal has already been brought back from oblivion, even if only briefly. The Pyrenean ibex, a subspecies of Iberian wild goat, went extinct when the last female, named Celia, was killed by a falling tree. A tiny skin sample was stored, and after three years' work a cloned calf was born. She sadly died after only a few minutes; born with an extra lung lobe crammed in her chest, she couldn't breathe.

Even if a complete success, with numerous clones raised, they would all have been females. Cloning still needs samples from different individuals and genders to prevent inbreeding after resurrection. Cloning only works when there is a closely related and extensively studied common animal whose reproductive intricacies are well known, to act in large numbers as surrogate mums. Cloning is feasible for many primates as they are related to humans, as well as wild cats, wolves, and hoofed animals related to cows, sheep or goats. Cloning won't be realistic any time soon for critically endangered Palawan pangolins, vaquita porpoises, or to resurrect the extinct Tasmanian thylacine.

Although we know the entire woolly mammoth genome, and have a reasonable knowledge of elephant reproduction, it appears impossible to keep hundreds of elephants to try implanting cloned mammoth embryos. For the mammoth, hope rests on building an artificial womb, so the foetus develops in a plastic bag, fed from tubes into its umbilicus. Researchers working to improve premature human baby survival have already used a plastic bag artificial womb to keep lamb foetuses alive for a month. Who knows what could be achievable in the future?

Despite huge media publicity and funding, wildlife cloning

has been limited to simply showing something is possible. No cloning has progressed to actually being useful in conservation or in increasing endangered animal numbers at all. The researchers working on Iberian ibex, banteng and some other animals immediately moved on to other species, rather than working to consolidate their work and build on it. Indeed, once something has been achieved, researchers seem to immediately lose interest, and search for a new project or world-first to achieve, like intellectual magpies. While the Apollo missions showed what was possible, we still are no closer to having cities on the moon than we were fifty years ago. So media reports of world-first reproductive successes in famous zoos haven't actually translated into any real-world use back in the wild. The support facilities and expertise needed are just too great, and the whole process just too complicated. Regular press releases, as researchers struggle to find funding, have given the public the unrealistic expectation that if we keep trashing the planet, we can simply clone animals back from cells in a freezer if it all goes horribly wrong. All the media attention could actually be making things worse.

There is technology even more exciting than potentially cloning extinct mammoths in giant plastic bags. We can't clone birds. Unlike frogs and wolves, all attempts to clone even the humble chicken have failed, and it is unlikely we can bring back the dodo before mammoths: another reason why resurrecting birds' close relatives, the dinosaurs, is not feasible yet, even if all dinosaur DNA wasn't totally degraded by the passage of 60 million years.

Imagine a field of chickens laying eggs, but on hatching, out come a bunch of endangered Vietnamese pheasants, happily raised by their chicken mums. This is what Mike McGrew and researchers down the road from my house in Roslin are working on. Bird germ cells, which give rise to the future eggs and sperm, form early in the embryo, usually only two or three days after an egg is laid. Sacrificing one newly laid egg means these cells can then be grown into millions of cells and stored frozen. Injecting these cells into sterile chicken embryos results in chickens that produce another species' eggs and sperm. Or at least the yolk, as the rest of the egg is deposited in the chicken's oviduct, a bird's version of a mammal's fallopian tube and uterus. Getting chickens to lay cassowary eggs isn't physically possible, but farmed ostriches could do this. Endangered birds could be reared at large scale as easily as farming chickens. Of all high-tech conservation breeding techniques, this is perhaps the most tantalising. Researchers can already make males producing sperm from another bird species, and are working towards getting the females to do the same. In the meantime, freezing primordial germ cells from endangered bird eggs is a possible ark for endangered birds.

Inbreeding and contraception

Spending so much time, effort and technology trying to get endangered species to reproduce, it then seems ironic that I actually spend a considerable amount of my own time doing just the opposite – trying to prevent many wild animals from breeding. A single male gelada baboon, with his beautiful bouffant mane, may be so successful that he risks swamping the captive population with his genes. As a result, inbred populations can develop all sorts of health problems. But removing the dominant male in a stable group can be disastrous, as young up-start males fight each other to take over, killing infants, breaking bones, and stressing the whole troop. If he has a vasectomy, the group remains stable and happy, and he continues his normal sex life, but the babies are actually fathered by other males, who sneak a quick copulation when he isn't looking.

In a rescue centre, a solitary yellow-cheeked gibbon and her son may depend on each other's company for their mental health and well-being. Confiscated pet gibbons can rarely be returned to the wild, but incestuously inbred babies are also far from ideal. Temporary contraception until more compatible partners are available, or permanent sterilisation, is best for gibbons needing lifelong care.

Many animals won't take a daily contraceptive pill reliably enough for it to actually work. We can sometimes dart them with longer-lasting drugs without needing anaesthesia. But darting a female blue-eyed black lemur with a progesterone contraceptive can cause problems from obesity to diabetes, and even heart disease. A female's cream fur colour will also abnormally become darker, more like a male's. Chimpanzees are similar enough to humans that oral contraceptive pills are an option, but a greedy bully may steal the others' food in which the pills were hidden, so it doesn't work. In sanctuary chimpanzees we often resort to a human contraceptive implant resembling a large microchip, given under the skin by injection every few years under anaesthesia.

Contraception can be variable, as human parents can attest. Giving the same hormonal implant to a tiny, red-bellied tamarin and a large red-river hog, the tamarin may be pregnant again in just six months, but a decade later the pig may still be infertile. Only two-thirds of tigers may conceive five years after being given a hormonal implant. And while more than three-quarters of golden-headed lion tamarins conceive again within two years after implant removal, they suffer far higher numbers of miscarriages and stillbirths. A plethora of different reproductive strategies, and the same hormones having different roles at various stages across species, means there is no universal solution.

The line between contraception and inadvertent sterilisation is not always clear. Permanent sterilisation also has its perils. Vets are only taught to sterilise domestic animals such as pet dogs, cats, horses and guinea pigs during our basic studies, and this is by removing the gonads. Castrating dogs or cats helps limit aggression and urine spraying, resulting in happier postmen and sweeter-smelling houses. Yet castration is not a great idea in many captive wild animals. If you castrate a lion, his mane will fall out, never to return, as it depends on testosterone production. You may then suffer stress-induced alopecia from angry staff and unhappy zoo visitors.

Gibbons change colour if you remove their gonads.

Yellow-cheeked gibbons are born a beautiful golden colour, blending into their mother's fur. They then turn black as they get older. Boys remain black for life, but at puberty girls again turn golden. Sterilised gibbons can change colour again, confusing the rest of the group. If adult red deer or moose are castrated they permanently grow soft, mishappen antlers resembling brown cauliflowers, which are easily injured. These perukes are named after the powdered wigs that King Louis XIV of France used to hide his patchy baldness from syphilis and rampant head lice. While red deer develop cauliflower antlers, mule deers' antlers look more like a cactus. The problem usually happens when a deer that has become aggressive is mistakenly castrated. Occasionally it happens in a wild deer that has castrated itself jumping a barbed-wire fence, or survived an incompetent hunter shooting its testicles off. If a deer really must be castrated, this needs to be done before puberty. Traditional Yamal reindeer herders, knowing this, castrate calves with their teeth to make them more docile as adults. I can sadly attest to the veracity of this. As a second-year vet student I was unfortunately selected to demonstrate the identical traditional technique of castrating lambs in the Karoo region of South Africa. Perhaps that explains my lack of a girlfriend for the rest of the year. Castrated reindeer still grow antlers, but as the only deer where females also grow antlers, testosterone is not essential.

Removing ovaries, as is done in pet dogs and cats, can be equally problematic. Hormones are important in behaviour. Sterilising male or female Barbary macaques disrupts a group's social hierarchy, and months of fights, bites and killed youngsters can result. In gorillas and great apes, removing ovaries can result in osteoporosis, just as in women after menopause.

For social primates, tubal ligation or vasectomy is best. Everyone has normal hormones, keeps their status, and gets to enjoy a normal sex life, but without any problematic breeding. Naturally, there are exceptions. I specifically removed the ovaries in one chimpanzee with low status that was gang raped once a month by all the males in her group and was clearly thoroughly miserable. After surgery she finally got some peace and a normal life. Keyhole endoscopic surgery is the best method in wild animals, which are impossible to bed-rest after operations. Clever and dexterous animals like rhesus macaques and bonobos can't then interfere with their wounds, remove sutures, or open themselves up to fatally explore their own innards. I have performed keyhole sterilisations, even the world's first robotic-assisted wildlife surgeries, on everything from tigers and lions to capybara and sea lions in sanctuaries and centres across the globe, with all their individual anatomical quirks. Using instruments thinner than a pencil helps, but for patients like ultra-intelligent orangutans I use 3 millimetre instruments the thickness of a pencil lead. The tiny instrument jaws make things slower, but the wounds are as small as from a microchip needle puncture, and don't always even need a suture. This is useful in patients like capybara and sea lions that immediately return to swimming in water after surgery. Few human surgeons would be brave enough to let their patients go swimming the afternoon of the surgery, yet I sadly have no choice and have had to develop special techniques to allow for this.

With the variety of reproductive cycles, hormones and anatomy among species, even vasectomies and tubal ligations can have downsides. Cheetah females only ovulate after mating. The cheetah penis is small but has fine spikes, like sandpaper, to stimulate ovulation. With tubal ligation or vasectomy, cheetahs mate, but with no pregnancy this repeats every few weeks, as females cycle throughout the year. A vigorous cheetah sex life may sound fun, but the continuous surging hormones dramatically increase the likelihood of malignant uterine cancer. African painted wolves are the worst, in my experience. Even under the best captive conditions a quarter of all female painted wolves will develop a serious uterine infection called pyometra, usually requiring an emergency hysterectomy if not to be fatal. Tubal ligation would make things even worse. The uterus is designed to expand as babies grow, but the cervix keeps everything closed to the outside world. Infection can be very serious as the uterus fills with bacteria and liquid pus that can't drain. I have operated on painted wolves where the uterus has contained 5 litres of pus. The very first animal that I ever anaesthetised, before even qualifying as a vet, was a painted wolf with pyometra. I have never forgotten the challenge, as she was so sick. These beautiful animals' complex social system, where only the alpha male and female breed but other females can also lactate to look after young, makes any contraception or sterilisation choice more complex than for most animals.

Contraception can sometimes help reduce conflict between humans and wildlife without needing to snare, poison or shoot wild animals to control their numbers. Growing up in South Africa, I found elephants to be a particular problem. Universally revered and loved by tourists from around the world, adult elephants are rarely preyed on by predators like lions. Their numbers depend on the availability of water. Waterholes congregate wildlife from zebra to rhinos in the dry season so that paying tourists can see them, keeping national parks economically viable. But maintaining artificial waterholes means elephant populations can explode, reaching far higher numbers than would be natural. In enclosed areas elephants can wreck the environment, pulling down trees and changing the whole ecosystem to the detriment of their and many other animals' survival. We imagine reserves as completely wild in nature, but this is far from the truth. Many Southern African reserves are highly managed, like giant zoo enclosures, with water and landscape management; rare animals like roan antelopes regularly vaccinated; and with animals transferred, tracked, tested, and constantly controlled to keep populations and their genetics healthy.

Closing artificial waterholes may naturally control an elephant population, but often isn't viable. Nothing outrages people more than shooting these highly intelligent animals to control numbers. To give one example, an elephant family unit was rounded up via helicopter and the entire herd darted. When all immobilised, the elephants from matriarch to babies were shot in the head at close range. Different-sized herd members became immobile at varying speeds, so by the time it was safe to land and shoot the elephants, some would tragically have suffocated to death. Some tourists bought elephant skin belts and handbags, but no one wanted the meat, so the elephant abattoirs at Olifantsrus, ironically meaning 'elephants' rest', and Skukuza made them into canned dog food. If you visit Ethosa, you can still see the rusting steel elephant abattoir, long abandoned.

One of my vet school professors, Henk Bertschinger, worked on an elephant contraceptive vaccine. Injecting pig zona pellucida, the layer surrounding eggs that sperm need to penetrate for fertilisation, caused elephants to make antibodies to their own zona pellucida, preventing sperm entering. Elephants could simply be darted from a helicopter. It never changed their behaviour. They cycled normally and were mated, but wouldn't conceive for a few years, before becoming fertile again. Darted pregnant elephants still gave birth, suckled and raised calves normally. The problem of needing two or three initial injections was ingeniously solved by a single dart with slow-release pellets containing the booster doses. Vaccination contraception has also been used in wild white-tailed deer and wapiti, as well as in bears and sea lions in zoos. Contraceptive-vaccinated elephants continue to have normal lives, but being able to lower the birth rate when needed can take the steam out of a destructive population explosion.

Preventing captive red-footed tortoises breeding, by contrast, is simple. Just keep them separate. Most tortoises are solitary. Keeping them in pairs simply results in the male becoming a sex-pest. Males can be so obsessed they bite and pester females to death, and will even mate shoes, bricks and garden gnomes when frustrated. Some female tortoises will still lay infertile eggs, even if no males are around. Stopping birds breeding needs a different approach. Removing a ferruginous hawk's eggs may stop them developing, but the mother will simply lay a replacement clutch. Repeated, this can run a female's calcium down dangerously, until her bones break. We can, however, carefully use this double-clutching to boost the numbers of Californian condor chicks, using incubators, calcium supplements and hand-rearing. Briefly boiling the hawk eggs, or replacing them with wooden dummies, usually keeps the mother happy, without her laying more eggs.

Shuffling eggs and birds helps foster eggs from poor parents or an elderly bird, prone to stumble and crush eggs. In zoo penguins, some pairs may be very fertile, but neglect or kick their eggs around. As there are often same-sex penguin pairs around, these make excellent foster parents to incubate eggs and raise chicks.

Cuckoos naturally foist their offspring on other unsuspecting birds, but fostering isn't just useful when captive-breeding endangered birds, like black stilt, Mauritius pink pigeon or hyacinth macaw, using other bird species as surrogate parents. Fostering can also be used for some mammals. Ornate tree kangaroos give birth to tiny joeys. Without a proper placenta, the jelly bean-sized foetus is born after only a few weeks, and must climb up its mother's fur and into her pouch, where it latches onto a nipple, remaining attached like a small fruit for months while it develops further. The ordeal can be likened to a new-born human baby crawling off the pavement onto a double-decker bus, up the stairs and onto the back seats on the upper deck. Tree kangaroos are very different to their land-living cousins, with hooked claws to live high in rainforest branches, and a diet of leaves rather than grass. But a common yellow-footed rock-wallaby mother will happily foster a tree kangaroo joey. Fostering endangered brush-tailed rock-wallabies to common tammar and yellow-footed wallabies leads to six times more babies raised than normal. Fostering works well and is relatively natural. Hand-rearing joeys in cloth pouches and bags as they grow, feeding them every four hours, using different milk replacers as milk changes so much during their development, is arduous. Yet so many volunteers raise orphaned joeys in Australia that commercial milk replacers specifically for marsupials are available, unlike for most orphaned wildlife elsewhere on the planet. But while wildlife carers and sanctuaries tend to fire-injured wallabies and kangaroos hit by cars, and hand-rear orphaned joeys, the Australian government allows a quota of over seven million kangaroos and wallaroos to be shot annually, a sixth of their entire populations.

Human–wildlife relationships seem doomed to vacillate wildly between frantically breeding rare animals and trying to exterminate similar species that are somehow successfully surviving in our modern anthropocentric world. The passenger pigeon went from five billion birds to extinct in the blink of an eye, thanks to hunters killing up to fifty thousand birds a day. Now researchers work at great expense to try and resurrect it through genetic engineering. Conservation of endangered Proserpine and black-flanked wallabies contrasts with the large-scale shooting of their close relatives in Australia. And while millions are spent trying to conserve the last remaining Scottish wildcats, red foxes are heavily hunted as vermin in the same areas. If red foxes were endangered, no doubt there would be huge fundraising and conservation efforts for a beautiful, intelligent and interesting animal. There appears to be little logic to our attitude to most wildlife. Common species are regarded as a nuisance or only of commercial value as food, medicine or fur, while anything rare is to be preserved at all costs: a modern equivalent of Victorian coin-collecting.

The murky world of species classification

There is one fatal flaw for many captive wildlife breeding programmes: species. The basic unit of biological classification, it may surprise you that there is no one agreed definition. Often taken to mean the largest group of animals that can successfully breed, that would not work for dinosaurs; no one knows who could breed with whom. Traditional classification was usually based on an animal's anatomy and morphology. Other classifications are based on evolutionary trees, or biological niches. Then genetics demonstrated that animals looking totally different, like cheetahs and king cheetahs, can be almost identical genetically, while the indistinguishable Scottish and common crossbills may look identical but are very different genetically. Scottish crossbills, the only endemic British bird, are only recognisable from their different call. A Scottish accent. And subspecies make everything even murkier. Siberian and Sumatran tigers are the same species, but classified as different subspecies, after thousands of years' evolution for their different environments. While one is much larger, they can still interbreed, so are not separate species. Everything in the natural world is on a continual scale, but we humans like to name and classify everything, from clouds to stock-market patterns. Animals are no exception. Many scientists disagree what a species is, let alone if red pandas have, after a recent paper, separate Himalayan and Chinese species or not. Babirusa were all believed to be the same species, until recent genetic analysis showed there are apparently several distinct species despite their almost identical appearance. Most zoo babirusa are a hopeless mish-mash, and possibly genetically useless for any future reintroductions. While most books and websites list seven or eight tiger subspecies, many experts think we should only classify tigers into two subspecies, which could make captive breeding and conservation much simpler.

I bet some irate readers have already penned angry letters telling me I have got the number of certain species wrong, or that the name for an animal I mention has changed, before getting this far in the book. It isn't my fault. Nothing is more frustrating than missing swathes of old scientific information, because species names have changed, as taxonomists play classification football with rival researchers: unless perhaps working your whole life with a subspecies that suddenly apparently no longer exists, and becomes of no conservation concern.

Perhaps with the state of the remaining natural world, and limited efforts and money already spread thin, focusing on subspecies may be a luxury we can't afford. Does the distinction between Bengal and Indochinese tigers, not even subspecies, just clades, make a real difference to saving tigers remaining in the wild? Could even the difference between Bengal tiger and Sumatran tiger subspecies be more of a hurdle than a help? I don't have the answer, but focusing on saving a single charismatic species can both help and hinder conservation of the environment. Tigers need forest and the whole package of plants, animals, even parasites, to continue to survive in the wild.

Politics doesn't help. The Scottish wildcat is the rarest wild mammal in the United Kingdom, with huge public and conservation interest. Trumpeted as critically endangered, most scientists don't even regard it as a separate subspecies of the continental European wildcat. Hunted to the brink by gamekeepers, the cats then decided to try to go extinct by having lots of sex with feral domestic cats. Any subtle genetic differences from mainland European wildcats has been swamped by far greater genetic pollution from domestic cats. Expensive conservation breeding programmes are mired in arguments about how many domestic cat genes are OK, or whether best to simply restart with cats from the continent instead. With no definitive answers, there are just extremely heated opinions. It is so much more difficult to fix something, than it is to not break it in the first place.

Despite constant zoo press-release excitement, breeding is a relatively minor part of species conservation. Tigers are as easy to breed as house cats; the main difference being your cat is unlikely to eat you. Captive breeding of tigers is so easy they are found everywhere, from drug barons' mansions to Thai tourist temples. Breeding tigers for photographic opportunities is far more lucrative than breeding lions for canned hunting. While reputable zoos globally hold half as many tigers as exist in the wild, North American pseudo-sanctuaries and pet tigers alone make up almost three times as many as live in the wild. According to some sources, there are actually more pet tigers in Texas than left in the wild on the entire planet.

Tigers are not in trouble because they don't breed. They are threatened with extinction because, in order to have viable wild populations, these large carnivores need massive areas of land and animals like deer readily available for them to hunt, while not being persecuted by people. In just over a hundred years, their numbers have plummeted from over 100,000 to less than 4,000. Humans and our domestic animals now make up more than 95 per cent of all mammal biomass on the planet's land. In an increasingly crowded planet, mainly filled with livestock and their people, there just isn't space for tigers left in our world anymore. The solution is not to breed more tigers. This is as oversimplified as suggesting the solution to a horrible, protracted war is simply for people in other countries to have more babies.

Nature has her own solutions to extinct animals. The Aldabra rail, extinct 136,000 years ago when sea levels rose, re-evolved again from the related white-throated rail subspecies 100,000 years ago when sea levels dropped. This may hold greater promise for South China tigers, Pyrenean ibex and Scottish wild cats than our current high-tech approaches. So long as there is sufficient good habitat remaining, related subspecies, such as Bengal tigers, Iberian ibex and European wildcats, may evolve back to the similar unique genetics of the original populations. But pristine environments rarely exist. Habitat destruction is the main extinction driver in our lifetime. It would take tens or even hundreds of thousands of years to see this pan out, something us humans with our fast-food lifestyle, 24-hour convenience stores and Zoom teleconferencing are unlikely to have the patience as a species to engage in. We can barely make a few years of environmental policy before elections yield a different leader who yet again tears it all up and starts in a different direction. *Homo sapiens* may no longer even exist within the time frame needed for things to re-evolve. Still, it remains a possibility when subspecies go extinct, if we can protect some land. It is difficult for humans to consider deep-time perspectives when considering reproduction, extinction and evolution, plugged into our 24-hour news feeds, social media updates and frantic pace of life. If all humans disappeared instantly tomorrow, plants overgrew crumbling concrete cities, and endangered animals boomed, with tectonic plate movements, solar flares, and constant change, over the next million years animals would continue evolving. Many endangered species we fret over would change, evolve into other species, or die out nonetheless. It may be worth considering this, when we put animals through extremely unpleasant reproductive procedures in captive breeding facilities. Does species conservation, treating animals as if they were valuable stamps in a collection, sometimes come at too high a cost to the individual animals themselves?

Conservation success

Sometimes captive breeding can however save endangered species from what seems to be an impossible situation – a single solitary individual left alive on the planet. The greatest conservation success story in which I have had the privilege to be involved is not with tigers, gorillas or elephants, but with a diminutive pale brown and white Polynesian tree snail, *Partula taeniata simulans*, which for many years I helped look after at the Royal Zoological Society of Scotland.

Found on the tiny French Polynesian islands off Tahiti, which are perhaps more famous for the *Mutiny on the Bounty*, Partula tree snails were first discovered on Captain Cook's 1769 expedition, and studied to prove Darwin's theory of evolution. Over a hundred different species, most less than a centimetre long, evolved on different islands, on different plants and at different altitudes. Hiding on the underside of plantain leaves, for centuries Polynesians used them in ceremonial dress. In an unfortunate early attempt at biological control that went disastrously wrong, in the 1970s the predatory Florida rosy wolfsnail was introduced to the islands, with the hope it would prey on the previously introduced giant African land snails, which were running amok and eating crops. Sadly, the wolfsnail decided the small unique tree snails were far better for eating, and within a decade the majority of these unique species had become extinct. Just over a dozen species were saved and taken to zoos, where they were carefully kept, studied and bred, being completely extinct in the wild.

The last known *Partula taeniata simulans* snail arrived at the Royal Zoological Society of Scotland in 2010. Thankfully, with astute care this snail, which had already been mated and fertilised before the others of the species had died, produced young. Starting in 2016, hundreds have now been returned to the wild. Now, it is once again possible, with much care and searching, to see these small pale brown and white snails on the undersides of leaves on the volcanic slopes of Mount Tohivea on Moorea Island.

While it is amazing to note that endangered animals can return from a single remaining live individual, this snail had already thankfully been mated and fertilised by another snail. Yet there are animals that can breed completely on their own. When I was working at London Zoo, the team there discovered that Komodo dragons could do this. Called parthenogenesis, an unfertilised female could actually produce fertile eggs on her own, containing female clones of herself, so was like the dragon version of Dolly the sheep. This is not the Komodo dragon's usual way of reproducing. It is advantageous for dragons, like most species, to mate and keep mixing genes in the population. This makes the species more resistant to diseases, and able to evolve, which is not possible with clones. But it is still useful occasionally when no mates are available, to keep the species going temporarily.

Even more interesting is the Brahminy blind snake, the smallest snake in the world. The size of an earthworm, for which it is commonly mistaken, it has been transported all over the world, often hiding in the soil of plants. You may have seen one and not realised it, mistaking it for a dark earthworm as it goes about looking for ant larvae and termite eggs to eat. Yet every individual ever examined of this most widespread of all snakes has been a female. They are all clones: a biological example of immortality, living in one of your plant pots. Next time you see what you think is a dark earthworm, take a closer look.

Convincing demure, endangered, wild animals to breed, resorting to sci-fi cloning, while preventing others' incestuous inbreeding attempts, can certainly keep a wildlife vet occupied, and be exhausting. But this is nothing compared to the nerve-racking preparation that surrounds actually returning animals to the wild where they belong. But before we get there, things can unfortunately still go wrong.

Examining the very last Captain Cook's bean snail from Polynesia alive on the planet in 2016. As they are hermaphrodites, there was a small hope right until the end that the species could still survive, if this individual had been fertilised at some point in its past.

15

Winnie-the-Pooh was shot

Nothing is as sad as seeing a dead, confiscated Chinese pangolin, rigid and cold on the autopsy table. It's a mystical creature, and one that I would love to see in the wild. After failing to keep the smuggled pangolin alive, violating the fragile body may seem pointless. The most heavily traded wild mammal in the world is one we still understand so little about. Over 100,000 pangolins may be smuggled each year, yet we have no idea how long they actually live for in the wild. They are nightmarishly difficult to keep alive in captivity, attempts to farm them have all failed, and few rescue centres manage to keep them alive for long. An autopsy is a final chance for us to learn from a patient's sad demise.

Death is inevitable for all animals. Sometimes with our treatments we delay it, sometimes we may actually hasten it. An autopsy is a teacher, marking our work, and informing us when we get it wrong. A zoo vet can tell if their diagnosis of an adrenal tumour in a blue-eyed black lemur was correct after cryptic test results; police can investigate if an otter was shot and dumped at the side of a road to cover up the crime; and examining black-footed penguins can help tell if they starved from local overfishing, suffered from bird malaria, or were poisoned by heavy-metal pollution.

A post-mortem examination doesn't seem an emergency. Yet occasionally, autopsy victims arrive with a police escort.

When a Tower of London raven died unexpectedly six months after the London terrorist attacks in 2005, it was feared this could be a coded message about upcoming attacks. Probably the most intelligent of all birds, ravens can even solve problems too difficult for chimpanzees. Tourists are told that if the ravens of the tower are lost, the monarchy will fall, and Britain along with it. Yet, contrary to popular opinion, the captive tower ravens were a Victorian invention, intended to portray the long continuous monarchy, and and to dramatise the tower's history as a site of execution. To everyone's relief, my raven autopsy found it had died of natural causes, and no Hollywood-worthy terrorist plot was under way.

A pangolin's hard keratin scales can protect it from a leopard attack, but its underside is soft and so easy to open for autopsy. Some animals pose more of a challenge. Even a tiny Egyptian tortoise needs an electric saw to open the shell and see inside. But getting an elephant's brain out of its monstrously thick skull using a chainsaw, while not injuring yourself fatally, and attempting to delicately remove an organ with the consistency of crème brûlée is worse. In contrast, after cutting a green anaconda's underside skin on either side with scissors, one tug and even the biggest snake is unzipped in a few seconds, revealing the organs perfectly in place. Despite its skin's armoured appearance, an Indian rhinoceros is also not difficult to open, the secret being a hooked carpet cutter blade. Once open, large patients are awkward. Examining a Masai giraffe's neck at autopsy, I have spent hours dissecting muscles, bones and nerves, as an injury the size of a coin can be enough to fatally paralyse it. Bulls use their massive necks to fight each other, yet with only seven vertebrae, the same as a gorilla's stubby neck, it is easily injured if they fall during anaesthesia.

There are even more challenging autopsy subjects: for example, sperm whales. Immediately after death, gas builds up dramatically in the intestines. You need to be very careful when making the first incision into the perilously bloated leviathan's body. If you don't want several tonnes of whale guts exploding out violently and ripping your arm off, you need to stand well clear and use a large knife tied to a long pole. One dead beached whale being transported on a truck dramatically exploded in a Taiwanese city centre, covering shop fronts, cars and pedestrians in blood, blubber and rotting whale intestines: a disgusting way to paint the town red. If an exploding 80 tonne whale doesn't sound hazardous enough, they frequently carry the zoonotic disease brucellosis. Sexually transmitted between whales, in people it can cause waves of fever and nausea that last months, and even cause arthritis and sterility in some unlucky victims. Unfortunately for vets, a higher infection rate is an occupational hazard. It is difficult to avoid getting soaked in muck, even wearing the best waterproof outfit, with the hundreds of litres of blood and body fluid sloshing around during a whale autopsy.

At the other extreme, a post-mortem examination of a centimetre-long Frégate Island giant beetle larva taxes my eyesight. Tiny brown spots on the tan rings of the chubby larvae may just be the invertebrate equivalent of a bruise, or instead a deadly fungal parasite invading and gruesomely eating the body from the inside. Adult beetles may look normal, but finding one dead in the morning with the white fungus bursting from the joints between the hard black plates of its body is disastrous. The invisible spores will have wafted everywhere, infecting other beetles. Examining an even smaller pine hoverfly for a re-introduction project, most organs are just too tiny to be examined by eye. After delicately opening the body and removing the internal organs as a blob, I can perform a squash post-mortem. This simply means sandwiching everything between two glass slides and looking at it under the microscope. I can see if the gut contains food or parasites, or if there are crystals in the fat bodies from a virus infection. For even more detail we can make paraffin-embedded slides and stain them with different dye concoctions to highlight different cells. A colour atlas of the microscopic anatomy of the flea is one of the stranger books on my shelf, and it's a handy guide when examining endangered insects.

Looking at cells isn't just useful for small patients. A black rhino may look frustratingly normal on autopsy, its stomach full of leaves. But peering down the microscope eyepieces at distinctive Prussian blue blobs and burst liver cells, you know the cause of death. The rhino has unfortunately stored too much iron from its high-quality zoo food. Without the bitter tannins found in its wild diet to bind it, iron accumulates, and, unable to cope, the liver has failed.

Under the microscope

Pondering cells down the microscope is often vitally important before you even lift a scalpel. Finding twenty dead common hippo next to a waterhole, it is tempting to start slashing open the bloated bodies in a heroic effort to find the cause. Instead, it is essential to first patiently take a drop of blood from the tip of an ear, smear it on a glass slide, and stain it with methylene blue, a dye first used to treat malaria a hundred and fifty years ago. Running your microscope off the car battery, if you see rows of blue brick-shaped bacteria with a faint pink halo, you definitely mustn't open the cadavers under any circumstances. The hippos have died of anthrax. Opening them would release millions of microscopic spores to waft in the air, contaminating surrounding soil and water, and ready to kill everything from buffaloes to lions. You could also fatally inhale the spores, just as with anthrax-laden terrorist letters. Fencing off a contaminated area is little help, as vultures can open the carcasses and spread the disease. Some of the toughest spores in existence, anthrax can remain viable for centuries in the soil. The tiny 2 kilometre long Gruinard Island off Scotland, used for a World War II anthrax bomb test, needed half a century of quarantine and 280 tonnes of formaldehyde before it again became safe for sheep. No vet wants to join the infamous anthrax club, of those who have mistakenly opened an infected carcass, causing ongoing deaths that will last longer than their lifespan. Susceptible animals like roan antelopes may need vaccination to prevent them all dropping dead, and infected bodies need to be burnt; not always easy in areas where trees are precious and wood is scarce.

Seeing bacteria down the microscope doesn't always mean they are a problem. Examining critically endangered Delosia cockroaches from the Seychelles, you will see clumps of bacteria inside fat cells. Resembling a nasty infection, these blattabacteria are actually vital for recycling the nitrogen that cockroaches battle to get from their plant diet. Antibiotics that kill the bacteria will also kill the cockroaches from protein starvation. This is perhaps similar to how mitochondria originated in animal cells two billion years ago. Even cockroaches have their own good bacteria. They just live inside their fat cells.

Cause of death

Interpreting what is abnormal is difficult enough. Deciding why a patient died is even more challenging. Performing detailed post-mortem examinations in the last remaining handful of Captain Cook's bean snails on the planet, I just couldn't figure out a cause for the snails' deaths. Despite help from snail experts Justine Gerlach and Paul Pearce Kelly, the very last snail sadly died in February 2016, and the entire species became extinct. It was extremely frustrating. I occasionally watch the video I took of the last lonely little snail to remind myself of why we do what we do.

Being unable to tell the cause of death, even after looking at hundreds of sample slides, is frustratingly common. Everything, even under the microscope, can look perfectly normal, yet the patient is dead: a reminder of just how little we understand life itself. But there still has to be a cause for the patient's demise. We just haven't been able to find it. A Western lowland gorilla may have an invisible tumour, only a millimetre in size, in her pancreas. Yet a surge of insulin from this microscopic insulinoma tumour can kill its 100 kilogram host. A favourite of crime writers, and real-life murderers, insulin was also popular in insurance fraud, to kill horses that could no longer race. We now have ways to detect insulin, but still have to at least suspect it, to test for it among the host of other possible causes of death.

Small and sometimes forgotten, amphibians are the wild animals with the fastest, most dramatic declines in my lifetime. More than a third are now endangered. Costa Rica's golden toad and harlequin frog populations crashed and went extinct in only a few years, despite pristine cloud forest reserves with no human disturbance. The mass extinctions in a few decades have been compared to that of the dinosaurs. Amazing species went extinct almost as soon as they were found. Australian gastric brooding frogs, the only animals to incubate their eggs in their stomach, had hardly been discovered when they went extinct. The northern gastric brooding frog went extinct within a year of its discovery. Its discoverer is now working on the Lazarus Project, trying to resurrect it from some old frozen specimens at huge expense and difficulty. Yet initially examining dead frogs under the microscope showed nothing obvious and the whole thing was a huge puzzle. Eventually, a team of scientists including one of my pathologist predecessors at London Zoo and my MSc supervisor, Andrew Cunningham, were able to show a unique fungus as the cause. This was a shock, as it wasn't then believed that infectious disease could cause extinctions. It was believed there was always a natural balance to infections. We still don't understand why it started to cause mass extinctions worldwide – perhaps a combination of climate change, water pollution, and global transportation. The chytrid fungus killer is itself fascinating. It forms tiny skin cysts that at first glance look just like normal mucus glands under the microscope. Yet these are enough to fatally disrupt the frog's ability to maintain its delicate water and electrolyte balance. The fungus spores actually swim in water, similar to microscopic tadpoles, before puncturing a new victim's skin, and starting their deadly cycle all over again. I find diagnosing infection down the microscope difficult and unreliable, so in order to be accurate we use PCR tests to detect the distinctive fungal DNA.

Autopsy samples are stored in formalin to preserve the tissues and cells, for later detailed perusal under the microscope. Surgery biopsies are treated the same way – a mini-autopsy of a live patient, to understand a disease and best treat it. In the field, samples can be preserved in alcohol. Operating in Myanmar on a bear with a bizarre 3 kilogram tongue that dragged on the ground, I preserved small cubes of tissue in a bottle of cheap vodka, to check for elephantiasis. While I was still operating, my friend Khyne U Mar, the famous elephant lady of Burma, took a break and in the dark mistook the plastic bottle for her water and took an unfortunate swig. At least the vodka had sterilised everything, and she had a laugh rather than being angry.

The autopsies on Captain Cook's bean snail didn't show any cause for the deaths that resulted in their extinction, probably because most died naturally of old age. We likely never really found the ways to make them thrive and breed well in captivity. Perhaps they preferred a slightly different humidity for part of a season, lower light levels, or something we couldn't replicate from their wild diet. Gradually the population faded into extinction, with nothing we could find on post-mortem to alter the course.

Sometimes it isn't the cause of death that is important, but rather what we don't find. It is with trepidation that I will open up the strangely named undertaker, or adjutant, bird in Cambodia. Looking like Dr Frankenstein's experiment to cross a vulture with a stork, and related to African marabous, they are sadly endangered. Once seen striding like arthritic army officers around small lakes, with their world disappearing you are now most likely to see them hanging out at a garbage dump, resembling hung-over Victorian tramps. Carefully cutting open the neck, I am hoping not to see fine red spots inside the windpipe, microscopic bleeds that hint at avian influenza. Arriving onboard migrating ducks, some avian influenza strains are a real risk to humans, especially in developing countries with patchy healthcare. But even if a flu strain is no threat to people, by the time I see the tell-tale red speckles, there is little we can do to stop most of the adjutants in the area dying, as they congregate in trees for their breeding season.

Wildlife vets are often the bearers of bad news. When animals are healthy, no one consults the vet. Pluck a patient back from the brink with your skills, and everyone just takes this as normal. But when a patient dies despite your best efforts, even if a condition is untreatable, the presumption is that you have failed. Afraid to face the reality of our own mortality, humans pretend that death is something abnormal, rather than the default final setting for all life. Thankfully, expectations are low when performing an autopsy. No one is under any illusion that we can bring a pangolin's corpse back to life.

Yet looking at dead animals can have the greatest conservation impact of all wildlife veterinary work. Treating snared Western chimpanzees, shot Sumatran orangutans or injured lowland gorillas, there is a limit to how many individuals one veterinarian can treat. Treating an individual and returning it to the wild undoubtedly can make its life better, yet it is only for the rarest of animals that this can meaningfully impact the survival of a species. But when half the world's population of critically endangered saiga antelopes suddenly drops dead over just two weeks, examining some of the 100,000 bodies is clearly essential to try to protect the species.

The Cyrano de Bergerac of the antelope world, a saiga's nose acts like an air conditioner in hot weather and a radiator in freezing temperatures, to protect their lungs. They are related to springboks and they live in massive herds that used to be millions strong, but they have almost completely disappeared through heavy hunting and loss of habitat. Until recently, one famous conservation charity even encouraged saiga hunting for traditional Chinese medicine, in a misguided attempt to reduce rhino poaching. The dramatic die-offs in recent decades happen when they congregate to give birth. With so few herds, they are now particularly vulnerable. And the cause is far from clear, with different contested theories. Wildlife vet Richard Kock's research seems to show a bacteria called Pasteurella as the cause. Normally a bacterial passenger in saiga, a combination of factors connected to global warming seems to have caused the organism to go rogue in this antelope.

Pasteurella is equally dramatic on the opposite side of the world where hundreds of thousands of snow geese densely pack along Hudson's Bay. Sick birds shed bacteria into the water, and in just a few weeks tens of thousands of snow geese and ducks can be found dead and dying. You will also find dead short-eared owls, northern harriers, and mice, which all mistakenly tried the tempting goose buffet. On autopsy we see liver spots and intestines full of yellow liquid, containing billions of the bacteria seeping into the water to infect other birds. To protect whooping cranes and other wildlife, carcasses need to be incinerated to stop contamination. Before then, cranes need to be persuaded to move away by harassing them with aircraft until the area has been cleaned up.

Infectious diseases may appear natural, but these epidemics are due to human disruption of the natural world. Animals congregate as people and farming displace them from the habitats they have occupied for hundreds of thousands of years. Evolution is slow. Species that evolved over millions of years struggle to cope with large man-made environmental changes that have occurred in only a few decades, an evolutionary blink of the eye. In just my lifetime the human population has doubled, and our impact is even greater, thanks to rampant consumerism. Many deaths, not due to diseases, are also unnatural. Autopsy investigations can mitigate some of this. My friend Raphael Molina examines thousands of dead birds every year in Catalonia, from bearded vultures and greater flamingos to hoopoes and alpine swifts. By monitoring problems such as the effect electricity pylon designs have on bird collisions, safer pylons can be selected for new projects.

The underwater realm is largely invisible, until thousands of dead fish suddenly float to a lake's surface. Rather than toxic chemicals, the cause is usually more humdrum. Heavy rains wash fertiliser off surrounding farm fields, providing an all-you-can-eat buffet of nitrogen for algae. The explosive bloom consumes the available oxygen in the water, suffocating all the fish within days. This is essential to diagnose and mitigate, lest the problem simply recur the following year when fields are sown. Fish are fascinating. If we humans stay underwater we drown, as our bodies can't get enough oxygen, while fish breathe fine when submerged. Yet take a fish out of water and it suffocates from not getting enough oxygen from the same air we breathe. Why do fish drown in air? Gills have thousands of thin finger-like projections, with even more projections on their surface, suspended in water. This gives these vital but small organs a massive surface area; essential as water contains less than a twentieth of the oxygen in air. Oxygen also diffuses out of air 10,000 times more easily. Fish drown out in air, because the wet gill filaments collapse with surface tension into a single blob. The now tiny surface area just can't cope, even with the oxygen in the air, and the fish suffocates. While the mudskippers I watched in the mangrove swamps of Gambia can absorb some oxygen via their wet skin and their mouth lining when exploring on land, their most important trick is to carry a pocket of water around in their gills when out of water. It isn't just fish that have gills. The Alabama waterdog and mysterious cave-dwelling olm are amphibians that keep their gills even as adults. Many crabs, just like mudskippers, have a gill chamber in which they carry water surrounding their gills when out on land so they can breathe.

Protected beneath a hard cover, their fronds pulsing with blood, the gills are the favourite hang-out of many parasites. Examining a gill sample under the microscope is an essential part of any fish post-mortem. Sometimes the slide resembles a minuscule zoo, with leeches, worms, and flukes hanging on with hooks, while a variety of hairy protozoa swim around frenetically. An occasional parasite is normal, as in any animal, but high numbers hint at poor water quality, stress, or other diseases depressing a victim's immunity.

Exploding whale guts; slipping on a bloody floor and plunging face first into an elephant's liver; cutting yourself while examining a hammerhead bat with Ebola; getting Crimean-Congo haemorrhagic fever from a tiny tick that crawled off the dead ostrich you were inspecting; and, despite protective clothing, still having to pick flecks of dried blood from your eyebrows in the shower. All these things are not very appealing aspects of wildlife pathology. Yet most autopsies are not gruesome affairs. I find a quiet dignity when examining dead animals, and it never ceases to fascinate me. While the aim of an autopsy is to discover the cause of demise, there is much else to learn and marvel at: all the organs, muscles, tendons and vessels, which in life make an amazing meat machine, are more complex or astounding than any clock full of cogs that I dismantled as a child.

Surgeon and pathologist

When I accepted the post of pathologist at the Zoological Society of London more than 15 years ago, my colleagues were somewhat surprised. With qualifications in surgery alongside my specialist training in wildlife medicine, my only operations would now be on dead animals. I had just turned down a job that would have involved working with wild tigers and leopards in the Russian far east as my mother had been diagnosed with breast cancer. It was easier visiting her from London than Vladivostok, and I had already been examining autopsy histopathology slides for zoos for half a decade. Despite the strange juxtaposition between surgery and pathology, I was far from the first to straddle the two fields.

Autopsy comes from the Greek word *autopsia*, 'to see for

one's self'. Throughout history, bodies have been opened, although you probably can't count the ancient Egyptians' removal of organs via small holes and mummification as an investigation into death or disease. One early high-profile autopsy was on Julius Caesar, which determined it was the second of his 23 stab wounds that proved fatal. Being as full of holes as a colander, his cause of death wasn't exactly difficult to determine. CT and MRI now mean the cause of a premature baby's death can be discovered without ever needing to lift a scalpel, and human autopsies are in decline. But autopsies are important in patients that not only can't speak, but which, like a Javan mouse-deer, tend to hide any signs of illness. Prey animals that are another's food hide any signs of weakness, lest a predator decides to single them out for its lunch date. There is also growing interest in why wild animals die, the health implications for us humans, and autopsy clues as to what is going on in the environment.

The word 'autopsy' is often reserved for humans, with some vets using the term necropsy. This Victorian approach misses the obvious fact that humans are just another animal; something opening any dead body irrefutably illustrates. As surgical examinations of cadavers, autopsies are historically linked to surgery, rather than to physicians' diagnostics, and their treatments by lotions and potions. Surgery was a colourful profession, with renown more dependent on anatomical discoveries than any actual ability to cure patients. But any advantage gained from anatomical knowledge was often negated by surgeons going straight from rotting cadavers to performing surgery in the same blood-splattered coats without even washing their hands. Delivering babies had horrific outcomes. Childbed fever killed not just the poor but also Henry VIII's mother and two of his wives. It also killed Mary Shelley's mother, so perhaps it isn't surprising she invented Dr Frankenstein to illustrate her opinion of men of science.

The first animal post-mortem reports are Aristotle's, although, like most early explorers of bodies' internal workings, he was more interested in anatomy, and less interested in diseases or causes of death. He was still trying to figure out what organs did. Animal anatomical vivisection by luminaries like Aristotle now appear terrible, yet around the same time Herophilos was performing dissections on 600 live human prisoners. While the Islamic physician Ibn Zuhr recorded the first proper human autopsies a thousand years ago, discovering the cause of scabies without a microscope, the origins of animal autopsy are lost in antiquity. The first wildlife autopsies were by hunting humans, before the existence of writing, domestic animals or farming. Removing the viscera of animals killed, trapped, or simply found dead, they had to decide whether it was safe to eat, or diseased and not to be consumed. This remained important as animals were domesticated for food, and still today vets inspect meat at abattoirs.

Today, wildlife autopsies can save human lives. When a few elderly people died with encephalitis in New York in 1999, it was chalked up to St Louis encephalitis, a virus only infecting about a hundred people a year in North America. Yet something didn't make sense to Tracey McNamara, pathologist at the Wildlife Conservation Society's Bronx Zoo. She saw the same encephalitis in wild crows and in the zoo's flamingos and worked out that what was killing the birds and humans was a completely new virus, not before seen in North America. West Nile Virus has since spread throughout the USA, infecting over three million people and killing large numbers of wild birds and horses.

The link between human and animal health

Understanding that human health is completely intertwined with animal and environmental health goes back to Hippocrates' time. The ancient Greeks recognised that these were inseparable. The coronavirus pandemic means everyone now knows what a zoonosis is, even if COVID-19 isn't strictly a zoonosis at all. True zoonosis, like rabies, Ebola, salmonella and bird flu, is spread directly from animals to humans.

While COVID-19 originated from a similar bat coronavirus, once in humans it has become a new virus that we now spread to each other without bats or other animals needed at all. Measles is actually similar. Spreading only between people, it originated about a thousand years ago, when a cattle virus called rinderpest found that medieval populations were big enough for it to make the jump from one species to another and become an entirely new disease. Humans now make up a third of the planet's terrestrial biomass, so it is no surprise that new diseases find us an appealing food source to exploit, just as locusts do with farmed crops. While measles is still common, and even increasing in wealthy countries thanks to anti-vaccination movements, the original disease rinderpest is now extinct; it is only the second infectious organism after smallpox to have been successfully eradicated. Yet its offspring is in rude health, thanks to the blossoming human population. More than 20 million people are still infected with measles every year.

While early zoological societies were more interested in the anatomy of the unfortunate animals that died in large numbers, some saw the potential to test theories about human health. Samuel Haughton, mostly remembered for mathematical equations on hanging for humane execution, performed dissections on animals that died at Dublin Zoo. He was interested in determining the causes of death so that he could improve the zoo's diets. At London Zoo, the high death rate from tuberculosis was blamed on damp enclosures with little ventilation. New enclosures were built, after the *Times* newspaper made unflattering comparisons to slums. Yet with better ventilation, many monkeys then died from the cold. Laudable as comparative pathology was, the actual cause of disease was completely misunderstood. Illness was still believed to be due to miasmas or bad airs. London Zoo lobbied for better drainage of the stinking sewage around Regent's Park for both human and animal health. This helped, but for different reasons to those imagined. Unbelievably, in a time of telephones, sewing machines and canned food, we were still clueless about infectious diseases. From the Roman Antonine Plague and the medieval Black Death, to cholera in Victorian times, everything was blamed on bad air. Enlightened individuals tried applying the scientific method to deaths as best they could. The first prosector at London Zoo, the surgeon James Murie, discovered almost a third of the zoo's animals died in his first year. He tried to study the causes of death in detail, using statistical analysis to examine specific symptoms before death, the enclosures, diets and husbandry practices: all visionary epidemiology. Nonetheless, the erudite zoo council couldn't see the benefit and insisted he focused instead on his other work. Eventually, exhausted and frustrated, he resigned. Succeeding prosectors felt no remorse in abandoning pathology entirely, and so had far happier careers at London Zoo.

Winnipeg, the black bear

Aside from discovering an animal's cause of death, I also learned the internal mechanics of everything from elephants to echidnas during my time as pathologist at London Zoo. After more than five thousand wildlife autopsies, my knowledge of anatomy, from polar bears to koalas, has proven invaluable for surgery. I still read old post-mortem reports for tips. Half a decade ago, I recognised a swallowed metal nail in the appendix of a confiscated female orangutan in Borneo, and safely removed this via keyhole surgery so she could be returned to the wild. The knowledge came from old zoo gibbon autopsy reports almost a century earlier, and I knew exactly what to expect from my autopsy experience. I spent many of my lunch times exploring the Society library across the road from the dreary, white-tiled autopsy room. One of my favourite places, 15 years ago it was somewhat forgotten, and the librarians let me explore historical documents in the basement in a way that would never be permitted now. That is how I found myself looking at the handwritten index card with details of the post-mortem on Winnipeg, a female American black bear,

323

who was shot due to decrepitude in old age. She would of course become the eponymous Winnie in the *Winnie-the-Pooh* books, and there are still a handful of photos of her at the zoo, including one showing a young Christopher Robin Milne feeding her a spoonful of honey. She was only twenty at the time of her death, although zoo bears often live into their late thirties.

Despite basement cupboards filled with jars of gruesome samples from decades of autopsies, you won't find answers to her demise there. You have to walk past the bronze statue of Winnipeg and Harry Colebourn, the Canadian army veterinarian who donated her to the zoo, and out of the gates to learn more. Heading through Regent's Park, and passing the British Museum, you eventually get to the Royal College of Surgeons. In a brown cardboard box in a backroom cupboard of the College's museum, you will find the skull of Winnipeg. With G.143.33 written in black marker on the bone, a large section of the skull is sawn open where the brain was removed. But it is the mouth that your eyes are immediately drawn to. Not a single tooth is present. Instead, the jaw bones are uneven and foamy, where bacteria malingered for years after all her teeth fell out. It is clear she would have struggled to eat, thanks to visitors feeding her honey for two decades: a sad end for the bear whose merchandise makes Disney $5 billion a year. Things didn't turn out much happier for Christopher Robin. He ended up hating the books and estranged from his father for most of his life.

Despite today's brass statue, London Zoo sold Winnipeg's body parts, and the skull was bought by the first president of the British Dental Association, Sir Frank Colyer. Some animal parts lead colourful lives after death. When 17-year-old Princess Charlotte married King George III, a belated gift a year later from South Africa was a mountain zebra. Visitors flocked to see it at Buckingham Palace, and it was even more popular than the elephant that was also housed there. Eventually, lent to a clockmaker's travelling menagerie, she died on her travels. Her body was promptly stuffed and displayed in the Blue Boar Inn in York – a far cry from Buckingham Palace. Queen Charlotte's ass, as it was called, ridiculed the long-lived British monarch. Inheriting the largest empire since Genghis Khan, George precipitated American independence, trouble in Ireland that still simmers, and resisted slavery abolition, between his periods of porphyria-induced insanity. No wonder the stuffed zebra, looking nothing like George Stubbs' portrait of the same animal, became a source for cartoonists' lampooning.

More recently, London Zoo's giant panda Chi Chi lives on in the World Wildlife Fund logo designed by Peter Scott, son of Sir Robert Scott, the Antarctic explorer. Natural History Museum visitors can still gawp at her stuffed body in a glass case. Her autopsy was performed at 3 a.m., immediately after death, by the late Ian Keymer. Long retired by the time I became Zoo pathologist, Ian was always helpful, with an encyclopaedic knowledge of everything he had seen. He told me Chi Chi's eyes were immediately removed – not how one usually starts an autopsy – and protected from light to allow investigation of the retina. Chi Chi lives on in the scientific paper written the following year in *Nature*, which described two light-sensitive pigments, and showed that giant pandas do have colour vision. A whole issue of the *Transactions of the Zoological Society of London* was devoted to her post-mortem findings. She lives on in the influence she's had on panda veterinary work today. Yet, when London Zoo's Guy the Gorilla died under anaesthesia for a rotten tooth removal only a few years later, the public was outraged at the thought of him being stuffed for the museum. Perhaps he seemed too similar to human beings.

While researching giant panda anatomy to try to support keyhole surgery training for Chinese giant panda vet colleagues, I discovered the giant panda Ming's brain in a jar at the Royal College of Surgeons in London, happily purchased from London Zoo in the 1950s. Ming had been a wartime symbol of hope for children in London, including Queen Elizabeth II, who visited the zoo as a child. Today, a donated statue of Ming has joined that of Winnie the bear in the zoo, their body part sales long forgotten. Still, I know colleagues who occasionally take part payment with an appealing skull or something else of curiosity. In many Asian countries, taxidermy is still an essential part of zoo veterinary work. It is not uncommon to be seated in a zoo restaurant, surrounded by stuffed giraffes, oryx and cheetahs; the zoo's previous inhabitants, resurrected into what Westerners often feel is a strange setting. Yet hunting lodges have rows of decapitated heads staring out mournfully at the dinner table, and in Victorian zoos stuffed animals were just as important as the live ones. Until its closure, the Zoological Society of London's museum had a larger collection than the Natural History Museum; even Charles Darwin reported it a better place to deposit important expedition specimens.

Museums struggle for space to include the biggest of all animals, but if they do have space, they invariably display a skeleton from a stranded blue whale. Yet one of the commonest whales to now strand on beaches, Cuvier's beaked whales, are a secretive deep-water species we know little about. When George Cuvier first saw a skull, he believed it to be an extinct prehistoric animal. Diving to almost three kilometres, possibly the deepest of all whales, these mysterious animals are very sensitive to noise. Strandings often coincide with regions of heavy ship traffic.

Seismic surveys and anti-submarine tests can generate 240 decibels, which is physically impossible in air. A jet engine only reaches 150 decibels. These sounds can kill nearby whales outright, and make those in the vicinity completely deaf, also with fatal consequences. We can now tell when a dead whale's hearing was damaged, using fluorescent dyes on dead hair cells in the inner ear which show if the damage to hearing occurred in the last ten days of its life. Whales also die from decompression sickness. Gas bubbles form in the blood from surfacing too quickly, after the whale has become disorientated and is in pain from the sound blast, which causes bleeding in their ears. While whales have stranded or washed up dead since ancient times, recent patterns are not natural. Yet most that die will simply sink at sea, so it is difficult to know the true causes.

The death of tiny inner ear hair cells may be a subtle change, but there is nothing subtle about 400 stranded pilot whales. Sociable caring animals that live in groups, stranded sick or disorientated pilot whales call out in distress, leading to large numbers of healthy pod mates also stranding. Rescuers may try to re-float healthier whales, but stranded companions call them back to shore with their distress cries. While enthusiastic volunteers in wetsuits and pontoons may re-float stranded dolphins and whales, without being able to assess their hearing damage, they possibly are simply re-floating them, only for them to subsequently die at sea and sink unseen to the seabed.

For many whales, the oceans must now be a lonely place. For millennia whale songs have carried thousands of kilometres underwater, and are used to find mates or keep in touch with friends. Beluga whales are songbirds of the sea with their complex clicks and whistles, while male humpback whale musicians, singing for hours, can bring females into breeding oestrus by their serenades. Yet even if not killing whales directly, we still drown out their conversations with our cacophony. Even blue whales have been changing their voices, making them lower and slower over recent decades, to try and cope. A whale's attempt at shouting.

Body parts and bones in zoos are now relegated to visiting school children, or left to museums to display. Good zoos have nothing like the death rates of early zoos where over a third of all animals would die every year. Yet things sometimes go to the opposite extreme. Some animals are injected and treated far past the point at which they have a life worth living, out of fear of poor publicity. Modern life has a fear of mortality, even of animals. Some zoos will treat advanced metastatic tumours, despite no benefit to the poor patient, who just has its pain prolonged. I have huge respect for my friend Hugo Fernandez at Barcelona Zoo who resisted attempts to prolong the life of Snowflake, the famous albino gorilla, when, inevitably, he developed malignant skin cancer.

It isn't just stuffed wild bodies that end up on display in Asian restaurants. Bush meat and wildlife markets pose the double damnation of human pandemic risk and environmental catastrophe. During my time at veterinary school in South Africa, there was a scandal where a pathology technician was caught selling meat from autopsy animals at the local market, instead of sending them for incineration. While cows and horses were most common, it included everything from hippos to zebras. Autopsy cases included anthrax and rabies, not the best meat sources to enter the human food chain. Autopsies are not without risk. With tuberculosis rife, early pathologists and zoo prosectors frequently developed red warts on their hands, due to tuberculosis invading the skin. Paul Langerhans, who first described the cells in the pancreas that secrete insulin, caught tuberculosis from autopsy work. He reinvented himself on Madeira, studying marine worms, and looking after fellow tuberculosis victims, before succumbing to the disease at only 41 years old.

After death some animal specimens still have other important roles to play. Shortly after starting as pathologist at London Zoo, I was presented with an Aruba Island rattlesnake for autopsy. As for any venomous snake, I had the identification card, anti-venom details, and hospital phone number before starting. Belinda, my long-suffering technician, quipped I'd better not envenomate myself just to get a long weekend off. Carefully removing the fangs, I performed a thorough autopsy, examining each small organ in detail, slicing it in thin pieces to ensure I missed nothing as I took samples for later microscope examination. I removed the tiny seed-sized brain, carefully chipping the skull bones away. After all was done and recorded, I packed the minced remains in a sturdy container for incineration. A few weeks later the reptile curator returned from a field trip and asked for the body. We were both horrified to find that I had minced and incinerated one of the original type-specimens, upon which the classification of the entire species was based. Critically endangered, with only 200 left in the wild and a handful in captivity, this was a monumental blunder on my part. Sadly, another snake later died and was saved from my mutilating hands for posterity.

Type-specimens can be rare and irreplaceable. Attenborough's long-beaked echidna is only described from a single animal, while all we know of the Somali golden mole is based on one jaw and ear bone recovered from an owl pellet over half a century ago. No one has ever seen the actual mole, or knows if it still exists. Deceased specimens can lead exciting lives. Lionel Rothschild, after whom Rothschild's giraffe is named, amassed the largest private zoological collection in the world. Rothschild was black-mailed by a mistress into selling most of the collection to the American Natural History Museum, but the remaining museum in Tring is still important for researchers. Things got interesting a decade ago when about 300 rare birds of paradise and quetzal skins disappeared. They were stollen by a student, who sold the feathers on Ebay for salmon fishing flies, to buy himself a golden flute. Thieves subsequently broke in and stole two rhino horns, but the museum had already replaced them with replicas. While Hollywood producers portray thieves in museum art heists, rhino horn makes a far more attractive target in real life. Worth more than gold, it is far easier to sell than a Rembrandt. Several were stolen from moth-eaten museum collections, before the remainders were all replaced by plastic replicas. A few years back, a rhino horn was seized at London's Heathrow airport hidden in a suitcase. Genetic tests showed exactly which deceased zoo rhino it had belong to, and those involved in smuggling the horn were caught.

Autopsies can take a considerable amount of work. I had 30 assistants, including 14 vets, helping me with one elephant autopsy, which still took all day. Sometimes there is an audience, hoping to glimpse why a popular animal has died. Often you are on your own, lost in trying to understand everything you are seeing. But a one-man Bactrian camel autopsy is not much fun. With a long list of samples, from frozen ark DNA and measurements, to tissue samples for bacterial cultures and microscope examination, even a Komodo dragon autopsy can take all day. A cosmetic autopsy may also be needed if your victim is destined for museum display. A chimpanzee's hair is carefully parted with a comb, before cutting the skin with your scalpel. To avoid damaging ribs, the heart and lungs are removed from the abdomen through the diaphragm. To reach the brain, the skull is freed from the neck, and the skin turned inside out to get to the back of the skull. Taking brain tissue for testing without being allowed to cut the skull is challenging, but you can even take your brain biopsy samples with a drinking straw.

While autopsies and surgical anatomy are linked, occasionally they are a continuum. I once operated on a giraffe, which had sadly expired on recovery from anaesthesia. With no time for commiseration, we had to then perform an autopsy between just the three of us, on the one-tonne patient. The owner, emotional from the incident, wanted a cosmetic post-mortem so they could get the animal stuffed. Not something a human surgeon would ever need to undertake. It was a long day, with the repressed emotions of sadness, disappointment, and frustration only surfacing on the trip home.

Man-made problems abound in wildlife autopsies. Sand tiger sharks with their stomach blocked with plastic, nets and large fishing hooks; white-tailed deer caught in fences; mute swans poisoned by lead fishing weights; giant anteaters hit by cars; and baby elephants drowned in a well. These are at least unintentional, even if careless. More sad is doing autopsies on animals that have suffered intentional malice. An orangutan blind from being shot in the eye with an airgun; a Canadian lynx that has chewed off its own foot to escape a metal trap; a hedgehog kicked to death like a football; a Javan spitting cobra bled out alive for traditional medicine; a red fox cub torn to pieces by dogs being trained to hunt; a black-backed jackal poisoned with strychnine; a sun bear, its paws hacked off for a distant restaurant. Yet sadly, only a few of these awful cases are actually crimes in the eyes of the law.

Still, environmental crimes generate over $200 billion a year, much more than illegal firearms. While half is for illegal logging and deforestation, this also dooms wildlife to death, even if the animals aren't directly trapped and sold.

Forensic autopsies can involve examining little more than a dried pile of bones and skin, X-rays for any signs of it being shot, and piecing together what happened to end the golden eagle's life. Yet the ultimate in decomposed autopsies goes to paleopathologists studying diseases in dinosaurs. Toe bone stress fractures are common in tyrannosaurs, as in human athletes, from over-exertion. With missing teeth, broken ribs, and torn tendon attachments, being a top predator was not easy in the Cretaceous period.

Sometimes only a fragment is available for autopsy. Testing for diseases and toxins is now amazing, yet even determining what animal was in a snare is a challenge. A hat band of black and white striped skin appears obviously from a zebra; but could actually just be dyed cow's hide. Genetics may be too slow for a few suspect hairs in a possible poacher's pick-up. Under the microscope though, a binturong has concave or c-shaped hairs in cross section, unlike a fishing cat's round hairs, or a Pallas's cat's oval hairs, which all look similar to the eye. The round surface of a hair shaft from a red panda has diamond petal scales, while the similarly coloured oval hair shaft from a ruddy mongoose has an irregular wave pattern. There are books and archives to help quick species identification from hair.

Sometimes hair patterns aren't enough. Some years ago, a black jaguar-sized animal tried to attack people through their sliding glass doors in England, and to the great excitement of cryptozoologists it left some hairs behind. The tiny follicle cells at the hair's base were submitted for genetic testing. Melanism is rare in big cats, yet common in supposed big cat sighting. As expected, the genetic results came back as a Labrador retriever. Sadly for the Scottish tourist board, there is almost certainly no monster hiding away in Loch Ness either.

From a dead whale to a fragment of faded hair, autopsies

tell us about wild animals' lives and health, and help us protect their living relatives. An autopsy may be the very last stop in a wild animal's life, but we have one other important hurdle to tackle as wildlife veterinarians. Everything we have undertaken thus far is often simply to get us to this point: returning our patients to the wild.

No matter how valuable the information gained from radio-collared animals like this snow leopard, this always comes at a cost to the individual animals tracked.

16

Die free

Catching an alligator may be perilous, anaesthetising a giraffe may fill you with trepidation, and operating on a tiger shark focuses your mind, but for me the ultimate stress is releasing an animal back to the wild. Watching a European otter explode out of its crate and disappear down a stream in a few seconds may be the culmination of all your work, but I find it the most difficult of all. Despite having treated a couple of hundred otters for return to the wild, I am always racked with self-doubt. Was he ready, fit and healthy to go back? Did we choose a good place, where he will find food and not be killed by a rival male? Is it sufficiently remote that he won't be hit by a car at night? And most importantly, does he have the survival skills to live back in the wild for any meaningful length of time, to have made what we put him through in treating him worthwhile? Born free, we also want wild animals to die free, but only after a good life.

Whether releasing a burnt koala back into a eucalyptus after treatment, bolstering the dwindling African penguin population by hatching abandoned eggs and rearing chicks for release, or re-introducing one-horned rhinos into northern Assam after local extinction, there is a huge amount of preparation before opening the crate door to release your patient, if it is to have a chance of surviving. Once released, some of the hardest work begins, tracking and monitoring how your discharged patient is faring: all while it makes every effort to avoid you or give trackers the slip. This is essential to understand if you have indeed done the right thing.

When wildlife releases work, it can be fantastic. As I write this, my friend Karmele Llano Sachez has just updated me on a young female orangutan that I operated on in Borneo half a decade ago. She had quickly recovered, and ended up as a foster mother for another orphaned infant orangutan. They had been released into the rainforest together, and all these years later were still doing well in the wild when tracked down.

Other outcomes are not so happy, despite your best efforts. Snowy owls are a rare sight in Scotland, only appearing every few years. The last time a snowy owl pair bred in Scotland was 45 years ago, on Shetland, barely closer to the mainland than to Norway. Years ago I was brought an injured male owl, from a newly arrived pair on the mainland – the only wild snowy owls that could possibly breed in the country in half a century. Male snowy owls are almost entirely white, while the larger female has black flecks on her chest, making them easily distinguishable. Everything was kept secret, while I treated him, lest the female was frightened away by enthusiastic birdwatchers. Eventually, after a month's treatment, rehabilitation, and checking his flight was perfect on slow motion video, he returned to his female partner in the wild. But there is little one can do to check an animal's Scottish street smarts. Only three days later, he got himself hit by a train. His long-suffering partner finally gave up after her boyfriend's fatal trainspotting efforts, and left Scotland. We sadly haven't had any other pairs since then.

Captivity for any wild-born animal, despite all good intentions, surgery or life-saving treatment, must carry the same level of distress we would feel if abducted and probed by aliens. An animal born and raised in a zoo is habituated to humans being around. Despite keeping most of its natural behaviours, it grows up close to people, familiar with their sounds and smells, and associates people with food, rather than being freaked out by our proximity. Many wild-born animals will never get used to us, and all our best treatments are hampered by an opposing force working against healing: stress. Survival hormones such as cortisol, essential for flight from predators or fights with rivals, have benefits. We use them in drugs like dexamethasone to treat coronavirus in people who can't breathe, or children with eczema. But any body is not designed to withstand a constant barrage of hormones designed for a brief survival boost. Sustained over the weeks we treat a puffin, these heavily suppress the immune system, working against antibiotics we may use to treat an infection. Even with preventative drugs, puffins frequently succumb to fungal infections of their lungs and air sacs. Caused by Aspergillus fungi, named after the holy water sprinklers they reminded the Italian priest of, who first discovered fungal spores 250 years ago, we each normally breathe in hundreds of these spores every day. Growing in compost heaps and other vegetation, they rarely cause a problem, unless animals are immunosuppressed. For a puffin, being treated in a cage is such high stress, their immune system ceases to function. It is as if they have stress-induced AIDS. So despite interesting animals we would never glimpse close-up in the wild, we always have to limit our contact with them to the minimum possible when treating them.

Holding a wild blackbird in your hand, you can see how absolutely terrified it is, and hear its desperate alarm calls. The only time in the wild it would ever feel a similar sensation would be in a predator's mouth as it is eaten. While we may want to stroke or reassuringly pat an Arctic fox we are holding, this would just make everything worse, with ripples of fear with each stroke, as the fox expects the pats to be the crunching of a polar bear's mouth eating it. Even large animals like brown bears are fearful of us. Bears living in proximity to humans in Scandinavia are far more stressed, even by the distant smells, sounds and lights of us humans, than bears living distant to humans. It has been described as them living in a landscape of fear. Yet how much worse being in a cage, in close proximity to the sounds and smells of other distressed animals, some of which could eat you, while hearing and smelling humans right there? The stabs of injections and cleaning of wounds are not understandable to the victim, just painful and distressing. Treatment centres for rehabilitating wild animals are also torture centres. Even if the outcome is good and they return to the wild, it is essential to get the balance of what we do and why right, otherwise we put animals through tremendous distress for nothing.

Survival after release

Despite television shows and news articles highlighting heroic successes in treating mangled wild animals, even in wealthy developed countries with the best veterinary treatment only half of all rescued, injured, and orphaned wild animals will make it back to the wild. Even less survive for any length of time once they get back there. There are some patients that do better than this. My friend Vijitha Perera in Sri Lanka receives orphaned elephant calves, often babies less than six months old with very severe injuries such as from being hit by a truck. Of those that make it to be released into Udawalawe National Park, more than 90 per cent will still be alive more than two years later, and many have gone on to raise healthy, normal elephant calves in the decades since being hand-raised. Yellow-footed wallaby reintroductions in South Australia also have a survival rate of over 80 per cent. In contrast, of over 500 black-footed ferrets captive bred and released into their former range, only about 30 per cent survive. Many fall prey to coyotes and raptors as they struggle to realise the risks of the wild, compared to their peaceful care in captivity. Others don't even do that well. Fewer than one in eight injured goldfinches will even make it through rehabilitation to the stage where they are able to be released.

Treating ill or injured animals is not the only reason for release. Grey wolves may be translocated to prevent inbreeding in a small population. Vancouver Island marmots bred in zoos are released to bolster the small number of these critically endangered rodents in the wild. Large blue butterflies have been returned to England. Most taxing is releasing animals that have gone completely extinct in the wild. There have been some dramatic successes. The Arabian oryx is the poster boy for the release of extinct animals. After decades of hard work and support, it has become the first species to be downgraded to vulnerable having being completely extinct in the wild only a few decades ago.

Other species, previously extinct in the wild, have also been successfully returned to the wilderness, such as the Przewalski's horse to the Mongolian steppes, the Californian condor to again soar over the Grand Canyon, the milu or Père David's deer in China, and the black-footed ferret in Arizona. There are also several species in the pipeline for return to the wild, such as Spix's macaw, Kihansi spray toad, and Socorro dove – a real cause for optimism in the ongoing fight against species extinction and the threats to the natural world.

Carefully managed reintroduction programmes

Disease risk analysis and health screening are crucial to these reintroduction programmes. Releasing a Socorro dove, carrying an invisible virus from a different bird species in a zoo, risks causing a disease outbreak in other critically endangered animals on the island, like the endemic Socorro mockingbird. Poorly planned reintroductions can not only fail, but even cause other species to go extinct. Anyone involved in species reintroductions will be familiar with the long process of meticulous planning, risk assessments, and endless meetings, all unseen but vital to a project's success.

The rarer the animal the less we know about its diseases, always a problem with endangered species. The most extreme are endangered invertebrates. As veterinarians we are more familiar with mammals and birds, while entomologists also rarely research endangered insect diseases. My fellowship of the Royal Entomological Society seems strange, when vet knowledge and interest is usually limited to the best flea treatment for pets, but it has helped when working with really small, endangered wildlife species, from pine hoverfly larvae to cave weta crickets. A problem with some early projects is that, saved from extinction just in the nick of time, we never managed to find what was normal. Decades after their extinction in the wild, when planning to return small Polynesian snails back to Tahiti, it was impossible to figure out if a microsporidia parasite had been normal in them for thousands of years, or if it had jumped from another species in the zoos we kept them in, and could pose a threat if released in Tahiti. When there are as few as 24 remaining Lord Howe Island stick insects, affectionately called tree lobsters, left on the planet, with just two pairs caught to try to save the species, it is near impossible to justify killing an extra one and placing it in preservative for future reference. But after tens of thousands have been hatched in zoos in the last two decades, this would have been ideal to ensure no new diseases go back to the wild. Dusty museum specimens impaled on pins in wooden cases are seldom much use, being little more than a crisp hollow shell. Autopsies can also be frustrating, as by the time a fen raft spider is found dead, the innards are already a decomposed bacterial soup. Much as we hate it, killing and preserving a small number of endangered insects that are perfectly healthy, to examine under the microscope in future, is usually a vital part of conservation programmes.

Enthusiasm can get the better of people. Tired of waiting for official reintroduction of the beaver to Scotland after four hundred years, well-meaning enthusiasts illegally released beavers into the River Tay. While the beavers thrived, there was a risk that they had also inadvertently reintroduced the *Echinococcus multilocularis* parasite to Britain. There was a real concern this could get into dogs and foxes and then spread to people. I spent two years with beaver expert Roisin Campbell-Palmer trapping and testing beavers, using blood tests, ultrasound and even keyhole surgery to check their livers, in makeshift operating theatres set up in barns. This was expensive, time consuming and not fair on the animals. We thankfully didn't find the disease, but did discover another parasite, the beaver beetle, which behaves similarly to a head louse despite being a beetle, and had inadvertently been introduced to Scotland.

With all the care and attention taken with planning and preparation to ensure wild animals re-introduced are healthy and pose no risk to other animals or people, it is frustrating to see 50 million pheasants and partridges bred overseas released into Britain every year for sport hunting. Almost a quarter don't even survive until the shooting season, and in the end less than a third are actually shot, the rest abandoned to their fate. There would be a scandal if even the smallest-scale wildlife reintroduction was undertaken with such poor risk management and animal suffering involved. Disappointingly, government bodies overseeing natural heritage sometimes seem little more than hunting and shooting licence administrators.

Despite best efforts, sometimes wildlife reintroductions don't succeed. The first attempts to return white-tailed sea eagles and large blue butterflies to Britain failed. Preventing the shooting, poisoning, and persecution that made the eagles extinct in the first place was vital. We also needed to better understand the complex needs of a butterfly that survives by its cuckoo-like larva fooling specific ant species into taking it into their nest and caring for it, while it eats their own larvae. I was very disheartened to see that after a decade's work to return beavers to Scotland, all the risk mitigation, and despite their popularity with the public, licences were given to shoot more than a fifth of all the beavers in just the very first year of their being recognised as native again. To try to reduce culling, Roisin and I have been trapping, health checking and translocating conflict beavers to England, but this could all still deplete the only recently reintroduced beaver population in Scotland. It will be shameful if beavers became the only mammals to go extinct twice in Scotland.

We have to bond with an orphaned baby otter so we can

get it to take milk. It needs to think that we are its mother, and we even give it fluffy toys to cuddle up with. But as soon as it is weaned we must return to our usual hands-off approach, putting cubs together so they revert to wild behaviour and learn to stay away from us humans before they are released. Even better if, as with hatchling Californian condors, you can rear them so that they remain oblivious to people. Videos of giant panda carers in China wearing panda costumes when feeding or cleaning are always amusing, but have a serious purpose. It is essential that pandas reared by their mothers for release in the Wolong mountains do not become habituated to people. The pyjama costumes may look nothing like a real panda to us, but with several released cubs now successfully living in the wild, it clearly works for the pandas. Despite criticism, giant panda conservation in China has been a major success, with the species classification downgraded from endangered to vulnerable. Protected areas are also saving a host of other species, from golden snub-nosed monkeys to snow leopards. While zoo-bred pandas act as ambassadors, they would never be candidates to return to the wild, being far too habituated to people.

Becoming habituated to humans during rearing is dangerous with orphaned male deer. Whether as large as moose, or as small as Chilean pudu, after puberty, driven by testosterone during the rut of mating season, they will attack people as rivals. Chinese water deer have no antlers, but hand-reared males can attack people with their sabre-like teeth during mating season. Antelope males may not have the same testosterone explosion of rutting deer, but I have still been attacked by a hand-reared Menelik's bushbuck.

Many species, from bonobos to beluga whales, teach their young the vital skills needed to survive in the wild. Of course there are exceptions. Spotted seals grow at a phenomenal rate thanks to their mother's fat-rich milk. She abandons them after a few weeks to go to sea, and they must make their own way in the world, learning how to catch fish while living off their stored blubber. Releasing hand-reared seals is no different to what would happen in nature. Hooded seal mums provide the shortest maternal care you can imagine, mothers usually abandoning pups after only five days. In contrast, many young seabirds like razorbills and guillemots cannot really be reared and successfully released, as they depend on help from their parents for months at sea, to learn to catch their own food with their parents. Magnificent frigate birds will still be fed and taught for over a year by their mothers after fledging, as they learn to catch their own squid and fish, and how to rob other seabirds of their catches, again making it very difficult to rear and release youngsters. The most extensive home schooling among birds is done by ground hornbills. With a lifespan into their seventies, youngsters depend on their parents for up to two years. Young male birds then spend six or more years as apprentices learning how to help raise chicks. Without this training they don't successfully breed themselves as adults. This makes rearing young ground hornbills for release problematic.

Among primates it isn't just humans and great apes that support their children and teach them social skills. Endangered golden lion tamarins have the appearance of a miniaturised Wizard-of-Oz lion, complete with squeaky voice. Unusual among primates in that they usually raise twins and sometimes even triplets, kids stay at home to help raise their younger brothers and sisters. This helps them learn to be parents themselves. Even the types of trees present in their forest are important, because the kind of play they develop there will help them develop the skills they will need to avoid predators later in life. When their numbers plummeted to fewer than 500 in the 1980s, the Smithsonian and other zoos bred, trained and released tamarins for several years. More than a year was spent in zoos getting them used to finding water in bromeliads and eating intact fruits, rather than eating chopped fruit and drinking from water bowls. After lengthy quarantine in Brazil, they were placed in enclosures in the forest to become accustomed to the sights and sounds while still protected, and when released months later were still provided with food and followed for more than a year. Despite all this time and effort, half didn't survive their first year. The wild is a rather unforgiving place. But the babies they managed to raise did considerably better, and numbers are now five times higher three decades on, although they are still sadly endangered.

If captive breeding wasn't complicated enough, getting released animals to survive and breed in the wild is even more challenging. This is seldom conveyed in ceaseless news stories about cute new-born zoo babies across the world. We may well be able to keep many species safe from total extinction in zoos, but getting them back to the wild is far more difficult. When a species habitat is gone, it is almost impossible.

Deciding to treat an injured wild animal for return to the wild is always a balance between stress, time and chance. Orphaned European otters need to stay with their mothers for over a year as they learn the skills needed to survive. Adult otters are solitary and territorial, and they will need to head off and find new unoccupied territory, if they are not to be killed. I sadly have done many autopsies on otters killed by others while dispersing, or having starved to death. They may appear as large as an adult, but their bones' open growth plates on X-rays show they are still young, and battling to learn essential life skills.

Thankfully the smooth-coated otters I treat in Asia, or giant river otters in South America, are social and live in family groups, so youngsters can be returned to their family as soon as recovered, to continue learning from the family's school on the river. Some animals even take care of others' babies. Adult herring gulls, spotting groups of young chicks in rescue centre paddocks, get so concerned they will keep returning and drop food through the net to chicks which they do not know at all. We can sometimes take advantage of the strong parenting instincts of our primate relatives. Infant Barbary macaques confiscated from markets in Morocco have been successfully fostered into wild macaque groups which are completely unrelated. It is the male macaques that tend to adopt the infant and look after it. This is quite unique. Barbary macaques are promiscuous, and a male has no idea which youngsters he may have fathered. Yet Barbary males are excellent fathers and uncles, and help carry and care for all youngsters in their group. While this helps us get an infant adopted, it does mean it has to already be weaned for this to succeed. Adoptions don't always work, but are a ray of hope for an endangered species that sadly has as one of its main threats the illegal capture of youngsters for pets and as photo props for tourists.

Orphaned European otters usually require over a year and a half's care before they are ready to be returned to the wild. Or as ready as we are able to get them. Hand-reared West Indian manatees take two to three years to rear and return, while my friend Vijitha, in hand-rearing Asian elephants in Sri Lanka, may need to look after them for over half a decade. Rearing these with even the best milk replacers is slower than their growth on natural mother's milk. A mother's milk is constantly changing in composition as a baby grows, and this is impossible to replicate artificially.

Returning an injured wild adult otter, or indeed most animals, from eagles to newts, back to the wild in the same location where they were found usually has the best chance of success. Adults have already learnt and used all the life skills they need to survive; finding food and mates, and avoiding predators and man-made harms. They will also know their territory, with places to find food, hide and shelter. Releasing a reared orphan baby is very different.

Some animals have fantastic survival rates in the wild. An adult griffon vulture returned to the wild has an almost 99 per cent chance of surviving a year. Andean condors have similar high survival rates, probably as scavenger animals often have high intelligence. Even adult golden eagles, which are far less bright, have a more than 90 per cent chance of surviving a year in the wild in Scotland. An adult osprey's life is, however, much more perilous. Only two-thirds of adults survive each year, thanks to arduous migrations to West Africa and back. While I was on my honeymoon in the Gambia, I watched ospreys fishing, and I wondered whether they might have been the same individuals I had previously seen and treated in Scotland.

With babies, it is a different story. A quarter of songbirds like blackbirds won't even survive their first week after leaving the nest. Most become food for other animals. Some are taken by birds of prey and wild mammals, but many are eaten by domestic cats. Cats kill two to three billion birds every year just in North America. Adult birds caught by cats also don't fare well. Even if rescued and given vet treatment, only a quarter of blackbirds with cat bites will survive, even if wounds don't look severe. It is probably the crushing trauma that does much of the damage and not just the punctures we can see.

When given one of these injured birds to treat, before reaching for painkillers and antibiotics, you have to really question whether it is fair on the bird. Blackbirds are not endangered, at least not yet. To save one blackbird injured by a cat means you will be prolonging the pain, suffering and distress of at least three others, which will die during their week or two of treatment, as you can't tell which will be the survivor. As vets we innately want to try saving everything, but this isn't always best for our patients. It is always difficult to euthanase patients, but we can cause far more harm by trying to treat everything.

Baby birds of prey and young owls fare better initially, as their parents help them with food and try to teach them life skills, much like human parents, after they leave the nest. But three-quarters of birds of prey will still not survive their first winter, when their parents' help is over, and their survival skills and ingenuity are put to the ultimate test.

To achieve good survival after release, it is essential to carefully choose which casualties to treat the first time you see them. We may treat the identical injury in adults and youngsters differently. A complicated wing fracture needing surgery and two months in care in an adult lesser spotted eagle makes good sense, when it is likely to live another decade or more after release. But treating precisely the same injury the same way in a recent fledgling, even if a more endangered greater spotted eagle that everyone is far more interested in, may not be wise. After months of captive care and the associated stress, it is unlikely to survive its first winter, whatever you do.

We also need to keep patients in a way that they don't harm their chances of survival. Heavy mute swans without pools to swim in will wear their feet through to the bones in just two weeks on concrete, while a lanner falcon in a cage will break its long tail feathers in just a few days. These feathers are crucial for its high-speed manoeuvrability, so we protect the tail feathers with a tail guard. Sometimes it is not clear what is essential. Burmese pythons are commonly kept as pets, often in what appear to be large enclosures but which are actually barely their length if they stretched out. While enthusiasts claim they appear happy, and there is endless debate, it is difficult to be certain. Considering they can have home ranges of more than 20 square kilometres, they probably need considerably bigger enclosures than they are usually forced to inhabit for decades when kept as pets.

Ensuring animals have sufficient food initially after release, while they learn where to find their own food, can help. If releasing red foxes, we aim for wet weather rather than the nice, hot, dry weather we ourselves prefer. Waterlogged soil forces large numbers of earthworms to the surface; an important food source for young foxes. This is also more natural than support feeding them with dog food and gradually weaning them off. After fixing a fledgling white-tailed eagle's broken leg, a week before its release we try to leave a road-kill deer somewhere near the nest area. This isn't just for him, but also to encourage the parents to hang around. They won't feed their progeny, but will let the fledgling follow them, so he will get a few weeks' valuable time to learn how and where they find food, even if much of it is scavenging from carcasses.

Tracking and monitoring after release

We need some way of knowing what happens to our patients once they are discharged; to know if all our veterinary ministrations were sensible and worthwhile. We can't simply phone an owner like domestic animal veterinary colleagues can. For many birds, this is as simple as applying a leg ring. Close to a million birds are rung every year just in the United Kingdom, almost entirely by volunteers. Bird ringing has ancient roots. Homing pigeons were used by ancient Egyptians five thousand years ago, and the Romans released crows with threads on their legs to convey messages during the Punic wars, or tell others about chariot-race winners. John Audubon, the American ornithologist, used threads on eastern phoebes' legs to see if they returned to the same nests the following year after migration. Serious bird-ringing schemes similar to those today have existed for over a hundred years. Yet only about one in 50 bird rings are reported, so it is slow and takes years to know if your bird patients are surviving, and at what rate compared to other wild individuals. Metal rings are small and usually only reported when a bird is found dead. No news is not necessarily good news. Your patient may still happily be alive, or could have died just a day after its release. While not always useful for our purposes, bird ringing generates vital data on how bird populations are faring.

Overall, the news isn't great. Bird numbers appear to be declining across most species, due to habitat loss, changing farm practices and climate change. Some birds have extended their range further north in the UK, like chiffchaffs, which now also start laying their eggs earlier, while kittiwake numbers are plummeting due to warming seas and heavy sand eel fishing for animal feed and fertiliser. Eventually, this may also cause our beloved puffins to become rarer. In North America alone, one in four birds has disappeared in the last fifty years, more than three billion fewer birds in the skies.

Understanding how birds move is important when trying to restore lost populations. If declining fish wasn't enough, puffins return to the island they hatched on to breed, and once a colony is lost they rarely come back. Project Puffin moved a thousand chicks to artificial burrows on Eastern Egg Rock and Seal islands over several years, feeding chicks and even using decoy puffins to encourage the young adults to return and dig burrows to breed. Ringing birds is important to know what is working and what isn't, lest everyone wastes huge amounts of time and effort.

Large, coloured leg bands with letters can be viewed through binoculars, and work well for larger seabirds, from wandering albatrosses to lesser black-backed gulls. Wandering albatrosses will mate for life, returning to nest on places like the South Georgia islands every two years. A chick rung with a colourful leg band may not come back to land for over a decade, but with time and persistence a good idea of how a colony is doing emerges, helping us understand the impacts of fishing, even if very slowly. A chick banded by one researcher can easily outlive them. Best of all, birds don't need to be caught or man-handled ever again.

Leg bands also tell interesting stories of more common birds. It isn't just survival that rings and leg bands help us understand, but often also movements. Releasing fledgling lesser black-backed gulls in Scotland, it amazed me to hear birds being spotted only weeks later enjoying the sun on a beach far away in Portugal. While lesser black-backed gulls are perhaps not as charismatic as an eagle, and ignored as common, following ringing data for one bird shows it flying all the way to West Africa and around Europe, a far more exciting life than most of us lead.

There is a whole army of volunteers spending their free time spotting and reporting these rings. It is the ultimate living treasure hunt. Everyone has touching stories of birds' amazing journeys, sometimes over decades. With all the dire news stories, it is easy to forget just how many people care about the natural world and give so much of their time to help in different ways.

While leg rings can help for gulls in the open, or albatrosses returning to nest, they can't be used for all birds. When monitoring king vultures, whose colourful faces adorn Mayan temples, you can't use leg rings. These birds have evolved a behaviour to urinate on their legs in hot weather, to allow evaporation to cool the blood flowing through. If you put a ring on their leg the uric acid in their urine can accumulate, corroding the ring and burning their leg. Instead, we may need to apply wing tags. These large, colourful tags are also easier to spot through binoculars when a vulture is soaring hundreds of metres above you. Tags can be applied to a feather, and so drop out when a bird moults in a year's time, or in some cases are attached through the wing membrane with a thin pin to make it permanent. They can also be read through binoculars when a critically endangered Indian vulture is perching on its inaccessible cliff nest hundreds of metres above you. Once the most common birds of prey on the planet, the populations of the three species of Indian vultures have collapsed from tens of millions of birds to only a few thousands in less than half my lifetime, and the slender bill vulture is predicted to go extinct in the wild in less than a decade. So intelligent is this species, we spent almost a month trapping in the Thar desert twenty years ago just to catch one bird. Even marking birds to follow them can be far from easy.

Leg rings or wing tags are useless tracking Amur falcons migrating across the ocean between Siberia and Southern Africa, or in trying to figure out where reintroduced bald ibis are dying from pesticide poisoning, when they disappear during migration. For that we need more sophisticated technology. When Sputnik 2 launched in November 1957, making the dog Kudryavka, more popularly known in the west as Laika, the first animal to orbit the Earth, the Cold War space race also inadvertently started modern wildlife tracking. A few American biologists complained that the Russians could tell more about a dog's movements in space than they could for wildlife a few metres outside their window. Initially it was difficult to get funding, until biologists convinced the US Navy of the potential military uses of tracking wildlife. Military jet operations were abandoned on Midway Atoll after a Laysan albatross had been sucked into an aircraft engine, and naval research was interested in studying the albatrosses, to see if moving them all to another island might work. The Navy quickly realised that miniature telemetry transmitters also had useful military and spying applications. Today, Laysan albatrosses are still breeding on Midway, the naval base long abandoned. Sadly, lead-based paint flaking off the old military buildings kills up to 10,000 albatross chicks a year, far more than aircraft strikes ever did.

The very first wild animals to be radio-tracked were ruffed grouse in 1960. It was a complete failure. The transmitters weighed about 50 grams, cutting-edge for the time, but far too heavy. They sat awkwardly on the back with an upright antenna, needing signal-receiving towers. The first bird's batteries only lasted a few days, and the researchers never found out what became of it. The second bird's transmitter also failed after a few days. The tower receivers didn't work, and when with a borrowed hand-held tracker they managed to locate the male grouse, they found it dead less than 50 metres from where it was released. The large antenna sticking up from its back had hit a branch in flight and the bird had crashed into the ground and died.

Undeterred, biologists decided the bulky transmitters were better suited to tree porcupines, and to stick to hand-held antenna receivers. Unlike the grouse, this at least worked. However, everyone was surprised to find radio signals often didn't travel in straight lines but were frequently reflected or refracted by landscape and trees, and they had to be very familiar with the typical distortions where they worked to have any hope of finding the porcupines. For the first decade, it appeared little more than a novelty and it wasn't clear it would ever be of much real use scientifically.

Today, everything from lynx to bald eagles has been successfully followed with the technology, with companies selling millions of dollars' worth of transmitters. Radio-transmitters can be found using drones to reach inaccessible cliffs and gorges. While collars are fine for large animals like leopards and rhinos, an expertly balanced back harness, adjusted for each individual, is essential for an Amur falcon trying to catch prey. Radio-collars won't work for most aquatic animals. Common seals with their conical head and shoulders are unsuitable for a collar, and a harness risks them becoming entangled underwater and drowning. One solution is to glue a transmitter to their head. This is the only part of the body to regularly exit the water when a seal breathes. Some seal transmitters simply use the mobile phone network when close to shore, to transmit their stored data. These seals literally phone home. The transmitter will last a year, falling off when they moult their fur coat. None of these methods will work for otters. There is no distinctive neck to attach a collar to, and any harness can either snag an otter fatally on underwater branches, break their fur and rub wounds in their skin if too tight, and if even slightly loose an otter will wriggle out Houdini-like in a few minutes. Gluing transmitters to their fur would be disastrous, as their fur is essential, not just for their waterproofing, but also as their insulation in freezing temperatures, as they don't have any blubber layer. Bears too are poor subjects for radio-collars. Polar bears can double their weight going into hibernation, but wake up in the spring half the weight, with a fluctuating neckline to match. Any collar risks strangulating the bear one month, only to fall off a few months later.

If monitoring is essential, we sometimes have no other option but to place the transmitter inside these animals' abdomens via a surgical operation. All surgery carries a risk, and even more so in wild animals, yet some biologists are blasé about how invasive this is for their study victims. Incredibly, many of these tags are placed by biologists in the field, with only a few hours' training. Until just a few years ago, even polar bear transmitters were in most cases simply fitted by the biologists. While they publish their scientific data on animals' behaviour and biology, it is difficult to estimate complication rates for these operations, as it is rarely ever published. But from the discussions I have had, and through trawling unpublished filed reports, it can be horribly high. When placed with strong ethical reviews, for meaningful reasons, radio-transmitter studies have been a way to engage the public with a host of endangered species and their threats. Small camera backpacks on animals from seals to steppe eagles give the public a glimpse into the animal's view of the world, helping build empathy for conservation programmes. Most camera harness footage, while appealing, has limited scientific value, but there are exceptions. Along with genetic sampling of droppings, we now know that gentoo penguins actually eat a large number of jellyfish in the wild. This was something we never knew from the old methods of stomach flushing to try to judge what penguins were eating, as jellyfish would digest so quickly they were never seen.

Radiotelemetry transmitters also show when things don't work as planned. After the *Free Willy* movies, there was a massive public campaign to return Keiko, the young male orca star of the movie, from his cramped quarters in Mexico back to the wild. Costing over $20 million and taking half a decade, it was a contentious project, and still is today. Captured when very young off Iceland, before being sold to the aquarium in Mexico, his return to the wild first entailed moving him to a large aquarium where he could get used to salt water, and improve his weight and body condition. He was then moved to a bay in Iceland and taken into the sea for supervised swims. When he eventually swam free, following some wild orcas, he was tracked for the 1,600 kilometres he swam to Norway, where he started approaching boats and people, even letting children ride on his back. Despite ongoing efforts he never managed to join any wild orca groups and had to continue to be fed, until he sadly died of pneumonia. Even after his death the conflict continued. Some claimed the release a success, as he spent five years in the ocean rather than a tiny aquarium pool turning trained tricks before his death. Others instead claim it was all a failure as he never managed to join a wild orca group, or even feed properly on his own most of the time. Captured as a youngster, perhaps he never learned enough survival skills before his captivity. Wild orcas are one of the most intelligent but also social of all animals. Living up to a century, you may find four generations of family members in a pod, and joining as a stranger, even with normal wild orca social skills, is difficult. While the lessons to be learnt from Keiko's release and death appear to be different to everyone, his monitoring and human help was only possible thanks to radiotelemetry tracking technology.

Keiko was followed using the classic radiotelemetry systems I used when a young vet, with high frequency radio waves that one tries to pinpoint using a receiver. Now we can also utilise satellite-tracking using GPS or the Earth-orbiting ARGOS satellites to accurately follow animals anywhere on the globe without ever laying eyes on them again, or needing to leave a comfortable office. They have been used on everything from savanna elephants and migrating caribou, to great white sharks in the ocean's depths and solitary jaguars hiding in the Amazon. Now, using a new system installed on the International Space Station, which orbits much lower than other satellites, we can use radio tags as light as 5 grams, on cuckoos migrating thousands of kilometres, or on straw-coloured fruit bats in West Africa in inaccessible roosts. Unfortunately, they still need a 10 centimetre long antenna pointing backwards. For bigger animals like hawksbill turtles, increasing miniaturisation means extra data can be gathered, such as swimming speeds, diving depth and water temperatures, which help us to understand continuing threats.

While detailed tracking by satellite helps us understand the long migrations of common cuckoos, we have also discovered some interesting avian behaviours. Plotting the flights of many birds on a map, it is clear they have adapted to aspects of the human-modified world. Cuckoos now often choose to follow major roads when navigating, which are easier to follow and more obvious than the clues they would previously have used. Golden eagles in Scotland don't navigate by following roads. When a satellite tag heads from a remote highland hill down

354

a vehicle track and onto a motorway before disappearing at sea, the bird has been illegally shot, the dead bird in a guilty gamekeeper's car until the evidence is dumped at sea. When presented with this evidence, gamekeepers in hotspots for wildlife crime ludicrously claim the eagles were actually killed by ornithologists.

But satellite tags are expensive, and radio-tracking takes a lot of time in the field, so we also use cheaper solutions. Microchips are probably the smallest, cheapest monitoring devices. Smaller than a grain of rice, they are called passive integrated transponders, or PIT tags. They have no batteries that can fail or leak. Consisting simply of a small electronic circuit in a glass capsule, they are completely passive, until activated by a radio scanner. They only respond to a narrow range of frequencies, and have to be near a scanner to be detected. The technology is identical to security labels used in clothes and books, or in your electronic passport. In wildlife, microchips were first used in fish to monitor their movements for waterways management. Similar radio-induced identification circuits are also used in ear tags of farmed cows to log how much food each cow eats, and how much milk they each produce, with low performers off to the abattoir.

Ear tags can be useful for monitoring hoofed animals like bighorn sheep, Rocky Mountain goats, and moose. Ear tags can even be useful for swimming Canadian beavers, or hairy-nosed wombats that spend most of their life down a burrow. Large yellow ear tags may be unsightly for wildlife photographers, but help identify individuals through binoculars from far enough away that the animal doesn't flee. Yet in regions of North America with significant deer hunting, there is a risk that animals may be shot and eaten only a few days after being anaesthetised. Anaesthetised animals are unfortunately off their game for a few days, as anyone who has had anaesthesia can attest. Farm animal medications and anaesthetics have strict withdrawal times before their meat is deemed safe for human consumption. Hunters may find their victim black-tailed deer or wapiti has a yellow ear tag with a reference number they need to check, to ensure it is safe for them to eat its meat. Hunter ear tag reporting in North America also gives some data to researchers on how long a deer has lived and how far it may have travelled since the tag was applied, despite an unlucky deer's untimely death.

Many wild mammals are far more difficult to monitor. Being nocturnal doesn't help. Microchips, while small and inexpensive, are only useful for some scenarios. In densely populated countries, it can be useful to recognise that an injured fox in the suburbs is one that you released back to the wild after treatment only a few months earlier, or that one found dead at the side of the road was another unfortunate releasee that failed to survive very long. Microchipped eastern diamondback rattlesnakes can be safely identified using a microchip reader on a pole. Rattlesnakes can appear lazy, lying curled up waiting for a meal to pass by before striking, but with home ranges as big as 5 square kilometres it can be almost impossible to find a camouflaged snake to check its microchip number.

Despite travelling hundreds of kilometres at sea, penguins are perfect subjects for microchip monitoring. Flipper bands used to be the main penguin identification when I started working with them, but even the best designs interfered with their wings' streamlined shape, which is so important for flying under water, and bands could rub and injure birds. Some penguin colonies have narrow paths between the rocks, and burying a microchip antennae beneath the sand in these natural gateways means we can monitor individual penguins' comings and goings over many years, building up good information on their survival. Microchips are inserted at the base of their tail, or in the skin over their stumpy ankles, to ensure it is close enough to the buried antennae to register.

There are even temperature monitoring microchips. To work, however, these need to be placed inside the abdomen. Penguins have been subjected to invasive large monitors inside their bodies in the past, as transmitters on backpacks would interfere with their swimming, in the same way an Olympic swimmer would never win medals wearing a child's school satchel during a race. These newer microchips help make biologists' procedures to study how far they travel, how deep they dive, and how their temperatures and heart rates change, less invasive.

Camera traps

The least invasive monitoring method doesn't even entail touching an animal. Camera traps are cheap and easily available, some costing little more than the memory card they need to record high-definition video. Yet this technology is one of the oldest of all wildlife monitoring techniques, and was first invented by a politician. George Shiras III was an American congressman, and the father of wildlife photography. Although circus and zoo animals and a few wild birds had been photographed before, he built large tripwire camera and flash systems to photograph animals living in the wild at night. The startled look of surprise in a moose's eyes, or in the eyes of a white-tailed deer caught leaping away from the flash in his early photos, is obvious. They must have got the fright of their lives when the bright flash, caused by the explosion of magnesium powder, went off. Within a few years, some of his glass plate photographs, such as a lynx sitting serenely, show the composition and skill of modern wildlife photography, and an entire *National Geographic* issue was dedicated to his photographs a hundred years ago.

Things are easier for both photographer and wild subject now. Instead of trip wires, motion sensors activate the camera. But if you're not careful with the placement of your camera, a fern waving in the breeze can fill your memory card with useless footage, which is not something that would have troubled Shiras. Some camera traps include a mobile phone card, and send photos to you instantly. Low-power modes mean a camera can work for months taking photos both at day and at night, and are waterproof enough to withstand monsoon rains. Unlike magnesium flash bombs, modern infrared LED

357

lights are invisible to our eyes, and almost indetectable to many animals. I say almost indetectable, as it is clear that some species, from spotted hyaena to honey badgers, can definitely see the light on dark nights, although they become accustomed to it, and learn to ignore it. Hyaenas, attracted by the faint light or investigating my smell, are always keen to chew up an expensive camera trap, and it is essential to use a protective metal box if you are to have any hope of retrieving non-masticated footage. But even a steel case isn't enough to save your camera from a determined Asian elephant. Thankfully they usually ignore cameras, with only the odd one destroyed now and then by an inquisitive teenager.

Drones are now sometimes used as a cheaper alternative to airplane surveys of large wildlife, as well as monitoring for poachers in remote areas. But animals are still just as wary of their sound as they are of helicopters, and even black bears will often hide from them. Like Adélie penguins, they exhibit fast heart rates when drones fly overhead, showing this is not a stress-free way of monitoring wildlife. Flying drones over seabird colonies when surveying elephant seals risks panicked birds flying into the drone, injuring themselves and causing it to crash. Drones' batteries are still very limited, and unless fitted with thermal cameras are not much use at night. It is still early days, and it remains to be seen if drones live up to some of the news hype around their proposed wildlife uses, or if they actually pose more of a wildlife menace.

Tasks previously done with radio transmitter collars, like national park Bengal tiger surveys, can now simply be done with camera traps; not only sparing animals trapping and anaesthesia, but often generating more robust data for far less cost. Camera traps can tell you things that no other monitoring methods can. Finding a dead golden snub-nosed monkey, there is no other way of telling what animals will scavenge it. From camera traps it turns out that other monkeys leave it alone. Thick-billed crows may steal a nibble, yet they usually simply prefer to eat the maggots. Masked civets eat the intestines, a common preference for civets, and strangely the face, while moon bears may eat the rest, and not just at night. Camera trapping has also helped us to understand that, despite their social nature and intelligence, none of the live monkeys came to see the body, unlike elephants with their dead.

Some animals have body markings as distinctive as finger-prints. From grey seals to whale sharks, photo-identification can tell hundreds of different individuals apart simply from body patterns on photos, and automated computer systems can analyse thousands of aerial photographs to add detail to a seal census on a rocky coast. Even red foxes have different enough facial markings that I can tell individuals apart from just photos.

Telling individual animals apart on night-time camera traps can be difficult, though. While some foxes I have monitored after release have distinctive facial markings, I am pretty hope-less at telling badgers apart, let alone the different females in a pride of lions. In some Southern African reserves, lions have been cleverly marked in a way that goes unnoticed by visiting tourists. Lions are branded, just the same way cattle are, to identify them. But instead of obvious letters and numbers, small marks, resembling healed fight wounds and scratches, are made over the shoulder area, using a pattern to represent different numbers. To those monitoring them, each lion's name is as clear as if written on its side, yet tourists remain bliss-fully unaware. A similar method, using ear notches, can be used to identify individual deer, without the need for an unsightly ear tag that could snag on a branch and rip an ear severely. Branding and ear notching are painful, and not some-thing one would contemplate on an otter. A scar with its missing fur would be disastrous for waterproofing. While we can microchip otters, only if a body is found or an otter returns to captivity would we have any idea what has happened to them. In most cases, an otter will simply disappear and we never know if it has died within a few days of release, or lived happily for many more years. Without surgically implanting a transmitter you can rarely be certain, but I have used a cheap and simple method inspired by Vivienne Westwood and Katy Perry. Hair dye. More specifically, bleach. Using a simple home hair-bleaching kit, we can dye a few small spots on the fur over a shoulder. One side identifies a male, the other a female. The pattern tells us which specific otter. The small spots are cinnamon coloured compared to the normal dark fur, but show up well on a camera trap with infrared lighting at night. They will last for several months until new hair moults through. It's not as good as radiotelemetry, but good enough for us to know whether an otter, after almost two years' care and rearing, is healthy, well, and established back in the wild after release. The application of bleach is a little more critical than that of your hairdresser. Overbleaching the hair dries and damages the hair shafts, causing the fur to be brittle and break. Even these small areas of fur damage can be enough to destroy the fur's waterproofing, allowing water to seep into the under-coat and chill the otter.

Monitoring animals in the wild can have a dark side, and not just when poachers use camera traps to locate moon bear trails in the forest to place their snares, or thermal cameras and drones to find white rhinos with long horns. I remember, when I was young, being amazed by Khoisan bushman trackers, who would reconstruct an animal's movements. In soft sand I can follow spoor from a lion, and in snow I can reconstruct the antics of an Arctic fox. I can even recognise when a car's starter cable has been bitten through by a beech martin rather than cut by a jealous ex-partner, the martin attracted to the fish oil in the rubber. But watching these trackers, it seemed they could see things that are invisible to other humans, following spoor across hard ground and rocks, with nothing visible for miles. Even then they were becoming a rarity. Used as army trackers in the wars apartheid South Africa picked with neighbouring countries, and displaced from traditional hunting grounds in the central Kalahari, ironically by nature reserves, as well as diamond mining, the traditional ways are almost gone. High-end tourism and private reserves, however, make it is essential for visitors with short stays and smartphone-induced micro-patience to see the big five. Gone is the patience of early mornings and long drives, with the real chance of seeing nothing at all. Economics often just can't permit this anymore. Attaching a radio collar to one of the lions made it easy to find the pride every morning for the visitors to be guaranteed a view, but large bulky collars are unsightly and spoil visitors' photographs. So now many private reserves get vets to fit an invisible abdominal transmitter. Wealthy tourists are none the wiser to how they are almost always guaranteed to see lions in their short stay. All is good while the batteries last. But after a year or two another transmitter needs to be fitted. As finding and retrieving an old dead transmitter would need a bigger operation, a new one is simply inserted instead. An older lion may have six or seven cigarette box-sized transmitters rattling around unseen inside its belly. While this practice is not as high profile as the business of lion cub selfies that feeds the canned lion hunt trade and the depressing export of about ten thousand lion skeletons to Vietnam and Laos for traditional medicine every year, there is clearly something questionable about the whole situation.

Invasive monitoring

All monitoring and marking of animals carries a risk. Even fitting a microchip can injure an animal. I will never forget looking in surprise at an X-ray of a collapsed Rodrigues flying fox many years ago, to find a microchip in the bat's brain, an unfortunate consequence of a small wriggling patient and an unlucky zookeeper's stumble. Radiotracking collars can catch on a branch, hanging their fossa victim, or slowly garrotte a growing sloth bear, cutting into its neck. Almost a quarter of savanna sparrows in one study got caught by their radiotelemetry devices in vegetation, often with fatal results. White-tailed deer in winter can build up kilograms of ice attached to their collar, and hunters, able to see their yellow collars more easily, are more likely to shoot them.

Intra-abdominal transmitter batteries can explode or leak acid and kill animals as large as grizzly bears. Or they may simply get infected, resulting in a polar bear dying during hibernation or an ill male lion being killed by a rival, which then also kills all the cubs to ensure his genes are the ones to form the future pride.

These problems can occur even when well-trained and experienced wildlife vets perform surgery, yet in most countries it is simply field biologists who amazingly are still allowed to perform these operations. I am unsure how many people would be happy if their caesarean section was to be performed by the hospital's IT administrator, rather than a surgeon. The ethics of when and why animals are monitored also needs constant scrutiny. Imagine waking up with a bright red box bolted through your arm, or a phone glued onto the top of your shaved head.

Ethically we try to choose the least invasive way of monitoring a patient that will do the job. While photos can be enough to identify several hundred individual whale sharks in the Philippines, this will not be sufficient to understand their movements in the ocean or the reasons for their decline. A buoyant satellite tag is used, as satellite signals will not work underwater. For large whales, satellite trackers are shot with a crossbow to embed in the tissue beneath their skin. There is no denying this is painful for the animal, and there is always a cost to the animal.

The individual's wellbeing is sacrificed for what is assumed to be the greater good, and it is for research ethics committees to carefully decide if the impacts of drilling and bolting a satellite tag through the dorsal fin of a dolphin or great white shark generates important enough data to justify its effects on the animal. Reading some research papers, this is clearly not always the case. In many studies animals that disappear are not reported, or presumed vanished due to transmitter failures, rather than deaths. Occasionally, when transmitters have been studied in captive animals the results are worrying. When captive massasauga rattlesnakes were surgically implanted with transmitters, a third developed serious infections during the first year, and another third developed inflammation in spite of no infection. When a handful of largemouth bass fish were recaptured after having tiny implants inserted, half had suffered complications that persisted even a year later, while 20 per cent still had infections or complications, even though implants weighed only 1 per cent of their body weight. And these were only a handful of the fish released a year before, and those that had survived. We can't presume this is due to snakes' or fishes' primitive immune systems or slow healing, as a third of American badgers with tracking devices implanted in their abdomens similarly suffer infections and major complications.

The majority of western grebes die after trackers have been implanted, despite a variety of devices and surgical techniques tried by different researchers. Even when just backpack harnesses were used in New Zealand takahe, more than two-thirds developed wing problems, some as serious as bone remodelling or wing fractures. Anyone suffering from chronic pain can testify how debilitating this can be, and these high complication rates certainly change behaviours even if not fatal, so we always need to carefully consider this.

Wild animals are like the sub-atomic particles described by Heisenberg. There is possibly almost no way to monitor them without influencing their behaviour in some way. This can lead us to make incorrect conclusions, but more important perhaps are the detrimental effects on the individual. Brown bears in Scandinavia have on several occasions been shot by hunters in the first few days after anaesthesia and surgical placement of abdominal transmitters, when still groggy and painful from their surgery. One radiotracking study of hedgehogs a few decades ago had a high death rate due to hedgehogs being hit by cars or eaten by badgers in the first few days. It transpired that the hedgehogs were anaesthetised and released the same day, and this is likely to have caused these deaths. Turkey vultures with wing tags or satellite tracker harnesses never fly the same, and are more likely to be mobbed and attacked by red-winged blackbirds. The extra weight of a satellite harness, even if small, may just cause an osprey to be too exhausted to make it back to land when migrating from Africa, or make an Amur falcon fall prey to hunters in northern India. Even camera traps, possibly the least invasive method of monitoring, can cause animals to fight or kill each other over the food that is sometimes needed to bait them to the camera.

Occasionally the adverse effects are to the researchers rather than the animals. When Russian ornithologists were tracking endangered steppe eagles, they used clever GPS tags that would relay their location data regularly via cell-phone texts. The eagles spend summer in Kazakhstan far from any cell-phone reception, and then send the backlog of data once they return to Russian cell-phone air space. Unfortunately, a few eagles decided instead to travel to Iran, Pakistan and even Sudan, where expensive roaming charges on thousands of text messages quickly used up the researchers' entire budget. Via crowd funding they raised enough to keep following the eagles, but learned their lesson for future studies.

There are also new and completely hands-off ways of learning of animals' movements and migrations. Stable isotope analysis can sometimes tell us where loggerhead turtles have been travelling and feeding, just using unhatched eggs. While this can't help us monitor an individual turtle we have treated for propellor injuries back in the wild, it can still be useful. If turtle nest sites decline on the coast of Japan we now know to look at what is happening off the coast of California where they feed. Thousands of turtles drown in fishing nets as bycatch every year, and linking the two can tell how severe the impact is from the nets on the other side of the world.

Monitoring animals in the wild can help us learn to do things better. While we worry that animals we return to the wild may not have the skills to survive, sometimes the problem is the wild itself. Some years ago we released two endangered sun bears back into the Cambodian Cardamom

Mountains after confiscation and treatment. They were fit, healthy, and appeared to have all the skills they would need. Yet within only a month of their release both had been caught in illegal wire snares, and were thankfully rescued due to their radio collars, although one still lost his paw. Despite animals being perfectly adapted, skilled and ready to go back to the wild, with our voracious consumption of the natural world, there may simply be nowhere for the animals to go back to. Wildlife tragically fared better under the genocide of the Khmer Rouge, when people feared to go into the mountains with the risks of landmines, being shot, or captured and tortured. After landmine clearance made life safer, poaching and snaring exploded, making tigers extinct in the mountains, and decimating the other wildlife. There has always been a rumour of a strange snake-eating antelope, called the kting voar, in these mountains. Easily dismissed as legend, it remains tantalisingly possible that there is a large herbivore unknown to science, as with the saola, the Asian unicorn, in the remote Annamite mountains of Vietnam and Laos. Sadly, if the kting voar does exist, it may well soon be extinct anyway, what with the rampant wildlife poaching in the Cardamom Mountains.

There is a similar problem for Borneo orangutans. Rescued from villages, shot for raiding crops, or left stranded when swathes of forest are burnt and bulldozed for palm oil plantations, they may appear the lucky ones, compared to the charred remains of proboscis monkeys, and other animals unable to escape the fires. Many are adults, with the skills and knowledge to return to the wild and live long, happy, and natural lives. Yet there are over a thousand orangutans currently stranded in rescue and treatment centres in Borneo, many destined to spend the remaining decades of their life in cages. Despite all efforts there is simply nowhere to release them. Their forests have been destroyed. Careful monitoring shows that simply releasing them into nearby forest doesn't solve much. Either they are harried and chased by the resident orangutans whose areas they have been dumped in, or they chase the residents off; the loser inevitably comes into conflict with villagers growing crops on the edges of the forest, or getting stranded with the ongoing destruction of forest edges, just to end up dead or being rescued again. It depressingly feels like a never-ending cycle for those of us involved.

Many Asian sanctuaries are filled with rescued and confiscated animals that would survive fine in the wild, if there was only enough suitable safe forest for them to actually go back to. Instead, they spend their lives in the centres, which despite everyone's best efforts will never be the same as a normal free life in the wild. While it is easy to blame the local population, it is usually our voracious Western consumption that is largely to blame.

Preparing animals for return to the wild can take a tremendous amount of time, work, cost and preparation, and still sometimes doesn't work. We may be returning an otherwise extinct animal like a scimitar-horned oryx to the wild in Chad, or trying to shore up the declining population of African penguins. On other occasions, our patients are not endangered at all, and we do this for the well-being of the individual itself. Whether trying to understand the effects of fishing trawlers on the population of loggerhead turtles, or evaluating our efforts to return beavers to the wild in England after being extinct for 600 years, trying to monitor and check on animals once back in the wild is fraught with difficulties.

As wildlife vets, we undertake an amazing variety of work, from diagnosing diseases just from a small dropping or clump of feathers on the forest floor, to performing complicated robotic-assisted surgery on an endangered animal in a nature reserve. The public can be overwhelmed and confused by so many charities begging for attention and donations for some very different purposes, and it is not always clear why we actually do all these different things. And that is where we turn our attention in the last chapter.

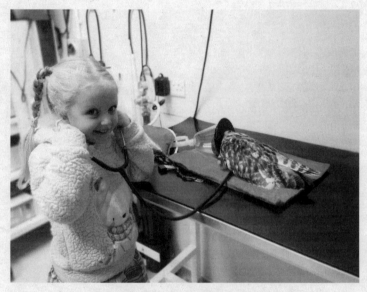

While we worry about leaving a better planet for our children, perhaps
we should also leave better children for our planet.

17

Why?

Because I grew up and qualified as a vet in South Africa, veterinary students regularly contact me about helping white rhino conservation. They are all very concerned about white rhinos going extinct from poaching for their horn, as we continuously hear on TV, and read in newspapers and magazines. Except white rhinoceros are not actually endangered. A quick trip to Wikipedia will show you they are only classified as 'near threatened' by the IUCN red list, the same conservation status as Alaskan moose, European otters, American bison and plains zebra. Are white rhinos the biggest con-job in conservation, or are they actually Africa's greatest conservation success story?

At the dawn of the twentieth century, the southern white rhino subspecies was the most endangered of all rhinoceroses. Fewer than twenty animals remained on the planet, huddled in a tiny area of what is now the Hluhluwe-Imfolozi nature reserve: the oldest proclaimed nature reserve in Africa, established in 1895 from a Zulu royal hunting ground, and managed to save the species from oblivion. Yet when tsetse flies brought cattle sleeping sickness in the 1940s, more than 100,000 wild animals inside the reserve were shot to reduce disease. The rhinos were spared, but it was still close, balancing wildlife in what even then were tiny pockets, versus vast surrounding cattle farming interests.

By the 1960s the reserve was filled to bursting with white rhinos, but was still the only place they survived, until rhinos were moved to other national parks and countries by pioneers with ropes, trucks and primitive dartguns, during Operation Rhino. Today, there are over 20,000 wild white rhinos across five countries and a thousand more in zoos. While heavy poaching by international criminal gangs has reduced the population, the white rhino isn't really at risk of extinction any time soon. So why all the constant media attention?

White rhinos in South Africa's plethora of private reserves and game farms are owned, and while poaching is a tragedy for the animals, it is also a heavy financial loss to the owners, like any theft. Some have invested very heavily in rhinos. John Hume, the world's largest private rhino breeder, has more than 1,600 white rhinos on his farm in North West Province, breeding and looking after them the same as cattle. A small private army of armed security personnel to prevent poaching is the only difference. Trimming each rhino's horn every two years makes them less appealing to poachers. He has over 6 tonnes of stored rhino horn, estimated worth a quarter of a billion US dollars, if he were allowed to sell them to Asia, but he is not. Hume and others have argued that farming rhinos, and legally selling horns, is the only way to ensure the species' ongoing survival. Others claim that legalising rhino horn would simply open markets for illegal trade, and actually make poaching worse, driving other critically endangered rhino species to extinction. A couple of hundred individuals now own over a third of all white rhinos on the planet. Whatever your opinion, the massive financial incentives mean white rhino poaching always gets huge media coverage. It is truly horrible, and tragic. But the white rhino is at no risk of going extinct at present. Yet thousands of caring people donate money or volunteer time to what are actually commercial businesses trying to trade rhino horn, run as a tourist attraction, or selling rhinos as hunting trophies. But love or hate this crazy capitalist rhino market, it is probably the main reason for the species' ongoing success.

While individual poached rhinos in South Africa are heralded by a storm of media coverage, the complete extinction from mainland Asia of what was the most widespread Asian rhinoceros species went almost unnoticed. Nature may be priceless, but without owners the only noticeable financial value is when someone hacks a dead rhino's face off, and sells the horn illegally. No one has anything to gain by trumpeting the failure of yet another conservation programme. Officials risk losing their jobs for embarrassing governments, and charities risk losing funding. That is how the extinction of the Vietnamese Sunda rhinos played out – with barely a whisper.

A subspecies of the Javan rhino, Sunda rhinos lived all over South-East Asia, even in India and China. Now the rarest and most critically endangered rhino species in the world, there are just over fifty Javan rhinos left on the planet. They only survive on the tip of Java, in a reserve after Krakatoa's eruption wiped out local villages in the area a hundred and fifty years ago. When I first visited Cat Tien National Park in Vietnam over a decade ago for rescued bear work, I secretly hope to spot a rhino. But there were rumours that the rhinos could already be extinct. A young and enthusiastic conservation ecologist called Sarah Brook was braving the dense terrain with a sniffer dog looking for rhino droppings for genetic analysis to see how many rhinos actually remained in their last foothold on mainland Asia. The results were not good, with only a single female found, in sharp contrast to the twelve rhinos claimed in travel guides. I never got to see her during my short trip, and a few months after returning home, it was confirmed that the Vietnamese Sunda rhino was indeed extinct.

Speaking to Sarah Brook years later in Cambodia, I could tell she was still very sad. Genetic testing confirmed all the droppings she ever found came from one lonely female. Then the droppings and footprint tracks ceased, and a ranger later found the skeleton of the decomposed rhino. With all the napalm, bombing, land mines and agent orange used in the area during the Vietnam War, it had been a miracle any rhino had initially survived at all. Rediscovered in 1988 when a local hunter shot one, only a dozen remained. Despite protection in a national park, their fate was sealed by the fact that Vietnam is the world's main market for rhino horn.

Discussing poached rhino's horn as an aphrodisiac in Vietnam, racism often bubbles to the surface. Yet, before blaming other cultures, we must realise the crisis originated in Europe. Rhino horn wasn't traditionally an aphrodisiac in Asian medicine. Medieval European beliefs were transferred by colonialism and rampant big-game rifle hunting that started the rhino's decimation. Seven thousand years ago, ancient Persians and Greeks believed rhino horn could purify drinks from poisons, and it was in demand by neurotic royals and religious leaders until surprisingly recently. While rhino horn is only keratin, the same as our fingernails, there is some truth to this belief. The horn's fibrous structure offers a large surface area, and some alkaloid toxins bind to it and are inactivated, or at least diluted. These include a variety of poisons, such as strychnine, opium, curare arrow poisons, psychedelic mushrooms, cocaine, nicotine, caffeine, and even the mouldy rye grain ergot toxins that perhaps caused the Salem witch trials. With few alternatives it didn't have to be a great antidote, just better than nothing. Somewhere along the line, the fact that kings could bed anyone they chose, while drinking rhino horn, got horn the mistaken reputation as an aphrodisiac. What appeared to be a magical property, from a creature confused with the mythical unicorn, laid the seeds for the rhino's decimation millennia later.

Returning to Cat Tien National Park years later, I went searching for the sad last rhino's remains. Eventually, forestry officials reluctantly let me in the locked musty room. Surrounded by a few forlornly stuffed animals, her skeleton was stiffly mounted in an upright robotic stance, in a massive dusty glass case. It was easy to see the distorted, thickened front leg bone, just below the elbow, with the AK-47 bullet fragment still embedded in it. The poacher's shot was rubbish, and it clearly took her months to die. Eventually, limping and ill, she appears to have fallen down a steep incline to her death. To add insult to injury, the first person to find her, hacked off her tiny almost non-existent horn and disappeared with it. A sad monument to another conservation failure.

I have come across many over the years, for example the rigid, stuffed body of a 200 kilogram Yangtze soft shell turtle at Hoan Kiem Lake temple in Hanoi, the largest, but also rarest of all freshwater turtles. I managed to glimpse the last solitary turtle, believed to be the legendary golden turtle god, a few years before it died in 2016. With only four alive on the planet, one in a Chinese zoo, and three in Vietnam, even living up to two hundred years old, the species is almost certain to go extinct. I have watched the short film fragment, the only one ever taken, of a kouprey, Cambodia's national animal seventy years ago. With no sightings in more than 40 years, they are almost certainly extinct. I take my children to see the stuffed quagga in the National Museum of Scotland: a bizarre half-striped zebra that went extinct in South Africa a hundred and fifty years ago. There are only a handful of skins in existence now, and only one photo of a living animal. While even children know about the dodo and thylacine, there is a long list of animals we have been unable to find in the wild for decades, which are almost certainly extinct: the Ethiopian water mouse, the imperial salamander, the Eskimo curlew, the Aru flying fox, the baiji, the one-striped opossum, the Javan lapwing, the skunk frog, the Christmas Island shrew, the crested shelduck, the cave squeaker, De Winton's golden mole, the Himalayan quail, the web-footed coqui, the Malabar civet, the peppered tree frog, the dwarf hutia, and the gloomy tube-nosed bat, just to mention a handful. Unlike the media surrounding white rhinoceros poaching, these animals have disappeared silently and unnoticed.

More confusion comes from the functional extinction of the northern white rhino. Two elderly females, a mother and daughter, are all that remain, at Ol Pejeta in Kenya. The northern white rhino never actually existed in Kenya, and so, despite appearances, with round-the-clock care, guards and individual carers, it is not much different to their previous zoo life. It is tragic to lose the unique genetics that white rhinos have evolved in the north range, but most believe them simply a subspecies, and their ecosystem roles could simply be played in future by reintroducing southern white rhinos. Over a long timescale, these would perhaps evolve a similar genome to the lost northern subspecies. Not all hope is lost for the northern subspecies. Nine frozen embryos have been created using sperm collected from two males years before their deaths. But breeding a few test-tube rhinos seems pointless when we can't protect them in the wild. A hundred years' hard work was needed to save the southern white rhino from the brink of extinction, yet northern white rhino, common a century ago, went in the opposite direction thanks to political instability, war, and the human tragedies that played out in their range countries of Uganda, Democratic Republic of Congo and South Sudan over the last half a century. But has the tragedy of the northern white rhino been highjacked for PR by the commercial interests of wealthy southern white rhino owners, as some suggest?

The strange case of the white rhino, one of the main pin-ups for wildlife conservation, despite not actually being endangered, is curious. In order to understand this we have to figure out what we actually mean by conservation, and, for us wildlife veterinarians, try to discern what we should actually be doing in our work.

Constantly moving rhinos between different game farms; darting and radio-collaring one month just to remove it a few months later again for tourism, sold as wildlife training for foreign vet students; there are more veterinarians working with rhino in South Africa than on the rest of the planet for all other rhinos combined. This is no surprise. There are 10,000 private game ranches that cover a tenth of South Africa, land double the size of Scotland. Game veterinarians move a third of a million wild animals between these ranches every year. While these are still dwarfed by 14 million cattle, the South African government has reclassified over thirty species, from lions and giraffes to buffalos and mountain zebra as farm

374

animals under livestock breeding laws. This includes rhinos. Even the government acknowledges the way many are managed makes them farm animals. With under 4,000 vets, and hundreds of game capture businesses, more vets work with wild animals than ever before in my home country. Almost all South African vets have laid a hand on a rhino at some stage. Thanks to myriad marketed wildlife courses for foreign vet students, there are also more vets across the world with hands-on rhino experience than will ever even see a wild European otter or an Alaskan moose. South African wildlife work is unlike anywhere else in the world, making these little more than expensive veterinary tourist holidays. Are rhino vet photos the equivalent of tiger cub selfies? Is all this actually just farm vet work, masquerading with appealing animals? With even a wildlife vet barbie doll on sale now, reflecting the profession's appeal, what a wildlife vet is, or should be, is far from clear.

What is a wildlife vet? The answer is not as simple as may first appear. While visions of vets treating koalas caught in bushfires, operating on shot orangutans, darting rhino from a helicopter, or freeing snared tigers may spring to mind, even what is meant by wildlife is not clear. While several thousand vets work with tigers, except for a handful these are all in zoos. So are vets working in zoos, 'wildlife vets'? The healthcare needs of a geriatric zoo tiger in a city zoo are a world away from an injured wild tiger snared in the Sundarbans mangroves. If a tiger in a Scandinavian zoo counts as wildlife, what about the same animal in a Las Vegas casino show, or kept by a wealthy celebrity in their mansion? Is this also 'wildlife'? The range of animals kept as exotic pets is usually taken to encompass everything that isn't a domestic dog, cat or farm animal. In the veterinary field, the supposed speciality of zoological medicine includes truly wild animals, zoo animals, and exotic pets. So is a specialist veterinarian seeing only pet rabbits, guinea pigs and tortoises a wildlife vet? The veterinary boards that oversee specialists in most countries bizarrely seem to think so. Everything is nonsensically lumped together. This makes ethical discussions between specialist vets really difficult. Some feel non-domestic animals should only ever live in the wild. Others believe that anything invasive we put an endangered animal in a zoo through to breed successfully is justified, while yet others support the international trade in wild caught animals for pets, which they enjoy working with. But the veterinary care for a lonely, obese, pet African grey parrot in a cage is very different to that needed for breeding parrots in a zoo, or the health care of confiscated traumatised parrots in Gabon needing rehabilitation and return to the wild. There are probably more than 10 million pet African grey parrots, but after decades of over 100,000 parrots caught yearly from even just one country, the species is now unsurprisingly endangered in the wild.

This also skews the scientific literature, upon which all veterinary decisions are based, towards pets and zoos. There are hundreds of references for treating arthritis and cancer in geriatric exotic pets and zoo animals, but not a single scientific paper on the best snare wound treatments in animals to be returned to the wild, despite millions of illegal snares set worldwide every year. Articles can be difficult to publish when editors are Western veterinarians and academics, taking resources in their affluent country for granted. Writing up operations in a South-East Asian rainforest a decade ago, we learned that journal reviewers didn't want to accept our article, as we hadn't performed an MRI scan. While available to an affluent Western zoo, there wasn't a single scanner in the entire country even for people, even had this been affordable. It is difficult to write a scientific journal paper on cheap, simple, basic techniques wildlife vets can use in the field where there may be minimal equipment and next to no funding, when reviewers use the gold standard of wealthy zoos and celebrities' exotic pets where money is not an issue. These animals are fortunate enough to have cataract surgery or custom 3D-printed implants available, when even basic facilities for treating gunshot wounds in wild animals in many countries is lacking.

Whatever one feels about increasingly intensive game farming in South Africa, there are always vets trying to improve things. My school friend Leith Meyer, now a professor of wildlife medicine in South Africa, patiently researches improvements in rhino anaesthetic to make it safer for the animals themselves. He has done hundreds of rhino anaesthetics, and I cringed years ago when, humbly presenting his findings at a conference, he was viciously criticised, as this didn't fit with the personal perspectives of a few prominent zoo vets, even if they had only anaesthetised a handful of rhinos. Anaesthesia in a zoo is very different to out in the field. Disparity in wildlife health care mirrors that in human health across countries. Whatever one's perspective on zoos, the treatment the animals receive mirrors the best private health care. Yet zoo management can be fickle, with huge sums of money spent treating everyone's favourite elderly gorilla, yet healthy red river hogs are culled for lack of space. Decisions may not be made by the veterinarian, but execution of them always is.

Even the assumption that all vets do good for animals is complicated. Modern whaling ships have veterinarians on board to certify a harpooned whale is dead before it is hacked up. Many veterinarians are avid bow hunters, shooters, and blood sport advocates. Bears that are illegally farmed for their bile have their extractions and operations performed by vets, and some veterinarians have even been implicated in illegal rhino poaching. Even pet veterinarians are not beyond reproach. The specialist vet caring for your beloved puppy with a broken leg in a university vet school may unbeknown to you have thirty experimental dogs in the back, whose legs are broken for research to help further their career..

The vision of an African wildlife vet darting an ill rhino from a helicopter is an illusion. Most interventions are not for the individual animal's benefit, but rather their owners. Most of the third of a million wild animals captured, darted and moved every year in South Africa are not for conservation but rather game farming on private land. Here, the work of a vet is purely economic in nature, little different to cattle and sheep production, although perhaps more photogenic.

Perhaps focusing on individual animals is nonsense, as many conservationists claim. Is it only populations we should be focusing on? With few exceptions, treating a single animal will never prevent extinction, and so is worthless in their eyes. So how do veterinarians fit in this picture? Realising that human health and wellbeing, animal health, and the environment are all intimately intertwined and depend on each other, should be common sense. Ancient Taoism recognised this long before James Lovelock's Gaia hypothesis, or the recent field of One Health.

The coronavirus pandemic has been a stark reminder. Climate change, chemical pollution, deforestation, human-wildlife conflict, bush-meat, dense human populations, and evolving diseases are all related and intertwined. Veterinarians working with doctors, epidemiologists, virologists, and climate scientists for the greater good under the umbrella of One Health is brilliant. Yet the term is often just co-opted by many researchers to continue doing exactly what they were before, with just a new appealing tag to help attract grant funding. A farm pig parasite researcher can tag on a reference to wild boar and One Health, and continue just as before. Sadly, One Health easily morphs into the old human and farm animal orientated perspective, where wildlife and the natural world are only seen as sources of diseases and inconvenience for people and food production, to be investigated or eliminated. Badgers are persecuted for cattle TB and bats for coronavirus, like African antelope were killed for rinderpest and sleeping sickness in cattle a century ago. Investigating PCB and mercury levels in striped bass has little to do with the marine environment, but rather with human risks from eating them. Leprosy in nine-banded armadillos is investigated for the risk it poses to humans, rather than any interest on its effect on interdependent wildlife species. And bird flu research is towards protecting farmed chickens rather than ecosystems. Most One Health research focuses on diseases, something that impacts us and our farm animals, but is usually of minor importance to wildlife population survival. Man-made chemical pollution poses a far greater threat to many wild species, yet often hardly gets a mention. The European Union has thankfully just banned lead shotgun shot, something most people will be unaware of. Over 20,000 tonnes of lead shotgun pellets contaminate the environment every year, poisoning over a million waterbirds annually in just Europe. Laudable as it is, One Health risks slipping back to focusing on just one species. Us. It risks missing the opportunity to take care of the entire planet's health, with humans as an interconnected piece rather than the entire focus.

Perhaps this is all too cynical, and everything does add up to help conservation, even if things get weird, wacky, and occasionally involve murky ethics. From this book, you have an idea of what we can do as wildlife veterinarians. But a more tricky question is, why? The usual answer is for conservation. But what exactly does this mean? Is everything claimed to be for conservation purposes actually so? And is conservation the only reason to undertake veterinary interventions on wildlife?

The word 'conservation' is so widely used that everyone thinks they know what it means, but in the media it has become almost meaningless. The word is weaponised in disagreements over anything from trophy hunting to climate change.

What is nature conservation? Turning to the sage of Wikipedia, as everyone does, yields a definition of 'a philosophy of managing the environment in a manner that does not despoil, exhaust or extinguish'. Yet everyone still means something different. Even those of us spending our entire working lives supposedly in the field of conservation can't agree. Is it simply trying to prevent as many species going extinct as possible? Or aspiring to return large tracts to pristine wilderness, as if humans had never evolved at all? Even leading scientists can't agree. Are we aiming for a mosaic, where how we live and farm has breathing space for wild animals to live among us? Or are we aiming for separation, where fenced areas contain the remains of the natural world and all wildlife lives out its life there? Does conservation mean aiming for complete non-interference with wild animals and their lives, or preserving them as a resource to be readily used for recreational hunting, fishing, and other economic purposes? If we can't even agree what conservation actually is, how can we ever aim for the same goals, let alone know if we have achieved them? Perhaps we should start by asking why we should conserve anything.

Everyone is concerned about Sumatran tigers going extinct. But much less so about the equally critically endangered Uluguru mountain grasshopper, or American burying beetle. Yet everything in nature is interconnected in ways too complex to disentangle. Perhaps we are best to see conservation as the preservation of biodiversity. Then tigers are just a mascot, only a tiny part of what we are trying to protect, if conservation is to have any meaning. If drumming up interest in the conservation of beetles is difficult, trying to explain the value of saving parasites is almost impossible.

Veterinarians are indoctrinated from day one of our studies that parasitic organisms from ticks to blood protozoa are all evil villains, always to be eliminated at any cost from our patients. Most domestic animal veterinarians make a significant part of their living from selling tick, flea, and worm treatments. Yet parasites are natural in wild living animals, just as predators are in an ecosystem. They will usually only cause problems if animals are ill, immunosuppressed, or have poor genetics. This is sometimes forgotten by wildlife veterinarians, aiming to ruthlessly eradicate them, just as we would in a pet kitten or farmed chicken. So-called parasites have often evolved alongside their hosts for millions of years. Wildlife parasites are often as endangered as their hosts. The endangered pygmy hog is far less charismatic than the tigers, rhinos and elephants living in Assam's Manas National Park. Found nowhere else, it is still difficult to inspire conservation efforts for this lovely, tiny, brown wild pig. But this is nothing compared to trying to illicit any sympathy for the unique and more critically endangered pygmy hog louse, which only lives on these endangered pigs. By ignoring unappealing members of the natural world, we risk making the whole concept of conservation and the preservation of biodiversity meaningless.

Some parasites are actually important for their host's health. Herbivorous tortoises like Asian forest tortoises actually benefit from intestinal worms. These worms don't appear to harm their host, but their movements mix and churn food in the flabby intestines, helping tortoises absorb their food better. Spur-thighed tortoises have eight species of intestinal worms, all living in different parts of the intestines, playing their roles.

Vets pose a biodiversity danger. Carelessly treating elephants will not only kill their ticks and intestinal worms, but also dung beetles and other insects trying to eat their droppings, affecting whole food chains. Rivers in England now have high levels of the insecticides fipronil and imidacloprid, five times higher than safety thresholds. Banned for use in agriculture due to their harmful environmental effects, the source is dog flea and tick treatments. Pharmaceutical marketing and pet health plans result in many dogs receiving these compounds whether needed or not, poisoning native wildlife, from tiny shrimps to fish, without dog owners or vets realising this.

We forget that even we relatively parasite-free humans still have more bacteria, protozoa, skin mites and other organisms living in and on us, than the entire number of our own cells. Strange when we think of ourselves as individual beings. All animals from pygmy hogs to elephants are more a mini moving ecosystem, than an individual. Mallophaga lice, eating dead skin and chewing microscopic bits of feather or hair, generally cause no harm, with several thousand species, most unique to a single host animal they have evolved with for millions of years. Researchers use these lice to study how different penguin species have evolved from each other. But wildlife vets have unfortunately made unique and harmless lice species on Californian condors, Iberian lynx and the little spotted kiwi extinct through thoughtless insecticide treatments, undermining our whole professional role in conservation.

Conservation is truly very difficult to achieve. It should not be an attempt to freeze everything in a magical time-warp as if humans didn't exist, but finding ways for humans to live that also allow the plants, animals, and other living species in their complex linked systems to coexist, is challenging. Vets tend to focus on diseases; reproduction scientists on resurrecting extinct species from a few frozen cells; reserve managers focus on fencing and protecting rhinos and elephants with armed guards; zoos focus on specific charismatic species and educators on local community awareness; and charities run consumer campaigns in distant lands. But without all working together, projects battle to achieve anything meaningful in the long term.

While zoologists study the fewer than 300 Ethiopian wolves left, vets vaccinate dogs in surrounding villages to reduce the risk from rabies and distemper. Ecotourism highlights problems to foreign visitors, while educators raise awareness in local children. Zoos believe that keeping wolves in captivity is their only hope, while geneticists believe that banking frozen cells is the ultimate insurance. While sitting one afternoon in Bale Mountains National Park, I watched a solitary Ethiopian wolf trot along a dry river bed, passing calmly through a handful of thin cows and mangy goats illegally grazing in the park, followed by a tiny boy in ragged clothes. The dry Afroalpine landscape is extremely poor grazing. But when desperate, one has little to lose. A faded pink plastic bag billowed past, a reminder of the crammed local buses constantly hurtling to villages inside the park. It is easy to get annoyed, and berate the government for not protecting the park and keeping grazing farm animals out of the small, sensitive Sanetti Plateau, a tiny ecosystem unique in all the world. Ethiopian wolves live in a minute area, only a thirtieth the size of the Galapagos islands. But it is in a politically unstable country, with half the population illiterate, and high population density surrounding the park. As local people battle to survive harsh conditions, encroachment and destruction of the park appears almost inevitable. Sad as this would be for Ethiopian wolves, many other species will also go extinct. Like the fascinating giant-headed mole rats, motley rodents the size of guinea pigs, with puffed-out cheeks, and frog eyes on the top of their heads. Or the endemic black-headed siskin, mountain nyala, or Bale monkey. None is appealing enough to protect the park if the wolves disappear. Loss of this ecosystem would also be disastrous for the surrounding 12 million people, who completely depend on the rain water system from the mountains. A tragedy of the commons. Small desperate actions by individuals destroys the environment everyone needs to survive. I saw this when I was working in India decades ago. Desperately poor families with no other option took small amounts of dead wood from the forest, until gradually there was nothing to fertilise the soil, with few of the insects or birds that depended on them left. The remaining trees battled and died and were slowly used when everything else had gone. Apocalyptic destruction by a million tiny cuts. Over the last few decades, entire forests and their animal inhabitants have disappeared worldwide, but often not through malice or large actions of greed. While diggers do destroy rainforest for palm oil, as I have seen while rescuing starving orangutans, it is the sum of all our own small individual actions; for example, not spending a few seconds to choose ethically sourced products at the supermarket. Nature is lost silently and almost invisibly in most places, not with a roar or a scream, just tree by tree.

The heavy commercialisation of wildlife has helped Southern and Eastern Africa's large wildlife species survive recent decades. But this only works when you can see wildlife easily, to sell this product to tourists and selfie photographers. It works for white rhinos and lions, mountain gorillas and Ethiopian wolves. It doesn't transfer to saving nocturnal clouded leopards in impenetrable rainforest, or spectacled bears in inaccessible mountain treetops, impossible to spot and show to tourists with shorter attention spans than a weasel.

Yet people are still interested in these species' fates, even if only seen on documentaries. Smaller creatures are less fortunate. Childhood memories of bug-smeared windscreens are something my children have never experienced. Intensive agriculture has sterilised swathes of the planet with its chemical arsenal, affecting all intricate food webs, even if they appear far removed. No one misses mosquitoes, but then still wonder where all the frogs have gone.

We suffer from taxonomic chauvinism. The word wildlife brings images of elephants and orangutans to mind, not the myriad insects and bugs making up the bulk of the planet's wild creatures. Just as Indian vultures have gone from being the commonest birds in Asian skies to almost extinct in a few decades, invertebrate numbers have plummeted catastrophically, undermining the food webs that sustain everything from imperial eagles to maned wolves.

Love them or hate them, zoos can make meaningful contributions to conservation. Almost forty animal species extinct in the wild, from Spix's macaw to milu deer, are still alive thanks to zoos. A few species like the Arabian oryx and Przewalski's horse have even been successfully returned to the wild. However, much of what most zoos claim is conservation, breeding and moving animals between zoos, is just maintaining the populations of animals for display to the public. Breeding elephants in captivity, despite all efforts, is simply not self-sustainable, let alone being able to ever meaningfully contribute to the species' conservation in the wild. One can hardly claim zoo king penguins are for conservation, when zoos still cannot maintain captive numbers without needing to catch more wild penguins. With over 4 million wild king penguins, and an increasing population, they are not endangered.

Stories of meaningful conservation projects helped by zoos are however insufficient for the constant PR churn to maintain interest and zoo visitor numbers. So occasional but important stories are swamped by an incessant barrage of nonsense, from polar bears opening Christmas presents, to the fictitious zoo censuses every January despite the existence of daily electronic records for decades now, to every new-born giraffe being hailed as crucial to the species' survival. It isn't, especially when surplus animals may be culled a short while later.

Zoos' aims are touted as conservation, research, and education. Education tries to raise awareness to threats facing the natural world, even if only by focusing on celebrity animals like tigers and giant pandas. But the impact is difficult to measure. While zoos educate millions every year, some studies show little impact on changing people's behaviour when shopping, commuting and other everyday choices. Yet nothing can replace seeing a real live animal, looking in its eyes, and trying to understand its view of the world with empathy.

But empathy also raises the main criticism of zoos – animal welfare. If animals are purely kept for education, then it is clear a zoo's main responsibility is to ensure they live the best lives possible. This is very difficult to achieve for a polar bear, which, awaking from hibernation, will instinctively roam hundreds of kilometres looking for food. Even feeding to obesity cannot switch off this strongly evolved need. Few zoos have enclosures even a thousandth of what a wild bear would roam. Having multiple zoo aims, these can pull in different directions. An individual animal's welfare may be sacrificed to the perceived greater good of a research project, or invasive artificial insemination for supposed conservation.

Most zoos believe their main role is conservation, and good zoos contribute to conservation programmes across the globe with a range of species. The practical expertise of zoo staff has helped many projects, from black-footed ferret reintroductions to protecting Indian one-horned rhinos. But only a small amount of the money raised by zoos goes to conservation work in the wild. Most goes to maintaining zoo buildings, feeding animals, and paying staff. However, those inadvertently contributing to wildlife conservation by having a day out with the kids probably weren't otherwise going to donate to the wildlife projects supported by the zoo. This is still a good thing. A quarter of a billion pounds each year is used for conservation work by zoos. But the impressive total masks the fact that most is simply the self-sustaining breeding of vulnerable species in zoos. Only a fraction goes to field conservation. The World Association of Zoos and Aquariums (WAZA) estimates that three-quarters of a billion people visit a zoo every year. So only a measly 30 pence per visitor goes to any form of conservation work, let alone conservation in the wild. WAZA itself urges zoos to aim for 3 per cent of their budget for field conservation, but most zoos do not achieve this. Some good zoos do better than this. The Zoological Society of London spent more than £15 million in 2019 on field conservation, just over 20 per cent of income. But digging through their accounts, it didn't come from zoo admissions at all, but through grants, legacies in wills, and specific donations. Zoo admissions just paid to run their two zoos. Most zoos' financial reports are so opaque it is impossible to know what they spend on conservation outside the zoo.

So it can appear disingenuous that zoos constantly fundraise for their conservation work, when so little often actually goes to conservation projects in the wild. Even more astounding, there have been several zoo CEOs paid salaries of over half a million dollars. One zoo and conservation society president and CEO's salary reached almost three-quarters of a million dollars a year a little under a decade ago before he retired, although these ludicrous salaries have thankfully been reined in somewhat. Yet several zoo and other conservation charity bosses are still paid similar to corporate CEOs, and more than some European heads of state. This verges on unethical behaviour, when you speak to an elderly pensioner forgoing basic necessities because they honestly believe their donations are essential, and going towards saving endangered animals, thanks to aggressive marketing. During the pandemic, zoos begged for funds to help feed their animals, while many zoo CEOs continued to collect pay packages larger than that of Members of Parliament.

Then there are real leaders you can't help being inspired by. Having a laugh with Matt Hunt after he fixed an oxygen cylinder that threatened to blow up during surgery in Cambodia, I can totally forget that he is the CEO of Free the Bears. Earning no more than he did decades earlier as a zookeeper, I discover he hasn't paid himself a salary for months, to ensure they have enough for the local staff and the bears' food, as funds are tight. Or, cleaning my surgical instruments after a long operation at the Animals Asia centre in Vietnam, I turn around to see CEO Jill Robinson happily sweeping the floor. I watch Shirley Curran, despite her broken ankle, hobble around feeding rescued lions every day, while Charlotte Corney patiently holds a tiger's leg for hours during an operation, making me forget she wasn't just a keeper. How can you not follow charity founders like Bala Amarasekaran who during the civil war in Sierra Leone insisted on staying in the battle zone to look after the chimpanzees in his rescue centre. Leaders like these have no need for staff Christmas bonuses or discount gym memberships to earn the respect of all those who work with them.

Many of us grew up observing local wildlife and birds and watching far-away wildlife on our TVs. But did natural history documentaries actually do more harm than good? Most made it appear there was far more wilderness remaining, brimming with wildlife, than was actually the case. Less than 4 per cent of the planet's land animals are wildlife, something you would never guess from TV. Watching seabirds pick off emerging hatchling turtles in dramatic slow motion as they frantically scramble to reach the sea, one has to pause and take stock. We tend to believe what we see. Yet watching eggs hatching underground is impossible. They are completely surrounded by sand and in the dark. What you are watching are eggs in a film studio set, with carefully positioned lighting. Seeing them emerge from the sand is also a lie. No documentary crew can watch a beach for months hoping to catch the brief moment when eggs randomly hatch, let alone knowing where in a beach eggs are buried. The studio-incubated hatchlings have simply been reburied in the sand for filming. And while turtles almost always emerge at night, this is no good for filming. But filmed during the day, the bright light disorientates them, and the film crew's presence alerts all the local seabirds to the free meal. Similarly, slow-motion footage of running tigers is often of trained captive cats running alongside a vehicle. I get too angry and can no longer watch most natural history programmes, but most viewers are oblivious to the subterfuge. Yet all this makes us think we know and understand wild animals.

Natural history television has undoubtedly had a huge positive influence, alerting many to the wonder of faraway wildlife species, and even inspiring careers in conservation. But documentaries are mainly filled with furious fights, frantic copulations, and dramatic chases. Yet writers from ancient times to Wordsworth instead speak about the tranquillity of nature. Even working my whole life around animals, these scenes are rare. Much of the time animals are hiding, and when you spot them, they are not usually doing anything very exciting. When tourists go on a safari, they are almost always disappointed. My children do not understand why it is so hard to even glimpse many wild animals, never seeing anything resembling what they have seen from the comfort of the sofa. Like some dystopian horror, we prefer the false flat wilderness we see on a screen to the actual natural world; the imaginary edited stories to the beauty of random nature. We watch magnificent slow-motion scenes of a cheetah running after gazelles, rather than going to the zoo to glimpse a slumbering feline. We can watch polar bears in close-up high definition pounce on a bearded seal, without the inconvenience of days of travel and freezing fingers. We forget the cameraman needed months to capture those few seconds of footage. Realistic computer-animated animals may now spare tigers and chimpanzees horrid lives as performing animals, but now they can do completely unnatural behaviours, just to help film plots. This all blends into a confusing melange of what is actually real about wild animals.

Even when we do see real wildlife, we choose to experience it through a screen. It is as if failing to film it on your phone means you haven't actually seen it. Yet concentrating on your screen, you fail to actually watch the real animal. You or I are unlikely to win wildlife photographer of the year. When I see something marvellous, whether an iridescent dragonfly or a leopard popping its head above the grass, I usually choose to drink every second in with my own eyes, ears and nose. Only I can replay my memories, but they are far better than any picture I have ever managed to take.

It isn't just TV that distorts our perspective. Powerful, influential countries such as the USA, Canada and Australia have very low population densities, with vast tracts of open space. Citizens, subconsciously, feel the rest of the world must be similar. But the tigers surviving in the Sundarbans inhabit a country over a hundred times more densely populated than North America. Wealthier developed countries, who make the most noise about conservation, also frequently do the least. One study a few years ago looked at different countries' efforts to conserve their large wildlife. Countries at the top of the league like Botswana, Namibia and Tanzania clearly gain from their tourist industries, but the Central African Republic, one of the ten poorest and least developed countries in the world, wracked by civil war for the last two decades, is still rated higher than the USA and most Western European countries, as were Rwanda, Mozambique and Estonia.

Still everyone believes the problem lies in developing countries. Many Westerners feel large land tracts should be fenced off, no matter the cost to local people. Having reached affluence, we aspire to pull the ladder up behind us, wishing that the rest of the world could be kept as a pristine safari park for our enjoyment: blatant neocolonialism.

It is often pointed out that there are simply too many people on the planet. It is true that even since my birth the human population on Earth has doubled, and this is almost too frightening to contemplate. Yet this easily slips into racism; that it is all the fault of other irresponsible people and their cultures in other countries. While families are larger in many developing countries, we miss the big picture. It is not how many children we have, but how much we consume. Thanks to rampant consumerism, the average North American has an environmental impact two hundred times that of an Ethiopian or Nigerian. A single-child family in North America has greater planetary impact than an Ethiopian family would have if they had 500 children. It is easy to blame others, but the problem lies closer to home. Cheap supermarket ice cream devastates orangutan forests in distant Indonesia; an obsession with the newest phones pushes gorillas closer to extinction; while cheap burgers burn the remaining Amazon down. Yet we keep our conscience clear by blaming distant foreigners.

Eschewing children for pets, as small hairy surrogates, also comes at a cost. In North America there is one dog or cat for every two people. Owning a dog has double the carbon footprint of your entire house's electricity for a year, and pets account for a third of all meat eaten in the USA. They also produce a third as much faeces as the entire human population, while domestic cats kill over a billion songbirds a year in North America alone. Americans spend $50 billion a year on their pets. The impact is a staggering 64 million tonnes of carbon dioxide a year just in the USA – the same as driving an additional 13 million cars. This somewhat deflates the belief that not having children, but instead a house full of dogs, is better for the planet. In full disclosure I have two children, and an old, rescued street dog. While the large human population is not great for the planet, a child could grow up to be Greta Thunberg, Mahatma Gandhi, or Nelson Mandela. They could go on to help save tigers from extinction, or win the Nobel prize for solving climate change. Something a cat can never do. While having pets has mental wellbeing benefits, there is no need for eight dogs. Or five cats, who are solitary by nature anyway.

If it isn't human overpopulation, then could climate change from fossil fuels be the biggest threat to wildlife? Unfortunately, many species are likely to be extinct before this truly affects them. Climate change is a huge existential threat for us humans and our current way of life. And we are correct to be very concerned and do everything we can to address this urgently. But while climate change will also harm wildlife, most wild species currently face greater threats.

When asked by enthusiastic students what they can do to save endangered wildlife, they have visions of rushing off to rescue injured orangutans or combat ivory poachers. But the biggest thing anyone, myself included, can do to save the planet's wildlife is not what usually springs to mind. Vet and zoology students happily fly halfway around the world, to Greta Thunberg's despair, to volunteer with pseudo-conservation elephant projects of questionable ethics, but most don't do the thing that actually makes the biggest difference: eating fewer animal products.

Only 4 per cent of the total mammal and bird biomass on the planet surface is now wild animals. From tigers to toucans, ostriches to okapi, roughly 20,000 wild species take up less than one-twentieth of the planet's land. We can't just blame human overpopulation; our food animals' weight on the planet is more than double our own. Almost two-thirds of all verte-brate animals on all the land surfaces of the Earth are farm animals. It seems there are too many cows, pigs, sheep and chickens rather than too many humans. Growing soya and food crops just to feed to animals, even with all modern inno-vations, myriad pesticides, genetic engineering, and factory farming, is an extremely wasteful use of land and water. It takes up ten to twenty times more land to feed your average Western meat-eater than a vegan. Reducing livestock by just 10 per cent could more than double the space on the planet for wildlife. Would this double tiger and orangutan figures? Of course not. Things are far more complex than that. But it would make a big difference to species like the jaguar, whose habitat is shrinking from growing soya for animal feed. But instead we are projected to need to produce another 5 per cent soya for animal feed by 2030, mainly due to us each eating more meat, rather than actual human population growth. I am not advocating you have to become vegan like me, but if everyone just ate a little less meat, even just two meat-free meals a week, the gains would be enormous. It is a travesty that over a third of all food produced is then thrown away as waste, and never eaten.

It is morally perverse that a whole frozen factory-farmed chicken often costs less than a large caramel macchiato, which is basically flavoured hot water in a paper cup. Overall, Americans and Australians eat over five times as much meat as they actually need nutritionally, with all the expensive associated health problems this causes. Meat consumption has doubled in only a generation. Land for livestock and their food needs to come from somewhere, and it comes from wild-life habitats, such as the Amazon. If you don't want to reduce your intake for your own health, or the cost to society, at least do it for the wild animals.

Being vegan can save twice as much carbon as the average person uses for all their gas and electricity. Eating a plant-based diet reduces your carbon footprint more than buying a hybrid car, recycling and installing energy-efficient lightbulbs all taken together, but it is true that fossil fuels are still a bigger overall contributor to climate change than animal agriculture, and living car free will have a greater climate change impact. Yet a carbon-neutral world does nothing to save space for wildlife on our crowded planet, even if helping mitigate our completely self-made existential crisis.

I admit a vegan diet is unnatural. But vegetarians from Pythagoras and Leonardo da Vinci to Gandhi and Jane Goodall have all lived healthy lives. Now vitamin supplements allow anyone, from Al Gore and Ariana Grande to Joaquin Phoenix and Venus Williams, to lead healthy vegan lives. Compassionate consideration for other species has been described as an expanded circle of concern as we become more highly evolved. Or perhaps not. But until we settle which it is, our search for intelligent extra-terrestrial life appears an extremely risky strategy to me. Why would aliens treat us any differently to how we treat chimpanzees, chickens or cockroaches? It is a deeply worrying thought.

While most veterinarians look after animals and care about the planet, without care in our profession's actions and lobbying we can easily become part of the problem. While vegan, I work closely with the local farming community, and support sustainable high animal welfare, and the production of food that has a lower environmental impact. Farmers are not the problem, they are the solution. If people are to eat meat, eating less, but more expensive high-quality products, ensures animals have better lives, while also lessening harmful impacts on the planet.

While we only get to vote for politicians once every few years, we all get to vote three times every day on the impact we wish to have on the planet, in choosing what we put in our mouths. And then every time we choose to buy anything. Is the palm oil in your chocolate from a sustainable source, and are farmers paid a living wage? Wage poverty is modern slavery, driving unsustainable illegal forest clearing and catching wildlife for subsistence. Our choices extend past food. When feeling hopeless in the face of environmental destruction, it is empowering to realise we can each have an impact with all our choices. Whether we are fooled by the hedonic treadmill of shiny new phones, or choose a less sexy repairable, sustainable model usable for years. Love it or hate it, the modern capitalist market responds, making less of the things we don't buy. Eventually sustainable, ethical products can become the norm. Every action we take is a vote for the planet we want to live in.

The endless stream of glamorous pictures, and supposedly amazing lives we see on social media, which make even millionaire models feel inadequate, hardly helps. Perhaps we can blame GDP. Everyone needs to sell more, and so everyone also needs to buy more. But happy, well-balanced people leading contented fulfilling lives need little, and buy less. A grandparent watching children playing in the mud; lying on your back looking at the clouds; gazing into your friend's eyes and wondering how they see the world; watching your children go to their first day at school; seeing a masked weaver frantically collecting twigs for its nest; wondering at the fragility of a small orchid in the wind; or just glimpsing a hedgehog late at night exploring your garden. These are all truly precious. And cost nothing. So useless for financial metrics. The word 'consumption' reveals what it does to the planet: chopping down forests, polluting the ocean, killing and squeezing wildlife into shrinking spaces to try to eke out a bleak existence.

To make us consume more, we need to feel unhappy, unfulfilled, inadequate, ugly, or unloved. Advertising does this perfectly. Endless pictures and programmes filled with young, beautiful, tall, rich, and supposedly happy people surrounded by some new shiny thing someone is trying to sell us, makes us all feel inadequate. Then we are sold the ultimate con-job. You may not be 22, with the looks of Adonis, immaculate suit, supermodel girlfriend, lounging on a yacht looking bored, but hey, if you buy this watch or soft drink, you will feel the same. Only after buying it, you don't. Perhaps a new phone, car, haircut, restaurant meal, or earrings is what you actually need instead. Feeling empty and inadequate inside, we work longer hours, neglecting friends and family, buying trinkets that clog up our cupboards, and binge on sugary processed food and social media late into the night, instead of sleeping well and enjoying cooking our own food.

All of us who aspire to a glamorous lifestyle, whether on a yacht off Cannes, or as a horseback game ranger as I secretly dreamed of as a teenager, need to remember the origin of the word 'glamour'. Dark magic. Witches and faeries cast a glamour, from the old Scottish word 'gramyre', meaning a spell to bewitch and deceive innocent observers. The next time you hear a celebrity described as glamorous, laugh and remind yourself of the reality. An insecure individual spending hours on make-up and lighting to try to appear very different. It sounds facile, but the planet is being destroyed because we buy too much crap we don't need, as a rubbish remedy for leading empty, unhappy, lonely and disconnected lives. But the destructive spending habits of several billion miserable people is not to be trifled with.

Why?

Our self-destructive consumerism is sadly part of our evolutionary inheritance. We are designed to frantically collect food and resources for lean times, something we battle to rein in with binge-eating and compulsive comfort-shopping. As social primates, we are also naturally extremely competitive for social standing, leading to dictators, greedy corporate executives, and an inability to stop pursuing meaningless promotions and empty job titles. No five-year-old child dreamed of being a director of process auditing. We could instead find purpose in living small but considered and meaningful lives, searching for fulfilment and happiness in our experiences and relationships, rather than running on the hamster-wheel of consumption.

We all become emotionally exhausted from the constant bombardment of negative messages about looming species extinction, climate change, pollution, overpopulation, and general planetary doom. So we switch off, turning our faces to our shiny pocket screens to anaesthetise ourselves to reality: far more effective than the Romans ever managed with colosseum gladiators. But saving the planet is not something we can just leave to politicians. Representative democracy is like being forced to choose between a punch in the face or a kick in the groin. You may want neither, but whichever you are forced to choose, you will be constantly reminded that you asked for it. Saving our natural world rests on all our individual actions.

After this rant, you may think I am a pessimist, despairing about the state of the planet and our hopeless attempts to improve. With shrinking rainforests, rampant wildlife crime, spiralling climate change, more species becoming endangered every day, and individual wild animals battling to survive, things can sometimes get you down. But I am actually a huge optimist. Never before in the history of humanity have so many people cared so much about the state of the natural world, and the wild creatures that share this planet with us. Not just concerned, but actively working to make things better.

While it is we humans that have got the planet into this mess, we are also the only species capable of fixing it. Who would have guessed five years ago that a quiet Swedish teenager with Asperger's syndrome would shake the world awake to climate change? Something even the vice-president of the wealthiest country on the planet couldn't manage. With frustration and burnout from the never-ending treadmill of long hours' work just to earn more income to spend on more pointless hedonic consumerism, many have wisely chosen to embrace more minimalist and thoughtful lives, not just for the planet, but also for themselves.

So with such huge problems confronting humanity and the planet, why on earth do I still treat and care about individual wild animals? Why do I operate on a single elephant or a rescued orangutan? Probably because I don't really have any other skills to contribute. I do believe that each animal, whether an Ethiopian wolf or a giant-headed mole rat, values its own life, just as we do our own. Both a golden eagle and a herring gull are intelligent, and have the same capacity to suffer and feel pain. Not caring about the suffering of individual wild animals harmed by man, and only focusing on species conservation, seems to me as callous as not caring about children suffering and dying in a war – it's like asking people in other countries to have more babies to fill the population numbers' deficit.

Treating an individual animal may not change the world, but for that animal its entire world is changed. Practising mindful consumption also helps reduce the adverse impacts I may inadvertently have on animals out of sight on the other side of the world. I will never win scientific accolades or conservation awards, but I sleep well knowing I have done all I personally can to reduce the burden of man-made suffering in wild animals.

So go on. Begin. Realise that your life is full of tiny daily choices, all votes which impact the planet. Each and every decision is a chance to really live your beliefs. A vote for a better world. Choose not to sleep-walk through life, inadvertently adding to the planet's woes with your lazy indifference. Every decision is a chance for a better planet and a happier, more fulfilling life for you too. And although you may never meet them or me, there are many millions of people on the planet who feel just like us. Together an invisible army. Together we can do amazing things for the natural world and all its wild animal inhabitants, with even the tiniest of steps. Every day, in every way, we can actually make things better and better.

Acknowledgements

This book would never have been possible without so many people. The brilliant Myles Archibald at William Collins, whose entire idea this book was – I wish I had come up with it, and am sure I haven't done it proper justice. Ben Clark, my ever-patient agent, who first thought I might actually have something interesting to write about, and made me take the first steps. Hazel Eriksson and Tom Whiting, who so patiently sorted out the manuscript mess I first gave them. I am completely undeserving of my ever-patient wife Yolanda, who has not only always been supportive, put up with my crazy international travels and adventures, largely raised our two beautiful children, but also forged her own path as a specialist veterinary cardiologist. I am immensely proud to be married to her. My mother and all her encouragement and support, despite my life-long unwillingness to wear a vest in cold weather. I also owe thanks to all the kind wildlife veterinary colleagues, vet nurses, surgeons, researchers and wildlife rescuers who have helped me across the world, and told me their stories and experiences. Lastly, to my wild animal patients: you had no choice but to put up with my fumbling attempts to treat you as best I could. It was always with your best interests at heart, even if you couldn't understand.

Index

Index

Index

Index